FIDUS ET AUDAX

CLAN CALLAGHAN

THE O CALLAGHAN FAMILY
OF COUNTY CORK

A HISTORY

JOSEPH F. O CALLAGHAN

CLEARFIELD

Originally Published by Irish Family Names
Dublin
2005

Revised Edition 2020
Copyright © by Joseph F. O Callaghan

Published for Clearfield Company by
Genealogical Publishing Company
Baltimore, Maryland
2020

ISBN 9780806359168

In time long gone by

poets and scholars were wont to appeal

to chieftains and lords to sustain their art.

A generous response often evoked a praise poem,

hailing the gift-giver's largesse, wisdom, beauty,

courtesy, loyalty, benevolence, and valor.

Not having the gift of poetry I must be content

to salute without lyrical adornment

my gracious patron and sponsors,

whose munificent bounty has enabled my words

to come to life on the printed page.

Míle buíochas dhaoibh go léir!

Joseph F. O Callaghan

WILLIAM J. O CALLAGHAN

IN HONOR OF MY FATHER

WILLIAM J. O CALLAGHAN

OF

DROMCUMMER, BWEENG, AND PHILADELPHIA

List of Subscribers

Michael O Callaghan	Mitchelstown, Co. Cork
Thomas G. O Callaghan	New Square, Medical Centre, Mitchelstown, Co. Cork
William J. Duffy	815 North Daniel Street, Arlington, Virginia 22201 U.S.A
Harold O Callaghan	87 Bedford Road, Katonah, NY 10536 U.S.A.
Helen O Callaghan Gibbs	303 W. State St., Apt 218 West, Doylestown, PA 18901 U.S.A.
RA Tony O Callaghan	1 Moss Run, White Plains, NY 10605 U.S.A.
William O Callaghan	50 County Street, Norwalk, CT 06851 U.S.A
Mons. Denis O'Callaghan	Presbytery, Bathview, Mallow. Co. Cork
Mary Gibbs Kershner	1354 West Hendricks Road, Pennsburg, PA 18073 U.S.A.
Mary O Callaghan	Bridge House, Meelin, Newmarket, Co. Cork

PATRON'S ADDRESS

As an O Callaghan whose roots are deep in the Cork soil it gives me, my wife Sheelagh, my son Brian and my daughter Zelda great pleasure to be associated with this unique book, while at the same time we feel a very deep sense of sadness that our daughter, Hazel, who died so tragically a few short years ago cannot be here to share our satisfaction.

Dr Joseph O Callaghan, the author, has produced a major work that has obviously taken years of painstaking research, and I must congratulate him on a splendid production. His attention to detail and his awesome grasp of his subject makes the book a pleasure to read. Rather than concentrating on a narrow depiction of the O Callaghan clan, Dr. O Callaghan chose to broaden the scope of the work to place the O Callaghans in the larger schemes of historically significant periods. This is a book, not alone about the O Callaghans, but a book about Ireland and how a Gaelic sept coped with the momentous changes from century to century.

What is most amazing about this work is the way in which the author was able to gather all the various strands together, giving us a glimpse of the importance of the family and the locations of the many branches and sub septs in ancient times. He was then able to trace the movements of many families or septs of the O Callaghans down through the centuries and in some cases right down to modern times. Naturally it would be quite impossible to trace every O Callaghan family from its early roots down to modern times in one book. By doing so with the substantial number of families as detailed in this book, Dr. O Callaghan has shown us that, with diligent research, it is possible for many O Callaghan families to trace their lineage back to Cellachán of Cashel.

The O Callaghans may not have been as prominent as some of the Munster septs, such as the O Briens of Thomond but they were a very powerful force at the time when they invaded Cork, along with their relatives, the MacCarthys. This event occurred following their defeat in Tipperary where they had lived for the two hundred years after the death of their primal ancestor, Cellachán, King of Cashel. Festering rivalry between the O Callaghans and the O Briens of Thomond led to their expulsion in the 12th century. From that time onwards the O Callaghans were based in Co. Cork where they displaced the Norse invaders of previous centuries.

When one reads about the very numerous branches of the O Callaghans and the vicissitudes they faced in their journeys through life, images of our own loved ones invariably come to mind. We can look back in joy and sadness upon their lives and deaths. In my case I remember my father James, a Ballinhassig man, and my mother, Nora, who was a Hurley from Newestown. I remember my grandfather, Owen, who passed his love of his race and name down through my father to me.

People who read this book will probably travel emotional journeys as I have done and will experience a sense of tranquility and a feeling of satisfaction that one has when the final pieces of a jigsaw fall into place. The real value of this book is that it gives every

O Callaghan a real sense of place in the continuum of history, a sense of belonging to a large family and a conceptual knowledge of lineage.

Another particularly gratifying aspect of the book is the way in which Dr. O Callaghan dealt with the wider O Callaghan diaspora, detailing the achievements of some of the many thousands who left their native Cork to find fame and fortune in many lands including the U.S.A. and Spain.

In conclusion I heartily recommend this book not alone to every O Callaghan but also to a wider public because of its intrinsic value as a true record of one Irish sept from the time of its inception.

OWEN O CALLAGHAN
FCIOB, MRICS
The Patron of this Publication
Blackrock, Cork

CONTENTS

List of Subscribers   vi

Patron's Address   vii

Illustrations   x

Maps   xii

Foreword by Juan O Callaghan Casas   xiii

Preface   xv

Preface to the Revised Edition   xix

1. Origins: Legend and History   1

2. The O Callaghans in the Tudor Age   19

3. The End of the O Callaghan Clan   33

4. *Le Case de Tanistry* and its Aftermath   49

5. The Confederation of Kilkenny   73

6. From Cromwell to the Wild Geese   101

7. The Penal Laws   125

8. Catholic Emancipation, the Famine, and the Land League   162

9. The O Callaghan Diaspora   193

10. Epilogue   222

Appendices   225

Genealogical Tables   230

Abbreviations   247

Bibliography   249

Index   268

Illustrations

William J. O Callaghan   ii

Shrine of St. Lachtín's Arm   10

Ballybeg Priory   35

Walls of Clonmeen Castle   58

Gunloop in Clonmeen Castle Wall   59

Dromaneen Castle   61

The Kilmallock Chalice   65

Clonmeen Churchyard Commemorative Plaque   83

Edmond O Callaghan of Kilgory   142

Dromaneen with Longueville in the Background   144

Clonmeen Church I   149

Memorial of Cornelius O Callaghan, Shanrahan   155

Cornelius O Callaghan of Shanbally, County Tippperary   157

Cornelius O Callaghan, Baron Lismore   160

Daniel O Callaghan Sr.   164

Clonmeen Church II   180

Col. John O Callaghan of Bodyke   186

Maryfort   187

Bishop Thomas Alphonsus O Callaghan   195

Michael O Callaghan, Lord Mayor of Limerick   198

Donal O Callaghan, Lord Mayor of Cork   199

Patrick O Callaghan, Olympic Gold Medalist   200

General William Callaghan   202

Cornelius O Callaghan, Viscount Lismore   204

General Sir Robert William O Callaghan   205

Shanbally Castle 206

Ramón O Callaghan y Tarragó 207

José O Callaghan, S.J., Biblical Scholar 209

Edmund Bailey O Callaghan, Historian 211

Fr. Eugene O Callaghan 213

Dromcummer in 2014 214

Rev. Joseph T. O Callahan, S.J., Naval Hero 216

Admiral Daniel J. Callaghan 217

Admiral William M. Callaghan 217

Investiture of Juan O Callaghan as Chief of his Name 221

Maps

Location of Families in County Cork (16th Century) from Ó Murchadha,

    Family Names of County Cork   18

Division of Duhallow among the Clans from Bowman,

    Place Names and Antiquities of the Barony of Duhallow   26

Ortelius, *Hiberniae Britannicae Insulae Nova Descriptio*   31

The Province of Munster according to Ortelius   32

Barony of Duhallow in 1655 from Bowman,

    Place Names and Antiquities of the Barony of Duhallow   72

FOREWORD

I am very pleased to introduce *The O Callaghan Family of County Cork: A History*, the result of many years of research by Dr. Joseph O Callaghan, in which he describes the history of the various branches of our family, from their common mythical origin to their present status throughout the world.

This book reflects the rigorous, extensive, and thorough work done in its preparation, the evidence of which is the wealth of bibliographical references that go beyond mere support of the book's contents. I am certain that it will be very useful in the future for further studies about our clan.

I hope that this book can help to revive the spirit of the 1988 family gathering, where my clan chieftainship was recognized. On that occasion, O Callaghans from all over the world met in Longueville House, close to the ruins of our ancestors' Dromaneen Castle on the Blackwater River in Ireland. I keep the memories of that gathering close to my heart; I was moved to meet the O Callaghans coming from all over the world to whom I send my warmest greetings. I hope that, by reading this book, the O Callaghans that could not come to Longueville in 1988 can revive the spirit of the gathering and accept the salutation that I could not give them on that occasion.

On behalf of all the O Callaghans I would like to thank Dr. Joseph O Callaghan for this book, a highly valuable source documenting the singular history of our family.

JUAN O CALLAGHAN CASAS

The O Callaghan

Chief of the Name

PREFACE

The origins of this book go back to my early teenage years when I first recollect developing an interest in my family and my family name. The fact that my name was spelled with both an O and a g (especially because it was silent) always elicited some comment in school and no doubt prompted me to think that there was something special about it. In the many years since then I have often had to spell my name for shopkeepers and all manner of other people. When I went to Spain to work on my doctoral dissertation I found that Spaniards always had difficulty with the name, in particular the double l, which they pronounced as y, and the gh, which they pronounced as a hard g; they also tended to transform the final n into an m. So my name often sounded like O Cayagam. In recent years I have been amazed at how telemarketers mangle my name or refuse even to attempt to pronounce it.

From my parents I learned that some families had dropped the O and others had dropped the g. I know that my grandfather was recorded as John Callaghan, but under the influence of the Gaelic revival he adopted the O about 1888 and when my father left Ireland in 1907 he was known as William O Callaghan. As I grew in age and wisdom I came to understand that these variations in spelling were not as important as they seemed. O Callaghan, O Callahan, Callaghan, Callahan (or other variants such as Callighan and Callihan) are all the same. Moreover, I learned that the apostrophe, of which so much was made, was not an essential element of the name. The name in its Irish spelling, Ó Ceallacháin, does not have an apostrophe; that came into use when English officials, transliterating the name from Irish into English in the seventeenth century, inserted it. The apostrophe is often dropped in Ireland, though it remains in general use in the United States. In this book I have opted to eliminate it.

My many hours of discussion about the name also led to inquiries into the family's origin. When I was about sixteen or seventeen I asked my father for as much detail as he could give me; I regret now that I did not ask more questions. As I wanted to know how our name was spelled in Irish, I wrote to the Genealogical Office in Dublin in the summer of 1945 and received a reply from the then Chief Genealogical Officer, Edward MacLysaght, who gave me the Irish forms of O Callaghan and O Sullivan (my mother's name) and of Dromcummer, the townland in Cork where my father came from. My mother, as it happened, provided much more information not only about her own family but that of my father as well. Most of that she had from my paternal grandmother who lived with us for a short time.

About the same time my brother Billy and I read my father's copy of Geoffrey Keating's *History of Ireland* in O Conor's translation. This book, chock full of the legends and history of ancient Ireland before the coming of the Normans, and sprinkled with names, many of which I found unpronounceable, told me a lot about Cellachán, king of Cashel, from whom the O Callaghans and the MacCarthys claim descent. Taking advantage of Keating, Billy and I were able to trace the family ancestry - or at least that of Cellachán - back to Adam! That was something of a feat for two teenage boys, but the many years that I have devoted since then to the professional study and teaching of history have given me a somewhat different understanding and perspective.

Preface

During the ensuing years, while completing my graduate studies, getting married, becoming a father to a family of my own, and trying to establish myself as a professor at Fordham University in New York and as a scholar in the field of medieval Spanish history, I also worked intermittently collecting data concerning the O Callaghans. As a consequence the chapters of this book have been written in fits and starts. If I had concentrated entirely on that task I could have finished it much sooner. Now that I am approaching the age of seventy-seven I realize that research could go on forever but since I cannot expect unlimited years for that purpose I resolved to bring this project to a conclusion. It may serve as a foundation for others interested in the history of the O Callaghan family.

The O Callaghans were settled in County Cork along the Blackwater River between Kanturk and Mallow in the barony of Duhallow until the end of the seventeenth century when they began the long journey that carried them to every corner of the globe.[1] My intention is to write a history of the family from the earliest times to the twentieth century. Attention will also be given to the O Callaghan or MacCallaghan family in the barony of Muskerry, south of Duhallow and north of Cork city, who also claimed descent from Cellachán of Cashel. The O Callaghans of Duhallow and Muskerry shared the same coat of arms. Place name references often enable one to distinguish between the two families, but in our time that is almost impossible. The O Callaghans of Clare are descended from the chief of the Duhallow O Callaghans who was transplanted there in the Cromwellian era. The name O Callaghan (often rendered Kealaghan, Kelaghan, or Keelan in English, from Ó Céileacháin in Irish) is also found in the northern Counties of Louth, Armagh, and Monaghan, but those O Callaghans or Callaghans have no connection with the Cork family and will not be considered here. John Cornelius O Callaghan, the noted historian of the Irish Brigades, belonged to that northern family. Nor is everyone who bears the name actually an O Callaghan; the family name of James Callaghan, the Labor Prime Minister of Great Britain, originally was Garoghan.[2]

The family members mentioned in this book were usually persons of wealth and prominence because they had the good fortune to be recorded in the documents. In this regard a comment by Diarmuid Ó Murchadha is worth repeating:

> There is a tendency in family chronicles to concentrate on the chief members or main line at all times - understandably, since records of the rank and file occur much less frequently. It must be borne in mind that an extremely rigid caste system obtained in medieval Ireland, with a small self-perpetuating aristocratic clique accorded the unquestioning service and respect of a large but obscure mass of commoners. Yet it was this silent majority of yeomen, husbandmen, labourers and others who, because they were not disturbed to the same degree, kept the family name extant from generation to generation.[3]

---

[1] Michael J. Bowman, *Place Names and Antiquities of the Barony of Duhallow*, ed. Jean J. MacCarthy (Duhallow, 2000), 4-5; Matthew Daly, "Duhallow," *SD* 1 (1976-7): 1-4.

[2] Edward MacLysaght, *Irish Families: Their Names, Arms, and Origins*, 3d ed. (New York: Crown, 1972), 71, and *The Surnames of Ireland* (Dublin: Irish Academic Press, 1980), 34, 170-171; letter to author from Ruth Thorpe, Personal Secretary to James Callaghan, 8 February 1977.

[3] Diarmuid O Murchadha, *Family Names of County Cork* (Dún Laoghaire: Glendale Press, 1985), 4-5.

Preface

Ó Murchadha also commented that because these ordinary people were usually not the victims of transplantation they remained in the same regions of County Cork occupied for centuries by their ancestors.

As male members of the family are mentioned most often in the documents they receive the greatest attention in this book, but obviously there would be no O Callaghan men without O Callaghan women. Only occasionally does one encounter references to the mothers, daughters, and sisters. In the eighteenth century Síle Ní Cheallacháin stands out because she transmitted the genealogy of the O Callaghans of Kilcranathan to a scribe who recorded it. How many other anonymous O Callaghan women also preserved the memory of the family, its genealogy, and its exploits?

The reader will soon discover that the O Callaghans had a distinct preference for certain personal names. When I was a child I heard from my parents that the Irish usually named the oldest son after his paternal grandfather and the oldest daughter after her paternal grandmother. The next children were named for their maternal grandparents. The rest were evidently named for uncles and aunts. One notices the recurrence of certain personal names: Tadhg (Teige in English, a poet), Donnchadh (Donough, brown lord), Domhnall (Donal, world-mighty), Conchubhar (Conor, wolf-lover), Mathghamhain (Mahon, bear-calf), and so forth. In the late seventeenth century English equivalents of these names began to appear, not translations, but names that sounded or looked similar to the Irish forms. So Tadhg became Timothy; Donnchadh, Denis; Domhnall, Daniel; Conchubhar, Cornelius; Mathgamhain, Matthew, and so on. Female names included Oiléan, in English, Ellen, Eileen (little sprite); Áine (radiance), Anna; Síle, from the Roman name Cecilia, transformed into English Sheila, or Julia; Siobhán, Joan, a name of Norman origin.[4]

No doubt God knows every hair on the head of every O Callaghan, but I do not and I cannot track them all. Nevertheless, dispersed throughout the world though they may be, all those who can trace their ancestors to the O Callaghans of Duhallow and Muskerry, can know that they are related to one another. DNA testing would likely demonstrate that conclusively. I recognize that my work is imperfect and incomplete but I believe it will be useful to countless O Callaghans and Callaghans throughout the world seeking to understand their own origins and to place their particular family in a broader historical context.

Several of the medieval texts mentioned in this volume have been published online by University College Cork under the rubric: CELT - Corpus of Electronic Texts (www.ucc.ie/Celt); in some instances translations have not yet been published. Lists drawn from a variety of modern sources such as the Tithe Applotment Books and Griffith's Valuation of Tenements may also be found online.

Townland names, mostly Irish but anglicized by English scribes of the sixteenth and seventeenth centuries, figure prominently in the text. Despite variations and distortions of spelling, with the help of logainm.ie and townlands.ie, I have been able to identify most names and provide their original forms in Irish. Whenever possible I have given the accepted modern spelling of townland names. Some, however, defy identification and are left as they appear in the documents.

---

[4] Donnchadh Ó Corráin and Fidelma Maguire, *Irish Names* (Dublin: Lilliput, 1990).

Preface

Without the assistance of many others I would not be able to present this volume to the reader. I am much indebted to Diarmuid Ó Murchadha for his kindness in reading the early chapters of my manuscript and saving me from multiple errors. C. J. F. MacCarthy generously called my attention to documents relative to the O Callaghans of Kilcranathan.

The directors of the Genealogical Office, the National Archives, the National Library, The Public Record Office, The Royal Irish Academy, The Registrar General, all in Dublin, the Cork County Library, the Archivo Histórico Nacional, and the Archivo General del Palacio, both in Madrid, and the Generallandesarchiv, Karlsruhe, Germany, kindly responded to my request for documents, as did Carol Quinn, curator of the Grehan papers in the Boole Library of University College Cork.

I am much indebted to the kindness of Teresa Bowman for permission to reprint two maps from her father-in-law's *Place Names and Antiquities of the Barony of Duhallow*. Diarmuid Ó Murchadha kindly consented to my use of a map drawn by Peter Tynan O Mahony showing the location of Irish families in Cork. Helen Davis of the Boole Library supplied me with a copy of a map of the barony of Duhallow.

Unless otherwise noted, photographs are my own or are in the public domain. The following consented to use of photographs: National Museum of Ireland (St. Lachtín's arm); Fr. Dermot Brennan and the Dominicans of St. Saviour's Monastery, Limerick (Kilmallock chalice); the O Callaghans of Longueville House and the photographer Patrick Casey (Edmond O Callaghan of Kilgory); Jay O Callahan (Joseph T. O Callahan, S.J.); the Pontifical Biblical Institute of Rome (José O Callaghan, S.J.); the Mitchelstown Historical Society (Shanbally Castle); the County Clare Library (Maryfort House; Col. John O Callaghan; Col. George O Callaghan-Westropp); the *Journal of the Cork Historical and Archaeological Society* (Bishop Thomas O Callaghan, O.P.); the Albany Institute of History and Art, Albany, New York (Edmund Bailey O Callaghan); the Limerick Athenaeum (Michael O Callaghan); Cork Corporation (Donal O Callaghan); Castlemagner Historical Society (Pat O Callaghan).

Rev. Robert Kingston, The Rectory, Mallow, and Ms. Pat Foott made inquiries concerning the O Callaghan chalice once held at Clonmeen but its current whereabouts are unknown. J. Aranza, Archivist of the Archivo Diocesano of Tortosa, Spain, and Juan J. Alonso Martín, Subdirector of the Archivo General del Palacio of Madrid, also responded to my questions concerning O Callaghans in Spain.

Over the years many members of the O Callaghan family provided me with information and I would like to record my debt to them and apologize for my tardiness in bringing this work to fruition: Veronica McLernon, Bishopstown, Co. Cork; Christine O Callaghan, Duarigle, Newmarket; Cornelius O Callaghan, Cork City, formerly of Lackendarragh; Canon Denis O Callaghan, Mallow, formerly of Maynooth; Ellen Geran, Geranville, Mallow; Commandant John O Callaghan, Glenbrook; Juan O Callaghan Casas, Barcelona; Mary O Callaghan-Dunne, Mallow; Mercedes Palau Ribes O Callaghan, Barcelona; Rita Callaghan Kraut and Thomas P. Callaghan, San Francisco; Terry O Callaghan, Blackburn, Victoria, Australia; Tim O Callaghan, Gloundine, Bweeng; Michael O Callaghan, Longueville, and Gary O Callaghan, Seattle, Washington, who organized the O Callaghan reunion in 1988.

Preface

Others who aided my research include Ruarí Ó h-Icí, Seandrom, Westfields, Limerick; P. J. Twohig, Freemount, Charleville; Paul MacCotter; Pat Twomey, Ballincollig; Con Tarrant, Banteer; John Kavanagh, Dromahane; Matthew Daly, Padraig Ó Suillebháin, and Dermot Kiely of *Seanchas Dúthalla, Duhallow Magazine*. I also want to thank Nora McCarthy, Margaret Lehane, and the Duggan family of Dromcummer for welcoming me.

Feast of St. Cellachán

22 April 2004

Preface to the Revised Edition

This revised edition includes new material relating to several members of the family: a praise poem by the Scottish poet, Maol Domhnaigh Ó Muirgheasáin, in honor of the chieftain Donough O Callaghan, who was transplanted to Clare; a portrait and funerary poem dedicated to Cornelius O Callaghan, progenitor of the Tipperary O Callaghans; some additional information about his sons Robert and Cornelius; a portrait of Cornelius, the first Viscount Lismore; some genealogical data concerning Daniel Callaghan of Lotabeg, a Cork merchant in the early nineteenth century. Also included is a map of Ireland by Abraham Ortelius (d. 1598), from the 1592 edition of his *Theatrum Orbis Terrarum.* Of particular importance is Eve Jennifer Campbell's extensive study of the O Callaghan lordship in her doctoral thesis, *Displacement and Relocation in Early Modern Ireland: Studies of Transplantation Settlement in Connacht and Clare* (National University of Ireland, Galway, 2012), and her article, *"Pobul Uí Cheallacháin:* Landscape and Power in an Early Modern Gaelic Lordship," *Landscapes* 18 (2017):19-36.

I want to thank the following for permission to use photographs in the public domain: Beinicke Library, Yale University (Ortelius map); National Gallery, Dublin (Cornelius O Callaghan); Sotheby's (Viscount Lismore; General Sir Robert William O Callaghan); National Library of Ireland (Shanbally Castle). I am also most grateful to Martina Madden of Fota House in Cork City for her kind efforts to locate a portrait of Daniel Callaghan Sr. and to the Irish Heritage Trust for permission to include it here. Chris Callaghan of Cork kindly sent me a copy of his family's genealogy.

In February 2017 my patron Owen O Callaghan went to his eternal reward. I shall always be grateful for his kind generosity that made the first edition of this book possible.

7 October 2020

CHAPTER 1

ORIGINS: LEGEND AND HISTORY

Legend derives the origin of the great Gaelic families of Ireland from Míl (or Milesius, as his name was Latinized), king of Spain, whose three sons, Heremon, Heber, and Ir, invaded the western island sometime between 1500 and 350 B.C. According to the *Lebor Gabála* or *Book of Invasions*, the Milesians, a Celtic race, conquered the peoples who had preceded them and divided the country among themselves. Modern historians, however, have shown that the history of Ireland prior to the Christian era is uncertain at best and that the theory of a Milesian invasion is a fiction devised to explain in a coherent manner pre-Christian history and to exalt the kingship of Tara. The settlement of the Gaelic-speaking peoples in Ireland is usually placed sometime in the fourth century B.C. A military aristocracy, they were a minority ruling over a much larger pre-Celtic population. Before the advent of St. Patrick, the country seems to have been divided into five kingdoms, apparently equal in power, corresponding more or less to Ulster (Ulaidh), Connacht, Munster (Mumha), Leinster (Laighin), and Meath (Mídhe). The kings of Munster, one of the five-fifths of Ireland, ruled from Cashel in modern Tipperary.[1]

During the ninth, tenth, and eleventh centuries, Irish historians set out to provide a unified, systematic, and comprehensive account of their history, tracing the descent of the principal Gaelic houses from Milesius and his sons. The *filí* or men of learning of ancient Ireland were held in high esteem because they preserved the memory of the race and the genealogies of the great families. It has been shown, however, that the genealogies for the pre-Christian era are largely invention and that many names even after the coming of St. Patrick are merely names and do not identify authentic historical personages. Some of the early ancestors of the Gaelic dynasties evidently were the gods of pagan times, the Tuatha Dé Danann (the people of the goddess Dana) such as Eochaid, who appears in the O Callaghan pedigree. The desire to make sense out of history and legend by means of the genealogies is reflected in Egan O Rahilly's poem on the death of Daniel O Callaghan in 1724, whose genealogy is traced all the way back to Adam![2]

---

[1] *Lebor Gabála Érenn. The Book of the Taking of Ireland*, ed. and tr. R. A. S. Macalister, 5 vols. (Dublin: Irish Texts Society, 1938-1956); Eoin MacNeill, *Celtic Ireland* (Dublin: M. Lester, 1921); Edmund Curtis, *A History of Medieval Ireland* (London: Methuen, 1938).

[2] *The Poems of Egan O Rahilly*, ed. and tr. Patrick Dineen (Dublin: Irish Texts Society, 1900), 66-87, no. XV.

Origins: Legend and History

The principal southern families, among whom are included the O Callaghans, were said to be descended from Milesius's son Heber, and more immediately from Oilioll Olum (Ailill Alum), who ruled the kingdom of Munster in the late second century A. D. By the twelfth century the legend had developed, without any historical basis, that Oilioll Olum determined that the succession to the kingship should alternate between the families of his sons, Eoghan Mór, the ancestor of the Eoghanacht, and Cormac Cas, the progenitor of the Dál Cais. The Eoghanacht controlled the kingship of Munster until it was wrested from them in the late tenth century by Brian Boru, the chief representative of the Dál Cais, and ancestor of the O Briens.[3]

Cellachán Caisil

In the early years of the tenth century the Eoghanacht dynasty was represented by Cellachán Caisil - Cellachán of Cashel - king of Munster (936-954), from whom are descended the MacCarthy (MacCarthaigh) and O Callaghan (Ó Ceallacháin) families. At that time Ireland was the scene of a mortal struggle between the Gaels and the Norsemen who had begun the conquest of the coastal areas in the preceding century. A seafaring people, the Norse established themselves in Dublin, Waterford, Wexford, Cork, and Limerick, ports from which they carried on trade with all the lands of northern Europe. They also penetrated inland, threatening to overcome the Gaelic aristocracy.[4]

An authentic historical personage, Cellachán Caisil appears in the annals as a warrior-king who ravaged far and wide, causing grief and destruction both among the Norsemen and his fellow Gaels. His first appearance in the annals is dated in 936 when, together with the men of Munster, he plundered the monastery of Clonmacnois in Westmeath shortly after the Norse of Dublin had done so. Three years later, joined by the Norse of Waterford, Cellachán and the Munstermen pillaged Meath, seizing the abbots of Clonenagh and Killeigh and laying waste the countryside as far as Clonard. His incursions into Meath in time brought down upon him the reprisals of the Uí Néill, the dominant family in the north, who sought to establish their supremacy over the whole of Ireland. Muirchertach mac Néill, heir apparent to the king of Tara, Donnchadh (919-944), forced the Osraige and the Déise, inhabiting modern Ossory and Waterford, to submit to him, but Cellachán perceived this as an unwarranted intrusion by the Uí Néill into his own dominions. Thus in 941 he led the Munstermen to plunder the country of the Osraige and the Déise, who in turn joined forces against him and inflicted a severe defeat upon him.[5]

---

[3] See the Eoghanacht genealogies in *Corpus Genealogiarum Hiberniae,* ed. M. A. O'Brien, 1 vol. thus far (Dublin: Dublin Institute for Advanced Studies, 1976), 1:195-234, and a list of the kings of Munster, *ibid.,* 1:360-361. Geoffrey Keating, *Forus Feasa ar Éirinn. History of Ireland,* 3 vols., ed. and tr. David Comyn and P. S. Dineen (Dublin: Irish Texts Society, 1901-1908).

[4] Several lists assign Cellachán a reign of ten years; *CGH,* 1:360; Kuno Meyer, "The Laud Synchronisms," *Zeitschrift für celtische Philologie* 9 (1913): 482; Donncha Ó Corráin, *Ireland before the Normans* (Dublin: Gill, 1972), 80-110.

[5] *Chronicon Scotorum. A Chronicle of Irish Affairs from the Earliest Times to 1135,* ed. and tr. W. M. Hennessy, Rolls Series 46 (London: Longman, 1866), 201, 203, s.a. 935, 938, 940; *Annals of the Kingdom of Ireland by the Four Masters from the Earliest Period to 1616,* 2d ed. and tr. John O'Donovan, 7 vols. (Dublin: Hodges and Smith, 1856), 2:631, 639, 641-643, s.a. 934, 937-939; *Annals of Inisfallen,* ed. and tr. Seán MacAirt (Dublin: Dublin Institute for Advanced Studies, 1951), 152-153, s.a. 941.

In the meantime, Muirchertach, intent upon exacting pledges of loyalty to the king of Tara, set out on a circuit of Ireland, stopping at Dublin where he took the Viking lord as hostage, and then Lorcán, king of Leinster. When he entered Munster, the Munstermen seemed ready to resist him but at length decided to surrender their king Cellachán, as a hostage:

> Muirchertach went to the south,
> To the beautiful, chalk-white, strong Cashel.
> And he brought with him Callaghan of troops.
> He would accept of no other hostage.[6]

The contemporary poem, *The Circuit of Ireland by Muirchertach mac Néill*, also described these events:

> We were a night at Magh Feimin
> Assuredly and certainly,
> A night at Cashel of Munster.
> There the great injury was inflicted on the men of Munster.
> There were arrayed against us three battalions brave,
> Impetuous, red, tremendous,
> So that each party confronted the other
> In the center of the great plain.
> We cast our cloaks off us,
> As became the subjects of a good king.
> The comely, the bright Muirchertach was at this time
> Engaged in playing his chess.
> The hardy Callaghan said -
> (And to us it was victory) -
> 'O men of Munster! Men of renown!
> Oppose not the race of Eoghan,
> Better that I go with them as a hostage,
> Than that we should all be driven to battle.
> They will kill man for man,
> The noble people of Muirchertach!'
> We took with us therefore Callaghan the just,
> Who received his due honour,
> Namely a ring of fifteen ounces on his hand,
> And a chain of iron on his stout leg.[7]

Given the evident superiority of Muirchertach's forces, the Munstermen concluded that they could not win a pitched battle and so agreed with Cellachán that the

---

[6] *FM*, 2:643, s.a. 939; *CS*, 205, s.a. 940; *Annals of Ulster*, 4 vols., ed. and tr. William Hennessy (Dublin: Her Majesty's Stationery Office, 1887-1901), 1:460-461, s.a. 940.

[7] *The Circuit of Ireland by Muirchertach mac Néill, Prince of Aileach. A Poem written in the year 942 by Cormacán Eigeas, Chief Poet of the North of Ireland,* ed. and tr. John O Donovan, in *Tracts relating to Ireland* 1 (Dublin: *Irish Archaeological Society*, 1841): 1-68, especially 20-21 (prose summary) and 41-49, lines 95-118; see the text online: www.ucc.ie/celt/published.html.

wiser course was to yield him as a hostage. Although Cellachán's status as a prisoner was manifested to all by the iron chain binding his leg, the gift of a ring for his finger acknowledged his kingly rank. He was carried off to Ailech in Tyrone where Muirchertach held him hostage for nine months before delivering him to King Donnchadh who eventually released him. By his circuit of Ireland, Muirchertach succeeded in impressing upon the Eoghanacht the power of the Uí Néill, but time and circumstance worked to thwart any attempt to unify the kingdom or to create a truly powerful monarchy. The rivalries between the northern and southern dynasties were too long established and the pressures of the Norse too strong to permit the establishment of an effective government for the entire island. In any case, Muirchertach enjoyed his triumph for only a brief moment, as he was killed fighting against the Norsemen in the next year.

Following his release, Cellachán levied war against the Dál Cais, gaining a victory over Cennétig mac Lorcáin at Magh Dúine in 944. This was the first recorded encounter between the two men whose descendants, the MacCarthys and the O Briens, became such archrivals in later times. Not until 951 do the annals refer again to the warlike activities of Cellachán of Cashel. Then he plundered Clonfert, Clonmacnois, Síl Anmchadha and Delbna Bethra, and burned the church of Gallen, in the modern counties of Galway and Offaly, perhaps with the hope of checking the pretensions of the Uí Néill to insular hegemony. The annalistic record ends very simply in 954 with the notation: Cellachán, king of Cashel, died.[8]

The evidence related above presents us with a king who carried fire and sword to both the Norsemen and the other Gaelic lords of his time. At first it seems difficult to determine any purpose to his actions, but as his predecessors and successors attempted to do, he sought to oppose the ambitions of the Uí Néill to lord it over the southern kingdom, while endeavoring to extend his own power beyond the confines of Munster. For this reason he apparently was willing to join the foreigners in plundering the northern regions, including the great monasteries that were the glory of the northern church. These were not merely religious houses, but small settlements of varied population and considerable wealth. Closer to home, Cellachán tried to maintain his dominance over the Déise in the southeastern extremity of his kingdom and to curb the growing power of the Dál Cais in the northwest. On the whole, he appears to have succeeded in achieving these goals. His "activity against the Norsemen," according to Eoin MacNeill, "is the last glory of the Cashel dynasty, the flame that shoots up from the candlestick before the candle goes out."[9]

Cellachán is also the hero of an epic tale, a historical romance, as it has been called, entitled *Caithréim Cellacháin Chaisil (The Martial Career of Cellachán Caisil)*. In this he is depicted as a great champion who delivered his kingdom from subjugation by the Norsemen. The historicity of this text is highly questionable, as it was written in the early twelfth century, primarily to exalt the Eoghanacht against their rivals, the Dál Cais, who, since the time of Brian Boru (976-1014), had seized the kingship of Munster from their grasp. Brian, who also forced the Uí Néill into submission, and claimed to be high king of all Ireland, won undying fame for himself and his family as the defender of

---

[8] *CS*, 207, 211, s.a. 943, 953; *FM*, 2:665, 671, s.a. 942, 949, 952; *AU*, 1:464, 472, s.a. 944, 953; *AI*, 154, s.a. 951, 954.

[9] Eoin MacNeill, *Phases of Irish History* (Dublin: Gill, 1919; paperback, 1968), 266.

Gaelic independence by his victory over the Danes at Clontarf om 1014. Even though the events described in the *Caithréim* have little or no historical foundation, the tale does have value as a reflection of twelfth-century notions of kingship and the political relationship between the O Briens and the MacCarthys. The memory of Cellachán as a vigorous king was evidently strong enough for later generations to propose him as the premier representative of Eoghanacht valor.[10]

Lamenting the oppressive tributes that the foreigners had imposed upon the land, the anonymous author began his story by citing the inability of the Eoghanacht kings to cast off this yoke. Cellachán, who changed all this, came upon the scene as the chief lords of Munster assembled at Glanworth (in County Cork) to elect a new king. After presenting Cellachán's genealogy, the author declared that his hero was illegitimate, his mother having begotten him "in violation of her marriage" to the coarb (secular lord) of Cashel. Illegitimacy in Irish literature, far from being a bar to kingship, often appears as characteristic of heroic figures. Cellachán is reported to have travelled about Munster in disguise for a year and a half, observing Norse settlements and fortifications in preparation for his later assaults upon them. The theme is one common to literature and is typical of the hero-king.

The chief aspirant to the kingship was Cennétig mac Lorcáin, the father of Brian Boru, representing the Dál Cais. The kingship, according to this tale, had alternated between the descendants of Eoghan Mór and Cormac Cas, but in fact this principle has no historical basis, and seems to have been put forward initially by the Dál Cais to justify their usurpation in the eleventh and twelfth centuries. The author now used the principle to support Cellachán's claims, as the chief representative of the Eoghanacht. His mother, who had been gathering troops, arms, and treasure on his behalf, challenged Cennétig's right, arguing that her son, as "senior by age and knowledge," as one who was "a king in figure and appearance," had the best right to rule. At this Cennétig withdrew from the assembly. The lords who remained proclaimed Cellachán as king and "put their hands in his hand [a pledge of loyalty], and placed the royal diadem round his head and their spirits were raised at the grand sight of him. For he was a king for great stature, and a brehon [jurist] for eloquence, and a learned sagaman for knowledge, and a lion for daring deeds." Interestingly, it was a woman, Cellachán's unnamed mother, who carried the day for him and routed the candidate of the Dál Cais. The ceremony of making a king seems to have entailed acclamation by the assembled warriors, who pledged their loyalty to him, very much in the same manner as vassals pledging homage and fealty to a feudal lord, and then placed a crown upon his head. These gestures may have been observed among the Normans and borrowed from them by the twelfth-century author of this tale.[11]

---

[10] *Caithréim Cellacháin Chaisil. The Victorious Career of Cellachán of Cashel*, ed. and tr. Alexander Bugge (Christiana, Sweden: J.Chr. Gundersens Bogtrykkeri, 1905); see the text online: www.ucc.ie/celt/published.html; John Ryan, "The Historical Content of *Caithréim Ceallacháin Chaisil*," *JRSAI* 71 (1941): 89-100, dated the text prior to 1118, but Donncha Ó Corráin, "*Caithréim Chellacháin Chaisil*: History or Propaganda?" *Eriu* 24 (1974): 1-69, placed it between 1127 and 1134. For a summary see Kathleen Hughes, *Early Christian Ireland: Introduction to the Sources* (New York: Cornell University Press, 1972), 299-300.

[11] *Caithréim*, 58-61, ch. 4-7; Katharine Simms, *From Kings to Warlords: The Changing Political Structure of Gaelic Ireland in the Later Middle Ages* (Wolfeboro, NH: Boydell, 1987), 21-40.

Following his election, Cellachán led his men in a series of triumphal attacks upon the Danish settlements at Limerick, Waterford, and Cork, and also expelled the foreigners from Cashel. As the power of the Danes was cast down, he then made a royal circuit of Munster to demand the submission of the lesser rulers of Gaelic stock. He also reconciled with Cennétig, whom he acknowledged as tanist (*tánaiste*), that is, as heir to the kingship after his death. Tributes were also demanded from the men of Ossory and Leinster. As Cellachán's power and reputation grew, the Danes of Dublin under their lord Sitric offered peace. Proposing that Cellachán marry Sitric's sister, they hoped to capture the king of Cashel when he came to Dublin for the wedding. The High King, Donnchadh, favored the scheme "for Cellachán had not consented to pay tax or tribute to him."

Evidently attracted by these proposals, Cellachán made preparations for the journey to Dublin, but when Cennétig learned that he planned to take his best troops, leaving the kingdom virtually unprotected, he urged him to take only a small guard instead. Seeing the wisdom of this advice, Cellachán set out for Dublin with only a token force. No accusation of treachery was made against Cennétig on this account. Meantime, Sitric's wife, who was in love with Cellachán, decided to warn him of the impending danger. Although he attempted to make his retreat, he was cut off by Sitric and taken prisoner to Dublin. Enraged that their king was a captive of the Danes, the men of Munster raised a large army and a fleet to rescue him. In the bay of Dundalk the southern fleet encountered the Danes and threw them into disorder. Cellachán, who was tied to the mast of Sitric's ship, was liberated and Sitric himself, along with many of his commanders, was killed. After burning the Danish ships the men of Munster advanced in triumph to Dublin and set it afire. As they began their return journey to Munster, the king of Leinster attempted to prevent their passage through his territory, but Cellachán was able to thrust him aside and to advance unmolested. After plundering Tara, the seat of the high king who had supported the Danes in this affair, Cellachán came in triumph to Cashel.[12]

While the annals do not present Cellachán as the fierce opponent of the Danes portrayed in the *Caithréim*, he was selected as the hero of this tale by a twelfth-century layman, probably in the service of Cormac MacCarthaigh, king of Munster (1124-1138), whose principal purpose seems to have been to exalt the Eoghanacht dynasty at a time when its fortunes were at a low ebb due to the ascendancy of the O Briens. Cellachán was extolled as an Eoghanacht hero, a champion of Munster, and a vigorous opponent of the Danes, in contrast to Brian Boru, the chieftain of the Dál Cais, whose exploits against the Danes were recounted in the twelfth-century *The War of the Gaedhil with the Gaill*. Indeed, this work seems to have served as one of the sources for the author of the *Caithréim*.[13]

Looking at Cellachán realistically, he probably required the Norsemen settled in his kingdom to acknowledge his overlordship and to send contingents to his hosts, but he did not destroy their power; nor did they hold him hostage in Dublin, nor did his men liberate him and gain a naval victory over them. His fellow Irish may have acknowledged

---

[12] *Caithréim*, 61-115, ch. 8-100. The *Toruighexcht Cheallacháin Chaisil* (an unpublished text) recounts Cellachán's subsequent adventures,

[13] *Cogadh Gaedhel re Gallaib (The War of the Gaedhil with the Gaill)*, ed. and tr. James H. Todd, Rolls Series (London: Longman, 1867); Ryan, "Historical Content," 89-91; Ó Corráin, "*Caithréim*," 57-69.

that he affirmed the subordination of subject peoples such as the Déise, but in the struggle for hegemony in Ireland (which, if it had not been interrupted by the Norman invasion in the twelfth century, would probably have resulted in the unification of the island) he was unable to resist the dominant power of the Uí Néill. Muirchertach not only defeated him, but he also carried him off as a hostage to the north. In effect, Cellachán was a typical king of the tenth century, warring against his immediate neighbors in the south, plundering districts in the central parts of the island, and attaining some modest success. He was not, however, the hero-ancestor that the author of the *Caithréim* made him out to be.

The Descendants of Cellachán Caisil

The death of Cellachán Caisil in 954 marked the high water mark of Eoghanacht power, as rulership in Munster soon passed to the Dál Cais. In the nine years following his death, four kings ruled at Cashel, each of them meeting a violent death, a sign in itself of the disorder of the times. The last of the four was Cellachán's son Donnchadh, who probably came to power in 961, only to be killed by his own people two years later. During those years the star of the Dál Cais was rising in Thomond or North Munster (County Clare) where Mathgamhain mac Cennétig ruled and soon began to extend his authority into the territory dominated by the Eoghanacht. Upon his death, his brother Brian Boru succeeded to the kingship of Cashel and eventually also obtained the high kingship of Ireland. In this way the hegemony that the Eoghanacht had exercised for so long in Munster was overthrown. Brian's descendant Muirchertach Ua Bríain in 1101 handed Cashel over to the church as a seat for the new archbishopric of Munster and so it passed out of Eoghanacht hands.[14]

The chief branches of the MacCarthy and O Callaghan families traced their descent from Donnchadh mac Cellacháin, the king of Cashel who died in 963. His son Saorbrethach was the progenitor of the MacCarthys, and another son, Murchadh, was the ancestor of the O Callaghans. Murchadh's son Domhnall is thought to have been the first to adopt the surname Ua Cellacháin or O Callaghan. The first instance when that patronymic appears in the chronicles is in 1053 when the *Annals of Loch Cé* recorded the death of Donnchadh Ua Cellacháin, "royal heir of Cashel," at the hands of the Osraige. Donnchadh was perhaps a brother of Domhnall and a son of Murchadh mentioned above.[15]

Eoin MacNeill has shown that the right of succession to the kingship was borne by all the male descendants of a king down to his great-grandsons; they formed the *derb fine* or true family of the king, those who had a right to be considered for the kingship. In the case of Donnchadh Ua Cellacháin, he was called *rigdomna* or royal heir, that is, an "eligible prince of the royal blood;" thus he was descended from a previous king, probably Cellachán of Cashel, whose great-grandson he may have been. But as MacNeill

---

[14] *AI*, 156, s.a. 963; *CS*, 214-215, s.a. 961; *FM*, 2:684, s.a. 961; *AU*, 1:478-479; *Cogadh*, 4, 71, 91, ch. 49, 60; Ó Corráin, *Normans*, 111-150, 176.

[15] *CGH*, 1:362-363; *An Leabhar Muimneach*, ed. Tadhg Ó Donnchadha (Dublin: Irish Manuscripts Commission, 1941), 150-159, 160-161, 203, 215, 217-218, 429; *Annals of Loch Cé. A Chronicle of Irish Affairs from A.D. 1014 to A.D. 1590*, ed. and tr. William Hennessy, 2 vols., Rolls Series (London: Longman, 1871), 1:50-51, s.a. 1053; *FM*, 2:862-863, s.a. 1053; *AU*, 1:594-595, s.a. 1053.

also pointed out, a *rigdomna* who never became king could not transmit claims to his descendants; thus Donnchadh's children were forever excluded from the succession. Furthermore, at this time, given the continued dominance of the Dál Cais, the royal heir of Cashel was only a potential claimant to the kingship of the Eoghanacht dynasty now reduced to the status of petty kings.[16]

The use of surnames seems to have developed in the course of the tenth century, but did not become common until the eleventh. There is a tradition that Brian Boru ordered everyone to adopt a surname, but there is apparently little basis for this. The patronymic Ua Cellacháin, in any case, appears from this time onward. The name is formed by two words Ua (Ó) and Cellachán (Callaghan), the latter, as we have seen, was the name of the tenth century king of Cashel. The meaning of the word Cellachán, composed of the personal name Cellach and the suffix -án, is a matter of dispute. Cellach has been interpreted to mean either a warrior or a churchman, clearly irreconcilable professions. Stressing that both interpretations are erroneous, Donnchadh Ó Corráin argued that the word derives from *cenn*, "a head," and *loch*, "shining, resplendent, bright." Cendlach (shining head), followed by the diminutive suffix -án (genitive -áin), gives the form Cendlachán or Cellachán. Parenthetically, it is interesting to note that one Cellachán, from the early Christian era, was honored as a saint and his feastday was celebrated on 22 April. The church in Ballyuachtrach near Midleton was dedicated in his honor. The word Ua means a grandson, or in a more general sense, a descendant. Thus the full name Ua Cellacháin means a descendant of Cellachán. Most Gaelic surnames were formed in much the same way by prefixing Ua or Mac to personal names of heroes or chieftains from the past. Female names, however, did not use Ua or Mac, but rather the prefix Ní or Nic, meaning daughter. So Síle Ní Chellacháin would mean Sheila, the daughter of Callaghan. Collectively the descendants of Cellachán are called the Uí Chellacháin. One might also speak of the Clann Chellacháin or children of Cellachán. Ó Ceallacháin is the later spelling of the name. The transliteration of the name in English is most commonly O Callaghan, but documents of the Tudor era also give the variants Callaghan, Callaghane, Callahan, Kalahan, among others.[17]

Given the dominance of the O Briens not only in Thomond, but also in Cashel, and their aspirations to the high kingship of all Ireland, the fortunes of the Eoghanacht of Cashel were at a low ebb during most of the eleventh and twelfth centuries. Displaced from the vicinity of Cashel through the pressures of the O Briens, the O Callaghans as well as the MacCarthys, along with other branches of the Eoghanacht of Cashel, established themselves farther south in County Cork. The MacCarthys seized control of the Norse settlement at Cork and made it their principal seat.

[16] MacNeill, *Celtic Ireland*, 114-143; Simms, *Warlords*, 53-54. *Derb fine* is pronounced derv-in-a; *rigdomna* as ree-ghowna. Paul MacCotter, "The Rise of Meic Carthaig and the Political Geography of Desmumu," *JCHAS* 111 (2006): 59-76.

[17] Ó Corráin and Maguire, *Irish Names*, 49; Edward MacLysaght, *Irish Families: Their Names, Arms and Origins*, 3d ed. (New York: Crown, 1972); Diarmuid Ó Murchadha, "The Formation of Gaelic Surnames in Ireland: Choosing the Eponyms," *Nomina. Journal of the Society for Name Studies in Britain and Ireland*, 22 (1999): 25-44. *The Martyrology of Donegal*, ed. J. H. Todd and W. Reeves (Dublin: A. Thom, 1864), 108-109, records the feast of St. Ceallachán on 22 April but without any further data. Eric A. Derr, "Episcopal Visitations of the Dioceses of Cloyne and Ross, 1785-1828," *Archivium Hibernicum* 66 (2013): 261-393p.

For the history of the O Callaghans during the high Middle Ages we must depend upon the very bare and infrequent notices found in the annals and the genealogy of the principal branch of the family; the genealogy, however, is often little more than a list of names without any historical data describing the accomplishments of the persons bearing them. In addition to those already mentioned, the annals tell us that Cellachán Ua Cellacháin in 1092 killed Donnchadh MacCarthaigh, king of Eoghanacht Caisil, and perhaps his brother Muiredach as well. Cellachán was probably the son of Domhnall Ua Cellacháin and grandson of Murchadh mentioned above. No reason was alleged in justification of this act, but one may suspect that it was an attempt on Cellachán's part to wrest the kingdom from a rival branch of the royal house. Cellachán himself was slain in 1115, perhaps a victim of the MacCarthaigh, though his assailant was unnamed. Cellachán's identification as "of Cashel" suggests that the family had not yet migrated to Cork.[18]

The O Callaghans of Uí Echach Muman

Some entries in the Irish annals, however, associate the O Callaghans with the Uí Echach Muman, a group of families belonging to the Eoghanacht of Raithlenn and settled in the southwest of County Cork. A poem by Cathán Ua Duinnín, probably of the early thirteenth century, detailing the genealogy of Uí Echach Muman, affirmed that the Uí Cheallacháin or O Callaghans derive from Ceallach, who apparently lived in the late tenth or early eleventh centuries. How much credence should be given this is difficult to say.[19]

Two O Callaghans cited in the *Annals of Inisfallen* evidently belonged to the Uí Echach Muman. The *Annals* tell us, for example, that a family quarrel resulted in the killing in 1112 of Cathal, grandson of Domhnall, son of Dubdá Bairenn, by his relative through marriage, Aed Ua Cellacháin. Inasmuch as Cathal and his family, from whom the O Donoghues are descended, belonged to the Uí Echach Muman, it seems reasonable to believe that Aed also belonged to that group rather than to the Eochanacht of Cashel. The *Annals* also record the death of Máel Sechnaill Ua Cellacháin, "king of the south of Ireland," at Cork in 1121. That description should be understood to mean that he was a ruler of some distinction, but certainly not one who dominated the southern half of the island. The Four Masters, a seventeenth-century source perhaps recording an earlier one, assessed his status more realistically by telling us that Máel Sechnaill, "the splendor of the south of Munster," was lord of Uí Echach Muman.[20]

Máel Sechnaill's name, together with those of Tadhg MacCarthaigh and Cormac MacCarthaigh, is inscribed on the shrine of St. Lachtín's arm, made between 1118 and 1127. A sixth century saint, Lachtín was the patron of Donoughmore in Muskerry where the shrine was preserved before being transferred to the National Museum of Ireland. The inscriptions are marred and cannot be read in their entirety, but the three names can be

---

[18] *AI*, 243-245, 274, s.a. 1092, 1115; *FM*, 2:943, s.a. 1092; *LM*, 160-161; *Poems of Egan O Rahilly*, XV, ll. 169-171.

[19] *LM*, 168-188, XXV, ll. 337-340; *CGH*, 1:251; John O Donovan, ed., *Leabhar na g-Ceart, or the Book of Rights*, ed. (Dublin: Celtic Society, 1847), 256-257, n. o.

[20] *AI*, 270-271, 280-281, s.a. 1112, 1121; *FM*, 2:1013, s.a. 1121. Aed son of Cenede, son of Cellachán, in *LM*, 160-161, and in *Poems of Egan O Rahilly*, 66-87, no. 15 (p. 79, line 168) probably belonged to the Eoghanacht of Cashel.

deciphered along with some additional phrases. Thus we are asked to say a "prayer for Máelsechnaill u Cellacháin the high king of the Ua Echach;" and also for "Cormac son of MacCarthaigh," the royal heir of Munster; and for "Tadg son of MacCarthaigh," king of Munster. The words that can be read following Máel Sechnaill's name suggest that he was responsible for having this shrine made.[21]

Shrine of St. Lachtin's Arm

(National Museum of Ireland)

---

[21] I rely on the transcription by Michael Ryan, Assistant Keeper, Irish Antiquities Division, National Museum of Ireland, communicated to me on 8 August 1979. See Françoise Henry, *Irish Art*, 3 vols. (Ithaca: Cornell University Press, 1965-1970), 3:103-106, pls. 38-40; *Treasures of Early Irish Art, 1500 B.C. to 1500 A.D.* (New York: Metropolitan Museum of Art, 1977), 214, plate 62; George Petrie, *Christian Inscriptions in the Irish Language*, 2 vols. (Dublin, 1871-1878), 2:104-105, fig. 95; George Coffey, *Guide to the Celtic Antiquities of the Christian Period preserved in the National Museum*, 2d ed. (Dublin: Hodges, Figgis, 1910), 53-54, pl. 12; Adolf Mahr and Joseph Raftery, *Christian Art in Ancient Ireland*, 2 vols. (Dublin: Stationery Office of Saorstat Eireann, 1932-1941), 1:161, pl. 99; A. T. Lucas, *Treasures of Ireland: Irish Pagan and Early Christian Art* (New York: Viking, 1974), 133, fig. 90, pl. 36. Margaret Stokes, *Early Christian Art in Ireland* (Dublin: Chapman and Hall, 1894), 74, 104-105; Edmund Hogan, *Onomasticon Goedelicum locorum et tribuum Hiberniae et Scotiae* (Dublin, 1910; reprint Dublin: Four Courts Press, 1993), 351; Ó Murchadha, *Names*, 66.

Origins: Legend and History

Tadhg MacCarthaigh (1118-1123) and his brother Cormac (1124-1138), both occupied the royal seat of Cashel, though the O Briens challenged their rights. As the O Connors of Connacht gained ascendancy in the twelfth century, they deliberately tried to weaken potential rivals by limiting the O Briens to Thomond and the MacCarthys to Desmond or South Munster. The linking of Máel Sechnaill with both Tadhg and Cormac MacCarthaigh in the inscription suggests a close relationship among them and it was perhaps with their support that he ruled. However that may be, Máel Sechnaill Ua Cellachán was the last member of his family to be described as king of Uí Echach. By the middle of the twelfth century the kingship seems to have passed into the hands of the O Mahonys.[22]

In 1283 Domhnall MacCarthaigh, king of Desmond, after suppressing an abortive attempt by some MacCarthys, O Mahonys, and O Callaghans to overthrow him, made peace with them. The linking of the O Callaghans with the O Mahonys and "all the Uí Echach" in this instance suggests that we are dealing here with the O Callaghans of Uí Echach. Griffin Ocallochan (Criomhthann Ó Ceallacháin), whose name does not appear in the genealogy of the O Callaghans of Duhallow, and who was charged as a felon in 1295, may also have belonged to the O Callaghans of Uí Echach.[23]

The MacCallaghans of Muskerry

Apparently distinct from the foregoing family were the MacCallaghans of Muskerry, a barony south of Duhallow. Although the *Book of Munster* affirmed that "the Clan Callaghan of Muskerry" (as well as the MacAuliffes) were descended from Tadhg MacCarthaigh, king of Desmond, it does not trace their genealogy nor does it establish a link with Tadhg. If the *Book of Munster* is correct, the MacCallaghans were a branch of the MacCarthys and like them descended from Cellachán Caisil. Not surprisingly the MacCarthys often used Cellachán as a personal name. Entries in the annals suggest that Tadhg had a son Cellachán, from whom the name MacCallaghan may have derived. Cellachán's descendants, killed in the wars among the MacCarthys or their neighbors, included five brothers: Mael Sechnaill (slain in 1161) and his son Donnchadh (slain in 1169); Muiredach (died 1172); Tadhg (slain in 1181); Murchadh (blinded in 1181); Cathal Odhar (slain in 1193) and his sons Muirchertach (slain in 1191) and Cellachán (slain in 1205).[24] This internecine warfare, prompted perhaps by territorial claims, n0o doubt also claimed the lives of many of their followers.

In modern times when the O and the Mac were dropped and all were called Callaghan, it became almost impossible to distinguish the O Callaghans of Duhallow and those of Uí Echach and the MacCallaghans of Muskerry. In the pages that follow I will attempt to do so where possible.

---

[22] *LM,* 204; Michael Dolley, *Anglo-Norman Ireland* (Dublin: Gill, 1972), 20-21, 25-26; Ó Murchadha, *Names,* 49-50, 229-230.

[23] *AI*, 383-385, s.a. 1283; *Calendar of the Justiciary Rolls, or Proceedings in the Court of the Justiciar of Ireland preserved in the Public Record Office of Ireland XXII to XXXI Years of Edward I,* ed. James Mills (Dublin Alexander Thom, 1905), 63; Ó Murchadha, *Names,* 66.

[24] *LM,* 150, 203, 214, 429; *AI,* 294, 302, 304, 314, 316, 318, 334, s.a., 1161, 1169, 1171, 1172, 1181, 1191, 1193, 1205; *CGH*, 1:362; "MacCarthaigh's Book," in *Miscellaneous Irish Annals* (A.D. 1114-1437), ed. and tr. Séamus Ó hInnse (Dublin: Institute for Advanced Studies, 1947), 14-15.

Origins: Legend and History

Territorial Adjustments after the Norman Invasion

Following the Norman invasion, Diarmait MacCarthaigh (1151-1185) did homage to King Henry II of England in 1171 for the kingdom of Cork, but just six years later Henry gave it to Robert FitzStephen and Milo de Cogan. Even so the MacCarthys remained in possesssion of the greater part of Desmond, although they and other Eoghanacht families had to contend with increasing Norman pressures over the ensuing decades. The O Callaghans eventually settled in the barony of Duhallow (Dúthaigh Ealla, the district of the Allow) in County Cork, where, after overcoming the peoples already living there, they settled in the present parishes of Kilshannig (*Cill Seanaigh*, Seanach's Church) and Clonmeen (Cluain mín, the smooth meadow) along the southern banks of the Blackwater River (Abhainn Mhór, the great river), as well as Castlemagner, Roskeen (Ros Caoin, the pleasant woodland) and Ballyclough (Baile Cloch, the town of the stone) on the north.[25]

At the same time it is possible that the O Callaghans of Uí Echach, located early in the twelfth century in the region to the south and west of Cork, as a result of Norman expansion and the rise of the O Mahonys, were limited to the barony of Kinalea, north of Kinsale and south of Muskerry. Settlement of the O Callaghans in Kinalea is indicated by the *Topographical Poem* of Giolla na-Naomh Ua h-Uidhrín (d. 1420), continuing the work begun by Seaghán Ua Dubhagáin (d. 1372) setting forth the lands of all the clans in Ireland. James Carney avers that the "two poems together constitute a compendium of the topography of Norman Ireland as seen, however, by poets who lived two centuries after the invasion." Ua h-Uidhrín writes:

Ar Cheinél Aodha an fhuinn te[26]	Over Cinel Aedha of the warm land
Ó Ceallacháin cláir Bhéirre,	Is Ó Ceallacháin of the plain of Bearra,
Fonn glaislinne go grian geal	A land of green pools with white bottoms,
Fiadh as fhairsinge inbhear.	Land of widest harbours.

After citing the O Callaghans in Kinalea, and the O Mahonys in adjacent Kinalmeaky, the poet then located the O Callaghans, together with MacAuliffe and O Keeffe, in Luachair, a region in northwest Cork, extending into Kerry and Limerick:

Ó Ceallacháin an chnis ghil	Ó Ceallacháin of the fair skin,
Do shíol Cellacháin Chaisil,	Of the race of Ceallachán of Caisel
Fir dár bhoing tuile thoraidh,	Man for whom a flood of fruit burst forth
Ós coill duibhe dearcnomhaigh.	Over the dark bearing wood.[27]

I doubt the conventional wisdom that holds that the O Callaghans were settled in

---

[25] John J. Kavanagh, *A Sense of History and Heritage of Kilshannig and Surrounds* (Kanturk: Kanturk Printers, 1996), 4-5.

[26] Cathán Ua Duinnín, in his poem on the Uí Echach, l. 69 used the same language: "Do chinél Aodha an fhuinn te . . ." *LM*, 172.

[27] *Topographical Poems by Seaán Mór Ó Dubhagáin and Giolla na Naomh Ó Huidhrín*, ed. James Carney (Dublin: Institute for Advanced Studies, 1943), vii, 47, 53, ll. 1253-1256, 1437-1441; *The Topographical Poems of John O Dubhagain and Giolla na-Naomh O Huidhrin*, ed. and tr. John O Donovan (Dublin: Irish Archaeological and Celtic Society, 1862), 103, 117, ll. 1253-1256, 1437-1441, and lxv, nn. 356-357. Ó Murchadha, *Names*, 67, believes that it was an "obvious mistake" to place the O Callaghans in Kinalea.

Kinalea in the twelfth century but were forced northward into Duhallow by the Normans. Rather I suspect that the poet is referring here to two distinct families, the O Callaghans of Uí Echach settled in Kinalea, and the O Callaghans of Duhallow settled in Luachair.

During the fourteenth century when the MacCarthys regained the greater part of Muskerry from the Normans, the MacCallaghans apparently also settled in that region.[28] Muskerry, extending north and west from Cork, was intersected by the rivers Lee and Sullane. To the north lay the barony of Duhallow; in the northwest rose the Boggeragh Mountains reaching northward toward the Blackwater River. Directly west from Macroom on the Sullane the Derrynasagart Mountains established the western boundary of the barony.

At the close of the Middle Ages MacCallaghans are found in the eastern sector of the barony of Muskerry, at Carrigadrohid along the river Lee, at Donoughmore abutting the barony of Duhallow, and at Carrignavar, north of Blarney and Cork City. For example, fifteenth-century ecclesiastical documents mention Cornelius Mackeallachayn (Conchubhar MacCeallacháin) vicar of Clonfert in Duhallow, who died in 1401. Donald Mackeallacayn (Domhnall MacCeallacháin), abbot of Gill Abbey (founded by the MacCarthys in the twelfth century in Cork), before 1469, is probably the same as Donald O Kellycharn [O Callaghan], abbot of Gill Abbey, who died in 1465. The pope entrusted Donatus Mickellachayn (Donnchadh MacCeallacháin), a canon of Cork cathedral, pastor of Knockavilla and Desertserges in Muskerry, with several missions from 1493 to 1512; he may be the same as Donald Veckcallaghan (Domhnall MacCeallacháin), the vicar of Garrycloyne in Muskerry in the sixteenth century.[29]

The O Callaghans in the High and Late Middle Ages

The genealogy of the O Callaghans of Duhallow recorded in the *Book of Munster* offers no clues as to the movements of the family during these centuries. According to a generation count, in succession from father to son, Cenede mac Cellacháin, Aodh, and Murchadh lived in the twelfth century. The annals tell us that in 1158 one of the sons of Aodh Ó Cellacháin, perhaps Murchadh, was killed by Brian Ó Briain and Donnchadh Ó Cearbhaill, king of Eoghanacht Locha Lein, a kingdom situated in Kerry about the Lakes of Killarney. Brian and Donnchadh then killed one another, surely a matter of indifference to the dead O Cellacháin.[30]

In the thirteenth century we have Mathghamhain, Maccrait, and Lochlann. The fourteenth century representatives of the name, in succession from father to son, were Maelseachlann, Maccrait, and Cinnédig. In 1345 McCraygh O Kaillaghan and Donoghwyth Ocaillaghan, - brothers perhaps - joined the MacCarthys, O Mahonys and

---

[28] Ó Murchadha, *Names*, 50-52, 58-62.

[29] *Calendar of Papal Letters relating to Great Britain and Ireland*, vol. 16, ed. Anne P. Fuller (Dublin: Irish Manuscripts Commission, 1986), 11-12, no. 20; vol. 19, ed. Michael J. Haren (Dublin: Irish Manuscripts Commission, 1998), 197-198, 244-245, 393, 395, nos. 334, 416, 702, 704; Evelyn Bolster, *A History of the Diocese of Cork from the Earliest times to the Reformation* (New York: Barnes and Noble, 1972), 101, 241, 502-503. Robert O Callaghan or O Huallachayn, named abbot of Tracton in 1467 and Dermot O Huallacháin named abbot of Mourne (pp. 146, 458) were not O Callaghans, but rather O Houlahans (O hUallacháin). Ó Murchadha, *Names*, 73.

[30] MacCarthaigh's Book," *Miscellaneous Irish Annals*, 40-41; Ó Murchadha, *Names*, 66.

the forces of the earl of Desmond in ravaging the king's lands. McCraygh may be identified with the Maccrait just mentioned. Cinnédig had two sons, Donnchadh, who succeeded him as head of the family, and Maelseachlann, whose successors are recorded in the *Book of Munster* as follows: Domhnall, Maelseachlann, Conchubhar, Diarmaid, and Donnchadh an Oileáin, of the Island, who was living in 1600, and married Eilis Ní h-Uaithne. With Cinnédig's son Donnchadh and his son Conchubhar Laighneach we pass from the fifteenth into the sixteenth century. Conchubhar Laighneach, who was living in 1469, married Ellen FitzGibbon and had two sons, Tadhg Ruadh and Maccrait. The latter's descendants are recorded as Cathaoir, Tadhg, Diarmaid, and Cathaoir. More will be said of Tadhg Ruadh in the following chapter.[31]

The genealogy discussed above is that of the head of the family. As it appears in the *Book of Munster*, it is a bare list of fathers and sons succeeding one another, without any indication of the dates when they lived or the events in which they participated. In considering the growth of this family, several points should be emphasized. Modern historians have spoken of expanding clans, including the O Callaghans. These were prolific families whose growth in numbers was encouraged by the loose marital bonds prevailing in medieval Ireland, to the extent that one could speak of polygamous relationships. The families that gained in strength were those where fathers had numerous sons, not necessarily by one wife; nor were the sons all legitimate, as one usually understands that term, though there was no stigma attached to illegitimacy. One must also suppose that along with many sons, there were many daughters, but neither they nor their mothers were recorded in the genealogies. Only in the early modern period do we encounter the names of the chieftains' wives. Wives were likely chosen with a view to cementing alliances with other important families. Given the tendency of chieftains to engage in numerous liaisons with women, whether sanctioned by the church or not, it is probable that each of the medieval heads of the family had other sons and daughters who are not recorded in the genealogy. Ultimately all of them derived from Cellachán of Cashel. Only in this way can one explain the growth of the family over the centuries and its ability to take over and dominate a significant stretch of land along the Blackwater in northwest Cork.[32]

While poets and historians focused their attention on the doings of chieftains, we have few notices of the activities of other members of the family. The medieval people of Ireland generally supported themselves by means of a pastoral economy, that is, the grazing of cattle and sheep. Students of Irish law pointed out that wealth and fines for infractions of the law were often calculated in terms of cattle, a sign of their significance.[33] As a consequence, the undulating land of Duhallow and Muskerry was not divided into neat farms owned by individual proprietors or held by tenants paying rent to a landlord; there were no towns or villages such as arose in later times. Place names are often descriptive of physical or geographical features: bally (*baile*), a town or settlement;

---

[31] *LM*, 160-161, 217; *Poems of Egan O Rahilly*, 78-79; Herbert W. Gillman, "The Chieftains of Pobul I-Callaghan, Co. Cork," *JCHAS*, Series 2, 3 (1897): 205-206, follows the genealogy compiled by Sir George Carew in the sixteenth century. Ó Murchadha, *Names*, 66-67; *Burke's Irish Family Records* (London: Burke's Peerage Ltd., 1976), 887.

[32] Ó Corráin, *Normans*, 28-46; Kenneth Nicholls, *Gaelic and Gaelicised Ireland in the Middle Ages* (Dublin: Gill, 1972), 10-12, 21-30; Nerys Patterson, *Cattle, Lords, and Clansmen. The Social Structure of Early Ireland,* 2d ed. (Notre Dame, IN: University of Notre Dame Press, 1994).

[33] Ó Corráin, *Normans*, 42-73; Nicholls, *Ireland*, 44-87.

carrig (*carraig*), a rock; drum or drom (*drom*), a ridge; gort (*gort*, a field), *garrán* (a grove of trees), *doire* (a wood or forest). Much of the area was wooded (for example, Kilmore, *an choill mhór* - the great wood). Over the course of centuries a great body of literature (*Dinnsenchas*) developed in Irish concerning the heroes and events associated with particular places.[34]

Nevertheless, the land was thought to belong to the clan, a notion emphasized by the term *Pobul Ui Cheallachain* used to describe it. *Pobul*, from Latin *populus,* meant the people, and *Pobul Ui Cheallachain* or the O Callaghan People also meant the lands they inhabited. From time to time, the chieftain assigned portions of it to his closest relatives. They ordinarily lived in a fortified enclosure - *dún, ráth, lios, cathair* - within which were usually several wooden buildings. Numerous place names beginning with *ráth* or *lios* as well as stone and earthenworks of many of these forts (most dating from the early Christian era) are found in O Callaghan lands. Oftentimes they were believed to be the haunts of the fairies, who would vent their anger on anyone who had the temerity to modify these structures. One who did so would have no luck thereafter.[35] The rank and file of O Callaghans were totally dependent on the chieftain for their sustenance and protection. Duhallow and Muskerry are known today as baronies, a term borrowed from the Normans of a later date; it is believed that the baronies were essentially identical with the *tuatha* or tiny kingdoms of ancient Ireland, each with its own *rí* or king. The baronies in turn were divided into smaller segments, called townlands or ploughlands. Cork, established by the Norsemen, was the closest thing to a town. Mallow (*Magh nAla*), the plain of the Ealla River, originally the site of an early Norman castle, also eventually developed into a town.

Christianity came to Ireland probably in the fifth century. Although St. Patrick was the most famous missioner, there were many others. The histories of such personages as St. Lachtín and St. Cellachán, who appear to have been early monastic saints, are scarcely known to us. Several place names, usually those with the prefix Kill or Kil (*Cill*) are reminiscent of early saints, who probably lived in the vicinity, though little is known about them. For example, Kilshannig (Cill Seanaigh), a townland of about 27,000 acres, was Seanach's church, probably near the Church of Ireland church at Newberry. We also find Kilpadder, Peter's church; Kilcolman, Colmán's church - St. Colmán was the patron saint of Cloyne; Kilgobnet, Gobnait's church; Kilpatrick, Patrick's church; Kilberrihert; Berrihert's church, named for an Anglo-Saxon saint who came to Ireland after the Synod of Whitby in 664; Kilmichael, Michael's church; and Kilcaskan, a church honoring a Welsh saint, Pascent or Cáscann. Donoughmore (Domhnach Mór) in Muskerry means the great church. Throughout O Callaghan's Country there are numerous archaeological sites of ancient churches.[36]

[34] John J. Kavanagh, "Some Places and Names in Duhallow," *SD* 7 (1989): 89-96.
[35] *AICC*, nos. 12027-13196 (ringforts); Bowman, *Names*, records numerous forts throughout Duhallow. My mother (who got the story from my grandmother O Callaghan) told me that my father's family cut into what seemed to be a fairy fort at Dromcummer and, she said, "they had no luck thereafter." John J. Kavanagh, "The Antiquities of Kilshannig," and "Some Kilshannig Place Names," *MFCJ* 1 (1983): 39-50, and 5 (1987): 30-33; David Buckley, "Two Stone Alignments in Kilshannig Parish," *SD* 7 (1989): 61-62.
[36] Padraig Ó Riain, *Corpus Genealogiarum Sanctorum Hiberniae* (Dublin: Dublin Institute for Advanced Study, 1985); Samuel Lewis, *A Topographical Dictionary of Ireland*, 2 vols. (London: S. Lewis,

In the twelfth century the church in Ireland was reformed and organized along the continental model. As a consequence, Cashel became an archiepiscopal see and the bishoprics of Cork and Cloyne, separated by the river Lee, were among its suffragans. Duhallow and most of Muskerry became part of the diocese of Cloyne, but Muskerry south of the Lee belonged to Cork. Openness to continental influences also brought Benedictine and Cistercian monks to Ireland, as well as Franciscan, Dominican, and Augustinian friars. Donough O Callaghan, evidently a Franciscan friar, in 1482 drew up the *Statutes of the Franciscans at Adare in County Limerick*. The O Callaghans reportedly established an Augustinian friary at Clonmeen, a townland of nearly 20,000 acres south of the Blackwater River and about two miles southeast of Kanturk. The west gable of a fifteenth-century church, larger than the usual parish church, still stands and was incorporated into the later Church of Ireland church there. Leading members of the O Callaghan family were buried in the church and many others were interred in the adjacent cemetery. The parish church was in the possession of the Knights of the Hospital of Mourne Abbey until 1577. In the late fourteenth century the Pipe Roll of the See of Cloyne indicates that David Magnel or Magner, whose family was Norman in origin, held five carucates or ploughlands in Subulter and Clonmeen from the bishop of Cloyne. In addition, the heir of Philip Omol (Aumale) acknowledged that he held the castle of Clonmeen from the bishop. In 1262 Bishop Alan of Cloyne granted patronage of the church of Kilshannig to John de Cogan; a century later Nicholas Barry held Kilshannig and David Barry held Dromore. As Clonmeen, Kilshannig and Dromore were held by the Normans in the late fourteenth century, the O Callaghans must have acquired possession after that time.[37]

Despite the christianization of Ireland ample evidence of the continuing influence of pagan customs exists. Throughout O Callaghan's Country there are numerous standing stones dating from prehistoric times as well as holy wells where the faithful came seeking healing for their aches and pains and sores. Holy wells, such as those near Banteer, Clonmeen, Curraghrour, Gortmore, Dromore, and Carrigcleena, were likely pagan in origin and and were christianized in later centuries. About four hundred yards north of Clonmeen church there is a holy well commemorating Fursa or Fursey, a sixth-century saint, said to be the patron of the parish. The faithful seeking cures visited there on 16 January; many left their crutches behind. At Carrigcleena More (*Carraig Cliodhna Mór* - Cleena's rock), about six miles south of Mallow, a circle of rocks surrounding one in the center was thought to be the favorite residence of Cliodhna, the *bean sidhe* or fairy woman. Regarded as the special protector of the O Callaghans, she was a goddess who personified the land and conferred sovereignty on the *ri* or king with whom she was joined in a symbolic marriage. So long as he ruled justly she favored the people with good harvests and prosperity. The inauguration of the chieftain of the O Callaghans may

1837), 2:208; *Census of Ireland 1851. General Alphabetical Index to the Townlands and Towns, Parishes, and Baronies of Ireland* (Dublin: Alex Thom, 1861), 87.

[37] Richard Hayes, *Manuscript Sources for the History of Irish Civilization*, 11 vols. (Boston: G. K. Hall, 1965), 3:559; *Rotulus Pipae Clonensis*, ed. Richard Caulfield (Cork: George Nash, 1859) 15, 23; Mervyn Archdall, *Monasticon Hibernicum. A History of the Abbeys, Priories and other Religious Houses in Ireland*, ed. Patrick F. Moran, 3 vols. (Dublin: W. B. Kelly, 1873-1876), 1:104; Lewis, *Dictionary*, 1:368-369; *AICC*, nos. 14411, 14567, 14713; James Grove-White, *Historical and Topographical Notes, etc. on Buttevant, Castletownroche, Doneraile, Mallow and Places in their Vicinity*, 3 vols. (Cork: Guy & Co. 1911) 2:221-224.

have been celebrated there.[38]

As late as the eighteenth century Egan O Rahilly (Aodhagán Ó Rathaille) saw nothing incongruous in using Cliodhna's voice to articulate his lament for Daniel O Callaghan. Although the power of the O Callaghan family by then had been broken, rendering the poet's language anachronistic, his words are reminiscent of praise poems written in honor of earlier chieftains. Cliodhna hailed Daniel as "the hawk of the Gaels of Erin,/ their hero in valour, their sword in battle/ . . . their high chieftain/ . . . their shield, their battle staff/ . . . their prince, their almoner . . . / their protecting chief . . . / their standard in battle, protecting them in the open day" (XV, ll. 45-60). "Cliodhna, from the white fairy rock," hailed "the noble warrior of bright Clonmeen . . . / the protecting robe of Ealla in the day of distress,/ protecting with the vigour of his strength and sword" (XVI, l. 3-8). Though written after the downfall of the Gaelic order these lines illustrate the virtues of leadership in battle and protection of their people that were construed as essential for a Gaelic chieftain.[39]

Now let us turn our attention to the vicissitudes of the O Callaghan family in the sixteenth century.

---

[38] Bowman, *Names*, 293-294, 309; AICC. 1:21, no. 9929; D. Franklin, "Cliodhna, Queen of the Fairies of South Munster,"*JCHAS* 3(1897): 81; Grove-White, *Notes*, 2:224; Kavanagh, *Kilshannig*, 60.

[39] *Poems of Egan O Rahilly,* no. XV, "On the Death of O Callaghan," and no. XVI, "On the Death of the Same."

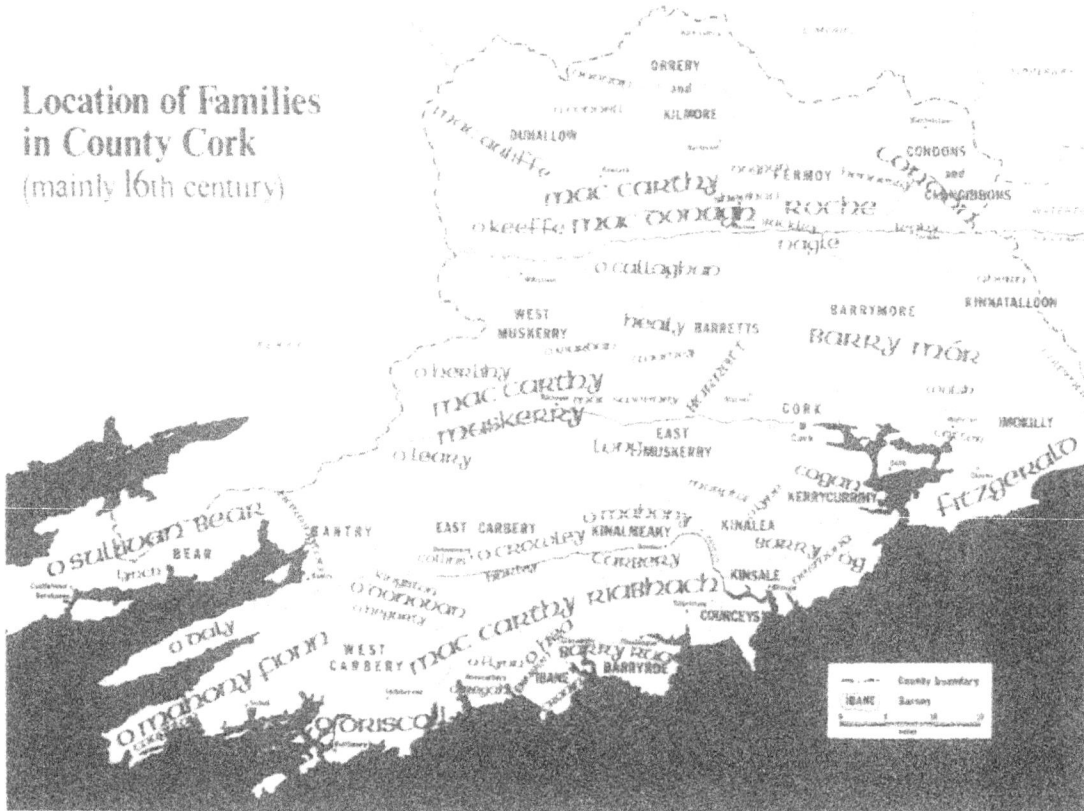

**Location of Families
in County Cork**
(mainly 16th century)

(From Ó Murchadha, *Family Names of County Cork*)

CHAPTER 2

THE O CALLAGHANS IN THE TUDOR AGE

Information concerning the O Callaghan family becomes considerably fuller in the sixteenth century, largely because of the extension of English authority through most of Munster and the attention given by the Tudor monarchs to questions of landholding, inheritances and the like. So much of what we know about the family's possessions and the links among its principal members comes from several *inquisitiones post mortem* or inquests carried out after the death of the chieftain; from royal pardons issued to rebellious members of the family; incidental references in official letters; and brief notes in the *Annals of the Four Masters*.

At the beginning of the sixteenth century Ireland had not yet been subdued by the English, though the Tudors would make more strenuous efforts to accomplish that goal than any of their predecessors. English government and English law were still confined mainly to the Pale, the region around Dublin, but there were important Anglo-Irish elements holding significant parts of the realm beyond that comparatively tiny area. The chief families of Anglo-Irish origin were the FitzGeralds, who held the earldoms of Kildare and Desmond, and their archrivals, the Butlers, earls of Ormond. In Munster, the most important Anglo-Irish family were the Geraldines or FitzGeralds of Desmond whose domains stretched across much of Cork, Limerick, and northwest Kerry. Given their territorial encroachments, a long-standing hostility existed between them and the MacCarthys of Cork and Kerry, who had once been kings of Munster, including the area now occupied by the FitzGeralds.

Among the several branches of the MacCarthys were MacCarthy Mór, whose domains reached from western Cork through Kerry, and who claimed lordship over all the rest; MacCarthy of Muskerry; and MacCarthy Reagh whose lands lay chiefly in Carbery. In the barony of Duhallow in northwest Cork, MacDonough MacCarthy was lord and counted among his principal followers O Callaghan, O Keeffe (Ó Caoimh), and MacAuliffe (MacAmhlaoibh), who all held lands along the Blackwater River from Mallow to the borders of Kerry. Territorial rivalries undoubtedly led to friction among them. A tradition of indeterminate date reported that when the MacCarthys attempted to build a castle at Gortrmore, the O Callaghans drove them off and then slaughtered them to a man in a battle near Drompeesh. As the MacCarthys used sledges or battleaxes to defend themselves, the place was known thereafter as Reaghnord (Reidh na nOrd), the plain of the sledges.[1]

O Callaghan lands extended along both banks of the river from a point slightly to the west of Mallow, to the junction of the Allow and the Blackwater just below Kanturk. Included in this territory were the parishs of Clonmeen and Kilshannig south of the river, part of Ballyclough, Roskeen, and parts of Castlemagner and Dromtariff north of the river. Butler estimated that the O Callaghan territory included at least fifty-one ploughlands or about 6,120 acres.[2] While MacDonough MacCarthy with his chief seat at Kanturk was the O Callaghans' immediate neighbor to the west, the lands of the Anglo-Irish Barrys and Roches bordered on the east. Barry, as viscount of Buttevant, had his residence there on the Awbeg River, while Roche was lord of Fermoy. The river Clydagh near Mourne Abbey divided O Callaghan holdings from the Roches. O Callaghan territory was commonly called Pobul Uí Cheallacháin, literally, the People of Callaghan, or O Callaghan's Country. The O Callaghans naturally intermarried with the MacDonoughs, O Keeffes, MacAuliffes, and MacCarthys of Muskerry, but as marriages were a convenient way of cementing political alliances they did not neglect their Anglo-Irish neighbors, the Roches, FitzGeralds, and Barrys.

Donal MacCarthy Mór (d. 1596), the most powerful of the Gaelic princes in Munster, whom Queen Elizabeth created Earl of Clancar or Clancarthy in 1565, claimed lordship over the others, including the

> countrey of McDonoghoe (called Duallo) which hath within it three other countries, O Callaghan's country, McAunlief's country and O Keeffe's country. He claimeth in these countries the giving of the rod to the chief Lords at their first entry, who by receiving a white wand at his hands, for which they are to pay him a certain duty, are thereby declared from thenceforth to be Lords of those countries. He claimeth also that they are to rise out with him when he maketh war, to maintain for him twenty-seven Galloglasses, besides to find him for a certain time, when he cometh to their countries.[3]

This report to Lord Burghley, Queen Elizabeth's Principal Secretary, stressed the obligation of MacDonough MacCarthy, O Callaghan, MacAuliffe, and O Keeffe to provide military forces (the gallowglasses were heavy-armed professional soldiers) and hospitality to MacCarthy Mór. By receiving the white wand from him, they were invested with their offices and were acknowledged as lords or chiefs of their name. As the earlier

---

[1] Gillman, "Chieftains," *JCHAS*, Series 2, 3 (1897): 203, n. 6 denied that O Callaghan, O Keeffe, and MacAuliffe were dependents of MacDonough, as alleged by Charles Smith, *The Ancient and Present State of the County and City of Cork*, new ed., 2 vols. (Cork: John Connor, 1815), 34-35. Gillman said that "all four chiefs are equally styled 'followers of the late Earl of Clancarr'" in British Library, Add. MSS no. 39, 873, State of Ireland 1578. In 1600, however, Sir George Carew described O Callaghan as a petty lord under MacDonough. *CSPIreland. Henry VIII*, 10:136; Bowman, *Names*, 269; *AICC*, no. 14692.

[2] William F. T. Butler, *Gleanings from Irish History* (London: Longmans, 1925), 12, 79-80, 97; Jean J. MacCarthy, "The Ancient and Noble Families of Duhallow," *SD* 10 (1996): 63-73; Con Tarrant, "The Chieftains of Pobul Uí Cheallacháin, Co. Cork," *SD* 5 (1984): 19-27; Kavanagh, *Kilshannig*, 6.

[3] Gillman, "Chieftains," *JCHAS*, Series 2, 3 (1897): 203-204, quoted Sir Warham St. Leger's letter to Lord Burghley, in the British Library, Add. MSS no. 39, 873, State of Ireland 1578. Sir William Herbert's "Description of Munster," *CSP Ireland*, 3:534, written in June 1588, quotes this text; C. B. Gibson, *The History of the County and City of Cork*, 2 vols. (London: T.C. Newby, 1861), 1:280-282.

title of *rí* or king had long since fallen into disuse it was common to refer to the chieftain simply as O Callaghan, or in more modern usage, The O Callaghan. English sources also describe the chieftain as chief of his name (*capitalis nominis sui*) or captain of his nation (*capitaneus nacionis sue*). Moreover, English spelling of Gaelic names now begins to appear in the many documents of the Tudor age. Thus O Callaghan emerges as the usual transliteration of Ó Ceallacháin, although English scribes often rendered the name in other forms, for example, O Kellaghan, O Chalghan, O Callaghane, this last an approximation of the Irish pronunciation of the last syllable, -aun. As with surnames, so also with personal names: Tadhg becomes Teige; Conchubhar, Conoghor or Conor; Donnchadh, Donough; and so forth. Occasionally latinized forms of these names appear, for example, Thaddeus for Tadhg, Cornelius for Conchubhar, Donatus for Donnchadh.

Tadhg Ruadh Ó Ceallacháin

In a broad context the sixteenth century was the age of the Tudors, the first of whom, Henry VII (1485-1509), came to power after the long civil war between the Lancastrians and Yorkists known as the Wars of the Roses. Ireland was involved only indirectly as the Anglo-Irish, especially the earls of Kildare and Desmond, gave their support to the Yorkist cause. What attitude the O Callaghans adopted in this, if any, is unknown. A laconic entry in the *Annals of the Four Masters* informs us that in 1500 David Barry, archdeacon of Cloyne and Cork, was slain by Thomas Barry and Muintir O Callaghan, that is the O Callaghan family. David Barry had previously killed his own kinsman Barry Mór, and the earl of Desmond subsequently ordered David's body dug up and burned. These several acts of vengeance probably were prompted by interfamilial divisions and rivalries of long standing but may also reflect the tensions between Yorkist and Tudor supporters. However that may be, the earl of Kildare, having convinced Henry VII of his loyalty, was confirmed in the post of Lord Deputy, and led an army into Munster in 1510, passing through Duhallow and taking MacDonough's castle of Kanturk; whether the O Callaghans participated in this affair is unknown.[4]

As the new century dawned, the head of the O Callaghan family was probably Tadhg Ruadh son of Conchubar Laighneach. Henceforth I will refer to these men by the anglicized forms of their names, that is, Teige Roe and Conoghor Reinagh. The former was also known as Teige Roe Bacach, meaning Red-Haired Teige, the Lame. His activities are scarcely known, but the date of his death can be determined approximately. An inquisition of 1594 stated that he died thirty-five years before his son's death in 1577, that is in 1542; but an inquisition of 1609 reported that "Thadeus alias Teige Roe alias O Callaghan, *principalis nationis suae*," that is, "O Callaghan, chief of his nation," died at Dromaneen (Dromanín) castle about seventy-two years before, or in 1537 While the inquisition of 1609 agrees with the pedigree given in the Book of Munster that Teige Roe's father was Conoghor Reinagh, the Four Masters affirm that he was the son of Owny (Uaithne) son of Cahir (Cathaoir). Accepting the evidence of the Four Masters, Gillman placed Teige Roe's death in 1568. On the contrary, Butler argued that the testimony of the two inquisitions is preferable and that Teige Roe should be identified as

---

[4] *FM*, 4:1257-1259; 5:1305, 1335, 1275; Gillman, "Chieftains," *JCHAS*, Series 2, 3 (1897): 208, misled by the Four Masters, thought that Cahir was the chief around 1500.

the son of Conoghor Reinagh and that his death should be placed somewhere between 1537 and 1542, probably before 1539.[5]

According to the inquisition of 1609 Teige Roe by lineal descent from his father Conoghor Reinagh held in fief in Poble O Callaghan, or O Callaghan's Countrie, the following places: the manors, castles, villages, and lands of Dromaneen and Clonmeen, each containing three carucates or ploughlands, as well as the following:

Property	Car.	Property	Car.
Ballyheen	1	Kilcaskan	3
Gortnagross	3	Gurteenbeha, Maine, Kippagh	3
Carrigolane	1	Roskeen, Cloonteens	3
Kilvealaton, Dromahane, Kilpadder	3	Pallas, Gearanaskagh, Gortbofinna	3
Gortvoclyne	3	Dromrastill	1.5
Gortroe	3	Kilcranathan	1
Rathcomane	3	Rathmore, Rathbeg	.5
Gortmore, Glawnyketenerick	1.5	Garranasath	.5
Banteer	3		

Also he received in capital rents forty shillings from the village of Ballymacmurragh (containing three carucates), and two measures of wheat, two chickens, four sheep, and three days yearly labor by each plough on the land. From the village and lands of Skarragh (3 carucates) he was entitled to yearly capital rents of forty-four shillings sterling, and three pounds sterling each year from Gortincowley (1.5 carucates; Gortincowley was later identified with Garrymcowney, and later still as Longueville. Gortvoclyne mentioned above may be the same as Gortincowley). The total area involved was about 40 carucates or about 4,800 acres (with approximately 120 acres to a carucate).

As English scribes had great difficulty in recording Irish place names in English there are numerous variations in spelling in the several inquisitions carried out in this period. John O Donovan copied the inquisitions as from the originals (lost in 1916), thereby contributing further confusion to spelling. While some places remain to be identified, those that are known include the castles of Dromaneen and Clonmeen, south of the Blackwater, the one to the east, the other to the west, at a distance of about four miles from one another. Running from east to west, Carrigolane (later known as Dromore), Kilvealaton, Dromahane, Gortroe, Rathcomane (this name seems to have disappeared), Gortmore, Banteer, Skarragh, and Glawneketnerick (Gleann an Chitinéaraigh, Glen North and South) lie south of the river. North of the river from west to east are Ballyheen, then southward to Ballymacmurragh, Kilcaskan, Maine (Money), Kippagh, Roskeen, Cloonteens, Pallas, Gearanaskagh, Gortbofinna, Gortnagross, Dromrastill, Garrymcowney, and Kilcranathan.[6]

Teige Roe, who married Oiléan or Ellen, daughter of Donough Óg MacDonough MacCarthy of Duhallow, left several sons, namely, Donough who succeeded him, Teige

[5] Dublin, Royal Irish Academy, Ordnance Survey Inquisitions, Cork, 1:137-148, no. 12, inquisition at Cork, 20 April 1609; *LM*, 160-161, 216; *FM*, 5:1695; Gillman, "Chieftains," *JCHAS*, Series 2, 3 (1897): 211; Grove-White, *Notes*, 3:65-69 gives the pedigree from Gillman. Butler, *Gleanings*, 81-82; *BIFR*, 888.

[6] RIA O.S.Inquisitions, Cork, 1:137-148, no. 12.

Óg, Cahir, Dermot, Conoghor, Owen, and Donal. His death probably occurred at Dromaneen in 1537. If each of his sons or even several of them had sons of their own we have a clear example of an expanding clan.[7]

Donnchadh Ó Ceallacháin (1537?-1577)

The concluding years of Teige Roe's chieftainship coincided with momentous events set in motion by King Henry VIII (1509-1547). Not only did he effect a permanent breach with Rome by declaring himself the Supreme Head of the Church of England, but he also initiated the Tudor effort to exercise greater control over Ireland. A docile parliament in Dublin in 1536-1537 acknowledged him as Head of the Church of Ireland and also ordered the dissolution of the monasteries. The dissolution seems to have been carried out over the next several years. The monastery of Augustinian friars at Clonmeen founded by the O Callaghans at some uncertain date was probably dissolved about this time. The Augustinian priory of Ballybeg about a mile south of Buttevant was also suppressed and its properties came under the control of Dermot, the son of Teige Roe, as commendatory prior.[8]

Henry VIII, furthermore, crushed the power of the Geraldines of Kildare, long the dominant family in Ireland, and was able to overcome the attempt of the Geraldines of Desmond to form an alliance with the O Neills and others to seek vengeance. Indeed, the Anglo-Irish and Irish lords recognized Henry VIII's new title, King of Ireland, and the most distinguished among them were rewarded with earldoms. Thus O Brien became earl of Thomond, Burke, earl of Clanrickard, and O Neill, earl of Tyrone.[9]

The Lord Deputy, Leonard Grey, had the responsibility of convincing the Irish to accept the new religious settlement and of pacifying the country. Intent on establishing James FitzMaurice FitzGerald as earl of Desmond against his rival James FitzJohn FitzGerald, Grey campaigned in Cork in November 1539. In doing so he apparently had the collaboration or at least the acquiescence of Cormac Óg MacCarthy, lord of Muskerry. The MacCarthys of Muskerry, seeking to achieve their independence both of MacCarthy Mór and the earls of Desmond, tended to favor the English government. For much the same reasons the new head of the O Callaghan family, Donough, the son of Teige Roe, seems to have followed Muskerry's lead. Thus Grey entered O Callaghan's Country, but was unable to cross the Blackwater River to engage James FitzJohn who stood opposite Dromaneen. Although Grey had to return to Cork, his expedition did have positive results.[10] A letter of 24 December 1539 indicates that Donough O Callaghan and

[7] *BIFR*, 888.

[8] Smith, *Cork,* 1:291, 315; Archdall, *Monasticon,* 1:96-97, 104; Lewis, *Dictionary*, 1: 122-124, 368-369; *AICC,* 14379; Brendan Bradshaw, *The Dissolution of the Religious Orders in Ireland under Henry VIII* (Cambridge: University Press, 1974).

[9] *FM,* 5:1477; R. Dudley Edwards, *Ireland in the Age of the Tudors: The Destruction of Hiberno-Norman Civilization* (London: Croom Helm, 1977), 39-63.

[10] Richard Bagwell, *Ireland under the Tudors,* 3 vols. (London: Longman, 1885-1890; reprint London: Holland Press 1963), 1:242; Gillman, "Chieftains," *JCHAS,* Series 2, 3 (1897): 208-209, said that in Henry VIII's time The O Callaghan was Donough, son of Cahir. Here he followed Connellan's translation of the Four Masters (Dublin, 1846) who related that in 1577 "O Callaghan, i.e., Donough the son of Teige Roe, son of Anthony [sic, recte Donogh] son of Cahir died." In the Irish text, instead of Anthony we read Uaithne, which O'Donovan translated as Owny. *BIFR,* 888.

others had made peace with the English. The earl of Desmond submitted fully in 1541. Then on 26 September 1542 Donough O Callaghan, *"suae nationis primus,"* or chief of his nation, joined MacCarthy Mór, Lord Roche, MacCarthy Reagh, MacCarthy of Muskerry, Barry Mór, Donal O Sullivan, and MacDonough of Duhallow in accepting Henry VIII as their natural and liege lord, promising to serve him against all others and to recognize him as Supreme Head of the Anglican and Irish Church on earth, "immediately under Christ." They also promised to maintain the peace, not to levy exactions for raising troops, nor to demand black rents (*duibhchíos*, illicit tributes) from the inhabitants of Cork, Youghal, or Kinsale, three towns largely English in population.[11] The lords of Munster, who bore their loyalty to the king lightly, gave no guarantees whatever that they would abide by their pledges. Their recognition of the king as Head of the Church probably meant very little to them. Henry VIII himself knew that their submission would last only as long as it suited their purposes.

Donough, the son of Teige Roe, was the subject of an anonymous poetic eulogy entitled *Caithréim Dhonnchaidh mhic Thaidhg Rua Uí Cheallacháin* or *The Warlike Career of Donough son of Teige Roe*.[12] The poem has little literary merit, as it is not much more than a listing of places plundered by its hero. The opening line conveys the theme: *"Deacair comhaireamh a chreach* - Difficult it is to enumerate his plunderings." As it now stands the poem is incomplete (although it runs to over 400 lines) and is totally lacking in any chronology. The editor, Eamonn de hÓir, pointed out that Donough's cattle raids and plundering expeditions ranged from Waterford to Kerry, a truly extensive area. While de hÓir questioned the veracity of the poet, he noted that the raids were launched principally against the Anglo-Irish such as the FitzGeralds and FitzMaurices of Limerick and Kerry and the Barrys and Roches of Cork. While it may be true that there is a degree of exaggeration in the poem, conflicts between O Callaghan and the neighboring families of Barry and Roche were undoubtedly quite real. The pillaging of Ballyclough and Buttevant to the north of O Callaghan's Country, pertaining to the Barrys, and of Castletownroche, one of the seats of the Roches, may very well have taken place. Intermarriage among the Barrys, Roches, and O Callaghans probably also occurred from time to time as a means of assuring peaceful relations. The poet also tells us that Donough attacked Maurice FitzThomas of the FitzMaurice clan (l. 258); defeated John of Kerry, another of the Geraldines (l. 289); besieged Ballincollig in Kerry and released O Keeffe from imprisonment (ll. 285-288); attacked MacCarthy Mór (l. 273) and MacDonough (l. 269); and killed Eoghan mac Taidhg (l. 281). The identification of these events and personalities poses a number of unresolved problems. One wonders, for example, whether Eoghan mac Taidhg was one of his brothers, perhaps the Owen of Dromore recorded in 1573. The poet, while referring to Donough as the son of Teige,

---

[11] Letter from William Wise to Walter Cowley in *CSP Ireland*, 1:51, no. 39; *FM*, 5:1419-1423; Gillman, "Chieftains," *JCHAS*, Series 2, 3 (1897): 209-210, citing Sir Richard Cox, *Hibernia Anglicana*, 2 vols. (London:, 1690), 1:273; Butler, *Gleanings*, 81-82; Edwards, *Tudors*, 42-43; Bagwell, *Tudors*, 1:267-268; *Early Modern Ireland 1534-1691* (Oxford: Oxford University Press, 1976), 1-69, vol. 3 in *A New History of Ireland*, ed. T. W. Moody, F. X. Martin, F. J. Byrne (Oxford: Oxford University Press. 1976).

[12] Eamonn de hÓir, "Caithréim Dhonnchaidh mhic Thaidhg Rua Uí Cheallacháin," *North Munster Studies: Essays in Commemoration of Monsignor Michael Molony* (Limerick: Thomond Archaeological Society, 1967), 505-525. I am deeply indebted to Mr. de hÓir for a summary, verse by verse, of the poem and a commentary upon its significance. Ó Murchadha, *Names*, 67.

also described him as the son or heir of Oiléan, that is, Ellen, daughter of MacDonough MacCarthy (ll. 29, 73, 202, 235). By saluting him as O Callaghan (ll. 2, 85, 197, 357) the poet acknowledged his status as chieftain of his family. Raids such as those described in the poem were a method of acquiring wealth through plunder, principally of cattle. The chieftain, thus enriched, could then extend his generosity to his followers.

We know nothing of Donough's attitude or policy toward the religious changes introduced under Henry VIII's successors, Edward VI (1547-1553), Mary (1553-1558), and Elizabeth (1558-1603), but in the latter reign more intensive efforts were made to subjugate Ireland. During Donough's chieftainship, Munster was thrown into turmoil partly because of the rivalry of the earls of Desmond and Ormond whose lands were contiguous on the borders of Cork and Tipperary, but also because of the rising of the earl of Desmond, challenging Queen Elizabeth's rights to the throne. Traditional hostilities between the Geraldines and the MacCarthys, however, were reflected in the opposition of Cormac Óg MacCarthy, tenth lord of Muskerry, to the rebellious earl. In this he seems to have had the alliance of Donough O Callaghan, though other members of the family clearly sided with the rebels. Perhaps, as Herbert Gillman pointed out, this was intended to preserve the chief's title to his lands against any charge of treason. In a memorandum of May 1562 concerning the conditions under which Gerald, earl of Desmond (1558-1583), would be received into the queen's favor again, it was stipulated that he "suffer the Lord Great Barry, the Lord Roche, Little Barry, Barry Roe . . . McCarthy More, McCarthy Reagh . . . O Sullivan Beare, O Sullivan More, McDonogho, O Callaghan and others in Munster to remain in the Queen's Peace." Among the victims of the innumerable wars among the Geraldines was Tadhg Ruadh Ua Ceallacháin (Teige Roe), killed in July 1568 near Lixnaw in a battle between James FitzGerald, grandson of the earl of Desmond, and Thomas FitzMaurice of Kerry. This Teige Roe apparently was a younger brother of the chieftain, Donough.[13]

The uncertain loyalty of the Irish chiefs was by now well known to the queen's representatives. As an ominous foreboding of things to come, a proposal was presented in March 1569 to plant the province of Munster with loyal Englishmen. As a means to that end, "all the lands belonging to the earl of Clancarthy [i.e., MacCarthy Mór], the O Driscolls, the O Donoghues, the O Mahoneys, the O Callaghans, the McSwinneys, and the O Sullivans," would be granted to those who would undertake to settle them. First, however, it was necessary to suppress the Irish rebels. In an assessment of the situation in 1569, when the presidency of Munster was established to subdue the area, we are told that "the meetest place to annoy McDonough, McCawley [MacAuliffe], McKeefe [O Keeffe], and O Kallaghan, if they should be out [i.e., in rebellion] is to place a garrison in Buttevant," about twelve miles north of Mallow. In the same text the comparative military strength of the lords of Duhallow is given. MacAuliffe could raise six horsemen and 200 footmen, "being a follower of McDonough;" O Keeffe could raise three horsemen and 100 foot; O Callaghan, seven horsemen and 100 foot, and MacDonough, eight horsemen and 100 foot. MacDonough MacCarthy, O Keefe, MacAuliffe, and O Callaghan would also be assessed 100 axes to pay for gallowglasses.[14]

---

[13] *CSP Ireland*, 1:195; *FM*, 5:1625-1629; Gillman, "Chieftains," *JCHAS*, Series 2, 3 (1897): 211-213; Bagwell, *Tudors*, 2:145; Edwards, *Tudors*, 104, 115-116.

[14] Peter J. Piveronous, "Sir Warham St. Leger and the First Munster Plantation, 1568-1569," *Eire-Ireland* 14 (1979): 24-25; *Calendar of Carew Papers in the Lambeth Library, 1515-1624*, 6 vols., ed. J. S.

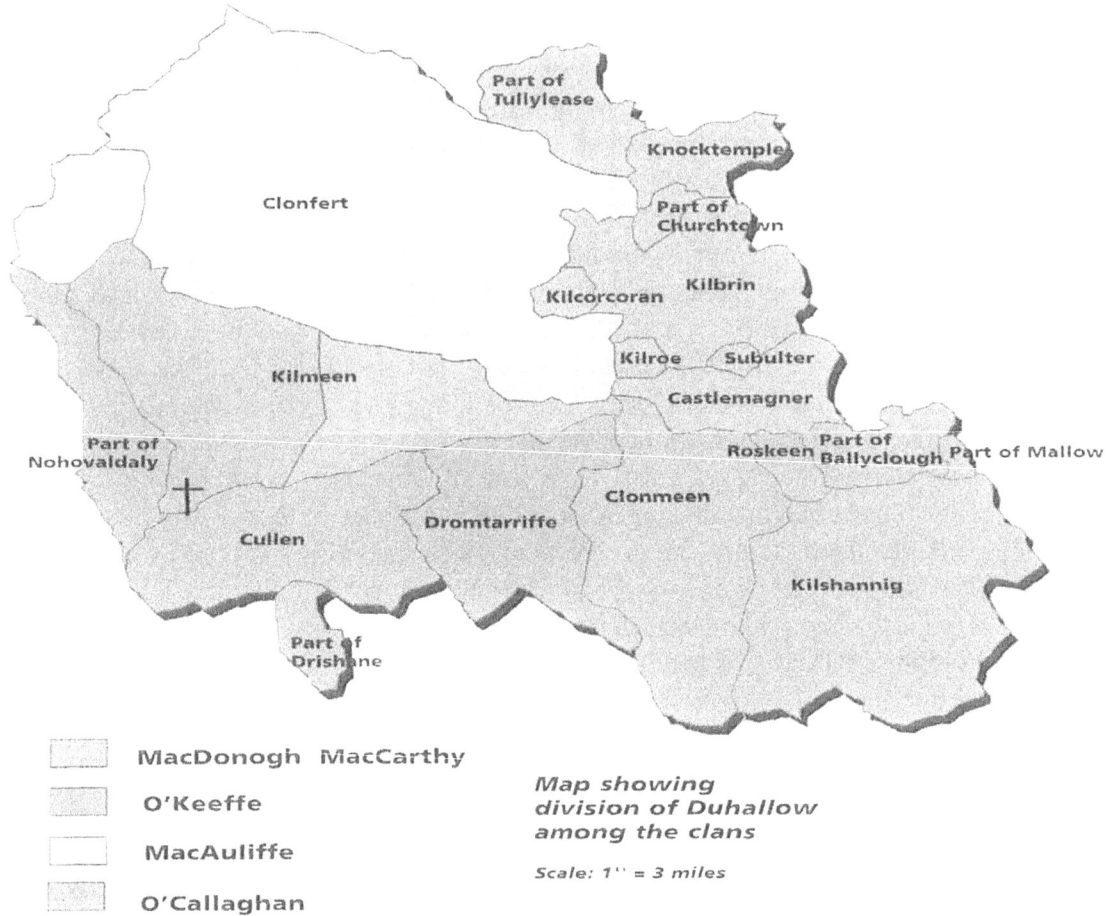

Part of Tullylease

Knocktemple

Clonfert

Part of Churchtown

Kilbrin

Kilcorcoran

Kilroe   Subulter

Castlemagner

Kilmeen

Part of Nohovaldaly   Roskeen   Part of Ballyclough   Part of Mallow

Clonmeen

Dromtarriffe

Cullen

Kilshannig

Part of Drishane

MacDonogh MacCarthy

O'Keeffe

MacAuliffe

O'Callaghan

Map showing division of Duhallow among the clans

Scale: 1'' = 3 miles

Division of Duhallow among the Clans

(From Bowman, *Place Names and Antiquities of the Barony of Duhallow*)

From the government's point of view, one of the principal causes of disorder was the earl of Desmond, but he had been kept in honorable confinement in London since 1565. As a condition of his release, he was required

> to suffer the Lord FitzMorice of Kerry, the Lord Great Barry, the Lord Roche, Young Barry, the Red Barry, the Lord Cursey, the viscount of Dessus, the earl of Clancarr, McArtereaghe [MacCarthy Resgh], Teige McCormocke, O Sullivan Beare, O Suleyvan More, McDonoghe, O Callaghan, and all the other noblemen and gentlemen of English and Irish blood within Mounster to live and to remain upon the queen's majesty's peace without attempting of anything against them.

Brewer and W. Bullen (London: Public Record Office, 1867-1873; reprint New York: Kraus, 1974), 1:391, 393, 395 (1515-74). On 26 October 1569 the Lord Deputy, Sir Henry Sidney, and his council sent a rather cryptic note to the Privy Council in London mentioning both MacDonough and O Callaghan, but without indicating their activities; *CSP Ireland*, 1:421.

Desmond responded on 21 January 1572/3 that he would not molest any of them, "saving such as hold their lands" from him. In the meantime, during his absence, his cousin, Sir James FitzMaurice, organized a Catholic confederacy against Queen Elizabeth. The rebellion was suppressed, however, and FitzMaurice left for the continent in 1573.[15]

In the aftermath of the rising, the government issued numerous pardons for offenses committed.[16] Although the chieftain, Donough, seems not to have participated in the rebellion, perhaps because he was aging, the following were among the more prominent O Callaghans receiving pardons:

Name	Place	Date
Cahir Óg, gentleman	Dromaneen; Banteer	1573, 1577
Conoghor	Dromore	1573
Donal	Pallas	1573
Owen	Dromore	1573
Donogh McCahir, gentleman	Dromaneen	1573
Teige McCahir	Buttevant, Kilpadder	1573, 1575
Dermod McOwen	Baron of Dromore	1573
Donal McThomas McOwen	Roskeen	1573
Callaghan McDermod	Leitrim, Condon's Country; Dromore	1574; 1577
Irrelagh McDermod	Leitrim, Condon's Country; Dromore	1574; 1577
Teige na Muchorie McDermod	Gortmore	1577
Callaghan McConoghor		1577

Cahir Óg, Conoghor, Donal, and Owen were sons of the chieftain, Teige Roe Bacach, and brothers of the current chieftain. Donough McCahir, Teige McCahir, Dermod McOwen, Callaghan McDermod, Irrelagh McDermod, and Teige na Muchorie (Tadhg na moichéirghe, Teige of the early rising?, also called Teige McDermod) were grandsons of Teige Roe Bacach; Donal McThomas McOwen was his great-grandson. Callaghan McConoghor was a grandson and successor of the chieftain, Donough. Condon's Country lay to the east of Mallow. In 1575 Teige McCahir was serving as a horseman with Cormac Óg MacCarthy, lord of Muskerry.[17]

As English authorities attempted to transliterate Irish names, they resorted to many phonetic variations. The name O Callaghan is spelled often with a K, sometimes with a final e. Personal names favored by the family with their Irish originals included the following: Cahir (Cathair), Callaghan (Ceallachán), Conoghor or Conor (Conchubhar),

---

[15] *CCP*, 1:431; *FM*, 5:1653-1665; Bagwell, *Tudors*, 2:237-238; Edwards, *Tudors*, 125-126, 131-132.

[16] This information is found in the *Calendar of Fiants* (warrants to the Court of Chancery for grants under the great seal) published in the *Reports of the Deputy Keeper of the Public Records and Keeper of the State Papers in Ireland*, vols. 7-22 (Dublin: Public Record Office, 1875-1890). These *Reports* will be cited by number and abbreviated *RDK*; thus *12 RDK* means the twelfth report.

[17] *12 RDK*, 92-98, 132, 138, 145, 193, nos. 2243 (5 May 1573), 2248 (6 May), 2251-2252 (6 May), 2257 (6 May), 2264 (8 May), 2464 (30 September 1574), 2515 (17 November), 2576-2577 (3 May 1575); *13 RDK*, 17, 29, 41, 44, nos. 2928 (16 November 1576), 2941 (21 November),. 3031 (20 May 1577), 3083 (6 September), 3095-3096 (7 September). See Appendices I-II.

latinized as Cornelius, Dermot (Diarmuid), Donal (Domhnall), Donogh or Donough (Donnchadh), Owen (Eoghan), Owny or Wohny (Uaithne), Shane (Seán), Teige or Thady (Tadhg), latinized as Thadeus. One also finds Kennedy (Cinnéide), John (Seán), Thomas (Tomás), and Irrelagh (Iorghalach). Given the constant repetition of certain names there had to be some way of differentiating one person from another. The word Óg or Oge, meaning the younger, could distinguish Cahir Óg (the younger) from his father Cahir Mór or More (the elder). A notable physical characteristic might be singled out as in Teige Roe Bacach (Tadhg Ruadh Bacach), the redhaired, lame Teige. Most often a short genealogy naming a man's father and oftentimes his grandfather was employed. Thus Donough McCahir McTeige Roe tells us that Donough was the son of Cahir, the son of Teige Roe, the chieftain who died around 1537.

The pardons also identify the residence of some of those mentioned, such as Dromaneen, Clonmeen, Dromore, the Pallas, Gortmore, Banteer, Roskeen, and Kilpadder, all lying within O Callaghan's Country on both sides of the Blackwater. It is evident that the custom of moving members of the chieftain's immediate family from one holding to another was still observed. Other persons cited in the appendix as residents of Carrigadrohid, Castle Hinchy, and Blarney probably were MacCallaghans of Muskerry. Individuals are sometimes described as gentlemen - these usually were the sons or grandsons of the chief - or as yeomen. Sometimes they were listed as gallowglass, meaning that they were professional soldiers.

Finally, it seems possible to make some estimate of the number of O Callaghans during the second half of the sixteenth century. According to the government's calculation in 1569, the O Callaghans could raise seven horsemen and 100 footsoldiers. Were these all O Callaghans? One cannot say, but if they were, would it not be within reason to say that there were perhaps as many women and children and older persons? If so, one could guess a total number of 300-400 O Callaghans. A smaller number might be more accurate, if one takes into account that the total of those pardoned over the years from 1573-1577 was about 45-50. If one doubled or trebled that number to account for women and children, then the totals would range from 90-100 to 135-150. My inclination is to believe that the number of able-bodied O Callaghan men and women at any given point was about 200, and if one included children and the old and infirm, then perhaps 300 to 400.

The chieftain, Donough, seems to have remained aloof from these wars, as much from age as from policy. The Lord Deputy, Sir Henry Sidney, reported that, on coming to Cork on 23 December 1575 he was visited by various earls and lords, including those of the Irishry, such as O Keeffe and "the sons (or heirs as they would have them) of McAwlive[MacAuliffe] and O Callaghan, the old men not being able to come by reason of age and infirmity; O Maghan and O Driscoll; each of these have land enough (with good order) to live like a knight here or there."[18]

As Donough had already been chieftain for nearly forty years, he must indeed have been of advanced age, perhaps in his sixties. In view of that fact, he made provision for the future in a conveyance drawn up at Clonmeen on 22 September 1574. According to this document, Donough McTeige O Callaghan of Dromaneen, chief of his sept, granted to Calvat or Callaghane M'Conoghor O Callaghan the manor of Dromaneen with all its rights and appurtenances, namely, the castle and lands of Clonmeen, Ballyheen,

---

[18] *CCP*, 2:39, no. 36; Gillman, "Chieftains," *JCHAS*, Series 2, 3 (1897): 213.

Dromore, Turcomerehie, Gortnagross, Gortmore, Gortnewolyne, Gortroe, Banteer, Kilcaskan, Rathcomane, Pallas, and the "entire country and lordship of O Callaghan in the County of Cork," to hold during his lifetime. After Callaghan's death these lands would remain with Donough until his death; thereupon they would pass to his heirs forever. From this it would seem that Donough's sons Conoghor and Teige Roe had both predeceased him and that his heir was his grandson, Callaghan, son of Conoghor and Katherine, the daughter of Maurice, Lord Roche. In the event of Callaghan's death without heirs, the estates would pass to his nephew Donough McTeige Roe McConoghor. Parenthetically it may be noted that Conoghor's marriage to Lord Roche's daughter may have been intended to foster better relations between the two families and perhaps create a political alliance.[19]

The properties mentioned include several cited in 1609 as pertaining to Teige Roe, namely, Dromaneen, Clonmeen, Ballyheen, Gortnagross, Gortmore, Gortnewolyne (Gortvoclyne in 1609), Gortroe, Banteer, Kilcaskan, and Pallas, but Dromore and Turcomerehie, and Rathcomane are not. Moreover, the identification of Turcomerehie remains a mystery.

The Inquisition of 1609 cited above records the substance of this document, noting that Donough enfeoffed Calvacius O Callaghan, otherwise called Callaghan McConoghor, with all the manors, castles, villages and lands of "O Callaghan's countrie alias Poble O Callaghan." The name Calvacius or Calvat (Ir. Calbhach) suggests that Callaghan was bald.[20] In accordance with Irish custom, Callaghan had probably been recognized as tanist to his grandfather.

Donough died in February 1577 at Clonmeen. The Four Masters record under that year the death of Donough, son of Teige Roe, son of Owney, son of Cahir, and the succesion of Callaghan, son of Conor, son of Donough. As already noted, this genealogy does not square with that given in the inquisitions and other sources where Donough is listed as the son of Teige Roe, son of Conoghor Reinagh. On this account Gillman has presented a highly confusing account of the succession to the chieftainship in the first half of the sixteenth century. He did point out that Donough was married to the daughter of John FitzGibbon of Mitchelstown, County Cork, known as the White Knight. Donough's sons Conoghor, Owen, and Teige predeceased him. His daughter Eilis (Alice) married David FitzGibbon, lord of Kilmore.[21]

Ceallachán Mac Conchubhair Ó Ceallacháin, 1577-1578

Ceallachán mac Conchubair, that is, Callaghan McConoghor O Callaghan succeeded to the chieftainship upon the death of his grandfather Donough. Sir Henry Sidney, in a letter to the queen in March 1576, alluded to Donough's designation of Callaghan as his heir. After commenting that Sir Cormac McTeige MacCarthy, lord of Muskerry, was on his way to London, "anxious that he should be the first of his family to

[19] *Calendar of the Patent and Close Rolls of Chancery in Ireland in the Reigns of Henry VIII, Edward VI, Mary, and Elizabeth*, 2 vols., ed. James Morrin (London and Dublin: Her Majesty's Stationery Office, 1861-1862), 2:393, no. 17.

[20] RIA, O.S. Inquisitions, Cork, 1:138-141, no. 12.

[21] *FM*, 5:1694-1695; RIA, O.S. Inquisitions, Cork, 1:138-141, no. 12; *LM*, 160-161, 216; Gillman, "Chieftains," *JCHAS*, Series 2, 3 (1897): 211-214; Butler, *Gleanings*, 81-82; *BIFR*, 888.

see his sovereign and that he may surrender his lands and take them again of your Majesty and yield you rent and service," he noted that "Young Ocaloghan who accompanies him likewise to surrender his lands and hold them of her Majesty is heir to his grandfather, who being old, has assured his lands to him."[22] This would seem to indicate an intention to surrender all the lands of the O Callaghans to the crown to be received back again in fief by the chieftain. This would in fact mean an overturning of traditional Irish law which did not acknowledge the chieftain as the sole owner of the lands, as seems to be implied here. In any case, there is no record that Callaghan effected such a surrender at this time.

Indeed, Callaghan McConoghor McDonough survived only one year as chief of his name, for he was drowned in the Blackwater river in 1578, according to the Four Masters: "and it was from a blemish of his revenge that he departed, before he had passed an entire year in the enjoyment of his patrimony, between the death of his grandfather and his drowning." No explanation of the meaning of "a blemish of his revenge" was given. The inquisition of 1609 recorded his death on 6 June 1578, without heirs of his body, although he did have a son, Cahir Modarta, who was apparently illegitimate. Nevertheless, he would have a significant impact on O Callaghan history.[23]

The sixteenth century ushered in a period of great transition marked by the steady encroachment of English authority on the Gaelic and Anglo-Irish lords. As the century drew to a close, even more substantive changes loomed for all of Ireland and the traditional clan system would be effectively destroyed.

---

[22] *Report on the Manuscripts of the Lord de L'Isle and Dudley preserved at Penshurst Place*, 6 vols. London: Historical Manuscripts Commission, 1925-1966), 2:53.

[23] *FM*, 5:1695; RIA, O.S. Inquisitions, Cork, 1:137-148, no. 12; *BIFR*, 888.

The following map of Ireland prepared by Abraham Ortelius in 1572 contains the earliest illustration of the O Callaghan lordship that I know. At that time the chieftain was Donough. The map places Ireland in a horizontal position so that the province of Munster is situated at the left side. The map locates O Calegane in North Cork on the Blackwater River. For reasons of space the first five letters of the name are written above the others and separated by a hyphen: O Cale-gane. This is one of the few clan names on the map. The area west of the name (toward the top of the page) is shown as wooded.[24] A better informed Ortelius, in his map of 1602, recorded O Callaghan, O Keeffe, and MacDonough in Duhallow. The full map is followed by a smaller one showing more detail.

Ortelius, *Hiberniae Britannicae Insulae Nova Descriptio*

---

[24] Beinecke Library, Yale University, *Hiberniae Britannicae Insulae, Nova Descriptio* Antwerp: Christoph Plantin, 1574).

The name O Cale-gane appears below a wooded area in the lower portion of the map.

The Province of Munster (Momonia) according to Ortelius

CHAPTER 3

THE END OF THE O CALLAGHAN CLAN

In the last decade of the sixteenth century the history of the O Callaghans underwent a profound change, as the lands that the family had held as a family, as a clan, were transformed into a personal lordship held by the chief and passed on to his heirs in accordance with the English law of inheritance. This effectively abolished the traditional Irish law regulating the utilization of the clan lands and the determination of the chief. Henceforth English law, rather than the Irish law of tanistry, would determine the head of the family. All of this was a foreshadowing of the eventual collapse of the relationship between the chief and the family in the Cromwellian period. Given the resolution of Queen Elizabeth and her ministers to subjugate Gaelic Ireland once and for all, the transformations just described were inevitable.

Conchubhar na Cairrge Ó Ceallacháin, 1578-1612

Upon the death of Callaghan McConoghor, his nephew, Donough, son of Teige, son of Conoghor, son of the deceased chieftain Donough, was intended to succeed according to the charter of 22 September 1574, cited in the previous chapter. At the time of Callaghan's death, Donough, born in 1566, was only twelve years of age.[1] That being the case, he was made a ward of the queen, and John, son of Viscount Roche, was named as guardian on 12 August 1578, just two months after Callaghan's death. As young Donough's mother was Katherine Roche, it was not surprising that her family assumed responsibility for upholding her son's rights. There probably was some concern about Donough's prospects and Lord Roche may have thought it possible to intervene in O Callaghan affairs to his own advantage. Traditional Irish law expected that the king or lord would be a fully adult male without physical blemish, who could effectively exercise the authority attributed to him. Donough thus had no claim in Irish law, though English law, which allowed inheritance according to primogeniture, even when the heir was under age, would have favored him.

The poet, Sir Edmund Spenser, then resident at Kilcolman castle, just north of O Callaghan's Country, summarized the Irish tradition of choosing a chieftain:

---

[1] *CPCRC*, 2:393, no. 17; *12 RDK*, 92, no. 3407 (2736).

It is a custome amongst all the Irish that presently after the death of any of their chiefe lords or captaines, they doe presently assemble themselves to a place generally appointed and knowne unto them, to choose another in his steed, where they doe nominate and elect for the most part, not the eldest sonne, nor any of the children of the lord deceased, but the next to him of blood, that is, the eldest and worthiest, as commonly the next brother unto him, if he have any, or the next cousin. . . . And then next to him doe they choose the next of the blood to be tanist, who shall next succeed him in the said captainry.[2]

The Inquisition of 1609 states that immediately upon the death of Callaghan, Conchubhar na Cairrge, or Conor of the Rock, son of Dermot, son of Teige Roe, the chieftain who died around 1537, "entered all the manors, castles, villages, and lands (except the villages and lands of Kilpader and Ballyhuine)." Teige McCahir, a grandson of the chieftain Teige Roe Bacach, held Kilpadder while Ballyheen was the dower land of Katherine Roche. Donal MacCarthy Mór, earl of Clancarthy, gave the rod or symbol of his authority to Conor, "notwithstanding that at that time there were others of his nation who were older," namely, Callaghan McTeige, Donough McCahir, and Cahir Óg O Callaghan. Two of Conor's five brothers, that is, Cahir Moyle and Dermot Óg, were apparently older as well. Although Gillman alleged that Conor seized the lordship contrary to the law of tanistry that is not correct. As the strongest among his male relatives, Conor was likely able to impose himself, but it would be wrong to charge him with usurpation of an office to which he had a very legitimate claim. Indeed, Sir John Davies, in his discussion of the dispute over tanistry treated in the following chapter, referred to Conor as "the last tanist."[3] Butler commented: "The fact that during his long rule of thirty-four years he brought his people and his country safely through all the perils of that troublous time, shows that he might well claim the title" [as the worthiest]. Conor was the last O Callaghan recorded as having received the rod of authority from MacCarthy Mór. The clan may have assembled for his inauguration at Carrigcleena, or perhaps at Dromaneen.[4]

Perhaps Conor assuaged his rivals by allowing Teige McCahir and his son Dermot McTeige to enter the village and lands of Kilpadder. Conor's brother Dermot Óg succeeded his father, Dermot, as prior of the monastery of Ballybeg. After the suppression of the monasteries, Dermot apparently got control of the revenues of that house and, though not a monk himself, was known by the monastic title of prior.[5]

[2] Edmund Spenser, *A View of the Present State of Ireland*, ed. W. L Renwick (Oxford: Oxford University Press, 1970), 16.

[3] Sir John Davies, "The Case of Tanistry," in *A Report of Cases and Matters in Law resolved and adjudged in the King's Courts in Ireland* (Dublin: Sarah Cotter, 1752), 85.

[4]RIA O.S. Inquisitions, Cork, 1:137-148, no. 12; Gillman, "Chieftains," *JCHAS*, Series 2, 3 (1897): 214-215; Butler, *Gleanings*, 83; Kavanagh, *Kilshannig*, 7.

[5] In a deposition of 1568 Cahir O Connor Faly referred to "the old prior O Callaghan;" Bagwell, *Tudors*, 2:135. On 12 December 1611 James I granted the tithes of Ballybeg nd its churches to Sir John Jephson and in 1613 full possession of Ballybeg as part of the manor of Mallow. Charles I confirmed Jephson in possession of the manor of Mallow, including Ballybeg, on 12 July 1630; Maurice Denham-Jephson, *Anglo-Irish Miscellany. Some Records of the Jephsons of Mallow* Dublin: Allen Figgis, 1964); *Calendar of the Patent and Close Rolls of Chancery in Ireland of the Reign of Charles I. First to Eighth Year 1631 Inclusive*, ed. James Morrin (Dublin and London: Her Majesty's Stationery Office, 1863), 562.

Ballybeg Priory

Conor's mother was Honor, the daughter of Edmond FitzGerald, lord of Clonlish, in County Limerick. In addition to Cahir Moyle and Dermot Óg, his brothers were Teige, Callaghan, and Irrelagh. Teige's appearance as tanist or presumptive successor in 1593 indicates that the regular transfer of power was planned. Conor's sister married Gerald FitzThomas FitzGibbon. Conor married Joan (Siobhán) (d. 10 March 1630), daughter of Turlough Bacach MacSweeney (Toirdhelbhach Bacach MacSuibhne), captain of gallowglasses, to whom he assigned as her marriage portion Gortmore, Gurteenbeha, Mohereen, and Kippagh. She died on 10 March 1630. Conor's children included Teige, Callaghan, Conoghor, Cahir, Donough (the last two were living in 1638), Calvagh (Calbhach), Kedagh (Céadach), Morgan, Elizabeth, and Eleanor. [6]

During Conor's chieftainship, the satirist, Aongus Ó Dálaigh (d. 1617), perhaps prompted by Sir George Carew, travelled about the country, describing in most unflattering language, the Gaelic lords whom he visited. He penned these barbed lines after his visit to O Callaghan:

Arán agus uisge lacháin
Mo chuid a d-tigh Uí Cheallacháin.
Is deacair croídhe o'n g-cuid sin slán.
'S gur dá thighe an t-uisge 'ná'n t-arán!

Bread and water from a pool
Was my supper at O Callaghan's house.
It is difficult to have heart after such a supper.
The water was twice thicker than the bread!

---

[6] *LM*, 162, no. 23; Gillman, "Chieftains," *JCHAS*, Series 2, 3 (1897): pedigree; *BIFR*, 888; *Poems of Egan O Rahilly*, 66-87, no. 15, lines 157-158. Eleanor married Lieutenant John Gillman with the Earl of Essex's forces in 1599. Townshend, *Clonakilty*, 351.

Banntracht chríche Uí Cheallacháin ar ló
Sean-mhná gan lón d'á d-táthad le gréin.
Is seirgthe seang-chliabhach a bhíd
Go h-ithe bídh a'tar a éis.

The women of O Callaghan's country
Are old women without store, basking in the sun.
Withered and slender-bodied they be
Till eating food and after it!

The translator, James Clarence Mangan, also paraphrased these lines:
The O Callaghan tribe turn out lots of old crones!
Whom I gazed on with pity. No blind alleyed city
Can shew such a group. With no flesh on their bones
They sit all day long in some lawny
Green sun shiny spot, and grow shriveled and tawny.

Among those I ate bread, which the great O himself
Sent me down by his daughter. I drank mud and water
Too, fetched from a ditch and which stood on a shelf
In a little brown earthen ware pitcher.
'Tis the beverage alike here of dame, duck and ditcher.

However well or poorly Aongus may have been treated in reality, there can be no doubt that he was not welcome again in O Callaghan's house. Indeed, his loathsome behavior stirred hostility among all those who offered him their hospitality only to be derided in his verses. When he showered his ridicule on the O Meaghers of Tipperary a servant of the family avenged the insult by plunging a dagger into his neck. As he expired he expressed regret for his false judgments on the lords of Munster.[7]

The Earl of Desmond's Revolt

The years of Conor's chieftainship were critical for Gaelic Ireland because of the steady advance of royal authority, hastened by the rebellion of the earl of Desmond and the Nine Years War, which greatly weakened the traditional autonomy of the Irish lords. In Munster the vast power of the earl of Desmond and his family was the principal obstacle to royal authority, but the FitzGeralds were still viewed as outsiders by the Gaelic lords. Thus it is not surprising that O Callaghan followed the lead of Sir Cormac

---

[7] Aongus O Daly, *The Tribes of Ireland. A Satire*, ed. John O'Donovan, tr. James Clarence Mangan (Dublin, 1852; reprint Cork: Tower Books, 1976), 68-69, 98. In the lines immediately preceding Aongus's complaint about O Callaghan's house he reviled the food he was given to eat at Cappagh: "Bread without being drowned in butter,/ And much chaff in its body/ In order to make me thankful/ This was my fare at Ceapach." Mangan paraphrased this "They are talkers at Cappagh - no more. If inclined/ You may swallow, as diet, the east or west wind,/ For you'll get little else; just imagine or map a/ Black briary desert out - that's cursed Cappagh." Ceapach, Cappagh, Kippagh in the parish of Castlemagner above the Blackwater, was part of O Callaghan lands.

McTeige MacCarthy, sheriff of County Cork and Lord of Muskerry, who realized that his adherence to the crown was the surest means of preserving his own lands. The alliance between MacCarthy of Muskerry and O Callaghan, so patent in the seventeenth century, probably was forged in the late Middle Ages, and was clearly operative at this time. On the other hand, while Conor O Callaghan, as chief of his name, may have followed a cautious policy during the Desmond rebellion, it is apparent that other members of the family threw in their lot decisively with the rebels.

A new stage in the struggle between the crown and the house of Desmond began when James FitzMaurice returned to Ireland in 1579, with promises from the pope and the king of Spain to help in overthrowing Queen Elizabeth. Landing at Smerwick near Dingle in Kerry in July, FitzMaurice was killed a month later, but members of his family continued the uprising.[8] For most of the summer, his cousin, the earl of Desmond, maintained an ambiguous posture, though others were less hesitant. Sir William Drury informed his superiors in August that "whosoever is discontented either for cause of justice or religion or for anie other respectes," was hastening to join the rebels. Parenthetically he reported that the castle of Dromore was taken, and two men killed there by O Callaghan "who is fallen to the rebell, and the poor subjectes do nowe generally fly with their cattell."[9] This remark seems to suggest that Conor of the Rock had adhered to the rebel cause. A skirmish had taken place at the castle of Dromore, situated about two miles southwest of Mallow, discomfiting those settled in that neighborhood. As Dromore appears to have been an O Callaghan castle (several O Callaghans were resident there in 1573 and in later years), it would seem that loyal troops had taken it, losing two of their men. Alternatively, it is possible that the crown may have taken possession of Dromore previously and O Callaghan may have attempted to recover it. Whatever the truth may be, if Conor of the Rock had joined the rebels, as Drury remarked, he shortly aligned himself with the crown.

Early in September 1579, as Drury marched through Muskerry and O Callaghan's and MacDonough's countries on his way to Smerwick, he took the castle of Lohort near Cecilstown in north Cork from the rebels and occupied an abandoned castle of MacAuliffe. He delivered Lohort to Sir Cormac MacCarthy, sheriff of County Cork, to hold for the crown and entrusted MacAuliffe's castle to MacDonough provided that it be surrendered on demand. Another document dated in September reveals the loyalty of O Callaghan and MacDonough to the crown. The earl of Desmond (who still had not declared hmself in rebellion), Lords Barry and Roche, and others prepared to oppose the rebels and arranged for MacDonough and the other lords of Duhallow, namely O Keeffe, MacAuliffe, and O Callaghan to gather their troops at Annagh and Ballingarry in County Limerick. The army thus assembled under the command of Sir Nicholas Maltby inflicted a terrible defeat on the rebels at Monasternenagh on 3 October. Bombarded by English cannon, the adjacent monastery was left in ruins. Given the silence of the sources, it is

---

[8] *FM*, 5:1713; Steven G. Ellis, *Tudor Ireland. Crown, Community and the Conflict of Cultures, 1470-1603* (London: Longman, 1985), 278-313; Edwards, *Tudors*, 140-152; G. A. Hayes-McCoy, "The Completion of the Tudor Conquest and the Advance of the Counter-Reformation, 1571-1603," in *NHI*, 3:103-112.

[9] "Lord Justice Drury and the Earl of Kildare to the Lord Chancellor and Archbishop of Dublin, 2 August 1579, Limerick," in *The Walsingham Letter Book or Register of Ireland, May 1578 to December 1579*, ed. James Hogan and N. McNeill O Farrell (Dublin: Irish Manuscripts Commission, 1959), 112-113; *FM*, 5:1717-1719.

impossible to determine the extent of the participation of Conor O Callaghan and his men in the victory.[10]

At this point, the earl of Desmond abandoned his pretext of loyalty and was proclaimed a traitor in November, but the other lords preferred not to commit themselves. In the spring of 1580, Sir William Pelham and the earl of Ormond marched into Limerick where they summoned the lords of Munster to consider how the war should be prosecuted. Pelham complained, however, that only Barry and Sir Cormac McTeige MacCarthy had appeared: "neither the earl of Clancartie, neither McCartie Reagh, the O Sullivans, McDonoghe, O Kiefe, O Callohan, McAullife, nor any of his country of Desmond would come unto us." Following that, Pelham advanced along the Blackwater, forcing the MacCarthys and O Callaghans and their cattle into the woods; he also evidently took hostages from the chiefs of Munster as surety of their allegiance. By June Clancarthy, O Callaghan, MacAuliffe, and others, chastened no doubt by this show of force, offered their services and joined Pelham at Castlemaine in Kerry. After the successful devastation of Desmond's lands there, Pelham returned to Cork where on 4 July, Clancarthy, Barry Mór, Barry Óg, Roche, Sir Cormac McTeige MacCarthy, O Sullivan, MacDonough, O Callaghan, O Keeffe, and others assembled to pledge their continued support of the crown.[11]

In the ensuing months the war degenerated into a series of raids, as Desmond was forced to take to the woods. By plundering Muskerry in 1581 and O Keeffe's country in 1582 he drove the lords of Duhallow, that is, MacDonough, O Keeffe, MacAuliffe, and O Callaghan, to journey to Cork, where they joined Clancarthy, Barry, Roche, O Sullivan Beare, MacCarthy Reagh and others on 10 July 1583 in renewing their pledges of allegiance to the crown's representative, the earl of Ormond. Desmond's forces steadily dwindled and his capture and execution in November 1583 brought the rebellion to an end.[12] Munster lay in ruins. Spenser, the poet, vividly described the horror of the war:

> Notwithstanding that the same [province of Munster] was a most rich and plentifull countrey, full of corne and cattle . . . yet ere one yeare and a halfe they were brought to such wretchednesse as that any stony heart would have rued the same. Out of every corner of the woods and glynnnes they came creeping forth upon their hands, for their legges could not beare them. They looked like anatomies of death; they spake like ghosts crying out of their graves; they did eate the dead carrions, happy where they could find them, yea, and one another soone after, insomuch as the very carcasses they spared not to scrape out of their graves; and if they found a plot of watercresses or shamrocks there they flocked as to a feast . . . that in short space of time there were almost no people left, and a most populous and plentifull country suddainely left voide of man and beast.

[10] "Lord Justice Drury and the Council in Ireland to the Privy Council, September 12, 1579, Camp near Aherlow Woods," and "The Note of the Plot sett downe by the Earl of Desmond, the Viscount Barry and Lord Roche, for the prosecution of the rebels (7 September 1579)," in Walsingham Letter Book, 165-167; FM, 5:1720-1721; Hayes-McCoy, "Tudor Conquest," 105-106.

[11] William Pelham to the Privy Council in England, 20 May 1580, Limerick, in CCP, 2 (1575-1588): 257, 265, nos. 394, 408; FM, 5:1727-1729; P. Grante to the earl of Ormond, 6 August 1580, Cork, CSP Ireland, 2:241, no. 17; Bagwell, Tudors, 3:46-47.

[12] FM, 5:1739, 1755-1757, 1787, 1795, 1799, 1817; Bagwell, Tudors, 3:112, n. 1.

The lands of the house of Desmond were confiscated and undertakers were authorized to settle colonists upon them. Nevertheless, the plantation of Munster did not directly affect O Callaghan lands, which remained intact.[13]

From the perspective of later centuries it is difficult to comprehend the attitude of Irish lords such as Conor of the Rock, who supported the government during the Desmond revolt. One should keep in mind, however, that the attitudes of later times had not yet developed, so it would be a grave mistake to judge sixteenth-century people by nineteenth- or twentieth-century standards. Given the longstanding lack of any political unity in Gaelic Ireland, Conor and the other Gaelic lords were primarily concerned to maintain themselves and their lordships as independently as possible. Until the sixteenth century, the crown scarcely intruded upon O Callaghan's authority. The principal threat to him and to the other Gaelic lords of Munster was the house of Desmond, which, for centuries, had sought its own aggrandizement at the expense of the Gaelic Irish. On the face of it, one could hardly expect the Gaelic lords to favor a rebellion led by their hereditary enemies. FitzMaurice presented his uprising in a somewhat different light, as a Catholic war to dethrone the heretic Elizabeth. In the confused religious situation of the sixteenth century, the Gaelic lords, while remaining firm in their allegiance to the Catholic Church, were not ready to embark on a Catholic crusade. Their principal concern, as already noted, was to preserve their lands and lordships, which they had no intention of risking in the name of Catholicism. Thus, they followed an equivocal course, trying to remain aloof, but giving allegiance to the crown when required to do so, and providing troops for the royal armies when necessary. By tacitly or openly supporting the government, they thought that they would be safe, but they did not realize that by allowing royal power to grow stronger in Munster, they were preparing their own inevitable destruction.

The concession of pardons in 1582-1585 to various members of the O Callaghan clan indicates that some of them had in fact participated in the rebellion, and that the adherence of others to the crown had not always been enthusiastic. Thus Conor of the Rock, his brother Irrelagh, and his cousins Teige McCahir McTeige Roe of Gortmabeare (Gortmolire?) and Donough McThomas McOwen McTeige Roe of Ballymacmurragh were pardoned in July 1585. On the other hand, Patrick Callaghan of Clonmeen was attainted of treason in 1588 for his role in the rebellion.[14]

As part of the general pacification of the country, royal commissioners persuaded the lords of Duhallow at Cork on 17 September 1592 to consent to an assessment of taxes. Duhallow, according to this accord, was divided equally into three parts, each of which owed an annual composition of £10: "Clancarties of Dowallie," that is, MacDonough's lands; "O Chalchane's country;" and "the third part is McAlie's, O Kiffe's and O Kirke's countries." O Kirke or Ó Cuirc was a family settled in Ballymaquirk, a townland on the Blackwater just south of Kanturk. The tripartite division

---

[13] Spenser, *View*, 101-102; D. B. Quinn, "The Munster Plantation: Problems and Opportunities," *JCHAS* 71 (1966): 29-40; A. J. Sheehan, "The Population of the Plantation of Munster: Quinn reconsidered," *JCHAS* 87 (1982): 107-117; Edwards, *Tudors*, 143-148.

[14] *13 RDK*, 175, no. 3974 (24 August 1582), and *15 RDK*, 25, 41, 69, 111, 120, 509, nos. 4318 (27 February 1583/4), 4469 (5 July 1584), 4564 (31 December 1584), 4722 (26 June 1585), 4751 (16 July 1585). See Appendix I. Smith, *Cork*, 1:51, n. 55, cited an inquisition held at Shandon Castle, Cork, 9 September 1588.

suggests that MacDonough's and O Callaghan's lands were richer than the rest. The document was signed by Conoghor O Callaghan alias O Kallaghan, Patrick Graunt, Brene [Brian] McOwen, and Art O Kiffe alias O Kife. Dermot McOwen MacDonough gave his consent by letter sent by O Keeffe. Brian McOwen, Conor's son-in-law, figured prominently in subsequent controversies over O Callaghan lands.[15]

Surrender and Regrant of O Callaghan Lands

In view of the terrible devastation resulting from the rebellion, Munster remained comparatively quiet for several years until the outbreak of the Nine Years War.[16] During that interval Conor of the Rock made the momentous decision to surrender O Callaghan lands to the crown and to receive them again under English law by a royal grant., requested that they be allowed to surrender their lands to the queen Employing Thomas Gould as their solicitor, Conor, "alias O Kallaghane of Dromynyne," Donall O Donovan, Conor O Mahony, both chiefs of their name, and Teige McOwen MacCarthy of Drishane and to hold them thereafter from her and her successors. Elizabeth gave her consent on 4 March 1593, authorizing a regrant of lands "with such liberties, jurisdictions, courts leet and franchises as in your [the Lord Deputy's] discretion shall seem meet, to be held of us, our heirs, and successors, by such tenure and services as you shall think convenient." Consequently the Lord Deputy on 26 June 1594 notified Sir Thomas Norris, Vice-President of Munster, of the queen's decision, and instructed him to summon a jury of twelve men, "most Englishmen, though indifferent [neutral] between him [Conor of the Rock] and his adversaries, and no freeholders," to determine "what castles, lands, seigniories, duties and services O Callaghan hath or of right ought to have in the County of Cork; to enquire concerning her Majesty's title, and of the rights of all subjects." The jury's findings were to be reported tro the Chancery two weeks after Michaelmas (29 September).[17]

Meeting at Mallow on 25 October, before Norris, William Saxey, Chief Justice of Munster, and Justice James Gould, the jury found that Conor held the castles of Clonmeen, Dromaneen, and Dromore, and twenty carucates or ploughlands situated mainly along the Blackwater in the parishes of Clonmeen and Kilshannig, and north of the river, in Ballyclough, and Castlemagner:[18]

Property	Car.	Property	Car.
Clonmeen, Gortmore, Drumrahye, Kilavoy, Koolekiltith, Ny Monane	4.5	Kilgobban	.5

---

[15] *CSP Ireland*, 2:68 from *CCP*, 69 (vol. 631, n. 15).

[16] See Eve Jennifer Campbell's doctoral thesis, *Displacement and Relocation in Early Modern Ireland: Studies of Transplantation Settlement in Connacht and Clare* (National University of Ireland, Galway, 2012), chapter 8: *Pobul Uí Cheallacháin*, and her article, "*Pobul Uí Cheallacháin*: Landscape and Power in an Early Modern Gaelic Lordship," *Landscapes* 18 (2017):19-36.

[17] *CPCRC*, 2:254, 260-262, nos. 30, 34. Thomas Gould had the first document enrolled in chancery on 29 January 1596. *CSP Ireland*, 68, no. 65; Butler, *Gleanings*, 83; Ó Murchadha, *Names*, 68.

[18] *CPCRC*, 2:260-262, no. 35, a summary; *16 RDK* 261, no. 5903; RIA O.S. Inquisitions, Cork, 1:52-54, no. 6 (partial transcription with the notation "the rest is defaced"). Butler, *Gleanings*. 84, 195-249.

Property	Car.	Property	Car.
Dromaneen, Kiletany, Kilvealaton, Kilroe, Dowkile, Kiltylane, Aldworth, Knocknamona, Kilebeg, Kilcolman	2	Gortroe, Drompeesh, Kilegortroe, Kilgobnet, Gortnygadderye, Kuolersye	3
Dromore, Kilpatrick, Carrigcleena, Knockycarig, Knockaney, Narroure, Shanyvyaloid, Byalahabwy, Carrigolane	3	Pallas, Gortenyclowny, Farredorisse	2
Kiletra, Dromahane, Coarrynvesye	3	Gortbofinna, Gearanaskagh	1
Kilevyaladae	1	Rathcomane, Trelair Tynytonyh, Gortnynagh, Kileaskith, Kilecurenane	3
Skarragh, quarter of; Kileknocke Igowney; Brittas, Cameraure, Kilberrihert	3	Gortnagross	2
Gortmolire, Lisyvogholy, Lackendarragh, Kilitraugh, Kiloutragh, Cappengyrryn (Garrane?)	3	Kilcolman	3
Banteer	1	Banteer Ieragh (West Banteer), Fermoyle, Knocknynenytadyry (Knockeenatuder?)	1
Kilcaskan, Dromcummer, Lismohilie, Killarush, Gurteenard	3	Kilpadder	2
Rathbeg, Rathmore	.5	Dromrastill, Tyhyngyeryh, Kilroe	.5
Kippagh, Gortinibrahalye, Coolnahane, Maine	3	Ballymacmurragh	.5
Cloonteens (Clonytinybeg, Clonitinymore)	.5	Ballyheen	1
Roskeen	.5	Gortnychonolye, Garrymcowney, Kilmichael, Ballynafeaha	1
Knockyveraghane (Kilbarrahan)	.5	Kilcranathan	1.5
Garranasath	.5		

Despite the tortured spelling of the townland names by the English scribe, many can be identified, though some place names apparently have fallen into disuse. Conor held demesne lands (that is, lands directly under his control) extending from west to east on the south bank of the Blackwater River from Banteer and Clonmeen, through Gortmore, Gortroe, Rathcomane, Gortmolire (now Lombardstown), Brittas, Drompeesh, Kilgobnet, Lackendarragh, Skarragh, Aldworth, Kilcolman, Kilpadder, Dromahane, Dromaneen, Kilvealaton, Carrigolane, Dromore, Kilpatrick, and Carrigcleena in the southeast. North of the river were the townlands of Gurteenard, Killarush, Ballymacmurragh, Ballyheen, Kilcaskan, Kippagh, Cloonteens, Dromcummer, Roskeen, Pallas, Gortbofinna, Gearanaskagh, Kilgobban, Kilmichael, Gortnagross, Dromrastill, Gortnychonolye and Garrymcowney (now Longueville), Ballynafeaha, Kilcranathan, and Kiletra (Kileoughteragh).

Identification of the following places is unknown, but their location can be determined from the neighboring townlands: Dromeragh or Drumrahye, Koolekiltith ny Monane, Kiletany, Kilebeg (Coill beag, the small wood), Dowkile (Dubh coill, the dark wood), Kiltylane, Knockycarig, Knockaney, Shanyvyaloid, Byalahabwy (Bealach buidhe, the yellow road), Coarrynyvesye, Kilevyaladae, Cameraure, Lisyvogholy, Cappengyrryn, Lismohilie, Gortnygadderye, Kuolersye, Gortenyclowny, Farredorisse, Trelair Tynytonyh, Gortnynagh, Kileaskith, Kilecurenane, Tyhyngyeryh, and Gortnychonolye.

The chieftain resided mainly in Dromaneen castle. Teige Roe and his son Donough are both recorded as living there, though Donough died at Clonmeen. His grandson Callaghan and Conor of the Rock, in his early years, lived there as well. As we shall see, possession of the two castles was later divided between contenders for power. The castle of Dromaneen was replaced in the late sixteenth or early seventeenth century by the structure, now in ruins, overlooking the Blackwater. Clonmeen castle was destroyed during the rebellion of 1641. There is no trace today of the castles of Dromore on the Clydagh River at the eastern edge of O Callaghan's Country; Gortmore on the Blackwater; and Gurteenkreen in the same townland.

The jury also found that "as O Callaghan is lord of the country, so there is a tanist, by the custom of the said country, and that tanist is now Teige O Callaghan," who by custom held Gortroe (3 carucates), the Pallas (2) and the Farderrise (unidentified). Pallas, on the northern bank of the River, may have been the tanist's principal residence. Gortroe stood opposite on the southern bank of the River. Teige, also called Teige na Muchorie, was Conor's brother. Callaghan McTeig O Callaghan, gentleman, and Donell McTeig McDonogh O Callaghan, yeoman, who were pardoned in 1573 while resident at Pallas, were perhaps sons of the tanist.

Furthermore, it was the custom that every kinsman of O Callaghan should have a "certain parcel of land to live upon, and yet no estate passeth thereby; but the lord who is now Conoghor O Callaghan, like his predecessors before, viz., O Callaghan for the time being, time out of mind, may remove him to other lands, according to custom." Thus Conor's brother Callaghan had three carucates in Rathcomane and Gortnagross, and another brother, Irrelagh, had a carucate in Kilcolman. Teige McCahir, a first cousin, had a carucate in Kilpadder; another first cousin, Callaghan McOwen, had a carucate in Dromrastill, Tinegherie (Tyhyngyeryh, unidentified but perhaps Woodpark), and Kilroe. Donough McThomas, a first cousin once removed, had three carucates in Ballymacmurragh out of which he owed Conor a seigniory or right of lordship amounting to two pounds, "and other duties." Dermot McTeige and others held the town and lands of Kilcranathan (1 carucate) at a yearly rent of four shillings and four white groats.

Finally, six quarters of land in Banteer, Kilcaskan, Gortroe, Skarragh, Rathcomane and Gortmolire were chargeable to MacDonough for the time being at an annual rent of sixty cows, or otherwise six shillings, eight pence for each cow; the quarter of Kilcaskan was also chargeable to MacDonough at a rent of fourteen shillings.[19]

In sum, the jury found that Conor of the Rock, as the O Callaghan and lord of Poble O Callaghan, held extensive lands in demesne along both sides of the Blackwater

---

[19] Smith, *Cork,* 1:34, n. 30; Butler, *Gleanings,* 85, n. 22; Campbell, *Displacement,* 106, 113, 121-122, 125-132. An inquisition of 1617 stated that in Elizabeth's time Owen MacDonough MacCarthy had certain lands from Donough O Callaghan to be redeemed whenever he gave security to pay the chief rent.

River, including the castles of Clonmeen, Dromaneen, and Dromore, and about 50.5 carucates. If each carucate consisted of 120 acres, then he held about 6,050 acres. However, he did not have direct control over all the acreage in each of the townlands cited. His brother Teige held the position of tanist, which in Irish law indicated that he was the designated successor to the lordship. As such he held five carucates or about 600 acres. Other kinsmen, Conor's brothers or first cousins, the ruling *fine* of the O Callaghans, held various lands, as they were entitled to receive sustenance of this sort, but they did not have any permanent right to them and could not bequeath them to their heirs. On the contrary, they were removable at the lord's will. Other O Callaghans were mentioned as holding lands subject to rents of various amounts.[20]

Conor of the Rock, in effect, proposed to surrender to the crown the demesne lands set aside for the maintenance of the lord of Poble O Callaghan and to receive them in return as a personal estate transmissible to his heirs. Although the lands held by other members of the family apparently were not included in this reckoning, the demesne lands, in Irish law, were not the lord's to give away. He was entitled to use them so long as he was lord, but he could not give them to his children or other heirs nor alienate them. A profound change in the law concerning the lands of the O Callaghan family was about to take place, but there is no evidence that any protest was made at this time.

The jury's findings were dutifully reported to the queen. Then, on 2 December 1594, Conor made a formal surrender of his lands extending from Glanda Ieyghe and Molyne Intremane on the west as far as the river Clydagh, to Bearnymoher and Bearny Inclynowe on the east, and from Portidieth and Bearicanhin on the south to the bog of Ballynoe (an old canal north of Blackwater) on the north. The Clydagh flowing northward into the Blackwater marks the eastern limit of Duhallow and also separates O Callaghan's country from the manor of Mallow. Aside from the Clydagh and Ballynoe the other boundary names are difficult to identify. The root *bearna*, meaning a gap and found in Bearnymoher and Bearny Inclynowe, suggests that those places were passes in the Boggeragh Moutains to the south. Bearicanhin may be the townland of Barrahaurin (Barr an Chárthainn) in the parish of Donoughmore. The western boundary "Glanda Ieyghe" may refer to one or another of the places in the Glen River valley and the Boggeragh Mountains flowing northward into the Blackwater through Banteer. Possibilites include Glentaneatnagh south of Nad between the Glen and the Nad Rivers, or Glannaharee in the valley of the river of the same name. Portidieth on the south is likely Portaghadav (*Portach na damh* - the bog of the ox) near Boula about a mile south of Bweeng.[21]

---

[20] Liam Ó Buachalla, "Some Researches in Ancient Irish Law," *JCHAS* 53 (1948): 76-77 pointed out that those mentioned in the inquisitions had a share "in the special estate attached to the chieftainship" because they were sons or grandsons of the former chieftain Teige Roe and formed the ruling *fine* or sept. He also noted that Donogho McThomas, as a great-grandson of Teige Roe, was not included in the ruling *fine* and paid a seignory to the chief. Other grandsons of Teige Roe, viz., Thomas, Conoghor and McCragh, sons of Donell, did not hold shares in the chieftain's estate, probably because they resided outside O Callaghan territory at that time. Thomas lived at Annagh in Orrery in 1600. Dermod Óg, brother of the chieftain, had no share either, probably because he was prior of Ballybeg in Orrery in 1594. The sons and grandsons of the chieftains Donough (d. 1577) and Callaghan (d. 1578) would also have been entitled to shares, but only Teige McOwen McDonough appears to have been alive, perhaps a minor; he is not mentioned in the inquisition. Butler, *Gleanings*, 85-86.

[21] Gillman, "Chieftains," *JCHAS*, Series 2, 3 (1897): 248.

Five days after Conor surrendered these lands to the queen, that is, on 7 December 1594 in Dublin, he received a grant of the castles and lands already cited, "with all houses, forests, waters, watercourses, court baron, advowsons of churches, view of frankpledge, and all things which to frankpledge appertain," to hold forever in chief by knight's service, that is, by the twentieth part of a knight's fee, at the rent of forty shillings yearly. Any composition imposed or to be imposed by the Council of Ireland was reserved, and the rights of other persons were not to be prejudiced. Henceforth Conor was freed of all Irish exactions and impositions, namely, cess (*cíos*, rent, tax), bonnaght (*buannacht*, billeting of troops), comry (*coinmhe*, coyne, maintenance), horseboys (provisions for a determined number often twice a year), shraagh (*sraith*, fine, tax), and so forth.[22]

As a consequence, Conor and his immediate family obtained an estate under English law that they would hold of the crown by an annual rent. Thereafter the English law of primogeniture would come into play, so that Conor's first born son would succeed not only to these lands, but in effect to the chieftainship as well. His brother Teige, the tanist, would have no right, as the law of tanistry was set aside. Gillman wrathfully denounced Conor's action as a "direct fraud on the clan" in which the government was a willing and knowing participant. Although the decision seems to have affected only the demesne lands of the chief, and not other lands held by the family, it undermined the family's traditional property base. Gillman concluded: "thus ended the existence of the clan O Callaghan as a clan. Thenceforward there is nothing to tell except the history of separate county families named O Callaghan." Probably other O Callaghans were able to secure ownership of their holdings also, as several of them held from the crown in Stuart times. Men of lesser rank became tenants of the new proprietors.[23]

An anonymous author writing in 1642 charged that Conor owed his new fortune to Sir Thomas Norris, the Vice-President of Munster. With his aid Conor and his family "have in time wrested out of the right line and gotten the whole Pobble to themselves, consisting of more than twenty ploughlands, whereof it is believed they would never have gotten one but by that introduction," that is, by Norris's intervention.[24]

An indenture dated 31 October 1593, just seven months after Elizabeth consented to Conor's petition for surrender and regrant, suggests the close relationship between Conor and Norris. Conor, "alias O Kallaghane of Pollykalleghan, gentleman," leased to Norris for twenty-one years, beginning at the following Easter, all the woods in Poble O Callaghan, especially those of Dromore, Killvillidge (1 ploughland), a third of the woods of Gortnagross (1 ploughland), and the woods of two ploughlands of Skarragh. Norris was authorized to open iron mines in the woods. Free passage for carts, horses, oxen, and workmen was guaranteed, as well as the right to build reasonable houses for the workers and other necessary buildings, with sufficient pasture for cattle. O Callaghan's rights and those of his tenants to pasture, plow, and manure the land, and to dwell thereon were reserved. Conor's rights to honey, acorns, timber, and hawks, valuable for hunting, were

---

[22] *CPCRC*, 2:335-336, nos. 8-9; *16 RDK*, 262, no. 5908; Grove-White, *Notes*, 3:61; Simms, *Warlords*, 129-146.

[23] Gillman, "Chieftains," *JCHAS*, Series 2, 3 (1897): 218-219; Butler, *Gleanings*, 85-86, 233; Ó Buachalla, "Some Researches," 75-81; C. J. F. MacCarthy, "Some Researches in Ancient Irish Law: A Complementary Note," *JCHAS* 54(1949): 11-16; Ó Murchadha, *Names*, 68.

[24] Gillman, "Chieftains," *JCHAS*, Series 2, 3 (1897): 219, citing British Library, Sloane no. 1008, fol. 98, also cited in *JCHAS* 2d series 2 (1896): 65.

also upheld. Norris's men had to take care not to spoil trees where hawks might breed. In return for all this Conor was to be paid at the rate of ten pounds sterling, and was also to have one hundred pounds of iron by the year "after there is a greate store made." If Norris wished to terminate the lease he had to give notice at Dromaneen castle. Conor subscribed this document and affixed his seal to it, as did Norris, but the seals seem to have disappeared.[25]

This document reveals a willingness on Conor's part to engage in the exploitation of O Callaghan lands on a more sophisticated level than in the past. The venture would, if successful, bring him increased wealth, but it required the cutting down of woodland that had stood for centuries and the opening of iron mines. In addition, workmen, who were probably Anglo-Irish or English, would be brought into the area and eventually would become permanent settlers there. Although O Callaghan rights were guaranteed, it would seem that they would have to make room for these newcomers. What reason there was to believe that iron was to be found there in any quantity is unknown, nor is it clear that this ever became a profitable venture for either Norris or O Callaghan. The rights to honey, acorns, timber, and hawks reserved to O Callaghan were probably traditional, dating back hundreds of years.

The Nine Years War

In the very year that Conor secured O Callaghan lands in full ownership under the crown, the outbreak of the Nine Years War signaled the beginning of the end of the old Gaelic way of life. The war began in Ulster under the leadership of Hugh O Neill, earl of Tyrone, and Hugh Roe O Donnell, who sought to rouse the rest of Ireland and to secure the assistance of Spain. In a report of 1596 concerning the attitude of the principal lords in Munster, Cahir O Callaghan, alias Cahir Modarta, dwelling near Mallow was described as "an instrument meet to be employed," and was "to be maintained in his possession at the least till these rebellions be assuaged."[26] Cahir Modarta was the son of the chieftain Callaghan who died in 1578. Illegitimate and perhaps under age, he had been passed over when Conor of the Rock gained the chieftainship. Clearly the government had its eye on him, possibly as a potential rival to Conor.

Prior to the general rising, several O Callaghans incurred the government's wrath for various transgressions. Among those pardoned in 1597 were Dermod McDonogh, Dermod Roe McCallaghan, Owen McTeige, Conoghor McTeige, and Kenedy and Donogh McDermod, both of Dromaneen. Owen O Callaghan, a nephew to Lord Barry, was charged on 13 March 1599 with having killed eleven principal leaders.[27]

After O Neill's victory at the Yellow Ford in August 1598, the lords of Munster rose in rebellion, and before the year was out O Neill's forces entered the province. James FitzThomas put himself forward as earl of Desmond and was so acknowledged by

[25] *The Lismore Papers (Second Series). Selections from the Private and Public (or State) Correspondence of Sir Richard Boyle, First and 'Great' Earl of Cork*, ed. Rev. Alexander B. Grosart, 5 vols. (n.p. 1897), 1:4-7, no. 2. In the transcription Oedrtynerosye should be Gortnagross; Vxemore is Dromore; Killvillidge may be Kilvealaton.

[26] *CCP*, 3:203-204, no. 264; G. A. Hayes McCoy, "The Completion of the Tudor Conquest and the Advance of the Counter-Reformation," *NIH*, 3:115-136; Edwards, *Tudors*, 155-172.

[27] *CSP Ireland*, 9 (1600), 37; *17 RDK*, 75, 83-84, nos. 6173 (25 November 1597), 6198 (17 February 1597).

MacDonough, O Callaghan, and others on 13 October about three miles west of Mallow, effectively in O Callaghan's Country. Although government forces were at Mallow, no conflict took place, as both sides withdrew. A computation of Irish forces in rebellion upon the arrival of the earl of Essex as Deputy in April 1599 indicated that 5,030 foot, and 242 horse could be raised in Munster. About 4% of the total, that is, 200 foot and 8 horse were to be raised by MacDonough, O Keeffe, and O Callaghan.[28] If that figure were divided equally among the three Duhallow lords, O Callaghan could provide about sixty-six footsoldiers and perhaps two or three horsemen.

What does that suggest about the O Callaghan population at that time? Taking into account young children, both boys and girls under fourteen, and men no longer able to serve as soldiers, as well as women, let us suppose that there were approximately five persons in the families of each of the sixty-eight or sixty-nine soldiers (or in round numbers, seventy); then we would have perhaps 350 men and women. Even if a larger number per family were assigned, there would still be less than 1,000 O Callaghans. Admittedly this is guesswork, but we must utilize whatever figures are available.

As Essex marched through Munster in May and June, reaffirming royal authority, many submitted to him and were pardoned, including Maurice Roche, viscount Fermoy, and the following O Callaghans: Teige Óg, Owen McTeige, Daniel McTeige, Dermod McTeige, Donogh McDermod, Dermod Óg, and Donogh McTeige. After Essex failed to crush O Neill and returned to England in the fall of 1599, Sir George Carew was named Lord President of Munster. Carew, who compiled the genealogies of the principal Irish families, set out to destroy crops and seize castles. He remarked to the Privy Council on 30 April 1600 that "the confusion and distemper" in the province was greater than ever, and complained that little could be expected from "the lords of the countries who are only in personal show subjects, as . . . Cormock McDermott chief of Muskerry . . . O Callaghan and all others . . . Most of them have either brothers or near kinsmen in actual rebellion." He went on to note that Florence MacCarthy, who claimed to be MacCarthy Mór, by reason of his friends, "as both the O Sulevans . . . the Carties of Desmond . . . most of the Carties of Muskery, all the Carties of Dowalla, O Kief, McAulyne [MacAuliffe], and many of the O Callaghans . . . is now the strongest and greatest force of any traitor in Munster."[29]

Within a few months, however, James FitzThomas and Florence MacCarthy were both captured and sent to London where they ended their days in the Tower. As a consequence, Munster was quieted and many of the rebels sought pardon. Carew informed Sir Robert Cecil on 2 May 1600 that he had received the submission of various gentlemen who gave pledges for their loyalty. "Amongst others of the best sort is O Callaghan and Barrett, lords of countries and chiefs of their names." Thus Conor of the Rock, "alias O Calghan of Clonmine, gent.," his wife Joan ny Tirrelagh, their son Callaghan McConoghor, Callaghan McOwen (a grandson of the chieftain, Teige Roe) and his wife Ellen ny Tirrelagh (probably a sister of Conor's wife Joan, and a daughter of Turlough MacSweeney), and Dermot O Callaghan alias Squyncy received pardons. By late August, MacDonough, O Keeffe, and MacAuliffe also indicated their desire to come

---

[28] *CSP Ireland*, 3 (1598-1599), 318; *CCP*, 3:298-300; Bagwell, *Tudors*, 3:302-307.
[29] *17 RDK*, 101-102, no. 5302 (24 July 1599); *CCP*, 3:385-387; *CSP Ireland*, 9 (1600): 128-129; Bagwell, *Tudors*, 3:324-328, 359-361.

to terms with the crown.[30] On 21 April 1602 Conoghor O Callaghan of Clonmeen posted 200 marks as a pledge of his loyalty to the queen. Owen O Diggenane [O Duignan] of Clonmeen, of whom nothing else is known, did so as well. Then on 17 October 1602 Conor provided bail of 200 shillings for John MacAuliffe so long as he "shall continue of dutiful behaviour."[31]

Keenly aware that such submissions were of transitory value, Cecil pointed out to Carew that the rebels would be "good subjects no longer than the sword hangs over them." Suggesting that some freeholders should not be received with pardons of lands, if their "countries be good and lie in no remote places," he indicated that O Callaghan was one whom he had in mind, especially as his country lay near Mallow, and was "fit to be adjoined and not parted." In other words, the queen's principal adviser was proposing that O Callaghan lands be confiscated because they were valuable due to their location near Mallow. The importance of that location was emphasized in a report on the state of Munster drawn up at the close of the year. O Callaghan, protected but not pardoned, held lands that

> are very great and good and very convenient for him that shall have Moyallo. It is a parcel of Dowalla called McDonogh's country and lying marvellous pleasantly and profitable on both sides of the river Blackwater. It hath three fine castles upon it and goodly woods and hawks. O Callaghan himself, being a petty lord under McDonogh is but a silly fellow and can do neither good if he be in nor any great hurt if he be out; for a strong man at Moyallo will always inhabit that country and never suffer any other to dwell there.

The report concluded that O Callaghan's Country, together with Mallow, might be kept in the queen's hands or, as an alternative that it be given to the earl of Desmond acknowledged by the government. As the earl was a Protestant, however, he was rejected by the Irish.[32]

Conor of the Rock, acknowledged in the documents just cited as O Callaghan ("alias O Callaghan"), who only six years before had achieved a great coup in securing for himself the bulk of the O Callaghan lands, now stood in jeopardy of losing them entirely. The description of O Callaghan's Country as pleasant and profitable, with three fine castles (Dromaneen, Clonmeen, Dromore), and abounding in woods and hawks, made it attractive for annexation to Mallow. Fortunately for Conor, his pardon extended not only to his person, but also to his property, and so he was spared the ignominy of confiscation.

As the pacification of Munster continued, additional pardons were given to other O Callaghans. The rather lengthy list suggests that most of the principal members of the

[30] *CSP Ireland*, 9 (1600): 145; *CPCRC*, 2:563-564, no. 51; *17 RDK,* 125, no. 6407 (15 June 1600). Thomas Stafford, *Pacata Hibernia. Ireland Appeased and Reduced or a History of the Wars of Ireland in the Reign of Queen Elizabeth,* 2 vols. (London, 1633; reprint, London: S. and R. Bentley, 1821*),* 1:141. James Barrett FitzWilliam of Lackenfeonyne, Co. Cork, and his wife Eliza ny Callaghan were also pardoned. *17 RDK,* 130, no. 6431 (11 September 1600); Caulfie;d Ó Murchadha, *Names*, 9-10.
[31] Richard Caulfield, *The Council Book of the Corporation of Kinsale from 1652 to 1800* (Guildford, Surrey: J. Billing, 1879). 323-324.
[32] *CCP*, 3: 450-451; *CSP Ireland*, 10 (1600-1601): 136.

family had been involved in varying degrees in the recent disturbances.[33]

The restoration of peace in Munster was interrupted, however, by the arrival of a Spanish fleet at Kinsale in September 1601. Various clans prepared for the renewal of warfare, while O Neill and O Donnell advanced to give comfort to the Spaniards who were besieged in Kinsale by government forces. Cormac MacCarthy of Muskerry was one of the Irish lords who supported the crown at this time, though as always the allegiance of an Irish lord was ambivalent. Quite possibly, Conor of the Rock, considering the threat of confiscation hanging over his lands, remained steadfast in his allegiance, and may have sent contingents to join Carew at Kinsale, where the Irish were routed on 24 December 1601. And yet O Callaghan, along with other lords of Munster, after the disaster of Kinsale, was thought to be favorably inclined if the Spaniards attempted a new landing, as he was "of the ancient race." In the ensuing months Carew mopped up the resistance in Munster, climaxing it with the capture of O Sullivan's castle of Dunboy in June 1602. O Neill submitted in March 1603, bringing the Nine Years War to a close.[34]

As a consequence of developments in the last quarter of the sixteenth century, Pobul Uí Cheallacháin, the lands inhabited and belonging to the O Callaghans of Duhallow, was transformed into an estate held by the chieftain and heritable by his descendants in accordance with English law. Nevertheless, the upheavals of the seventeenth century eventually brought about the downfall of the O Callaghans and other families of the Gaelic aristocracy.

---

[33] *17 RDK,* 147-149, 152, 165, 187-190, 245, 264, nos. 6465 (27 January 1600), 6467 (1 February 1600), 6481 (18 March 1600), 6499 (25 April 1601), 6539 (29 May 1601), 6555 (22 June 1601), 6558 (5 July 1601). See Appendix I.

[34] *CSP Ireland,* 2-3 (1606-1608), 313, no. 423; Bagwell, *Tudors,* 3:398-406; John Silke, *Kinsale. The Spanish Intervention in Ireland at the End of the Elizabethan Wars* (New York: Fordham University Press, 1970).

CHAPTER 4

LE CASE DE TANISTRY AND ITS AFTERMATH

The death of Queen Elizabeth early in 1603 brought to the thrones of England and Ireland the first of the Stuart dynasty, James I (1603-1625), who was already king of Scotland. The hopes of Irish Catholics that he would show greater tolerance than his predecessor immediately proved to be false. The Act of Uniformity was enforced and the plantation of Ulster increased the Protestant population. English law and administration were continually extended throughout the country with the consequent dismantling of Brehon or Irish law and custom. As a result of these developments the Gaelic Irish and the Anglo-Irish (the descendants of the twelfth-century Normans) drew closer together because of their common adherence to Catholicism and a new concept of Irish nationality began to take shape. Together the two groups, so long hostile to one another in the Middle Ages, endeavored to resist increasing encroachment upon their lands by newcomers from Britain.

Le Case de Tanistry

In the government's effort to obliterate Brehon law with its distinctive ideas of chieftainship, tanistry, and equal inheritance among male heirs, the O Callaghan family played no small part. *Le Case de Tanistry*, or *Case of Tanistry*, adjudicated in 1608 and reported by Sir John Davies, James I's Attorney-General for Ireland, provides valuable details about the crisis in the O Callaghan lordship at the close of the sixteenth century.[1] Davies described an Irish lordship in this manner:

> But by the Irish custom of tanistry the chieftains of every country and the chief of every sept had no longer estate than for life in their chiefries, the inheritance whereof did rest in no man. And these chiefries, though they had some portions of land allotted to them, did consist chiefly in cuttings and cosheries and other Irish exactions whereby they did spoil and

---

[1] Richard Bagwell, *Ireland under the Stuarts and during the Interregnum*, 3 vols. (London: 1909-1916; reprint London: Holland Press, 1963); Aidan Clarke, *The Old English in Ireland 1625-1642* (Ithaca: Cornell University Press, 1966); Brendan Fitzpatrick, *Seventeenth-Century Ireland: The War of Religions* (Totowa, NJ: Barnes and Noble, 1989).

impoverish the people at their pleasure. And when these chieftains were dead, their sons or next heirs did not succeed them, but their tanisties, who were elective, and purchased their elections by strong hand. And by the Irish custom of gavelkind, the inferior tenanties were partiable amongst all the males of the sept, both bastards and legitimate, and after partition was made, if any one of the sept had died, his portion was not divided among his sons, but the chief of the sept made a new partition of all the lands belonging to the sept and gave everyone his part according to his antiquity.[2]

In effect, the chief held office for life, receiving various tributes from the clan or sept for his support, but he had no right to bequeath his lands to his sons. Rather the tanist, who was the chosen and designated successor to the chieftainship, now advanced to that position. The other male members of the family, legitimate and illegitimate, by order of seniority, each received a portion of land upon which to live, but their sons did not have the right of inheritance. Upon the death of the incumbent, the chief took possession of his lands and gave them to whomever he would. Davies concluded that because no one had a full right of ownership and the right to leave his holding to his heirs, Irish lords did not build stone or brick houses, nor plant gardens or orchards, nor enclose nor improve their lands. "For who would plant or improve or build upon that land, which a stranger, whom he knew not, should possess after his death?"[3]

As so many other Irish lords, Conor of the Rock took the steps necessary to transform the O Callaghan lordship into a personal estate heritable by his heirs. He surrendered to the crown O Callaghan lands, which were not his to give and received a grant of the same lands from Queen Elizabeth in 1594. Though he survived the revolt of the earl of Desmond and the Nine Years War with his holdings more or less intact, the high-handed manner in which he had manipulated the O Callaghan patrimony to his own private advantage displeased other members of the family who challenged his rights. The chronology of the conflict is not entirely clear, but it may be outlined as follows.

The Entry Book of Orders or Decrees of the Court of Castle Chamber, Dublin, reported that on 27 June 1605 at Cary Hospital the justices heard a suit involving "Cahir O Callaghane of Dromynyne, co. Cork, gent., r. John Barrie, esquire, late sheriff of co. Cork, Brien McOwen of Castlemore and Conagher O Callaghane of Clonemyne, same county, gents."[4] Sir John Davies, the Attorney General of Ireland, explained the origin of

---

[2] Sir John Davies, *A Discovery of the True Cause why Ireland was never brought under Obedience of the Crown of England* (Dublin, 1787; reprint: Shannon, Irish University Press, 1969) 127-128; Nicholls, *Ireland*, 21-67.

[3] Davies, *Discovery*, 128; Sir John Davies, "The Case of Tanistry," in *A Report of Cases and Matters in Law resolved and adjudged in the King's Courts in Ireland* (Dublin: Sarah Cotter, 1752), 78-115; also in *Les reports des cases et matters en ley resolvés et adjugés en les courts del rey en Ireland 1604-1612 collect et digest per Sir John Davies, chivaler, atturney generall del rey en cest realm* (London: E. Flesher at al, 1674), fol. 29v-42r; Liam Ó Buachalla, "Some Researches in Ancient Irish Law," *JCHAS* 53 (1948): 75-81; C. J. F. MacCarthy, "Some Reseaches in Ancient Irish Law. A Complementary Note," *JCHAS* 54 (1949): 11-16; Fred Buckley, "The Case of Tanistry," *MFCJ* 2 (1984): 44-54, reprinted in Kavanagh, *Kilshannig*, 22-25.

[4] Decree of the Court of Castle Chamber, Dublin; *Report on the Manuscripts of the Earl of Egmont*, 2 vols. (London and Dublin: Historical Manuscripts Commission. 1905-1909), 1:30.

that suit in *Le Case de Tanistry*. After summarizing the family history from Donough MacTeige Roe, he noted that Conor of the Rock had surrendered the clan lands to Queen Elizabeth who granted them to him as a personal estate. Conor, who was resident at Clonmeen in 1600, at some unspecified date enfeoffed a person named Fagan with the castle of Dromaneen, and he in turn enfeoffed Brian McOwen, who then leased the property to his son Murrough McBrian.

Both Herbert Gillman and William Butler believed that Brian was Brian McOwen O Callaghan, whose father Owen McTeige and his parents Teige McOwen and Sheila NyOwen were pardoned on 15 June 1600. Teige McOwen was a grandson of Donough, the chieftain who died in 1577 and a first cousin once removed of Conor of the Rock. In English law, Brian McOwen's family represented an older branch of the family than Conor, but whether that was grounds for demanding a share in the family estates is unknown. However, the Entry Book cited above referred to "Brien McOwen of Castlemore." He may be identified as Brian mac Owen MacSweeney, a member of a gallowglass family settled in Cork around the middle of the fifteenth century. He held the castles of Castlemore and Clodagh (adjacent to Crookstown) for MacCarthy of Muskerry. The ties between the O Callaghans and MacSweeneys were close. Conor's wife was a daughter of Turlough Bacach MacSweeney and Brian's daughter Mary married Conor's son Teige, and after Teige's death, Conor's son Callaghan.[5]

Conor may have chosen to move to Clonmeen and to construct a new mansion there on the site of an earlier castle (though only the external walls are standing today). He may have entrusted Dromaneen to Brian until such time as his son Callaghan McConoghor was of age and fully capable of maintaining the place. The grant may also have been a guarantee of a future marriage between Callaghan and Brian's daughter.[6]

On the other hand, the family of Donough McTeige McConoghor, the great-grandson of the chieftain Donough, could allege that they had been unjustly deprived of their inheritance. Young Donough, designated as the ultimate heir of the chieftain Donough in 1574, died ten years later without heirs of his body. Though Irish law did not admit inheritance in the female line, the family of his aunt Eleanor, sister of Callaghan, the chieftain who died in 1578, could assert a claim. Eleanor (who died 18 October 1593) was married to Art O Keeffe, chief of his name. Their several children included Daniel (who died in 1594 without heirs) and Manus, who succeeded to the lordship of the O Keeffes as well as to his mother's claims to O Callaghan lands. Perhaps realizing the difficulty of occupying Dromaneen, at some distance from O Keeffe's country, Manus enfeoffed Cahir O Callaghan with that property.[7]

Cahir, known as Cathaoir Modarta, the surly, was an illegitimate son of the chieftain Callaghan who died in 1578, and a great-grandson of Donough, the chieftain who died in 1577. He was also Eleanor's nephew and a first cousin of Manus O Keeffe.

---

[5] *BIFR*, 888; Gillman, "Chieftains," *JCHAS*, Series 2, 3 (1897): pedigree, makes no mention of Teige's or Callaghan's marriage to Mary MacSweeney; he cites an inquisition *post mortem* recording the death of Teige McConoghor on 31 May 1624 at Banteer. Butler, *Gleanings*, 89-90; Ó Murchadha, *Names*, 69, 298.

[6] On 5 September 1601 Brian McOwen McSwyny of Cloghda posted 100 shillings as a pledge of loyalty; Caulfield, *The Council Book of the Corporation of Kinsale*, 322.

[7] Eleanor's sister, Honora, who married Sir Thomas Barry Óg of Rincorran died on 31 January 1586 without children. *BIFR*, 888. The Inquisition of 1609 stated that Eleanor died on 18 October 1598. RIA O.S. Inquisitions, Cork, 1:137-148, no. 12; Ó Murchadha, *Names*, 69.

His illegitimacy was in no way an impediment in Irish law to succession to the chieftainship. In 1596 the English authorities described him as a gentleman settled near Mallow, "a meet instrument" to be employed to further the government's interest. On this account he was "to be maintained in his possessions at the least till these rebellions be assuaged." Three years later the earl of Essex supplied him with muskets and powder so that he could hold Dromaneen in the queen's name, "but within two dayes after he turned traytor." He was resident at Dromaneen in 1601 and while living there in 1603 and 1605 he served as a juror.[8]

Thus, it would seem that while Conor enfeoffed Brian McOwen with Dromaneen, Cahir had effective possession of the castle in 1599, 1601, 1603, and 1605. Apparently sometime between 1600 and 1603 (probably in 1602), Sheriff John Barry of County Cork, Brian McOwen of Castlemore, and Conor O Callaghan of Clonmeen, with two hundred men, assaulted Dromaneen castle, "breaking down the doors, thrusting out the plaintiff's [Cahir's] servants, and taking thence goods and chattels to the value of sixty pounds." Conor of the Rock's alliance with Brian against Cahir was manifest to all and signaled a major split within the family.[9] On 4 March 1603 the President and Council of Munster ordered the sequestration of Dromaneen and six ploughlands "to the hands of Walter Coppinger of Cork, gent." until the quarrel between Brian McOwen and Cahir Modarta was resolved in court. Meantime, Brian was authorized to lease the castle to whomever he wished.[10]

According to a suit brought by Cahir in June 1605, Brian pressed his claims and unfairly obtained a writ of restitution in the name of Owny McRowrie O Mory, "a notorious traitor who was slain in rebellion two years before," from Chief Justice William Saxey of the province of Munster. The writ required the delivery of the castle and lands of Dromaneen to Brian. Owny MacRory O More, chieftain of the O Mores of Laois, who was killed in 1600, joined the rebellion against the English in the Nine Years War and, in an attempt to gain support in Munster, advanced through Tipperary and as far as Limerick. Perhaps Brian McOwen acknowledged his authority and asked him to issue a writ of restittution that would effectively evict Cahir from Dromaneen. However that may be, the court referred the case for trial in the Court of King's Bench or that of Common Pleas in Dublin by the writ of ejectment (*de ejectione firmae*) that could be obtained by the person ejected. At the same time, Cahir obtained a writ of *supersedeas* from the Court of Common Pleas, effectively setting aside the writ of restitution.[11]

Cahir, considering the damage done, brought suit in the Court of Castle Chamber on 27 June 1605 against John Barry, Esq., former Sheriff of County Cork, Brian McOwen, and Conor O Callaghan. The court fined Barry £200 for disobeying the writ of *supersedeas* and "for gathering so great a multitude around him unlawfully to commit so great and manifest an outrage, misdemeanor, and riot." If he could certify that he had already been fined £100 by the Court of Common Pleas, he would not be subject to this fine, but he would have to appear before the Lord Deputy and Council. Brian McOwen was also fined £200 and imprisoned "during pleasure" and ordered to make restitution to

---

[8] *CSPIreland. James I*, 1:68, no. 83 (6 June 1603); Ó Murchadha, *Names*, 69.

[9] Decree of the Court of Castle Chamber; *Report on the Manuscripts of the Earl of Egmont*, 1:30.

[10] Caulfield, *The Council Book of the Corporation of Kinsale*, 306, 323.

[11] *Egmont MSS*, 1:30; Hans S. Pawlisch, *Sir John Davies and the Conquest of Ireland. A Study in Legal Imperialism*, (Cambridge: Cambridge University Ppress, 1985), 76; Bagwell, *Stuarts*, 1:9, 17.

Le Case de Tanistry *and Its Aftermath*

Cahir for all damages and to cover his costs and expenses. Conor of the Rock, "being one of the principal setters on" of the riot was fined £100 and was to appear to answer for the outrage. Whether any further action was taken against him is unknown.[12]

Although no reason was stated, a general pardon issued by James I on 18 February 1607 to Cahir O Callaghan, gentleman, of Dromaneen, and several of his relatives may have been prompted by the assault on Dromaneen. Cahir's relations included Owny McDonnogh McCahire, Donnill McTeige, otherwise Donill ni Sawine, Conoghor McDonnogh otherwise Connoghowre Entedane, Dermod McDonnogh McConnoghowre Reagh, John McDonnogho McConnoghor Reagh, Dermod McDonnogho McTeig, and Teige McShane McDermod. All were yeomen and probably his tenants there.[13]

I suspect that at this point, Brian McOwen, faced with the prospect of spending an indeterminate period in prison, enfeoffed his son Murrough McBrian with Dromaneen, as reported in *Le Case de Tanistry*. Cahir ejected Murrough, who then brought suit, *in ejectione firmae*, in the Court of King's Bench. The suit was probably initiated in 1605, as *Le Case* reported that it was argued in King's Bench several times over three or four years. Richard Bolton, Recorder of Dublin (later lord chancellor) and Sir John Meade were counsel for Cahir, while Sir John Davies, who later wrote a report of the case, acted for Murrough McBrian. Judgment was rendered in Hilary Term, in the fifth year of King James, that is, in the winter of 1608.[14]

Le Case de Tanistry, as this suit came to be known, and whose repercussions on Irish law were profound, focused on the nature of the Irish customs of inheritance and succession to power, summed up in the word tanistry. The question before the court was whether tanistry was void in itself or whether it was abolished by the Common Law of England. The court had also to decide whether tanistry was destroyed by the enfeoffment which created an entailed estate and whether Conor of the Rock, who came to power by reason of tanistry, gained a better estate by his surrender to Queen Elizabeth.[15]

The text begins by recording the transmission of authority among the O Callaghans from the time of Donough McTeige Roe, chief of his name according to tanistry, who died in 1577, and his nomination of his great-grandson, Donough McTeige Roe McConoghor, as his heir. As already indicated, the lordship of the O Callaghans was assumed by the elder Donough's grandson, Callaghan McConoghor, who died in 1578. At that point, Conor of the Rock, "being the oldest and most worthy of the blood and surname of O Callaghan," entered the land and claimed to hold it as lord or chieftain of "Publi Callaghan" [Pobul Uí Cheallacháin], according to the law of tanistry. After he surrendered his lands to Queen Elizabeth, she regranted them to him in 1594.[16]

Davies, the attorney for Murrough McBrian, the plaintiff, argued that tanistry was

---

[12] *Egmont MSS*, 1:30; Pawlisch, *Sir John Davies*, 76; Daniel Coghlan, *The Land of Ireland* (Dublin: Veritas, 1931), 58-61.

[13] *Calendar of the Patent Rolls of the Chancery of Ireland. 1 James I – 22 James I* (Dublin: A. Thom, 1800), 97.

[14] Davies, "The Case of Tanistry," 115; Bagwell, *Stuarts*, 1:119; Aidan Clarke, "Selling Royal Favours, 1624-32," *NHI*, 3:237.

[15] For a summary of the legal arguments see the master's thesis of Adam Donald Pole, *Customs in Conflict Sir John Davies, the Common Law, and the Abrogation of Irish Gavelkind and Tanistry* (Queen's University at Kingston, Ontario, Canada, 1999), esp. 88-121.

[16] Davies, "The Case of Tanistry," 79-80.

ancient, continual, and reasonable, and so in conformity with the Common Law; nor was it overturned by Queen Elizabeth's grant of an estate to Conor, because the person holding by tanistry did not have an estate that could be alienated in perpetuity, but only during his lifetime. According to this reasoning, Conor succeeded to the lordship by tanistry and gained a personal estate by virtue of Elizabeth's grant, but the law of tanistry continued to operate, so he could not alienate that estate in perpetuity. Yet, as he was still alive, he could alienate Dromaneen to Brian McOwen and Murrough.[17]

On the contrary, Cahir, the defendant, argued that the custom of tanistry was void, and that Conor did not gain an estate by the letters patent issued by Queen Elizabeth. Tanistry was said to be unreasonable and contrary to the commonwealth which "cannot subsist without a certain ownership of land" and a definite right of inheritance of land by a specific person. Due to this uncertainty of inheritance, no one would ever undertake to improve the land or build houses of any value or educate the children. (Compare this with Sir John Davies's comments recorded above). The custom of tanistry was interrupted in fact when the chieftain, Donough McTeige Roe (d. 1577), executed an estate tail according to Common Law, in favor of Donough McTeige, the younger, in 1574.[18]

The court annulled and abolished tanistry, concluding that it was prejudicial to the king and contrary to the rules of Common Law. Furthermore, inasmuch as Conor, who claimed O Callaghan lands by the custom of tanistry, had no estate of which the Common Law took notice, the court decided that he gained nothing by Queen Elizabeth's grant. His entry into O Callaghan lands therefore was only an abatement or intrusion after the death of Donough McTeige the younger. The grant made by the queen in consideration of his surrender of his lands was declared void in law. The rules for making the surrender do not seem to have been observed.[19]

Although this decision apparently justified Cahir's claim to Dromaneen, it would seem to have left Conor of the Rock without any right to any of the lands that he had surrendered to Elizabeth in 1594. As tanistry was declared void, and the queen's grant failed to convey an estate, he had no title at all to his lands. Thus, possession of the greater part of the O Callaghan lands was still much in doubt. Recognizing this difficulty, the litigants, with the court's approval, "came to an agreement by which a reasonable division was made of this territory amongst them." Cahir O Callaghan obtained Dromaneen and other lands and all the parties secured grants from the king "by virtue of a commission for strengthening defective titles."[20]

The resolution of this matter was apparently the reason why an inquisition was carried out at Cork on 20 April 1609 before the Chief Justice, Sir Dominick Sarsfield. The jurors determined that Teige Roe O Callaghan, "chief of his nation - *principalis nationis sue*" (d. c. 1537) had possessed both Dromaneen and Clonmeen and other lands in O Callaghan's Country, and that these had then passed to his son, Donough McTeige Roe, who held the O Callaghan lordship until his death in 1577. They related the history already discussed concerning the respective rights of Callaghan McConoghor (d. 1578), his nephew Donough McTeige (d. 1584), and Manus O Keeffe. Conor of the Rock, who had received the rod of authority from the earl of Clancarthy, had enjoyed the lordship of

---

[17] Davies, "The Case of Tanistry," 81-86.

[18] Davies, "The Case of Tanistry," 86-108.

[19] Davies, "The Case of Tanistry," 108-111.

[20] RIA O.S. Inquisitions, Cork, 1:137-148, no. 12 (20 April 1609).

the O Callaghans until about nine years before, that is, about 1600, when Cahir O Callaghan had entered Dromaneen, Dromore, Kilvealaton (Killebealady), Dromahane, Gortnagross, and Gearanaskagh. Apparently, as a consequence of this inquisition, Conor and Cahir came to agreement, leaving the latter in possession of Dromaneen and its dependencies, while Conor had to be content with Clonmeen and its lands.[21]

In order to secure an undisputed title to Dromaneen for Cahir, the three principal claimants, Conor, Cahir, and Brian McOwen of Cloghda (just south of Castlemore) on 23 March 1610 surrendered these lands to the crown: Carrigolane, Gortmolire, Rathcomane, the castle and lands of Dromaneen, a quarter of Dromore, a half quarter of Kilvealaton and Dromahane, two carucates in Skarragh, and a quarter in Gortroe. A quarter apparently consisted of three or four carucates or ploughlands. Two months later, on 18 May Cahir received the regrant of Dromaneen, Dromore, Kilvealaton, Dromahane, Kilpadder and other lands to hold as a manor with 600 acres in demesne and the right to hold a court at an annual rent of £13 4s. Intent on resolving other claims, Cahir and Art O Keeffe of Dromagh, representing Eleanor O Callaghan and her son Manus O Keeffe, proposed to surrender Dromaneen and other lands to the crown and to receive a regrant. Considering "the good service done by the said Cahir to the late queene," James I on 16 October 1610 authorized Sir Arthur Chichester, the Lord Deputy, to regrant the castles, manors, and lands of Dromaneen, Dromore, Gortnagross, Ballywine (Ballyheen), Ballyhostie (Ballyhest), Ballynafeaha, Garrymcowney, and other holdings to Cahir and Art O Keeffe to hold in common socage (a non-military tenure) of Dublin Castle, either jointly or severally, as they wished, and subject to the present rents.[22]

Conor, the Last Chieftain of the O Callaghans

Two years later, on 31 May 1612, Conor of the Rock, then in his fifties or sixties, died at Clonmeen, leaving his property to his son Ceallachán or Callaghan.[23] Conor, who had become chief of the O Callaghans thirty-four years before, was the last person to hold that position under the old order, which he helped to bring to an end. There is no evidence that any O Callaghan thereafter was chosen or designated by the clan as its chief, nor is there any evidence that anyone ever again received the rod of authority from MacCarthy Mór. No longer could any man claim to be "captain of his nation," as the Tudor documents had it, because there was no longer a "nation" or clan in the old Gaelic sense. Nor was anyone recognized thereafter as tanist with the right of succession to the chieftainship. The chieftainship of the O Callaghans died with Conor of the Rock. Henceforth there were two leading branches of the clan, each with power and influence, and with some vestigial claim to the allegiance of the lesser members of the family.

Pobul Uí Cheallacháin, or O Callaghan's Country, moreover, existed now only as a geographical term, rather than as a family patrimony. The demesne lands of the chieftain had been transformed into a family estate, heritable in accordance with English law. Nevertheless, Conor's attempt to seize all those lands for his own benefit resulted in

---

[21] RIA O.S. Inquisitions, Cork, 1:137-148, no. 12 (20 April 1609).

[22] *CSPIreland. James I*, 3:584, no. 966. The same text appears in *ibid.*, 4:292, no. 536 (16 October 1612); Grove-White, *Notes*, 3:61-62; *BIFR*, 888; Gillman, "Chieftains," *JCHAS*, Series 2, 3 (1897): pedigree; Butler, *Gleanings*, 298.

[23] RIA O.S. Inquisitions, Cork, 1:325-331, no. 40 (26 August 1618).

a bitter court battle and the effective division of the properties between himself and his cousin Cahir. Conor's residence at Clonmeen and Cahir's at Dromaneen symbolized that rupture. From the crown's standpoint the future belonged to the Perceval family. In 1615 James I named Sir John Perceval lord of Duhallow and of Poble O Callaghan and Poble O Keeffe. If it was his intention to subordinate O Callaghan and O Keeffe to Perceval, that does not seem to have occurred. In time, the Percevals were among the most successful beneficiaries of the confiscations following the rebellion of 1641.[24]

An inquisition concerning Conor's holdings taken at the King's Castle in Cork on 26 August 1618 showed that he possessed the castle and village of Clonmeen, and carucates in the following townlands with their annual value:[25]

Property	Car.	Value
Clonmeen, Dromeragh, Coolroe, Coolkilty (Coolekeelt), Kilavoy	3	20s
Banteer (East and West), Fermoyle	3	20s
Kilcaskan, Dromcummer	3	20s
Gurteenbeha, Money, Kippagh	2	20s
Roskeen, Kilbarrahan, Cloonteens (Clontyneroe, Clontynebane)	3	20s
Gortmore, Glankitinere	1.5	20s
Rathcomane	3	20s
Carroghnybroe, water mill; part of quarter of Gortmolire.	.5	5s
Clonquin, Lisaghvohilly, Lackendarragh, part of quarter of Gortmolire	2.5	13s 4d
Gurteenbeha, Gurteenbeha, Money, and Kippaghe, chief rent		4s 4d

Identification and/or location of several of these places is still problematical. Dromeragh, and Coolkilty were near Clonmeen; Rathcomane was above Gortroe and Glankitinere was south of Coolroe; Carroghnybroe, claimed by Dermot McTeige O Callaghan, probably should be identified with Curraghbower south of Gortroe. Clonquin and Lissaghvohilly were likely near Lackendarragh south of the river.

The jurors also found that Conor leased or mortgaged various properties, which were probably in effect at the time of his death:

Property	Mortgagee	Date	Car.	Value
Roskeen (1), Knockkillavaher (.5)	Conoghor Garvane	17/1/1608	1.5	£40
Clohentyncree (Cloonteens)	Donough McConoghor O Garvane	10/11/1605	.5	
Clonquin, Lissaghvohilly, Lackendarragh	Nicholas FitzChristopher Gould, Cork merchant			£40
Banteer East	Teige McConoghor Garvane	1611	1	

---

[24] Rowley Lascelles, ed., *Liber Munerum publicorum Hiberniae ab anno 1152 usque ad 1827 or The Establishments of Ireland from the nineteenth of King Stephen to the seventh of George IV*, 2 vols. (London, 1824-1830), 2:11 (Lodge's Peerage).

[25] RIA O.S. Inquisitions, Cork, 1:325-331, no. 40 (26 August 1618).

Le Case de Tanistry *and Its Aftermath*

Property	Mortgagee	Date	Car.	Value
Currygnylane, Shanevolaghe, Bealebuy	Thomas Norris		1.5	£30
Gortmore, Money, Gurteenbeha, Kippagh (.75 car. each); Carrough ny Brough (.5 car., water mill)	Conoghor Óg O Garvane Donough O Daly		2.75	
Rathcomane	Sir John FitzEdmond FitzGerald	26/9/1607		£60

Knockkillavaher probably is Kilbarrahan less than a mile above Roskeen north of the Blackwater; Clohentyncree appears to be Cloonteens, also north of the river. Currygnylane may be Carrigcleena. Shanvevolaghe and Bealebuy (Bealach Buidhe) were likely in the same area.

In all Conor held nineteen carucates (about 2,280 acres) worth about £12 or 145 shillings annually. His lands on both sides of the Blackwater stretched from Banteer and Clonmeen eastward through Roskeen, Gortmore. Gortroe, Gurteenbeha, Kippagh, and Coolnahane to Gortmolire (Lombardstown). Rathcomane, we are told, contained "three ploughlands betwixt the littell watter or brooke comonly called Sylloyd [unidentified] on the east, the brooke or blackwater on the north, the runynge watter betwixt Gorteroe and Rath Comane aforesaid on the west, the lands of Portyedove on the southe." Gortroe is south of Lombardstown and Portyedove probably is Portaghdav near Boula about a mile south of Bweeng.[26]

The persons to whom Conir leased property included Sir Thomas Norris, the Vice-President of Munster, who made a contract in 1593 for the exploitation of iron mines in the woods of O Callaghan's Country, as mentioned above. By 1618 Currygnylane, Shanevolaghe, and Bealebuy had passed into the hands of Sir John Jephson who married Norris's daughter and heir. Sir John FitzEdmond FitzGerald, formerly High Sheriff of Cork and a loyal servant of the crown, was probably Conor's uncle. Nicholas FitzChristopher Gould belonged to a notable merchant family of Cork. The O Garvan family, headed by Conoghor, and his sons Donough and Teige also received land in fief from Conor of the Rock. After his death his widow Joan ny Tirrelagh entered this enfeoffment in Gortmore, Gurteenbeha, Money, Kippagh, and Carrough ny Brough and was still in possession at the time of the inquisition.[27]

At his death in 1612 Conor held in demesne six or more carucates (about 720 acres) as follows:

Property	Car.	Value
Kilcaskan	1	
Clonteenbane	.5	

---

[26] Conor mortgaged Rathcomane to Sir John FitzGerald; Edward MacLysaght, "Survey of Documents in Private Keeping: Second Series. Doneraile Papers," *AH* 20 (1958): 58 (26 September 1607).

[27] RIA O.S. Inquisitions, Cork, 1:325-331, no. 40 (26 August 1618); MacLysaght, "Doneraile Papers," *AH* 20:1958): 58 (26 September 1607).

57

Property	Car.	Value
Skarragh, Kilknockgowne, Mohereen, Kilberrihert, Glantane	2.5	5s
Banteer West, Fermoyle, Knockenloderey, Grantyshersted, Inshiquintine	2	
Gurteenbeha, capital rents		4s 4 d

Kilcaskan, Clonteenbane (Cloonteens), and Gurteenbeha were north of the Blackwater. Kilknockgowne (Derrygowna?), Mohereen, Kilberrihert, and Glantane were situated around Skarragh south of the river. Banteer and Fermoyle, and the carucates of Knockenloderey (Knockeenatuder?), Grantyshersted, and Inshiquintine lay at the western edge of O Callaghan's Country. All Conor's castles and lands were held of the king in chief (that is, in direct dependence on the crown) by military service at an annual rent of forty Irish shillings.[28]

Conor probably had erected a castle or fortified mansion at Clonmeen on the foundation of an earlier structure but the building no longer stands. In 1844 James Roderick O Flanagan remarked that "a little to the west, the south bank [of the Blackwater] displays prostrate relics of feudal times. Half a ruined flanking tower, portion of a lofty wall, and remains of a parallel, constitute all that remains of Clonmeen Castle. This castle was destroyed during the wars of 1641, and several of the cannon balls which battered the walls have been found. It presents a melancholy spectacle of faded glory, as it must have been of great strength, presenting, even in decay, the lingering traces of former might."[29]

Walls of Clonmeen Castle

---

[28] RIA O.S. Inquisitions, Cork, 1:325-331, no. 40 (26 August 1618).

[29] James Roderick O Flanagan, *The Blackwater in Munster* (London: J. How, 1844), 153; Gillman, "Chieftains," *JCHAS*, Series 2, 3 (1897): 202 and n. 4; Grove-White, *Notes*, 2:236; *AICC*, no. 14354; Kavanagh, *Kilshannig*, 7-8.

About fifty years later Herbert Gillman, an O Callaghan by descent, described the remains of Clonmeen castle:

> The castle was built on lime-stone rock, about a field distant from the southern bank of the river Blackwater in the townland of North Clonmeen, a mile and a-half east of the present railway station of Banteer, on the Mallow-Killarney railway. The bawn was nearly a square, each side being about two hundred and seventy-five feet in length, and this was enclosed by a strong curtain wall, three feet outside. This wall was guarded at each of its angles by round towers of two (possibly three) storeys high. The north-western tower has disappeared, but portions of the other three remain. They were fourteen feet in internal diameter, with walls five and a-half feet thick, and each floor has loops for hand-guns, not only towards the field but also two looking into the bawn itself. The entrance to each tower was at the inner angle of the bawn. The keep has wholly disappeared; some of its stones appear to have been used in building a limekiln of a quarry close by to the east. The remains of the castle indicate a structure of date 1590-1610, and its builder was, therefore, probably Connoghor O Callaghan, the chieftain who got a regrant in 1594 of the lands from the Crown. He is known as 'Conoghor of the Rock' and may have used an earlier building than the one whose remains now appear. Possibly the building was added to and rendered stronger by works erected by Donogh, husband of Connoghor's grand-daughter, a famous man in Cromwellian times.

The bawn (*bó dhún*, cow fort) was the enclosed area where cattle were pastured. The keep was usually a fortified tower, either rectangular or round, that served as a residence and also as the last line of defense if the exterior walls were breached. The gunloop was an angular space piercing the castle wall and gradually tapering to a gap in the outer surface of the wall. An archer or man armed with a musket could stand or kneel in that space and fire his weapon at the enemy. The opening in the wall was so narrow that his body was well protected from enemy fire.[30]

Gunloop in Clonmeen Castle Wall

---

[30] See the detailed description in Campbell, *Displacement*, 106-112.

Le Case de Tanistry *and Its Aftermath*

The End of Cahir O Callaghan of Dromaneen

Conor's great adversary, Cahir Modarta lived some years longer, dying about 1636. By his wife Ellen, daughter of Callaghan MacCarthy of Carrignamuck in Muskerry, he had several sons: Donough, Teige, Callaghan, and Conor, and at least one daughter Katherine who married Teige O Brien of Killenecurra.[31] The last references to him suggest something of his importance in the political and social life of County Cork and of his effort to expand his holdings even further. For example, in 1631 Cahir O Callaghan of Dromaneen, esquire, and William Bryen of Kilnecurry, gent., arbitrated a dispute between William St. Leger and Robert Shynan of Castlepooka and his son Nicholas concerning certain lands. Three years later Thomas Bettesworth, writing to Sir Philip Perceval, mentioned the possibility of the appointment of Cahir O Callaghan to serve on a commission with Sir William Fenton, Richard Fisher, and John Burgatt. In the following year complaint was made that Cahir was encroaching upon Perceval's lands at Dromdowney, northeast of Gortnagross, an O Callaghan holding.[32] An inquisition concerning Cahir's estate carried out at the King's Old Castle in Cork before Walter Coppinger in 1637 showed that, in addition to Dromaneen he held in fief 1.5 carucates in Gortnecolly, otherwise called Garrymcvouhy, Rossard, Kilmichael, Kilgobban, Ruanes and Ballymcohny (Garrymcowney?), valued at twenty shillings yearly. Gortnecolly or Garrymcvouhy (identified elsewhere as Gortincowley, or Gortnachonolye) was adjacent to Garrymcowney (later Longueville). Kilmichael, Kilgobban, and Ruanes were just north of there. Without having obtained a royal license, Cahir alienated all these lands in 1611 to David, Viscount Roche of Fermoy; the latter, after receiving royal authorization, in turn alienated them to Cahir in July 1613. An inquisition taken at Mallow before Sir Philip Perceval in 1638 recorded that Cahir held in fief a carucate in Subulter (less than a mile north of Castlemagner), worth ten shillings yearly, as well as half of three carucates in Ballymacmurragh (Lackaliegh, Croghty, and Rathmaher) and half of Killavallig worth fifteen shillings. He enfeoffed with these lands Sir William Fenton, Conoghor Óg O Garvane of Kippagh, Daniel O Keeffe of Dromagh, and Tulagh O Conbae of Dromaneen. The inquisition also revealed that Cahir's son-in-law Conoghor McTeige O Callaghan of Banteer held a carucate in East Banteer, half a carucate in Inchidaly (less than a mile northeast of Banteer) mortgaged at £155 and valued at eleven shillings yearly. Cahir enfeoffed his son Donough O Callaghan with the mortgage of £155, *sub condicione redempcionis*. All the aforesaid were held of King Charles I but by what service was unknown.[33]

Cahir was also authorized to hold a market at Dromaneen every Monday and two annual fairs on the feasts of St, Mark (25 April) and St. Bernard (20 August) and on the day after each.[34] Those dates were likely established long ago. The fairs were festive occasions that drew crowds from all about, as livestock were sold, children played games, young people engaged in romance, and, if the evidence of the nineteenth century can be

---

[31] Caulfield, *The Council Book of the Corporation of Kinsale*, 343.

[32] *LM*, 161, 216; Dublin GO, MS 177, pp. 458-459; *BIFR*, 888; MacLysaght, "Doneraile Papers," *AH* 20 (1958): 65-66 (20 April 1631; on 1 July 1631 Cahir witnessed a quitclaim issued in light of that award). *Egmont MSS*, 1.1:77 (14 April 1634), 81 (24 February 1635).

[33] RIA O.S. Inquisitions, Cork, 5:77-78, 184-185, nos. 413 (13 April 1637), 464 (9 April 1638). Lord Barry purchased eight ploughlands in Subulter from the crown and sold them to O Callaghan.

[34] Caulfield, *The Council Book of the Corporation of Kinsale*, 347.

transposed to an earlier time, faction fights often broke out especially at nighttime.

Just as Conor probably developed the castle of Clonmeen, Cahir, or more likely, his son Donough, was responsible for the transformation of the castle of Dromaneen into the fortified house that "occupies a bold and romantic situation" on a cliff overlooking the Blackwater. Some portions of an older tower house enclosed in a small bawn may have been incorporated into the new structure. Writing in 1844, the Irish antiquarian John Windele remarked on the interminable, lonely road "buried in solitude" leading to the castle of Dromaneen:

> [The castle] is a specimen of the last phase of the castellation in the descent from the lofty moated keep to the simple manor house. It presents an irregular shell with high gables, massive chimneys, and one or two machicolated projecting parapets peeping out above the ivy, which thickly clothes the building, and resting on rounded corbels. The interior is quite ruinous, the floors and stairs all departed. The execution of the carved doorways, mullions, dripstones, and elaborate mantel-pieces is excellent - a taste for that illegitimate Italian style which began to pervade at the beginning of the 17th century seems prevalent in the frames of the doorways and fire places of this structure, and would refer us for the date of the building to the close of the reign of Elizabeth.[35]

Dromaneen Castle

About fifty years later Gillman commented:
> The remains of the Castle of Dromaneen still stand on the south bank of the river Blackwater, about two miles west of Mallow. The external curtain walls, which are about three feet thick, enclose a space about 186 feet from east to west, and 77 feet from north to south. A road still called *bohereen-na-spridda*, or the "boreen of the spirits" (the origin of the name

---

[35] Cited by Grove-White, *Notes*, 3:69-70; Henry F. Berry, "The Parish of Kilshannig and Manor of Newberry, Co. Cork," *JCHAS* 11 (1905): 34-35; Kavanagh, *Kilshannig*, 9-10. For an aerial view see https://www.youtube.com/watch?v=56k5QBQ_N74

being lost), leads from the east of the barbican entrance which is protected by a round tower and a guard room, both loopholed for hand guns. West of this tower is the outer ward, a space of about 70 feet from north to south, and 21 feet transversely. A passage 12 feet wide leads from this past a large building to the inner ward, in which are two other buildings, one to the north 65 x 24 feet, and one to the west 41 x 20 feet . . . . South of the whole pile is a space of about six acres, which was all paved over up to recent times and which is still enclosed by a wall all round, strengthened with half-round towers, crenellated for hand-guns. The whole structure is probably of date about the first half of the seventeenth-century, but there is in the interior an ancient wall, 5 1/2 feet thick, which appears to be a remnant of an earlier castle.[36]

Much more recent is the description by the Cork archaeological survey team. The castle stands on a limestone cliff above the Blackwater in an area of about five acres. South of the castle as the ground rises there is a bawn (from *bó dhún* - cow fort) in which cattle were sheltered from potential enemies. A wall with round towers at each corner and in the middle of each of three sides gave protection; only four ruined towers, each with gun loops for defense, still stand. On the cliffside low walls connect three rectangular structures, namely, the castle or main residence, an attached wing, and a building to the east. The castle consisted of three storeys and an attic with high chimneys at each gabled end. Entry was through doors on the ground and first floors, with two rooms, one larger than the other, on each floor. Underneath the small room was a basement. One large room, probably used for receptions and festive occasions, extended the length of the second floor. Windows were located on the north and south walls and the end gables and there were several fireplaces. The floors, which have entirely disappeared, were of wood. Extending southward at a right angle to the main edifice is a two-storey building with a kitchen and a fireplace on the ground floor; the upper floors were probably used to accommodate residents or guests. Connected to this on the southwestern corner is a square tower, provided with gun loops on the ground level. The entire complex has an L-shape. On the northwest corner of the castle are steps, known as 'Lady's steps' leading to the flat land on the riverbank. More than likely the river was used for communication with Clonmeen and other places. East of the main structure is a third building with two storeys, an attic, and gabled ends. Walls connecting the buildings form an inner and an outer courtyard. An arched doorway gives access through the outer courtyard wall. Denis Power suggested that the castle was constructed around 1630 when the heirs of Cahir and Conor of the Rock were married. John Kavanagh commented that the "narrow, winding, and well sheltered" *bóithrín na sprioda* or "road of the ghost" leading from Kilshannig church to Dromaneen "could easily instill an eerie feeling; but the ghost was probably a fabrication, created by the O Callaghans to ward off any intending intruders!" He also reported the local tradition that "the O Callaghan gold is buried deep in the watery caves under the foundations of Dromaneen Castle."[37]

---

[36] Gillman, "Chieftains," *JCHAS*, Series 2, 3 (1897): 218; Smith, *Cork*, 1:300; Lewis, *Dictionary*, 2:208; Grove-White, *Notes*, 3:64.

[37] *AICC*, no. 14375; Denis Power, "Dromaneen Castle: An O Callaghan Stronghold," *MFCJ* 17 (1999): 5-17; Campbell, *Displacement*, 113-121; John J. Kavanagh, "Kilshannig, Mythology, Tales and

Dromore, the third O Callaghan castle, once stood on the west bank of the Clydagh River. Marked on Jobson's map circa 1589, it was probably situated between Dromore Lodge and Old Dromore House. The tenth-century *Book of Rights* cited Dromore as one of the royal seats of the kings of Munster.[38]

Callaghan O Callaghan of Clonmeen, 1612-1631

Meantime, following Conor of the Rock's death in 1612, his son and heir, Callaghan O Callaghan, then over twenty-five years of age and married, took possession of his father's estate.[39] Conor's widow, Joan ny Tirrelagh, resided in her dower lands of Gortmore, Gurteenbeha, Mohereen, and Kippagh until her death in 1630.

An inquisition of 1617 reported that MacDonough claimed from Poble Callaghan meat, drink and wages for twenty-seven gallowglasses with their boys and meat, drink and lodgings for a third of all strangers whom MacDonough pleased to entertain as often as occasion required. Another inquisition of 1631 recorded that Callaghan O Callaghan owed MacDonough sixty beeves to be levied on six quarters. The earlier claim to food, drink, and lodging for twenty-seven knights and their squires and also for a third of those whom he wished to entertain was repeated.[40] Florence MacCarthy, claiming to be MacCarthy Mór, but imprisoned in the Tower of London, in 1589 named as one of his sureties "Callaghan McConoghor, son and heir to O Ceallaghain chief lord of the O Callaghans that stands in the Co. of Cork by the town of Mala." In 1613 in the trial of Con McCahir for robbery, Callaghan and three other jurors, namely, Donell McTeige Carty of Dysert, Owen McDonough of Ballymacmurragh, and Donell McDonnagh Sassynagh of Twonagh, were fined £40 each and imprisoned at the pleasure of the court for refusing to join other jurors in convicting the defendant. That is an interesting commentary on justice in Ireland.[41]

Like other landlords pressed for cash, Callaghan mortgaged various lands:

Property	Date	Mortgagee	Car.	Value
Dromcummer, Lisnaherey, Killarush	28/11/1615	James Lombard, Cork merchant	2	£100
West Banteer, Fermoyle	9/3/1615?	Thomas FitzWilliam Gould of Cork		£135
Killavoy, Coolroe	25/9/1617?	James Lombard	.5	
Dromeragh, Curraghrour, Cowlenykilty	25/9/1617	James Lombard	1.5	
Nadmore, Nadbeg	10/1/1607?	Nicholas Fitz James Lombard	.75	

Beliefs," and "Excerpts from the History of Kilshannig,"*MFCJ* 9 (1991): 18, and 2 (1984): 59.

[38] Grove-White, *Notes*, 3:81; Smith, *Cork*, 1:300-301; *AICC*, no. 14309; O Murchadha, *Names*, 68-69.

[39] If he were just twenty-five in 1612 then he was born in 1587, but he was given as surety for Florence MacCarthy in 1589 which suggests that he was probably in his early forties.

[40] Butler, *Gleanings*, 95.

[41] *The Life and Letters of Florence MacCarthy Reagh, Tanist of Carbery, MacCarthy Mór*, ed. Daniel MacCarthy (London: Longmans, 1867), 70; Gillman, "Chieftains," *JCHAS*, Series 2, 3 (1897): pedigree; *Egmont MSS*, 1.1:42 (14 May 1613).

Dromcummer, Lisnaherey and Killarush were located north of the Blackwater east of Kanturk. West Banteer, Fermoyle, Killavoy, Coolroe, Dromeragh, Curraghrour, Cowlenykilty (also called Coolekeelt), Nadmore, and Nadbeg were south of the river and west and south of Clonmeen. James Lombard and his son Nicholas belonged to a notable Cork family originally from Lombardy in Italy who later gave their name to Lombardstown, formerly known as Gortmolire in the heart of O Callaghan'ss Country. Because he alienated property to James Lombard, and also to David Lombard (with his brother Donough) without royal permission, Callaghan had to seek a royal pardon in 1625. Thomas FitzWilliam Gould belonged to an important family of Cork merchants. Callaghan also witnessed a conveyance of the town and lands of Rathcomane containing three ploughlands in O Callaghan's Country by Maurice Roche, gentleman, of Cork, and his brother James Roche of Cork, merchant, to Daniel O Keeffe of Dromagh, Oliver O Grady of Foreroaght, Cork, John O Sullivan of Rosse I Craw, Cork, all gentlemen, for £220. Other witnesses included Donough O Callaghan and Dermod O Callaghan, probably Callaghan's brothers. In 1620 Callaghan was High Sheriff of County Cork.[42]

Callaghan first married the widow of his brother Teige, namely, Mary, the daughter of Brian McOwen MacSweeney of Mashanaglass (southeast of Macroom), probably the same Brian who joined Conor of the Rock in the assault on Dromaneen around 1602. After that marriage was annulled, Callaghan married Joanna Butler, the daughter of James Butler, second Lord Dunboyne (d. 1624), and the widow of Maurice FitzGibbon (d. 1608), son and heir of Edmund, the White Knight. The union of the O Callaghans with the Butlers, one of the leading Anglo-Norman families, had significant consequences in the next generation during the Confederation of Kilkenny. After Callaghan's death Joanna married Thomas FitzGerald, the knight of Glin. Her three husbands surely found her an attractive bride, perhaps because of her youth and beauty, but also because of the political advantages of a connection with the Butlers.[43]

Prior to his death Callaghan and Joanna had a chalice made for the Dominican convent of Kilmallock in County Limerick. The Latin inscription reads:

Dom. Callaghanus O Callaghan et Juana Butler uxor eius fieri fecerunt pro convento Killocensi Ord. Praed. Req[uie]s[can]t in pace.

Sir Callaghan O Callaghan and Joanna Butler, his wife, had this made for the convent of Kilmallock of the Order of Preachers. May they rest in peace.

The date 1639 inscribed on the chalice must refer to another inscription on the base, because Callaghan died in 1631. The chalice,now in the Dominican monastery of St. Saviour in Limerick, is silver gilt, nine and a quarter inches high; the cup is three and

[42] *Calendar of State Papers relating to Ireland preserved in the Public Record Office, 1625-1670*, 8 vols., ed. Robert P. Mahaffy (London: Public Record Office, 1900-1910), 1:77, 248. The manuscript dated the two mortgages to James Lombard on 25 September 1607 and 25 September 1617. The mortgage to Nicholas, James's son, was dated on 10 January 1607, but I am inclined to think all three were made in 1617. Callaghan received a pardon on 26 January 1625 for alienating property to James Lombard; his brother Donough obtained a pardon on 28 November 1627. MacLysaght, "Doneraile Papers," *AH* 20 (1958): 64 (22 December 1630); *BIFR*, 888.

[43] *LM*, 216-217; Dublin GO, MS 177, p. 457; *BIFR*, 888; J. Anthony Gaughan, *The Knights of Glin. A Geraldine Family* (Mount Merrion: Kingdom Books, 1978), 53.

three-quarter inches wide, and the base is six inches. The chalice was used at the mass celebrated by Father Denis O Callaghan of Maynooth during the O Callaghan reunion at Ballybeg in 1988.[44]

The Kilmallock Chalice

(St. Saviour Monastery, Limerick)

Callaghan died on 28 May 1631 at Clonmeen, while swimming, presumably in the Blackwater River. He was mentioned on 3 July 1632 as "late of Clonmeen." His brother Conor, who settled in Abbeydorney, County Kerry, died probably in 1638, leaving three children by his wife Dorothy: Teige, Donough, and Eleanor.[45]

The Church in the Seventeenth Century

At that time the great majority of the O Callaghans were likely faithful Catholics. The Kilmallock chalice evinces Callaghan's continued adherence to the faith of his ancestors. A visitation of the diocese of Cork, Cloyne, and Ross in 1615, commissioned by the crown, provided some evidence of the impact of the Protestant Reformation at the beginning of the Stuart monarchy. Some thirty-five years before, in 1581 the bishop had replaced a rebellious vicar of Kilshannig by appointing Dermot McWogny O Callaghan (Dermitius McWogny Y Kalghan; Diarmaid Mac Uaithne Ó Ceallacháin), who had likely

---

[44] Rev. J. Crowe, "Notice of the Kilmallock Chalice," *JRSAI* 9 (4th series 1889): 216-217; Robert Day, "Additional Notes on the Kilmallock Chalice, with a Notice of the Midleton chalice," *JRSAI* 9 (4th series 1889): 217-220.

[45] *CSP Ireland 1625-1670*, 1:602; *BIFR*, 888. Conor's will, dated 3 April 1637, was proved on 14 November 1638; Dublin PRO Testaments.

---

conformed to the Established Church. In 1615 the commissioners described the state of the Church of Ireland parish churches of Clonmeen, Roskeen, and Kilshannig all in O Callaghan's Country. The church and chancel (the sanctuary) of Clonmeen were said to be "well repaired," but the church of Roskeen was "down." Clonmeen and Roskeen were valued at £6 and Kilshannig at £8. Emmanuel Phaire, the vicar of Clonmeen, Roskeen, and Kilshannig, was in residence, and received £3 from Clonmeen and Roskeen and £4 from Kilshannig. He also ministered at Castlemagner north of the Blackwater where the church and chancel were "down." The church at Clonmeen was "out of repair" in 1676 and in ruins in 1694 because of "the Irish in the late war."[46] From time immemorial O Callaghans were buried in Clonmeen churchyard.

Catholic clergy were usually educated abroad. A catalogue dated 1621 of Irish priests, "exiled from their country for the Roman, Catholic, and Apostolic faith - *exilez de leur pays pour la foy catholique, apostolique et romane,*" and educated at Bordeaux in France included Eugenius (Eoghan or Owen) Callachan of the diocese of Cloyne, and Thadeus (Tadhg, Timothy) O Challachan of the diocese of Cork. Another Thaddaeus Callaghan was ordained for the Irish province of the Dominican Order in 1629. Of particular interest is Kedagh or Ceadach O Callaghan, born in Clonmeen, a son of the chieftain Conor of the Rock. He studied near Cork under the masters Daniel Flynn and Richard Prendergast, before going to Bordeaux to study philosophy; from there he went to the Irish College in Salamanca in 1626. When he took the entrance examination he was "considered middling and passable;" two years later the examiners agreed that he and his fellow students had been attentive and gave a good account of the subject matter. Initially he used the Latin name Carolus or Charles as an alternative to Ceadach, but in 1628 he called himself Caietanus or Cajetan O Callaghan.

By chance we have more information about Derby (an anglicized form of Diarmuid) Callaghan, a native of Mallow, who lived in the household of John Wallis, Esq., Clerk of the Council of Munster, and then attended grammar school for two years and the Irish College at Bordeaux for eleven weeks. After ordination and service in Ireland for thirteen years he lived in Paris for four years before going to Bordeaux. He sailed for Ireland from La Rochelle but his ship was driven to Plymouth, England where he was interrogated by the justices of the peace on 9 January 1636. He and his companion, another "Romish" priest, at first denied that they were priests "in order to save trouble." He explained that the crucifixes and indulgences in his trunk were intended for his Irish friends. As a papal notary he also carried a papal letter for the deanery of Cloyne as well as a letter of excommunication against Daniel Leaghey to be given to Leaghey's bishop. The fate of Fr. Derby Callaghan was not reported, but perhaps he was allowed to return to Ireland. Around 1663 Callaghan O Callaghan was described as "a learned, upright and remarkable man from a distinguished family of Cloyne diocese, [and] is aged about forty years." A Franciscan, Cajetan Callaghan received holy orders at Prague in 1681-1683.[47]

---

[46] W. Maziere Brady, *Clerical and Parochial Records of Cork, Cloyne and Ross*, 3 vols. (Dublin: A. Thom, 1863-1864), cited by Grove-White, *Notes*, 3:342; "Royal Visitation of Cork, Cloyne, Ross, and the College of Youghal," *Archivium Hibernicum* 1 (1913): 173-215; *AICC*, no. 14411, 14713.

[47] *CSPIreland. James I,* 5:320, no. 733, and *CSPIreland. Charles I,* 2:120; Thomas Burke, *Hibernia Dominicana sive Historia Provinciae Hiberniae Ordinis Praedicatorum* (Cologne, 1762; reprint Westmead, England: Gregg, 1970), 114-117; D. J. O Doherty, "Students of the Irish College, Salamanca

Le Case de Tanistry *and Its Aftermath*

The Other Descendants of Teige Roe Bacach

In addition to the principal branches of the family established at Dromaneen and Clonmeen, other descendants of Teige Roe Bacach (d. c. 1537), especially his younger sons, Cahir, Dermot, Owen, and Donal, acquired permanent holdings in the old lands of Pobul Uí Cheallacháin. As noted above, the chieftain customarily alloted family lands to his closest male relatives, but they did not enjoy full rights of ownership and could not bequeath them to their children. On the contrary, when one died the chieftain could divide all the family lands again among the surviving members according to age and rank. In the last quarter of the sixteenth century the names of several descendants of Teige Roe appear in royal pardons, but their place of residence often varies, suggesting that they did not have a permanent title to the property in question. However, by the seventeenth century, in much the same way as Conor of the Rock created an estate under English law for himself and his descendants, some of his cousins also appear to have acquired hereditary ownership of certain lands. They included the O Callaghans of Rathmore, Pallas, Gortmore, Ballymacmurragh, Roskeen, Kilpadder, Kilcranathan, and Banteer. These families all seem to have survived until the rebellion of 1641, but most of them were dispossessed as a consequence of the Cromwellian settlement.

Cahir, the third son of Teige Roe, tanist by Irish law to his brother Donough (d. 1577), was the ancestor of the O Callaghans of Rathmore (Ráth mór, the great fort), situated north of the Blackwater. Royal pardons of 1573, 1585, and 1603 indicate the succession through Cahir's son Donough, and Donough's sons Owny and Callaghan. Of Owny's five sons, Cahir Roe, pardoned in 1600, died in 1622, holding Rathmore of the crown in chief (that is, directly from the king) by the service of one-twentieth of a knight's fee. His son Donough inherited his estate and likely was the father of Loghlan O Callaghan, who together with Robert Magner, forfeited eighty-four acres in Rathmore and Rathbeg after the rebellion of 1641. Two other members of the family "Tady mac Morrogho O Callaghane and Morrice mac Teige O Callaghan," both attainted of treason in the reign of King James I, held a quarter of a carucate or ploughland in Rathmore.[48]

Teige Roe's fourth son, Dermot, was described as prior of Ballybeg, a title enjoyed by his son, the chieftain, Conor of the Rock, and later by another son, Dermot Óg. Teige na Muchorie, Dermot's fourth son, living at Gortmore in 1577, and tanist to his brother, Conor of the Rock, had several sons, but apparently none of them created a permanent estate.[49]

More fortunate in that respect was Dermot's sixth son, Irrelagh. Resident in various places, he was pardoned in 1574, 1577, 1585, and in 1601; in 1594 he held certain clan lands under Conor of the Rock. On the death of his uncle Donal in 1602 Irrelagh was assigned the lands of Pallas, nearly seven miles west of Mallow in the parish of Roskeen. He married Ellen, daughter of Art McMahon O Keeffe, the chieftain of the O Keeffes. An inquisition following his death at Pallas on 2 February 1609 revealed that he

---

(1619-1700)," *Archivium Hibernicum* 3 (1914): 96, and 4 (1915): 13; Benignus Millett, "Calendar of Volume 16 of the Fondo di Vienna in the Propaganda Archives, Part 3, ff. 217-280," *CH* 41 (1999): 10-35, citing ff. 243r-244v; Matthäus Hosler, "Irishmen ordained at Prague, 1629-1786," *CH* 33 (1991): 16-18.

[48] Gillman, "Chieftains," *JCHAS*, Series 2, 3 (1897): pedigree; *LM*, 161, 217; Dublin, PRO, Books of Survey and Distribution, vol. 3 Barony of Duhallow; Ó Murchadha, *Names*, 69.

[49] Gillman, "Chieftains," *JCHAS*, Series 2, 3 (1897): pedigree.

held of the king, but by what service was unknown, Pallas, Gortencloney, Fardorush (unidentified), Gortbofinna and Gearanaskagh. Irrelagh's son Dermot, over twenty-five, and married at the time of his father's death, succeeded to his estate. Ten years later, however, Dermot's appeal to King James I to confirm his title seems to have been denied. Instead, the king, on 4 December 1619, granted to Sir James Blunte Irrelagh's lands of Pallas, Gortneclony, Farderashe (1.75 carucates), Gortroe (3 carucates), Gortbofinna, and Gearanaskagh (1.25 carucates) "in his highnes' hands for want of livery sued by Dyermott O Callaghan sonne and heir of said Irrelay alias Irrelagh." The annual rent for approximately 720 acres payable to the crown was £17 Irish, due at Easter and Michaelmas. Dermot seems to have recovered possession, but his failure to pay the rent from Michaelmas 1620 until Easter 1623, jeopardized his title to the land. Whether he lost the property to the crown at that time is unknown. During the siege of Mallow in 1642 Dermot of Gortroe was charged with stripping naked two of the English settlers. Irrelagh, probably Dermot's son, outlawed in 1642, was transplanted to Clare where he appears in 1659. In 1641 Donough O Callaghan of Clonmeen, the head of the family, was listed as the forfeiting proprietor of Pallas (about 396 acres).[50]

Owen of Dromore (Drom mór, the great ridge), the sixth son of the chieftain Teige Roe, was the ancestor of the O Callaghans of Gortmore and Ballymacmurragh. Gortmore lies on the southern shore of the Blackwater, southwest of Roskeen Bridge, while Ballymacmurragh (Baile Mac Murchadh) stands farther west on the opposite side of the river. There seems to have been a castle at Gortmore on a rocky outcrop overlooking the Blackwater, but there are no remains visible today. Local tradition affirmed that the MacCarthys tried to build a castle there but were driven off by the O Callaghans. Many old swords and several cannon balls were found near the remains of the castle. The castle of Dromore, also disappeared, stood on a height overlooking the Clydagh River valley. Owen's son Dermot was described as baron of Dromore in 1573.[51]

Another son, Teige McOwen, may perhaps be identified with "Teigg Ettarremon mac Owen" who, together with "Donyll Keigh mac Thomas mac Teigg of Pobble Ycallaghan" was accused by a presentment jury in 1575 "not only to be notoriouse theefes but also wrongfully came in August with force and armes, viz., in the night time, to Barnehelly and then and their thre caples [three horses] . . . there found, feloniously toke and lead awaye contrarie to her Majesties peace." Barnehely is a village near Ringaskiddy on Cork Harbor, so the two men were at some distance from Pobul Uí Cheallacháin. Ó Murchadha provided their Irish names: Tadhg a'tearmainn, suggesting a connection with glebeland, perhaps church land; and Domhnall Caoch meaning Donal the blind, a handicap, however, that did not impede him from participating in the crimes charged. However that may be, Teige McOwen was probably dead before 1601 when his two sons, Conoghor and Donal, yeomen living at Gortmore, were pardoned. Dermot of Gortmore, perhaps Conoghor's or Donal's son, was outlawed in 1642. It is likely that

---

[50] According to *LM*, 162, Iorghalach had two sons Iorghalach and Eoghan. Iorghalach Óg in turn had two sons Diarmaid and Ceallachán. Gillman, "Chieftains," *JCHAS*, Series 2, 3 (1897): pedigree. *Inquisitionum in Officio rotulorum Cancellariae Hiberniae asservatorum Repertorium*, 2 vols. (Dublin: George and John Grierson and Martin Keene, 1826), 1, Dublin, no. 19 (19 September 1624); Henry F. Berry, "The English Settlement in Mallow under the Jephson Family," *JCHAS* 12 (1906):1-26, esp.22; Dublin, PRO, Books of Survey and Distribution, vol. 3 Barony of Duhallow.

[51] *AICC*, no. 14309-14311; Bowman, *Names*, 114-115; Grove-White, *Notes*, 3:151; Lewis, *Dictionary*, 1:369.

Gortmore was held in dependence of Donough O Callaghan of Clonmeen, the forfeiting proprietor in 1641 (about 458 acres). Donough, a son of Thomas McOwen McTeige Roe, resided at Ballymacmurragh in 1585, 1594, and 1600. Owen O Callaghan of Ballymacmurragh, perhaps another son of Thomas, lost about 213 acres in the Cromwellian settlement.[52]

Still other O Callaghans were established at Roskeen (Ros caoin, beautiful wood), about three miles southeast of Kanturk on the Blackwater River. Donal, the seventh son of Teige Roe, lived at Pallas in 1573, but after his death early in 1600 his lands there were assigned to his nephew, Irrelagh. Of Donal's several sons, the eldest, Thomas Reagh (Tómas Riabhach, the swarthy), dwelt at Roskeen in 1573, as did his son, Donal. Teige Roe of Roskeen, perhaps another son of Thomas Reagh, accused of plundering during the siege of Mallow in 1642, was subsequently attainted and lost his estate (about 370 acres) in the Cromwellian settlement. Daniel O Callaghan of Roskeen was listed in the subsidy rolls of 1662 with property valued at £17 1s 8.5.d.[53]

Another branch of the family acquired an estate in Kilpadder, west and south of Dromahane, and Kilcranathan (north of the Blackwater). Teige McCahir, a grandson of the chieftain Teige Roe (according to Gillman), or of his brother Maccraith (according to other sources), resided at Kilpadder in 1575. After Conor of the Rock gained the chieftainship, Teige McCahir obtained a royal grant obligating him to the service of one-fifth of a knight's fee. Upon his death around 1623, his son Dermot Roe inherited that estate and on 8 July 1633 Charles I granted Kilpadder to him.[54] Dermot Roe also held Kilcranathan of the crown by one-twentieth of a knight's fee. When Dermot died on 13 February 1636 he was interred in the parish church of Clonmeen. At that time his sons Cahir of Kilpadder and Donough of Kilcranathan were married and of adult age. Cahir forfeited about 313 acres in the Cromwellian Settlement as did Donough's sons, Callaghan and Owen.[55]

Cahir of Kilpadder, however, seems to have recovered some of his property before his death around 1680 when he made his will. Identifying himself as Cahir O

---

[52] *LM*, 162: "Eoghan mac Taidhg Ruaidh dias mhac aige i. Ceallachan agus Diarmaid an Ghaorthaidh." MS Ga has "Eoghan mac Diarmada mic Taidgh Ruaidh." *BIFR*, 888 states that Dermot macOwen was of Drumdorry. Dublin, PRO Books of Survey and Distribution, vol. 3 Barony of Duhallow; Ó Murchadha, *Names*, 67-68.

[53] Berry, "English Settlement," *JCHAS* 12 (1906): 22; Dublin, PRO, Books of Survey and Distribution, vol. 3 Barony of Duhallow; Grove-White, *Notes*, 4:185.

[54] Gillman, "Chieftains," *JCHAS*, Series 2, 3 (1897): pedigree; *BIFR*, 887; 12 *RDK*, 2576 (2101), 3 May 1575; 17 *RDK* 6762 (5428) 1602. McCragh McTeige McCahir of Kilpadder was pardoned on 7 December 1603; *CPR James I*, 14:25-26, no. 13. McCragh may have been another son or perhaps may be identified with Murrough. Richard Hayes, *Manuscript Sources for the History of Irish Civilization. Supplement I (1965-1975)* (Boston: G. K.Hall, 1979), D26008, *Sarsfield Papers*, Associated Families.

[55] *LM*, 217, no. 56; Dublin, GO MS 177, pp. 455-456, 463 (inserted page); Gillman, "Chieftains," *JCHAS*, Series 2, 3 (1897): pedigree; *BIFR*, 887-888; Dublin PRO, Books of Survey and Distribution, vol. 3 Barony of Duhallow. Dermot married Sara, daughter of Fineen O Mahony of Kinelmeaky. Cahir McDermot Roe first married Ellen, daughter of John Power of Carrickphilip, Co. Waterford, by whom he had a son, Teige; his second wife, Jane, daughter of Teige MacCarthy of Aglish, gave him three sons, Dermot, Donough, and Callaghan. Teige McDermot married Ellen, daughter of Teige MacCarthy of Killballyverrihy, and had a son Dermot McTeige of Glanaketterry. Dermot's third son Callaghan was described as "beyond seas;" the fourth son Connor married Ellen, daughter of John Daly of Cloyne, and a fifth son Donough married Mary, daughter of Paul Mallorie of Castlemore. A daughter Elinor married Dermot MacCarthy of Dounine; a second daughter Joan was unmarried.

Callaghan of Curragh, County Cork, Gentleman, he bequeathed his estate in Kilpadder (where his family had possessed one to three carucates - 120 to 360 acres - at least since 1575) and Gortboly (Corbally), as well as a farm of three ploughlands in Roskeen, two ploughlands in Curragh and Knocknacolan, north of Kanturk and part of Sir Philip Perceval's estate, with "my interest in a parcel of mountain land held from my Lord of Broghill [Roger Boyle] , to my son and heir Teige O Callaghane." He provided also that his body should "be buried in my ancestors tomb in Cluonmeene Church if it can be done; if not where my executors shall think fit in the said church." He also entrusted £100 to the safekeeping of Colonel Robert Phaire. Referring in 1680 to "Callaghans farm of Corragh," Sir John Perceval expressed his preference for English tenants instead of Irish ones. Perhaps because Cahir's son Teige McCahir supported James II during the Glorious Revolution, Richard Newman got a patent for Kilpadder under the Act of Settlement in 1694. Another son, Major Dermot O Callaghan of Curragh was outlawed in 1691.[56]

Finally, the O Callaghans of Banteer descended from Conor of the Rock's third son, Teige McConoghor of East Banteer and Inchidaly, about a mile west of Clonmeen. His older brother Callaghan alienated these lands to him, for which a pardon was given on 7 February 1631. When Teige died on 31 May 1624 his son Conoghor McTeige McConoghor (born circa 1594) was married apparently to a daughter of Cahir Modarta. Conoghor, called Cornelius in the text, received livery of possession of his father's lands in Banteer on 7 February 1631. An inquisition of 9 April 1638 showed him holding lands in Banteer and Inchidaly. He probably held them in dependence on the head of the family, his brother-in-law, Donough of Clonmeen, who was listed as the forfeiting proprietor of Banteer (about 1,386 acres) in the Cromwellian Settlement. Teige O Callaghan who obtained Dromalour just west of the Allow, about a mile and a half south of Kanturk, confiscated from Dermod Óg McCarthy, the proprietor in 1641, probably was Conoghor's son. Teige, or perhaps his son Teige, sold Dromalour to John Longfield in 1700. Teige's children likely included Cornelius Senior of Banteer, Teige of Coolroe More, and Sheila of Banteer, who will be treated in the following chapter.[57]

Two others probably related to the chieftain's family are Charles Callahane (probably Cahir) of Ballynamona (on the Awbeg River, east of Doneraile) and Thady Callaghan of Carrignameragh (unidentified). In 1685 Charles Callaghane of Moorestown, County Cork, Gentleman, received a lease from John St. Leger, ancestor of viscount Doneraile, for ten years of 10.5 acres in the manor of Moorestown, alias Ballynamona, at an annual rent of £5 payable on 1 May. Charles owed suit to court and had to grind his corn in the manor's mills. Kennedy Callaghane (probably Charles's father), now deceased, had previously held that property.. In his will of 28 April 1698 (proved on 13 May), Thady Callaghan of Carrignameragh, Gentleman, provided for Christian burial "according to the discretion of my friends," and asked that his brothers Dermod and Callaghan and Edmond Condon of Marshalstown serve as overseers of his wife Margaret

---

[56] Dublin, PRO, Prerogative Will 13 July 1680; Welply, "Colonel Robert Phaire," *JCHAS* 30 (1925): 20-26, esp. 22; *Egmont MSS*, 2:102 (11 December 1680). Curragh is about a mile south of Kilbrin; Knocknacolan is about three miles southwest of Kilbrin and two miles northeast of Kanturk; Gortboly or Corbally is less than a mile north of Knocknacolan.

[57] Gillman, "Chieftains," *JCHAS*, Series 2, 3 (1897): pedigree; *CPCR Charles I*, 590; RIA O.S., Inquisitions, Cork (9 April 1638); Dublin PRO, Books of Survey and Distribution, Barony of Duhallow, vo.l. 3; Joseph F. O Callaghan, "The O Callaghans of Kilcranathan, County Cork," *JCHAS* 92 (1987): 106-112; Grove-White, *Notes*, 3:60.

Callaghan and their children, though he did not name them. He bequeathed a few cows, sheep, and lamps to Ellen Murphy, Nell Murphy, and Nelly Condon, probably servants. Edmond Condon regained his property at Marshalstown in 1699.[58]

The MacCallaghans of Muskerry

In addition to the O Callaghans of Dromaneen and Clonmeen and their various branches settled in the barony of Duhallow, pardons of the Elizabethan era present us with the MacCallaghans of Muskerry, a branch of the MacCarthy clan descended from Cellachán Caisil. Identified by their father's name, for example, Teige McDonogh, they were described as kern or professional soldiers, husbandmen or farmers; they resided principally at Blarney, Carrigadrohid (four and a half miles east of Macroom), Carrignamuck (on the Dripsey river, less than a mile from Dripsey castle), Carrignavar, Castle Inch (about two and a half miles east of Ballincollig), all in the valley of the River Lee. There was even Fineen McOwen, a clerk, that is one in Holy Orders, perhaps a priest.[59]

Two documents illustrate the links between the MacCallaghans of Muskerry, the O Callaghans of Duhallow, and the MacCarthys of Muskerry. An inquisition taken in April 1641 after the death of Cormac MacCarthy, Viscount Muskerry and Baron of Blarney, relates that he had enfeoffed Teige Óg O Callaghan with Raheen and Keilknockavilly (Knockavilla) in Muskerry. In consideration of the dowry paid to his daughter on the occasion of her marriage in 1635 Cormac enfeoffed Donough O Callaghan of Clonmeen and others with various estates.[60]

Although the families of Duhallow and Muskerry survived the turmoil of the late sixteenth century, the civil wars in the middle of the following century disrupted their lives more profoundly than ever before.

---

[58] MacLysaght, "Doneraile Papers," *AH* 20 (1958): 78-80; Dublin, PRO Testaments; Ó Murchadha, Names, 103.

[59] See Appendix II.

[60] John Collins, "Some MacCarthys of Blarney and Ballea," *JCHAS* 59 (1954): 83, 86.

This map of Duhallow is based on the map drawn at the direction of Sir William Petty between 1655-1656 as part of the mapping of Irelamd after the Cromwellian conquest.

Dromanig
Polleratullales
Maulran
TULLYLEASE
Carnatulleles
Rathrany
TowerMacAuliffe
Knocknaskehi
Knockglasse
Knahali
Tullauffe
Lisnacrany
Killeen
Knockankilly
KNOCKTEMPLE
Knockamanacan
CLONFERT
Garnanskehy
Kilballinmurrihy
Knockanacassop
Killinakan
Kilbrohort
Gortnashareny
Knockaphelleven
Garricastle
Knockancrig
Garriheen
Cullen
Clonfert
Lismoyer
Ballinaballa
Glorelan
Knockavscane
Corrgan
Lycloroe
Knockavelly
Coolvetta
Garricummane
Rosanarney
Scarteen
Killone
Ballibane
Rathnagroll
Caunonbeg
Knockalohert
B. Grandig
Tallevonlegory
Corraduff
Dwaragan
Curraculberiff
KILBRIN
Ballychusty
Ballincor
Glanarnoy
Ballimacpierce
Ballinedorine
Garanavarig
Clonrobbin
Coolemaghen
Garean
Castle Macauliffe
Curranmcgarrett
Dromnecrore
Lisrobbin
Castlecor
Knockballimarti
Killinbollogh
Lismeelcony
Ballinoe
Sohulter
Ballinrashin
Knockrowork
Dromoraig
Clongeel
Knocknacola
Balleheen
KILMEEN
Corbally
Raghmagh
Derrygallen
Clonturk
Ballitubber
Knocknanos
Balliwollegian
Rathmona
CASTLEMAGNER
Ballivollig
Derrintubbrid
Gortamarta
Ballinemoragh
Drumlour
Killrush
Killcolman
Killcaskanbany
Knockardrahan
Drumcumer
Knockangrenagh
PART OF
Killunan
Ballimaquirke
KERRY
Corletaher
DROMTARIFFE
Cooleclogh
Clonebane
Dromnoynagh
Monacrona
Clonemena
NOHOVAL
Knockanagehy
Dromagh
Banteire
Gortmore
PART OF
Knockanagree
Umeriboy
Desert
Dromtarriffe
BALLYCLOUGH
Drumskehy
Dromineen
Cullen
Islandohilly
Mauleran
Kilboleday
Lisnaboy
Dromahow
CLONMEEN
Gortmalire
Dromahane
Gortnageen
Curran
Fermoyle
Brittas
Ahane
Dwargan
Lissitragh
Rathbrasil
KILSHANNIG
Carrigolane
Nohavell
Curran
Killvoy
Dromsecane
Ballimor
Cooleroe
Rathcomaine
Dromore Castle
Allort
Carigcag
Commons
Prowis
Rathcoole
Gortroe
Killedav

Barony of Duhallow in 1655
(copied from Petty's Map of Cork, in U.C.C.)

Glankittner
Lackandara
Orolort
THE BOGGRA

(From Bowman, Place Names and Antiquities of the Barony of Duhallow)

CHAPTER 5

THE CONFEDERATION OF KILKENNY

The comparative tranquility of James I's reign was shattered when a bitter conflict erupted between King Charles I (1625-1649) and the English parliament. A monarch with an extraordinarily high concept of royal power, a strong attachment to the Anglican Church, and an antipathy toward the Puritans (Presbyterians and non-conforming Protestants), Charles I refused to admit any constitutional limits on his authority. As the old barriers between the Gaelic Irish and the Anglo-Irish began to come down because of their common attachment to Catholicism, they joined in an attempt to secure an amelioration of laws restricting their religious practice. Charles I was not particularly attentive to their pleas, unless they were willing to pay substantial sums in taxes in return for the graces, as these civil and religious liberties were called. Meanwhile, the English parliament was becoming restive under the high-handed rule of the king and his refusal to concede anything to Protestant non-conformists. From 1629 to 1640, he tried to rule without parliament, but eventually he was compelled to summon that body to ask for financial aid. The upshot was the beginning of a struggle that ended with his deposition and execution in 1649. These events had tremendous repercussions in Ireland and the O Callaghan family did not escape unscathed.[1]

The Union of the O Callaghans of Dromaneen and Clonmeen

The O Callaghans, despite the alterations of Elizabeth's time, still remained in effective possession of their ancestral lands on both sides of the Blackwater from Mallow to Kanturk. The division within the family, however, symbolized by the twin castles of Clonmeen and Dromaneen, each the seat of a rival branch, was a weakness. Recognized as such, it fortunately was not allowed to continue. Around 1638, upon the death of Cahir Modarta, whose seat was at Dromaneen, his son Donough, reportedly thirteen years of age at that time,[2] succeeded to his inheritance. He also married his cousin Ellen O Callaghan, the daughter and heiress of Callaghan O Callaghan of Clonmeen and his wife, Joanna Butler, the daughter of James, earl of Dunboyne. Thus Donough effectively brought the two branches of the family together by virtue of his marriage and through his

---

[1] R. F. Foster, *Modern Ireland, 1600-1972* (New York: Penguin, 1989), 1-78.
[2] Dublin, GO, MSS 147, pp. 459-460.

wife had an important connection to the Butlers, whose chief representative, the earl of Ormond, was to play such a powerful role in the next thirty years.[3]

Donough and Ellen were the subjects of a praise poem in thirty-seven stanzas by the Scottish poet Maol Domhnaigh Ó Muirgheasáin. During a visit to Ireland he wrote poems in honor of Domhnall Ó Donnabháin (1640); Cú Chonnacht Ó Dálaigh (1642), and Seafraigh Ó Donnchadha an Ghleann (1643). Although the poem dedicated to Donough is undated, it probably was written about the same time. Maol Domhnaigh may have accompanied the Scottish warrior Alasdair MacDonnell, who came to Ireland about the outbreak of the rebellion of 1641. The poem is typical of the genre, full of rhetorical flourishes extolling the virtue of liberality and references to bygone heroes, the most important of whom was the tenth-century king, Cellachán of Cashel. Hailing Donough as the son of Cahir, he emphasized that he had lawfully acquired his lordship and had not violated the rights of his family. That perhaps referred to the recent conflict between the Dromaneen and Clonmeen lineages. "Scions of their seed," Donough and Ellen represented "two noble branches from one plant; of the same house are they" (v. 35). Clonmeen, Ellen's patrimony, a place of abundant gift-giving, was a "bustling house well suited to poets" (v. 23). He described Clonmeen as a "fine dwelling," an "indestructible board-white beautiful house" (v. 33).[4] Concluding, the poet hailed that "generous lady of Cluain Mín," whose "beautiful, gentle disposition has added dignity to her fine race" (v. 37), In other words, at a time when the old order was passing away, Maol Domhnaigh lauded his hosts who rewarded him through their generous hospitality. His editor, Ronald Black, commented that his description of Clonmeen "is the finest thing he has left us."[5]

Donough's five sons may have been too young to participate in any significant way in the events of that momentous era, but his brothers, all sons of Cahir Modarta, were actively involved, as we shall see. His younger brother, Cahir, participated in the siege of Mallow and was outlawed in 1642. Married to Joan Ny Teige MacCarthy, by whom he had several children, Teige, Dermot, Donough, and Callaghan, Cahir may have died by 1678. A third brother, Teige Roe, also outlawed in 1642, had three sons, Conor, Donough, and Cahir. Callaghan, the fourth brother, a lawyer active in the affairs of the Confederation of Kilkenny, in 1644 promised to marry Mary, daughter of Edmond FitzGerald of Ballymartyr, the seneschal of Imokilly, who gave her a marriage portion of £600. Callaghan's father Cahir of Dromaneen, his brother Donough of Clonmeen, and Daniel O Keeffe of Dromagh bound themselves to Edmond FitzGerald in the sum of £2,200. Cahir also gave Callaghan mortgages of £440 on Clonmeen, Coolroe, Dromraghy, and Curraghrour, £500 on a ploughland and a half of Skarragh, and £140 on Ballynafeaha and £50 on Kilmichael. Callaghan was still alive in 1666 when he was named in a chancery bill. He had two sons, Callaghan and Kennedy. The latter may be that Kennedy O Callaghan mentioned below who reported a conversation of Lieutenant

---

[3] *Poems of Egan O Rahilly*, lines 154-155; Sir Bernard Burke, *A Genealogical and Heraldic History of the Landed Gentry of Ireland*, new ed. A. C. Fox Davies (London, 1912; reprint London: Burke's Peerage, 1958), 519-520; *BIFR*, 887; R. O Donovan, "To Hell or to Clare: Donogh O Callaghan, Chief of his Name, A Transplanter," *The Other Clare* 9 (1985): 68-75.

[4] Although we have to guard against taking the poet literally, we could assume that the walls of Clonmeen were of white stone; it seems unlikely that they were of wood as the phrase "board-white" suggests.

[5] Ronald I. Black, "Poems by Maol Domhnaigh Ó Muirgheasáin (III)," *Scottish Gaelic Studies* 13:2 (1981): 289-301. For the other poems see *ibid.* 12.2 (1976): 194-208, and 13:1 (1978): 46-55.

John Chinnery in 1674. A fifth brother, Conor (or Cornelius), participated in the siege of Mallow, was outlawed in 1642, and was likely a Lieutenant-Colonel under General Purcell in 1649; he had several sons: Cahir (who was killed in Ulster), Conor, Callaghan, and Teige, who married Mary, the widow of Donough Óg (Donough of Dromaneen's heir), and died in 1703.[6]

The Siege of Mallow, 1642

The lives of Donough O Callaghan and of the Irish generally took a radical turn with the outbreak of rebellion in 1641. Prompted by the bitter conflict between King Charles I and the English parliament over the twin issues of royal authority and religious liberty, and by the king's failure to make concessions to the Catholics, Rory O More and Felim O Neill organized a rising in Ulster and Leinster in October 1641. Ireland quickly divided into several factions. The Old Irish, that is, the descendants of Gaelic families, and the Old English or Anglo-Irish, the descendants of the Normans, were drawn together by their common adherence to Catholicism and their continued allegiance to the king, from whom they still hoped to gain the right to practice their religion freely. They regarded with hostility the Puritans, mostly New English or Scots Presbyterians, who had settled in Ireland in the sixteenth or early seventeenth centuries, and who strongly favored the parliamentary cause.[7]

Soon after the rising in Ulster, the insurgency spread into Munster. The whole province was out by March 1642.[8] An anonymous contemporary reported that the Catholic leaders in Duhallow, namely, Dermot MacDonough MacCarthy, Donough O Callaghan, Donal O Keeffe, and others either in person or through their proxies, came with most of their forces to join the rebel general Richard Butler, Viscount Mountgarret, at Twopothouse near Buttevant on 10 February 1642. Suggesting that Mallow be used as a base of operations, they promised that the army would not be lacking provsions, as they had already plundered the English settlers in the neighborhood. MacDonough brought 200 men and O Callaghan and O Keeffe another 200. Our anonymous reporter expressed a negative view of their appearance, character, discipline, and readiness for combat. About half of them, he remarked, were "loose unarmed robbers, pillers, strippers, preyers, drivers of men, women and children," and the other half, though supposedly military men, were "roguishly armed, falsehearted, ignorantly disciplined, penuriously powdered

---

[6] *LM*, 161, Dublin, GO, MS 177, pp. 458-460, and MS 144, pp. 16-19 (Bill in Chancery, Richard FitzGerald v. Callaghan O Callaghan, 12 November 1666); *BIFR*, 888; Burke, *Landed Gentry*, 519-520. Variant manuscripts of *LM* give Cahir four sons: Cathaoir Ruadh, Calbhach, Ceadach an Brathair (perhaps a Franciscan friar), and another who is unnamed. According to his will, probated on 12 July 1680, he had two daughters: Ellen, married to Dermot MacAuliffe, and Catherine married to Teige O Brien of Kilcar, County Cork.

[7] Aidan Clarke, *The Old English in Ireland 1625-1642* (Dublin: Four Courts Press, 2000); M. Perceval-Maxwell, *The Outbreak of the Irish Rebellion of 1641* (Montreal: McGill-Queen's University Press, 1994).

[8] Richard Bellings, *A History of the Irish Confederation and the War in Ireland, 1641-1643*, 7 vols., ed. John T. Gilbert (Dublin, 1882-1891; reprint New York: AMS, 1972), 1:64-77; Michael P. Linehan, *My Heart Remembers How, being the Story of Muscraidhe O Donegan* (Dublin: J. Duffy, 1944), 133-137; Patrick Corish, "The Rising of 1641 and the Catholic Confederacy, 1641-1645," *NHI*, 3:294-295; Micheál Ó Siochrú, *Confederate Ireland, 1642-1649: A Constitutional and Political Analysis* (Dublin: Four Courts Press, 1999).

[poorly supplied with gunpowder], carelessly commanded, and barely conditioned."[9]

As the rebels laid siege to Mallow, Lord Roche, MacDonough, and O Callaghan supplied them with about "1,400 English sheep . . . besides great store of beeves, plenty of beer and bread sent in every day." One of their objectives was to take the stone house in the middle of town where the English had taken refuge. Captain Henesie, assisted by Donough's brothers Callaghan and Conoghor, commanded the O Callaghans in an assault on the house. Some of those within were tenants of Cahir Modarta O Callaghan (now deceased) and had built upon and improved the lands they held from him near Mallow. Now persuaded to surrender on the promise that their goods would be restored, they were plundered again when they did so on 14 February. The rebels captured the Short Castle of Mallow on the next day, but when Roche and MacDonough quarrelled over possession of the town the troops abandoned the siege two days later. Reports that the Lord President of Munster, Sir William St. Leger, was advancing to relieve Mallow prompted the rebels to evacuate the town.[10]

Some years later after the collapse of the rebellion, namely, in 1652-1653, the English who suffered losses during the siege of Mallow presented their claims. A widow alleged that Donough O Callaghan's people killed her husband and robbed her of goods valued at £134. Another declared that the soldiers of Cahir O Callaghan (perhaps Donough's brother) murdered William Lynes and his wife near Mallow. Donough McCahir O Callaghan (the chieftain) and Dermot MacDonough MacCarthy were accused of driving off property belonging to Thomas Bettesworth. Still another stated that he had seen O Callaghan at the head of his own company at the taking of the Short Castle and the attack on the Great Castle. Two men reported being stripped by Dermot O Callaghan of Gortroe and "turned naked to the garrison of Mallow." Another saw O Callaghan (probably the chieftain) wearing arms at Dromaneen. Conoghor Reagh O Callaghan was seen at the siege of Mallow and Teige Roe O Callaghan of Roskeen was accused of injuring his neighbors. Others settled on lands in O Callaghan's Country reported losses in varying amounts. Edward Harris of Kilshannig parish, who "heard the said Callaghans discussing together about these troublesome times," avowed that "he . . . heard them severally say that they had his Majesty's commission for what they did or words to that effect." Whether or not these depositions were exaggerated, they do reflect the intensity of feeling that had been aroused by English settlement in and around Mallow.[11] James Foord of Kanturk not only complained of being plundered, but also detailed the debts owed to him that he did not expect to recover because of the rebellion, His debtors included Cahir O Callaghan of Drishane, Donough O Callaghan of Castlemagner, Owen O Callaghan of Kilbrin, and Donogh O Garvan of Roskeen.[12] Also lamenting the loss of

---

[9] Herbert W. Gillman, "The Rise and Progress in Munster of the Rebellion, 1642," *JCHAS* 1 (1895): 529-542, esp. 539, 541-542. The author of the manuscript (London, British Library, Sloane 1008) edited by Gillman evidently was a partisan of the parliamentary cause, familiar with the area around Mallow, and perhaps a Protestant clergyman.

[10] Gillman, "Rise," *JCHAS* 2 (1896): 14, 19-20, 22-24, 26-27, 63; Smith, *Cork*, 1:325-326; Joseph F. O Callaghan, "The O Callaghans and the Rebellion of 1641," *JCHAS* 95 (1990): 30-40.

[11] Berry, "English Settlement," *JCHAS* 12 (1906): 14-15, 18-22; Nicholas Canny, "The 1641 Depositions as a Source for the Writing of Social History: County Cork as a Case Study," in Patrick O Flanagan and Cornelius G. Buttimer, *Cork History and Society: Interdisciplinary Essays in the History of an Irish County* (Dublin: Geography Publications, 1993), 278.

[12] https://www.maths.tcd.ie/~sweetnam/bisse.txt, fol 52r-53 v.

---

property was Emanuel Phaire, of Kilvalide, rector of the Church of Ireland parish of Kilshannig and his son Robert Phaire who asserted that he was robbed by Thomas McConoghor of Kilvalide, a servant of Cahir O Callaghan of Dromaneen.[13]

As Lord Mountgarret left Roche and MacDonough to quarrel over Mallow, the rebels in Cork required a new leader. Donough MacCarthy, Viscount Muskerry, thus far uncommitted, now concluded that the rebels were loyal to the king and placed himself at their head. According to our anonymous source, he had an annual revenue of £7,000 and an inheritance of £30,000. By contrast Roche, MacDonough, O Callaghan, and O Keeffe were so deeply in debt that their revenues served only to meet their interest payments.[14]

The Confederation of Kilkenny

In June 1642 the Old Irish and the Anglo-Irish Catholics formed the Catholic Confederation of Kilkenny. A professedly royalist body, the Confederation was not directed against the king, nor did it seek to gain the independence of Ireland; it did hope to secure religious freedom and the removal of the civil disabilities that weighed upon Catholics. As its principal operative organs, the Confederation established a Supreme Council consisting of twenty-four members, six from each of the four provinces, and an Assembly including eleven bishops, fourteen lay lords, and two hundred and twenty-six commoners.[15]

Donough O Callaghan of Clonmeen was among the twenty-four members of the Supreme Council. Indeed, he was one of the few Gaelic Irish to have such a notable position. He and his brother Callaghan O Callaghan, then resident at Castle MacAuliffe, near Newmarket, were among those who swore the oath of the Confederation in June 1642. Callaghan was described as "not long since came from the Inns of Court in studying the law, a pertinacious young fellow." Recognizing the value of having a trustworthy person trained in English law to defend the family's property rights in an age when no man's title was safe, Callaghan had probably been sent to London to study law by his father, Cahir Modarta. In close alliance with Donough MacCarthy, Viscount Muskerry, both men played an influenial role in the events that unfolded in the next few years. Allied with the Butlers by marriage, Muskerry and Donough O Callaghan seem to have concluded that cooperation with the Anglo-Irish and continued allegiance to the crown was the best way of retaining their possessions and the wellbeing of their families. James Tuchet, earl of Castlehaven, and a member of the Supreme Council, after reviewing the causes of the war in Ireland, commented that among "those very ancient Milesians" who "sided with such other confederate Catholicks . . . to bring back the whole nation to their former obedience to the King and his laws," Viscount Muskerry (afterwards earl of Clancarthy), "the O Callaghans and some other gentlemen thereof

[13] W. H. Welply, "Colonel Robert Phaire, "regicide". His ancestry, history and descendants," *JCHAS*, Ser. 2, 29 (1924): 76=8-, esp. 79-80.

[14] Several letters to Sir Philip Perceval in January and early February 1642 indicate that Muskerry had still not joined the rebels; on 15 February one correspondent reported that Muskerry, Roche, and O Callaghan "I hear are out, but no certainty of it." *Egmont MSS*, 1.1:161-164, 173; Gillman, "Rise," *JCHAS* 2 (1896): 17-18.

[15] Foster, *Modern Ireland*, 79-100; Corish, "Rising of 1641," *NHI*, 3:298-299; Charles P. Meehan, *The Confederation of Kilkenny*, new ed. (Dublin: J. Duffy, 1882); Thomas L. Coonan, *The Irish Catholic Confederacy and the Puritan Revolution* (New York: Columbia University Press, 1954).

(men of note in Munster) were eminent."[16]

Participation in the Confederation brought certain hazards as Donough learned shortly. After landing at Kinsale in July 1642, Lord Forbes and his English army terrorized the southwest, advanced inland and, according to reports, "took also great O Callaghane's castle lately." "Great O Callaghan," or O Callaghan Mór, the Irish would have it, meant Donough, the chieftain. Clonmeen, the more westerly of the O Callaghan castles, presumably was meant, but the O Callaghans must have recovered possession by 1645 when they entertained the papal nuncio there. In mid-summer, Edward Vauclier, sent by Sir Edward Denny to warn the defenders of Ballycarty Castle in Kerry that relief was on the way, was captured in Slieve Lougher by Teige MacAuliffe of Castle MacAuliffe, Conoghor Ceogh of near Liscarroll, and Owen O Callaghan of near Newmarket and about 500 men. At that time Humphrey O Callaghan (whose Irish name was likely Amhlaoibh or Auliffe) was serving as an ensign to Lieutenant John MacWilliam O Reardon, Muskerry's commander at Blarney. In addition, Donough O Callaghan and sixteen of his relatives were among those indicted of treason at Youghal on 2 August 1642 and outlawed by the Court of King's Bench:

Name	Place	Name	Place
Cahir	Dromaneen	Owen McDonough	Kilbranty
Teige Roe	Dromaneen	Dermod McDonough	Kilbranty
Callaghan	Dromaneen	Cornelius Reagh	Coolageela
Cornelius	Dromaneen	Irrelagh	Clonmeen
Dermot	Gortmore	John	Coolavota
Cahir	Kilpadder	Cahir	Skarragh
Teige	Kilpadder	Teige	Ruanes
Donough	Kilpadder	Cahir	Dromlegagh

Cahir, Teige Roe, Callaghan, and Cornelius of Dromaneen were Donough's brothers. Cornelius or Conoghor Reagh of Coolageela (Kilbrin parish) was an agent of Sir Philip Perceval and Irrelagh of Clonmeen was a great-grandson of the chieftain, Teige Roe. Kilbranty apparently is Kilcranathan; Coolavota is in Kilcorcoran parish; Ruanes is in Ballyclough parish; Dromlegagh is unidentified.[17]

The Irish suffered another setback when Morrogh O Brien, baron of Inchiquin, who was acting on behalf of the crown, defeated Mountgarret at Liscarroll in late August 1642. It was later reported that Conoghor Reagh O Callaghan (that Cornelius Reagh of Coolageela outlawed in August), an agent of Sir Philip Perceval, and his company did mischief at Liscarroll at that time. At Cloghleigh, north of Fermoy, on 4 June 1643 the Confederates, led by Generals Barry and Purcell, Castlehaven, Muskerry, Donough O

[16] Bellings, *History*, 1:1-8, 86-88, 111-114, and 2:212, 214, 217; Gillman, "Rise," *JCHAS* 2 (1896): 19; Earl of Castlehaven, *Memoirs or his Review of the Civil Wars in Ireland* (Dublin, 1815; reprint, Delmar, NJ: Scholars Facsimiles, 1974), 21; Meehan, *Confederation*, 93.

[17] Philip D. Vigors, "Rebellion 1641-2 described in a Letter of Rev. Urban Vigors to Rev. Henry Jones, with a note of Officers engaged in the Battle of Liscarroll (From a Manuscript in Trinity College, Dublin)," *JCHAS* 2 (1896): 305. The letter was dated 16 July 1642; Brady, *Records*, 2:330, 346; Inquisition of 21 March 1642/3, in Mary Hickson, *Ireland in the Seventeenth Century, or the Massacres of 1641, their Causes and Results*, 2 vols. (London: Longmans, Green, 1884), 2:127, 137; Bellings, *History*, 3:351-352; *BIFR*, 889. Caulfield, *The Council Book of the Corporation of Kinsale*, 330, 333.

Callaghan, and others thwarted the forces that Inchiquin sent to plunder the province of Munster. Donough recognized the English colonel, Sir Charles Vavasour, and saved him "from the fury of the common soldier by his very great care."[18]

Meanwhile, the earl of Ormond, whom Charles I had named as lord lieutenant in Ireland, offered a truce to the Confederation. After a second general assembly met at Kilkenny on 20 May 1643, a cessation of hostilities for one year was agreed upon on 15 September 1643. During that time Donough O Callaghan and Viscount Muskerry were appointed commissioners to resolve complaints of the seizure of land, cattle, and other livestock in violation of the truce. Tensions were evident, however, as an English officer protested that "Donogh O Callaghan . . . and others for the Irish . . . came to the meeting [at Ballybeg] with 200 armed men." Writing to Sir Philip Perceval on 24 February 1644 from Mallow, Thomas Bettesworth, the English commander at Liscarroll, remarked: "In truth, to give him his due (for that the devil must have), I find Do. O Callaghane, in our intercourse of quarter, to be one of the moderatest, most rational men amongst them, and a strict observer of the Articles of Cessation, or a seemer to be so." Nevertheless, that last phrase suggests a lingering suspicion of Donough's trustworthiness. Lord Inchiquin also told Donough that he had "always found you more reasonable than most."[19]

In a letter written to Captain Thomas Reymond at Clonmeen on 12 April 1645, Donough expressed his own desire for peace. Though he had not been informed officially that the truce had been prolonged, he commented:

> yet such was and is my desire of peace and quiet with my neighbors that I gave order to my own people to sit quiet till I give order to the contrary. I am loath to begin hostility with my neighbours if not forced unto it, after the fair quarter and correspondency held between us since the beginning of the cessation. If you will acknowledge and serve our sovereign lord the king against his enemies, as I found you were resolved to do, and obey the Lord Lieutenant's commands, I see no reason you should be held an enemy to our party who serve his Majesty and will live and die in his quarrel.[20]

In the meantime, Donough's brother Callaghan was in England on business of the Confederation. General Edmund Ludlow reported that two "Irish Papists," who were "very zealous to justify the king's cause and to condemn that of the Parliament," came to see him at Oxford in 1644. They had been "sent over by the rebels in Ireland to treat with the king on their part, about assisting him against Parliament. This I afterward understood from one of them whose name was Callaghan O Callaghan, when together with the brigade commanded by the lord Musquerry he laid down his arms to me in Ireland."[21] It

---

[18] Lord Inchiquin to Sergeant Reymond, 13 August 1642, Mallow, and letter of John FitzNicholas Barry, 28 April 1645; *Egmont MSS*, 1.1:180, 253; Bellings, *History*, 1:92-93, 156-157.

[19] *Egmont MSS*, 1.1:190, 196 (8 December 1643), 197-203 (4, 10, 16, 24 January 1643/4; 3, 12, 24 February), 230 (12 May 1644); 206-209, 244; Corish, "Rising of 1641," *NHI*, 3:308-309.

[20] *Egmont MSS*, 1.1:250.

[21] *The Memoirs of Edmund Ludlow, Lieutenant-General of the Horse in the Army of the Commonwealth of England, 1625-1672*, ed. C. H. Firth, 2 vols. (Oxford: Clarendon Press, 1894), 1:85. John Cornelius O Callaghan caustically dismissed Ludlow, pointing out that "Colonel Callaghan O Callaghan, and the powerful Munster sept of which his elder brother, Donough O Callaghan of Clonmeen was the head, were from the beginning of the troubles in 1641, remarkable for their solicitude to put an end

is ironic that Ludlow asserted that Callaghan and those he represented were in rebellion inasmuch as they professed allegiance to the king.

Among those seeking restitution was Conoghor Reagh O Callaghan who asked Lord Muskerry to order the removal of certain persons who had seized his lands. As already mentioned Conoghor Reagh, resident at Ballybahallagh (Béal Átha Bathlach, the Mouth of the Ford of Bathlach) in the parish of Knocktemple, about two and a half miles east of Liscarroll), was an agent for Sir Philip Perceval. Cited as Cornelius Reagh O Callaghan of Coolageela (parish of Kilbrin, about a mile and a half south of Ballybahallagh) he was outlawed in 1642 for his conduct at Liscarroll.[22]

A genealogy, hereafter cited as *C*, compiled in 1844 by Daniel Callaghan Jnr. of Lotabeg House, connects his Cork merchant family with Donough Mór, the chieftain who participated prominently in the Confederation of Kilkenny, and his brother Conoghor Reagh, or Cornelius of Ballybohalough. The genealogy affirms that Cornelius married Ellen, daughter of "Dermod McCarthy styled MacDonogh of Kanturk Castle," and had at least four sons, namely, Dermot Reagh, Teige, Cornelius, and Owen. Dermot Reagh married Honora, the daughter of Cornelius O Callaghan of Banteer.[23]

MacDonough's relationship with Conoghor Reagh, his son-in-law, however, was not a cordial one. A clearly hostile Dermot MacDonough MacCarthy on 11 March 1643/4 charged that Conoghor Reagh

> while professing to be a member of the true Catholic cause and enjoying all privileges and freedom within the Catholic quarters has been all his life a chief instrument to Sir Philip Percival, Sir James Cragg, and other evil ministers of the State and gave them continual false intelligence and information whereby many gentlemen and families in Co. Cork and especially in the barony of Doohally [Duhallow] were ruined.

MacDonough, who lost his own lands at Kanturk to Perceval, cited five instances of Conoghor's treachery. (1) He thwarted Lord Mountgarret's capture of Mallow castle by providing information to the defenders. (2) He relieved the garrisons at Newmarket and Liscarroll with provisions, including thousands of sheep especially after the defeat of Rochfordstowne in 1642. (3) He abandoned his own house to take refuge with the garrison at Newmarket. (4) Following the cessation he occupied enemy lands in the Liscarroll region and opted to favor the enemy rather than the Catholics. (5) He distrained his neighbors' cattle at Kilberrihert, impounding them at Liscarroll castle, an act implying mutual confidence between him and the enemy. Conoghor's treachery threatened the safety of the Catholics and as "in peace time [he] was an open and known instrument of their destruction and ruin, so in the war he will be a hidden and close viper in their bosom if not prevented." Therefore MacDonough asked that Conoghor be obliged to answer these accusations under oath and to suffer the appropriate punishment.[24]

---

to these troubles." See Charles O Kelly, *Macariae Excidium*, ed. and tr. John Cornelius O Callaghan, in *Narratives Illustrative of the Contests in Ireland (1641-1690)*, ed. Thomas Crofton Croker (London: Camden Society Publications, vol. 14, 1841), 474.

[22] Egmont MSS 1:1: 63-91 (especially 63-64, 82-83, 112-113, 142), 200, 204-206, and 1:2: 533, 556, and 3:370; Vigors, "Rebellion" *JCHAS* 2 (1896): 305.

[23] I am grateful to Chris Callaghan, a descendant of Daniel Jnr., who gave me a copy of this genealogy.

[24] *Egmont MSS*, 1.1:204-205 (11 March 1643/4).

Meantime in support of Conoghor Reagh's claim for restitution, Owen O Callaghan (probably of Newmarket) and Donnell Óg O Dowgane testified that prior to the recent conflict he held lands in Coolageela "as of his own inheritance by way of mortgage" and other lands by long leases from Sir Philip Perceval, namely Ballybahallagh, Kilberrihert, Gortneleiragh, Bawnmore, Rathenane, and Gortnascragga. Throughout the war Conoghor and his tenants paid rent for those lands, and occupied them until about 20 September. The Supreme Council of the Confederation of Kilkenny ordered him to be reinstated in possession and to receive compensation.[25]

MacDonough, however, claimed that Conoghor held some of his lands from him and that "being of an unsettled disposition and little affecting the Catholic cause and more inclined to the adverse party," he was "a known instrument to Sir Philip Percivall and other malignant persons in those parts, to receive and give intelligence and intimations of the acts of the nobility and gentry of that county from time to time, to their great prejudice." Conoghor reportedly said that the charges on the lands in question were greater than the profits and so relinquished them to MacDonough. As the lands were laid waste and Conoghor was "always wandering between ours and the enemy's quarters," MacDonough, by authority of the army commissioners in Cork, gave the lands to the persons said to be in illegal occupation. He asked the Supreme Council on 10 June 1644 to suspend its order and require Conoghor to make good his claims. When the Council referred the matter to the Cork army commissioners, Conoghor protested that he could not expect a fair judgment as all the commissioners were related to MacDonough and appealed to the Council. The Council's decision is not known, but Conoghor appears as resident at Ballybahallagh in subsequent years and he was enrolled among the Innocents in 1662 whose lands were to be restored. His son appears in possession of the lands mentioned early in the eighteenth century.[26]

The Papal Legate in Ireland

The situation changed fundamentally following the arrival of the papal nuncio, Archbishop Giovanni Battista Rinuccini, in October 1645. Invited by the Confederation to restore papal authority in spiritual matters in Ireland, he landed at Kenmare in Kerry, bringing money and arms from Pope Innocent X and King Louis XIV of France. Accompanied by Richard Bellings, secretary of the Confederation, his journey from Kerry to Kilkenny was a triumphal one, as he passed through Macroom, Lord Muskerry's seat, then to Dromsicane, the residence of Dermot MacDonough MacCarthy, and thence to Clonmeen, the castle of Donough O Callaghan, "the chief of his most noble and ancient tribe, whose singular magnificence and humanity both the nuncio and the others in such a great multitude experienced." In 1976 while visiting Clonmeen Churchyard, I spoke to Tom Mannix, a very old man, who described the nuncio's coming as though it had happened only yesterday. According to local tradition, that likely was well founded,

---

[25] *Egmont MSS*, 1.1:230-231 (25 May 1644). Kilberrihert is about one and a half miles north of Ballybahallagh and about a mile east of Gortnascragga; Bawnmore is about one and a half miles west of Ballybahallagh; Gortneleiragh is probably Meelaherra and Rathenane may be Rathranna both about two and a half miles south of Bawnmore.

[26] *Egmont MSS*, 1:1:232-233 (10, 19 June 1644); *The Statutes at Large passed in the Parliaments held in Ireland, 1310-1785*, 20 vols. (Dublin: B. Grierson, 1786-1801), 2:245-263 (30 November 1660), 264-348 (1662). On 6 March 1685/6 he also mentioned Dennis Callaghan of Ballybahallagh.

"the dinner service used . . . for the occasion was gold plate."[27]

Rinuccini's arrival unfortunately widened the breach between the factions. The bishops and many of the Old Irish wanted to push the war more vigorously but the Anglo-Irish, most of whom were laymen and in the majority, wanted to negotiate with the king and with Ormond. The division was typified by the hostility between Owen Roe O Neill and Sir Thomas Preston, the two principal generals of the Confederation. Following the lead of Viscount Muskerry, Ormond's brother-in-law, Donough O Callaghan favored an accommodation with the king. The possibility of gaining concessions seemed greatly enhanced when Charles I suffered defeat at the hands of the parliamentary army in England in July 1645. Anxious to secure military support from Ireland, the king instructed Ormond to offer limited religious toleration to the Catholics. For that purpose Ormond negotiated the so-called Ormond Peace on 28 March 1646.[28]

Owen Roe's great victory over the parliamentary forces at Benburb in Tyrone on 5 June, however, gave heart to those who wished to press the military effort with greater vigor. Thus when Ormond published the peace on 30 July and the Supreme Council did so at Kilkenny on 3 August, Archbishop Rinuccini repudiated it, threatening with excommunication those who assisted its implementation. In February 1647, the assembly of the Confederation rejected the peace. A new oath of association stressing the rights of Catholics and calling for the restoration of lands recently seuzed by the Protestants was drawn up and signed by Donough O Callaghan of Clonmeen and his brother Callaghan O Callaghan of Castle MacAuliffe as representatives from Cork.[29]

The royalist cause suffered severely when the parliamentary army in England seized the king, prompting Ormond to surrender Dublin to the Puritans in July 1647. In Munster, Murrough O Brien, Lord Inchiquin, now enlisted in the parliamentary cause, took Dungarvan in May and Cashel in September. His campaign of devastation and destruction gained him the sobriquet, Murchadh na d'tóiteán, Murrough of the Burnings. Next, he destroyed the Confederate army under Lord Taafe at Knocknanuss (Cnoc na nOs – Hill of the Deer) about four miles east of Kanturk on 13 November.[30] Among those who fell in battle was Owen O Callaghan of Kilcranathan in the Parish of Ballyclough; his son Donal Mór was wounded. They descended from the chieftain Teige Roe Bacach.[31] A most notable participant in the battle was Colonel Alasdair MacColla Chiotaich MacDómhnaill or MacDonnell, known as Colkitto, a member of the MacDonald clan, who were lords of the Hebrides. After the battle, he was taken prisoner

---

[27] *Commentarius Rinuccinianus: De sedis apostolicae legatione ad foederatos Hiberniae Catholicos per annos 1645-1649*, ed. Fr. Richard [Barnabas O Ferrall] and Fr. Robertus [Daniel O Connell], new ed. Fr. Stanislaus Joannes Kavanagh, 6 vols. (Dublin: Irish Manuscripts Commission 1932-1949), 2.1:13-17; O Donovan, "To Hell or to Clare," 69.

[28] Donough O Callaghan signed many of the orders of the Supreme Council issued in 1646; Bellings, *History*, 5:279-280, 282-283, 286-308 (text of the peace), 330-332, 338-340; *CSP Ireland, 1625-1670*, 2:441. *The Embassy in Ireland of Monsignor G. B. Rinuccini. Archbishop of Fermo in the Years 1645-1649*, tr. Annie Hutton (Dublin: A. Thom, 1873), 119, 137, on Muskerry's role.

[29] Burke, *Hibernia Dominicana*, 884 (10 March 1647); Patrick J. Corish, "Ormond, Rinuccini and the Confederates, 1645-1649," *NHI*, 3:320-322; Jerrold Casway, *Owen Roe O Neill and the Struggle for Catholic Ireland* (Philadelphia: University of Pennsylvania Press, 1984), 172-173.

[30] James Buckley, "The Battle of Knocknanuss, 1647. (From a Tract in the British Museum, Cat. E. 418.)," *JCHAS* 5 (1899): 109-132.

[31] See the testimony of Silé Ní Cheallacháin given in 1762 in Joseph F. O Callaghan, "The O Callaghans of Kilcranathan, County Cork," *JCHAS* 92 (1987): 110-112.

and then slain at the Chieftain's Ford over the Awbeg River near Rathmaher. Major Nicholas Purdon, who shared in the later confiscation of O Callaghan lands reportedly shot him to death. He was buried there at first but his body was transferred three days later to the O Callaghan tomb in Clonmeen graveyard. Local legend affirmed that Ellen O Callaghan, wife of the chieftain Donough O Callaghan, arranged his interment with the O Callaghans, though there is no contemporary written evidence to support that statement. Another legend attributes his burial there to his lover Kathleen O Callaghan.[32] In the eighteenth century Robert O Callaghan of Clonmeen related that his family had one of Alasdair's spurs but that it was subsequent ly mislaid. His great sword was displayed for many years at Lohort castle. The Banteer, Lyre and District Community Council in 1996 erected a commemorative plaque on the wall of Clonmeen churchyard.

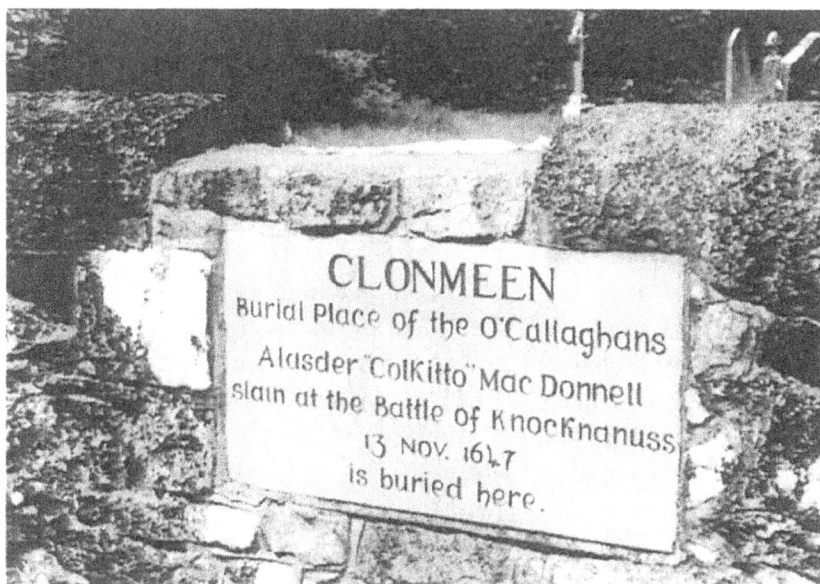

Clonmeen Churchyard Commemorative Plaque

The shifting political currents were clearly illustrated when Lord Inchiquin abandoned the parliamentary cause in favor of the king in April 1648 and declared his readiness to conclude a truce with the Confederation. Callaghan O Callaghan and Sir Richard Everard were appointed to negotiate the terms which highly displeased a contemporary who remarked caustically that "The Supreme Councell, men beyond example for falsehoode, had now, contrarie to their severall oathes of union, association and confederacie, inclined to a contracte of friendshipe and association with the Baron of Inshishuyne [Inchiquin, and] for this purpose employed privately Sir Richard Everard, Baronett, and Callaghan O Callaghan Esq."[33] The title of Esquire given to Callaghan was

---

[32] *Commentarius Rinuccinianus*, 2:784-786; Corish, "Ormond," *NHI*, 3:323-325; Meehan, *Confederation*, 236-237; *AICC*, nos. 14694, 14697; Con Tarrant, "Alaster MacDonnell," *SD* 2 (1976-77): 38-42; Rennie McOwan, "Alasdair MacDonald," *ibid.* 11 (1997): 11-14. Edmond O Donoghue, "McAlasdrum - Sir Alasdair McColla Ciotach McDonnell," http://castlemagner-his-soc.com/mcalasdrum-sir-alasdair-mccolla-ciotach-mcdonnell/

[33] *A Contemporary History of Affairs in Ireland 1641-1652*, ed. John T. Gilbert, 3 vols. (Dublin: Irish Archaeological Society 1879), 1:190.

in recognition of his status as one educated in the law. The same title might also be used of landowners such as his brother Donough who were considered to be of knightly rank, even though they had not formally been knighted.

Despite Rinuccini's objections, the Supreme Council appointed representatives, including Donough O Callaghan of Clonmeen, to sign the Articles of Concord establishing a truce with Inchiquin on 20 May 1648. Together with William Ryves, governor of Mallow, Donough, now identified as both *armiger* (squire) and Lieutenant-Colonel, was named commissioner for County Cork with authority to resolve disputes that might prejudice the truce. Presumably he was also included among those whom Rinuccini excommunicated on 27 May for supporting the truce. Patrick Corish described the legate's action as a "political disaster . . . an irrevocable declaration of war on the Supreme Council." The Council decided to appeal to Rome on 31 May against the legate. When the assembly met at Kilkenny in September 1648, Owen Roe O Neill was declared a traitor to the Confederate cause. Despite the commonplace that the Old Irish adhered to the legate and to O Neill, Donough MacCarthy, Viscount Muskerry, Donough O Callaghan and his brother Callaghan were among the Old Irish who remained steadfast in their adherence to the moderate course, seeking to come to terms with the king and his representative, Ormond.[34]

When Ormond returned to Ireland in September 1648, Callaghan O Callaghan was one of twelve commissioners whom he named to advise him concerning the establishment of a general peace in Ireland. On the other side, Donough O Callaghan was one of the committee appointed by the Confederation to consider Ormond's proposals. An accord was reached on 17 January 1648, assuring Catholics of religious liberty and of the king's promise to consider legal recognition of the Catholic Church in Ireland. The treaty dissolved the Confederation, replacing it with twelve "commissioners of trust," among whom was Donough O Callaghan, Esq. Article 2 provided that a free parliament should be held within six months or as soon as the commissioners should decide.[35]

The Cromwellian Conquest

The treaty was made meaningless by the execution of Charles I on 30 January 1649. England was declared a Commonwealth, but Irish royalists proclaimed Charles II who designated Ormond as Lord Lieutenant. Rinuccini, whose high hopes for the restoration of Catholicism in Ireland were in ruins, left for good in February. When the Munster royalists were mustered in the spring of 1649 General Patrick Purcell commanded the infantry; his Lieutenant Colonel was Conner Callaghan, probably a younger brother of Donough of Clonmeen. The cavalry, commanded by the Earl of Castlehaven, included Major Callaghan O Callaghan, probably Donough's other brother, long active in the affairs of the Confederation. Another Major Conoghor O Callaghan served in the regiment of Colonel Donough MacNamara.[36]

---

[34] Burke, *Hibernia Dominicana*, 887-889, art. 15; Corish, "Ormond," *NHI*, 3:328-331; Casway, *Owen Roe O Neill*, 226-228.

[35] *A Contemporary History*, 1:191; Bellings, *History*, 7:154-155 (19 December 1648), 163-164 (27 December), 184-199, 235 (29 January 1649), 249-250 (9 February), 255 (10 February), 266-267.

[36] *The Manuscripts of the Marquis of Ormonde preserved at the Castle of Kilkenny. Historical Manuscripts Commission, Fourteenth Report, Appendix, Part 7* (London: Historical Manuscripts Commission, 1895), 1:200, 214, nos. 64, 75.

Events moved swiftly but unfortunately for the royalists, who were defeated at Rathmines in August 1649, a few days before the arrival of Oliver Cromwell with an army of 12,000 men. After the sack of Drogheda in September and Wexford in October, Cromwell marched from Youghal through Mallow to Kilkenny, which surrendered in March 1650. Ormond was meeting simultaneously with Donough O Callaghan and the other commissioners of trust at Limerick concerning the breakdown of governmental functions. Meanwhile, Lord Broghill in April effectively crushed the royalist resistance in Munster when he routed Lord Roche near Macroom. After the surrender of Clonmel in Tipperary on 10 May 1650, Cromwell departed for England two weeks later, leaving his son-in-law Ireton to complete the conquest.[37]

The royalist party disintegrated rapidly especially after Charles II, hoping to win support among the Scots, in August repudiated the peace concluded at the beginning of the year with the Confederation. Ormond, accompanied by many of the royalist faction, sailed for France in December, after yielding his authority to the Earl of Clanricard. Donough O Callaghan evidently remained in Ireland, but his brother Colonel Callaghan O Callaghan went to France on behalf of Lord Muskerry to try to obtain funds from Charles, Duke of Lorraine, to maintain a force of 400 or 500 horse and 1,400 foot. Richard Bellings, who informed Ormond on 19 May 1651 of "Colonel Callechan's" activities on behalf of Muskerry, expressed the fear that without money, the troops would "disperse and either turn irregular tories [guerillas] or serve the enemy." Two months later, on 26 July, Lord Muskerry, hoping to raise the siege of Limerick, was routed at Knockiclashy or Knockbrack about three miles southwest of Banteer, by Lord Broghill and the parliamentarians, who had crossed the Blackwater at Clonmeen. Clonmeen castle reportedly was destroyed after the battle.[38]

The Duke of Lorraine's scheme to intervene in Ireland was a last straw that the Catholics tried to grasp as Ireton moved inexorably to victory. Limerick surrendered on 27 October 1651 and the fall of Galway on 12 May of the following year completed the conquest. Among the very last to surrender was Lord Muskerry, who held out for three weeks at Ross Castle on the lower Lake of Killarney, before finally yielding to General Edmund Ludlow. Muskerry appointed Callaghan O Callaghan as one of the commissioners to conclude the articles of surrender on 22 June 1652. Muskerry's son and Lieutenant-Colonel Conor O Callaghan, probably a brother of Donough and Callaghan, were given as hostages to Ludlow to guarantee observance of the articles, which allowed Muskerry and the 5,000 men under his command to go abroad.[39]

Muskerry and Callaghan O Callaghan seem to have gone to the continent, but it is

---

[37] Patrick J. Corish, "The Cromwellian Conquest, 1649-1653," *NHI*, 3:336-347. T. C. Barnard, *Cromwellian Ireland. English Government and Reform in Ireland 1649-1660* (London: Oxford University Press, 1975); D. M. R. Esson, *The Curse of Cromwell. A History of the Ironside Conquest of Ireland, 1649-1653* (Totowa, NJ: Rowman and Littlefield, 1971).

[38] Bellings, *History*, 7:371; Smith, *Cork*, 1:296; Lewis, *Dictionary*, 1:368; Bowman, *Names*, 174-175; Corish, "Cromwellian Conquest," *NHI*, 3:348-351; Pádraig Lenihan, *Confederate Catholics at War, 1641-1649* (Cork: University Press, 2001), 202-203; Kavanagh, *Kilshannig*, 8; Con Tarrant, "The Battle of Knockbrack," *SD* 6 (1986): 54-56.

[39] Ludlow, *Memoirs*, 1:320-322; Ludlow's letter of 14 June 1652 to William Lenthal (*ibid.*, 1:524-525), mentions Lieutenant-Colonel Knocher (i.e., Conoghor or Conor) O Callaghan; *A Contemporary History* 3.2:324-329; Robert Dunlop, *Ireland under the Commonwealth being a Selection of Documents relating to the Government of Ireland from 1651 to 1659*, 2 vols. (Manchester: Manchester University Press, 1913), 2:318.

uncertain whether they took any large body of troops with them. The parliamentary commissioners reported on 19 February 1653 that they had learned of the return of Muskerry and Colonel O Callaghan "and of their declining their former intentions for the transporting of men," a phrase that suggests that they had decided not to attempt to transport soldiers to the continent. Apparently they had gone to Spain where they discovered that because of their adherence to the Ormondist faction in the Confederation of Kilkenny, they were not received with great warmth by other Irish exiles and decided to return to Ireland to take their chances there. The commissioners instructed Colonel Robert Phaire, the governor of Cork, "immediately to send both of them up with a safe convoy to Dublin, that so we may understand something more fully from themselves of their present resolutions; in the doing whereof we shall desire you that all civil respects may be shown unto them." Both were lodged in Marshalsea prison in Dublin and by December Muskerry was brought to trial for the murder of various persons. Colonel Callaghan O Callaghan, who seems not to have been tried, appeared in Muskerry's defense, reporting that on one occasion while he was with General Barry at Limerick or Kilmallock, Barry read a letter to General Purcell from Muskerry concerning the murder of English ladies travelling from Macroom. Muskerry "was much grieved at that murder, desiring the General to prosecute the murderers to justice, but [O Callaghan] did not hear what was then done thereupon."[40] Lord Muskerry was acquitted of the accusation and of a second murder charge in May 1654, when he was allowed to go into exile.[41] The trial documents also refer to Teige O Callaghan, the provost marshal, responsible fpr bringing offenders to military justice, appointed by General Barry.Teige was probably another brother of Donough and Callaghan.[42] In effect, as the war came to an end, Ireland awaited the retribution that came swiftly enough.

The Transplantation to Clare

Eleven years had elapsed since the rising of 1641. During the intervening years the Confederation of Kilkenny, in which Donough and Callaghan O Callaghan had been most intimately involved, had tried to win from King Charles I basic religious and civil liberties without repudiating his sovereignty. The Puritan and parliamentary party had triumphed in both England and Ireland and now the day of reckoning was at hand. The English parliament passed an Act of Settlement in August 1652, ordering the aristocracy, both Old Irish and Old English, who had participated in or abetted rebellion to remove themselves from their ancestral lands and go west of the Shannon to Connacht and Clare where they would be allotted land hitherto considered wasteland. In effect, the landowners who had not displayed a steadfast loyalty to the parliamentary cause were to

---

[40] Hickson, *Ireland*, 2:238-239, no. 345 (the reference to Colonel Callahan probably meant Callaghan O Callaghan); *ibid.*, 2:196 (1 December 1653). Lieutenant Richard Beare asked John Perceval on 11 December 1653 "whether you have put in your suit against O Callaghane, who, I hear is now at Dublin." He also said that he had written to Perceval by Col. Callaghan, presumably Colonel Callaghan O Callaghan, but there is no clear indication of the nature of the suit. *Egmont MSS*, 1.1:530; Ludlow, *Memoirs*, 1:341.

[41] Dunlop, *Commonwealth*, 2:436, no. 520; Peter Berresford Ellis, *Hell or Connaught! The Cromwellian Colonisation of Ireland 1652-1660* (New York: St. Martin's Press, 1975), 69, 96-97.

[42] Jennifer Wells, "Proceedings at the High Court of Justice at Dublin and Cork, 1652–1654, part I," *Archivium Hibernicum* 66 (2013):63-260, esp. 152, 164-165, 168, 170-171,177,

be transplanted.[43]

The commissioners appointed to apportion land to those being transplanted met at Loughrea in County Galway and by decree of 12 June 1656 ordered Donough O Callaghan of Clonmeen and his wife Ellen to transplant themselves. By a final decree of 29 August 1657, Donough was assigned 2,497 profitable acres in County Clare in the parishes of Tulla, Killnoe, Killuran, Clonlea, and Killaloe in the baronies of Bunratty and Tulla. Ellen was allotted 2,503 acres in the parishes of Templemaley, Kilraghtis, Clonlea, Doonry, and Killnoe in the same baronies. Their portion in Clare was about a quarter of the 19,888 acres they had possessed in Cork in 1641.Together with their sons Teige, Donough, and Cahir, they settled at Mountallon, in the parish of Clonlea and barony of Tulla; nineteen O Callaghan proprietors were recorded there in the census of 1659. More than likely they made the journey from Dromaneen and Clonmeen to Mountallon, a distance of about fifty-five miles, sometime after the summer of 1657, possibly in the spring of 1658. In addition to their families, they were accompanied by their domestic servants and retainers and carted away many of their household goods.[44] They likely settled in a tower house at Mountallon, erected by the MacNamaras, the former proprietors. They had now to familiarize themselves with a new environment and new neighbors who were not overjoyed by their arrival.

In 1699 the English Parliament established a Court of Trustees to dispose of estates forfeited by James II's followers, who registered their claims. The Court conducted its business at Chichester House in Dublin until 23 June 1703. Many buyers gained great wealth by the acquisiton of these forfeited properties.[45] For example, in 1663 the Court of Claims determined that the lands assigned to Ellen in Templemaley rightly belonged to Lady Elinor Blake, the widow of Sir Valentine Blake, and her son John. As a consequence of that loss and other transactions, by 1703 the O Callaghan estate had been reduced to about 3,035 acres.[46]

By a similar decree of 21 June 1656 Conor O Callaghan of County Cork was also transplanted and was assigned 400 acres. He was likely Donough's younger brother and probably should be identified with Lieutenant-Colonel Conor O Callaghan mentioned in the muster rolls of 1649 and by General Ludlow. In 1659 he was settled in Ballyquin in the parish of Killokennedy and barony of Tulla. The O Callaghans of Clonloum were his descendants.[47] Donough's brother, Colonel Callaghan O Callaghan, who was so active in

[43] C. H. Firth and R. S. Rait, *Acts and Ordinances of the Interregnum, 1642-1660*, 3 vols. (London: His Majesty's Stationery Office, 1911), 2:598-603; R. C. Simington, *The Transplantation to Connacht, 1654-1658* (Dublin: Irish Manuscripts Commission, Irish University Press, 1970), vii.

[44] "An Account of Lands set out to the Transplanted Irish in Connaught," *Calendar Ormonde*, 2:127; Simington, *Transplantation*, 6; Seamus Pender, *A Census of Ireland circa 1659 with Supplementary Material from the Poll Money Ordinances (1660-1661)* (Dublin: Irish Manuscripts Commission 1939), 172-174; O'Donovan, "To Hell or to Clare," 68-75; Campbell, *Displacement*, ch. 3: Historical Background. A 'Social Revolution.' See the doctoral thesis of Teresa Shoosmith, *Settlement and Social Change in the Barony of Tulla, c. 1650-1845* (Galway: Nationl University of Ireland, 2015), 4

[45] John T. Gilbert, *An Account of the Parliament House, Dublin: With Notices of Parliaments Held There, 1661-1800* (Dublin: Hodges, Figgis, 1896), 14-15.

[46] Campbell, *Displacement*, 232-238, citing Geraldine Tallon, *Court of Claims: Submisions and Evidence, 1663* (Dublin: Irish Manuscripts Commission, 2006), 373.

[47] Cornelius O Callaghan, one of the executors of James Butler (5 January 1722, may have been one of them; Sir Henry Blackall, "The Butlers of County Clare," *North Munster Antiquarian Journal* 7:2 (1955): 19-45, esp. 29-30, 34-35; Shoosmith, *Settlement*, 93.

the affairs of the Confederation, does not appear in the list of the transplanted Irish. Perhaps he opted to settle in France in support of the exiled Charles II; or, more than likely, he may be that Callaghane O Callaghane, resident at Dromanure in the parish of Dromcliff and Island barony, west of Ennis, in 1659. Still another O Callaghan proprietor, Israel O Callaghan (Israel was probably a transliteration of Iorghalach or Irrelagh, who was outlawed in 1642) took up his residence at Ballyally in the parish of Templemaley and barony of Bunratty.[48]

The removal of the aristocracy now allowed the government to settle Cromwell's soldiers and others on confiscated lands. New Protestant colonists moved in, establishing farms, enclosing the land, clearing woodland, developing iron mines, and other industries. The agent for John Perceval, one of the principal proprietors in North Cork, fully expected that the immediate effect of transplantation would be an abrupt drop in rents, as "you will have few or no tenants this next year by this proclamation of transplanting, which clearly extends to all papists without exception." In point of fact the majority of the Catholics remained on the land in Cork, now in dependence on the adventurers who took over O Callaghan lands. In the poll-tax (Census of 1659) probably carried out by Sir William Petty's surveyors there does not appear to be a section devoted to Duhallow where O Callaghan lands lay, but there are indications of their presence elsewhere in Cork and Limerick. In Cork City and in Mallow, ten O Callaghans were recorded, and in the barony of Connello in Limerick, there were seventeen. The fifteen MacCallaghans in the barony of Barretts apparently belonged to the Muskerry family.[49]

The details concerning the distribution of forfeited lands are recorded in the *Books of Survey and Distribution*. The names of the proprietors in 1641, usually identified as Irish Papists, and the new proprietors around 1670 are listed, together with the extent of profitable acreage allotted to each. Unprofitable acreage, that is, bogs, woods, and barren mountain land, was also set down. The purpose was to enable the government to assess an annual quit rent on landed property (so-called because it freed the landholder from the performance of other services). The tables below illustrate the redistribution of O Callaghan lands in the parishes of Kilshannig, Clonmeen, both south of the Blackwater, and Ballyclough, Castlemagner, and Kilbrin, north of the river.[50]

The following table shows that Donough O Callaghan was the proprietor in 1641 of lands in the Parish of Kilshannig running from east to west, namely, Carrigolane, Kilvealaton, Dromore Castle, Dromahane, Kilcolman, Oulert (Aldworth), Dromaneen, Mohereen, and Skarragh. Counting profitable and unprofitable acreage he held about 4,933 acres. Cahir O Callaghan (a grandson of the chieftain, Teige Roe) had about 313

[48] Also transplanted were Katherine Stapleton, alias Callaghan, of County Cork who was assigned fifty acres (21 May, 13 August 1656); Evelyn Callahan of no original address was assigned thirty-nine acres in County Galway, Barony of Dunkellin, Parish of Killeenin; *Calendar Ormonde*, 1:214, 2:127, 174; Simington, *Transplantation*, 52, 107; Ludlow, *Memoirs*, 1:524-525; Pender, *Census*, 165, 172, 178.
[49] Lieutenant Richard Beare to Perceval, 11 December 1653, *Egmont MSS*, 1.1:530; Pender, *Census*, 195, 201, 233.
[50] Dublin, PRO, Books of Survey and Distribution, vol. 3 Barony of Duhallow; John O Hart, *The Irish and Anglo-Irish Landed Gentry when Cromwell came to Ireland* (Dublin, 1884; reprint as *The Irish and Anglo-Irish Gentry*, New York: Barnes and Noble, 1969), 285 lists the following O Callaghans among the forfeiting proprietors in 1657 in Cork: Donough, Callaghane, Owen, Dermod MacShane, Dermod MacTeige, Donogh MacDermod, Donough, Cahir, Lehland [probably Loghlan], Dermod and Teige Roe.

acres in Kilpadder, while John O Mullane possessed Brittas, once O Callaghan land. Dermot O Callaghan (who took part in the siege of Mallow) had 3,062 acres, a substantial total, including 1,034 acres in Lackendarragh, 421 in Gortmolire, and 1,607 in Gortroe. The principal beneficiaries of the confiscation were Sir Richard Kyrle and Richard Newman who obtained Dromaneen; John King, created Baron Kingston in 1662, who acquired Dromore Castle; and William Lombard, who secured Lackendarragh and Gortmolire. References to Donough O Callaghan as nominee mean that, according to the royal list of 1662, he should be restored to his estates. That did not happen.

Parish of Kilshannig:

No.	Proprietor in 1641	Property	Unprofitable Acres	Profitable Acres	Proprietor c. 1670
1	Donough O Callaghan	Carrigolane		417.2.16	Lord Kingston, Richard Newman, Donough O Callaghan nominee
1b	"	Carrigolane	167.2.154		
2	"	Kilvealaton		328.0.32	Sir Richard Kyrle Richard Newman
3	Donough O Callaghan	Dromore Castle		734.3.08	Luther Walton (85.3.21); Thomas Morris (204.3.34); Lt. Thomas Smithies (23.3.19); Lord Kingston (386.3.26); Capt. William Harmer (57.3.13)
3b	"	Dromore Castle	401.1.24		
4	"	Dromahane		194.0.32	Sir Richard Kyrle, John Strange
5	"	Kilcolman		212.032	Donough O Callaghan nominee
5a	"	Kilcolman	250.0.32		
5b	"	Oulert (Aldworth)		101.0.32	Sir Richard Kyrle, Richard Newman Donough O Callaghan nominee
5c	"	Oulert	98.1.24		
6	"	Dromaneen		866.0.0	Donough O Callaghan nominee, Sir Richard Kyrle, Richard Newman
7	"	Mohereen		242.2.16	Donough O Callaghan nominee

No.	Proprietor in 1641	Property	Unprofitable Acres	Profitable Acres	Proprietor c. 1670
8	Donough O Callaghan	Skarragh		464.3.0	Sir Richard Kyrle, Richard Newman
a	"	Skarragh		38.0.0	Sir Richard Kyrle, Richard Newman
8b	"	Skarragh	421.3.8		
9	Cahir O Callaghan	Kilpadder		169.2.16	Sir Richard Kyrle, Richard Newman
9a	"	Kilpadder	144.0.32		
10	John O Mullane	Brittas		304.2.16	William Lombard
11	William Lombard	Glantane		209.3.08	William Lombard
12	Dermot O Callaghan	Lacken-darragh		527.0.32	William Lombard
12a	"	Lacken-darragh	68.3.08		
12c	"	Lacken-darragh		89.2.15	William Lombard
12d	"	Lacken-darragh	350.0.0		
13	Dermot O Callaghan	Gortmolire		421.0.32	William Lombard
14	"	Gortroe		1083.0.0	Sir Richard Kyrle, Viscount Baltinglass, Richard Newman (611.0.05); (472)
14a	"	Gortroe	348.0.0		
14b	"	Gortroe	176.1.24		
		The Great Bog, or Bogra	9045.0.0		
	John St. Leger	Rathcomane, unprofitable mount			

In the Parish of Clonmeen Donough's lands extending westward from Kilshannig included Gortmore, Clonmeen, Killavoy, Coolroe, Banteer, and Fermoyle south of the Blackwater. To the north were Pallas, Dromcummer, Killarush, Kilcaskan, Gurteenard, Dromeragh, and Island. In all, he held about 8,827 acreas. Teige Roe O Callaghan had about 398 acres in Roskeen. Dame Elizabeth Fenton and her husband, Sir William Petty, Roger Brettridge, Lord Kingston, and Sir Peter Courthorpe benefitted from the confiscation. Clonakillenore does not appear on current maps of the area, but it likely lay between Gortmore and Clonmeen and may have consisted in part of mountainous land. The table below illustrates the distribution of lands:

Parish of Clonmeen:

No.	Proprietor in 1641	Property	Unprofitable Acres	Profitable Acres	Proprietor c. 1670
1	Donough O Callaghan	Pallas		396.2.161	John Hodder (88); Lord Kingston (61.1.16); Samuel Pomeroy (247.1.0)
1a	"	Pallas	66.0.0		
2	"	Gortmore		458.1.0	Dame Elizabeth Fenton
2a	"	Gortmore, part called Mullahaleere (Mt. Hilary)	438.1.0		
2c	"	Clonakillenore		1216.1.24	Philip Cross and wife, Protestants (921.1.24); John Hughes in preemption, by name, Glannileuerig (295)
2d	"	Clonakillenore	143.3.08		
2e	"	Clonmeen		880.0.0	Dame Elizabeth Fenton (841); Sir William Petty (29)
2f	"	Clonmeen called Killavoy and Coolroe	617.0.00	116.1.24	William Lombard (9 gneeves of Killavoy, 58.0.32); Sir William Petty (116.1.24)
2g	"	Clonmeen called Killavoy and Coolroe	320.0.00		
2h	"	Mullahaleere Mount (Mt. Hillary)	738.3.08		
3	"	Banteer		651.1.24	Sir Peter Courthorpe (213.0.09); Sir Peter Courthorpe (438.1.13) to Richard Nagle to Abraham Dixon

No.	Proprietor in 1641	Property	Unprofitable Acres	Profitable Acres	Proprietor c. 1670
3a	Donough O Callaghan	Banteer	459.3.08		
3b	"	Banteer	276.0.00		
4	"	Fermoyle		273.2.08	Sir Peter Courthorpe to Richard Nagle to Abraham Dixon
4a	"	Fermoyle	85.0.00		
4b	"	Fermoyle	715.0.00		
5	"	Dromcummer		401.3.08	Roger Brettridge (200); Dame Elizabeth Fenton (59); Lord Kingston (96); Samuel Pomeroy (57.3.20)
5a	Donough O Callaghan	Dromcummer	38.0.00		
5b	"	Killarush part of Dromcummer		70.1.24	Roger Brettridge
6	"	Kilcaskan		250.3.08	Dame Elizabeth Fenton (129); Lord Kingston (122) to Richard Conran
7	"	Gurteenard, part of Kilcaskan		135.3.08	Lord Kingston (55.1.03) to Richard Conran; Richard Strongman (80.3)
7a	"	Gurteenard	74.1.24		
7b	"	Part of Dromery and Island	12.3.08		
8	Teige Roe O Callaghan	Ballyroskeen (Roskeen)		370.1.24	Dame Elizabeth Fenton
8a	"	Ballyroskeen	28.3.08		

In the Parish of Ballyclough north of the Blackwater and west of Mallow, Donough O Callaghan possessed some 1,233 acres in Gortnagross, Garranasath, and Dromrastill. Callaghan and Owen O Callaghan, probably brothers, had about 314 acres in Kilcranathan, while Callaghan McDermot and Dermot McDermot O Callaghan, also brothers, held 424 acres in Gortnecloghy or Garrymcowney. Sir Nicholas Purdon acquired most of these lands, but in 1698 his descendants sold Garrymcowney, Kilgobban, Kilmichael, Ruanes, Ballynafeaha, and West Dromrastill to John Longfield, a native of Wales, whose family subsequently bestowed the French name Longueville on their estate.[51] After Alasdair MacDonnell was taken captive in the battle of Knocknanuss, Sir Nicholas, identified as Major Purdon by an anonymous English officer, shot Alasdair in the head, killing him. The officer commented: "For I am confident, that after an Enemy having surrendered his Sword and Armes, and is a Prisoner, 'tis murder to kill him."[52]

Parish of Ballyclough:

No.	Proprietor in 1641	Property	Unprofitable Acres	Profitable Acres	Proprietor c. 1670
1	Donough O Callaghan Irish Papist	Gortnagross		812.0.32	Sir Nicholas Purdon (120); Col. Richard Clayton (261) to Lawrence Clayton; Jerome Beaseley (43.2.34); John Comins (125.1.14); Richard Curtis, Richard Hockney (73.2.14), Lord Kingston (188.2.10)
2	Donough O Callaghan	Garranasath		90.3.08	Donough O Callaghan nominee (55); Sir Nicholas Purdon (90.3.08)
3	"	Dromrastill		331.0.00	Sir Nicholas Purdon
4	Callaghan and Owen O Callaghan, Irish Papists	Kilcranathan		314.0.32	Sir Nicholas Purdon
5	Callaghan McDermot and Dermot McDermot O Callaghan, Irish Papists	Gortnecloghy or Garrymcowney (Longueville)		424.0.00	Sir Nicholas Purdon

---

[51] Grove-White, *Notes*, 4:58-59; Kavanagh, *Kilshannig*, 12-19 (facsimiles for Clonmeen, Kilshannig, Ballyclough, and Castlemagner), 32-35.

[52] *The History of the Warr of Ireland from 1641 till 1653, by a British Officer of the Regiment of Sir John Clotworthy*, ed. E. H. Hogan (Dublin: McGlashan & Gill, 1873), 73.

Lying west of Ballyclough and still north of the Blackwater river were lands in the Parish of Castlemagner, a stronghold of the Magners. The previous proprietors were Donough O Callaghan, the head of the family, who had about 1,013 acres in Island and Gurteenbeha, Killavallig, Kippagh, and Bannagh; Owen O Callaghan who held about 213 acres in Ballymacmurragh; and Loghlan O Callaghan (whose personal name seems to be unique among the O Callaghans) and Robert Magner with 84 acres in Rathmore and Rathbeg. In addition to the lands cited, Robert Magner, the leader of the Magner clan, escaped execution on Cromwell's orders, but was dispossessed of the family's chief seat at Castlemagner. It fell to Roger Brettridge who eventually transferred it to Sir Standish Hartstonge.[53] Captain Walter Yelverton acquired a goodly share of those lands, but, as before, Dame Elizabeth Fenton, John, Lord Kingston, and Roger Brettridge were among the principal beneficiaries of the confiscation. In his last will of 1685 Yelverton mentioned his holdings at Rathmore, Rathbeg, and Killavallig.

Parish of Castlemagner:

No.	Proprietor in 1641	Property	Unprofitable Acres	Profitable Acres	Proprietor c. 1670
1	Donough O Callaghan, Irish Papist	Island and Gurteenbeha	69.0.00	343.2.16	Elizabeth Fenton (197.3.19; 145.3.02)
2	"	Killavalig		287.1.24	Lord Kingston (169.0.10); Captain Walter Yelverton (70.1.14; 48); to William Lombard (287.1.24)
3	Owen O Callaghan	Ballymacmurragh		213.3.08	John Groves
4	Loghlan O Callaghan and Robert Magner	Rathmore and Rathbeg		84.0.00	Lord Kingston (3); Walter Yelverton (81)
5	Donough O Callaghan	Kippagh, part of Island		170.0.00	Roger Brettridge (122); John Casey, Richard Cox (32.1.14); Lord Kingston (15.2.25)
6	"	Bannagh, part of Island		144.1.24	Captain Walter Yelverton

---

[53] Smith, *Cork*, 1:296.

In the Parish of Kilbrin north of Castlemagner, Donough O Callaghan's 1,279 acres included Subulter, Lackaleigh, Ballyrusheen, Rathmaher, Ballyheen, Curragh or Curraghelanbarriffe (north of Ballyheen and south of Ballyhest), Garrane (Garranmacgarett, adjacent to Curraghelanbarriffe), and Ballyhest. Roger Brettridge, the Earl of Cork, and Captain Richard Burnell's child obtained most of these lands.

Parish of Kilbrin:

No.	Proprietor in 1641	Property	Unprofitable Acres	Profitable Acres	Proprietor c. 1670
1-2	Donough O Callaghan Irish Papist	Subulter and Lackaleigh		354.0.32	Captain Richard Burnel's Child (330.1.32); Quartermaster John Chinnery (23.3)
3	"	Ballyrusheen		201	Captain Richard Burnel's Child
4	"	Rathmaher		73.1.24	Roger Brettridge
5	"	Ballyheen		282.1.24	Roger Brettridge
6	"	Curraghelanbarriffe (Curragh)		137.0.00	Captain Burnel's Child (105.3.21); Lord Kingston (31.0.19)
7	Donough O Callaghan	Garrane		93.1.24	Captain Richard Burnel's Child
8	"	Ballyhest		139.0.00	Earl of Cork (131); Quartermaster John Chinnery (40.2)

From the foregoing it appears that Donough O Callaghan possessed about 17,285 acres on both sides of the Blackwater River. Deducting 5,387 acres judged unprofitable, he had 11,898 profitable acres. Sir Richard Kyrle and Richard Newman acquired Dromaneen, while Clonmeen was divided between Dame Elizabeth Fenton and her husband Sir William Petty. Also dispossessed were Cahir O Callaghan of Kilpadder who lost his estates to Kyrle and Newman; Dermot O Callaghan whose estates in Lackendarragh, Gortmolire, and Gortroe were allocated among several persons including Kyrle and Newman; and Teige Roe O Callaghan of Roskeen, now ceded to Dame Elizabeth Fenton. Others forfeiters included Owen O Callaghan of Ballymacmurragh; Loghlan O Callaghan of Rathmore and Rathbeg; Callaghan and Owen O Callaghan of Kilcranathan; Callaghan and Dermot O Callaghan of Gortnecloghy and Garrymcowney. Among the new proprietors were Lord Kingston, Lord Baltinglass, Sir Philip Perceval, Sir Nicholas Purdon, Sir Peter Courthorpe, Quartermaster John Chinnery and several former Cromwellian soldiers.[54]

Father John Callaghan

After the collapse of the Confederation of Kilkenny there ensued a bitter quarrel among the Irish exiles grouped about the court of the future Charles II in France. The controversy pointed up the divergent views of those who favored the Muskerry policy of accommodating to Ormond - a policy to which the O Callaghans adhered - and those who followed the uncompromising position of the nuncio, Archbishop Rinuccini. One of the personages figuring prominently in this debate was Father John MacCallaghan or Callaghan of Carrigadrohid in East Muskerry. Patrick Corish described him as "the noted Jansenist polemical writer, who had adhered to the Ormondist faction in the 1640s and whose clerical career Lord Muskerry . . . had attempted to further while serving on the Supreme Council of Kilkenny."[55].

Fr. John related that he was the fifth son of Dermot MacCallaghan and his distant cousin, Catherine MacCallaghan, and was born in 1605 at Killone (unidentified; perhaps Killowen, in Drishane Parish) in County Cork. The *Commentarius Rinuccinianus* says he came from Carrigadrohid. Among several MacCallaghans living there who were pardoned in Elizabethan times, was Dermod Buy McTeige (1585), who may have been his father. The others - Callaghan McDonogh McCallaghan, yeoman (1576), Callaghan McWohny I Kallaghan, yeoman (1573, 1576, 1577), Donogh MacCallaghan (1576), and Teige McDonnell, husbandman (1585) - were likely his cousins, and one of them was perhaps his grandfather.[56]

He explained that his family, a branch of the MacCarthies, were vassals of Lord Muskerry, and more than 200 gentlemen of the family participated in the rising of 1641. He also acknowledged the more numerous O Callaghan family of Duhallow, whose chief was a member of the Supreme Council of Kilkenny. Although his family was of noble rank, the death of his father while John was still young left the family in a difficult situation. At twenty-one, he went to France in 1627 to study in colleges conducted by the Oratory of Divine Love and the Society of Jesus. Apparently he did not gain admission to any of the Irish Colleges and so was reduced to poverty, but about 1636 or 1637 he received a doctorate in theology from the Sorbonne. He was known thereafter as Callaghan or Calaghan. In subsequent years, when he had become something of a lightning rod because of his polemical writings, it was alleged that he had fraudulently obtained his degree, a charge that he vigorously rejected; on the other hand, it was reported that he was a brilliant student. He was probably ordained in Paris for service in the diocese of Cloyne and likely returned to Ireland thereafter.[57]

---

[54] Foster, *Modern Ireland*, 101-116; Karl Bottigheimer, *English Money and Irish Land. The Adventurers in the Cromwellian Settlement of Ireland* (Oxford: Oxford University Press, 1971).

[55] Patrick Corish, "The Irish in Paris," *Irish Theological Quarterly* 21 (1954): 32-50.

[56] 8 May 1573, *12 RDK*, 98, no. 2264 (1837); 21 November 1576, *13 RDK*, 17, no. 2941 (2348); 6 September 1577, *13 RDK*, 41, no. 3083 (2321); 1585, 15 *RDK*, 128-129, no. 4764 (4958). Fineen McOwen was probably a priest (1577). Ó Murchadha, *Names*, 73.

[57] "Lettre de Monsieur Callaghan docteur en theologie de la Faculté de Paris et curé prieur de Cour Cheverny, a un docteur de Sorbonne de ses amis, touchant les principales impostures du P. Brisacier Jesuite. Avec une lettre d'un Seigneur Catholique d'Hibernie [Richard Bellings], qui le justifie . . . de toutes

Nevertheless, by 1642 he had returned to Paris where his influence with the papal nuncio drew fire from several Irish Jesuits who expressed their misgivings in several letters addressed to the Franciscan scholar Luke Wadding, guardian of St. Isidore's College in Rome and an active agent for the Confederation at the papal court. In August 1642 a Capuchin friar, Fr. Michael Cullain, arrived in Paris from Cork bearing letters from the Confederate leaders, General Barry, Lord Muskerry, and others. According to Fr. Matthew O Hartigan, S. J., the Capuchin "takes to his coadjutor (as he calls it) [his assistant] a batchelor [a student in the university] here named John Callogan priest." The presence of so many agents, in Fr. O Hartigan's view, gave rise not only to jealousy but also to confusion.

On 3 October 1642 Fr. Dermot Dwyer, S. J. wrote to Wadding enclosing letters from his brother saying:

> All my brother's hope it is you; the reason why the Nunce [the papal nuncio Rinuccini] hindered him is as it is thought for not keeping himself secret both here and in his way, which is not true, except only what Dr. Callaghane published upon conjectures had from there from Dr. Connell. He [Fr. Callaghan] is a man full of ambition or at least taken for such a one. He whispers daily at the Nunce is [the papal Nuncio's] ears to have more access into matters of state. He said here after my brother's departure he wondered how the court there was mistaken in sending such a man with any matters of consequence, who had not *pondus rationis* [common sense, or good judgment]; wherein Dr. Connell should be sent. It is enough he is a Caribricia [a native of Carbery]. This only I write to inform you of the man, for he forces acquaintance at every part, thinking someday to wear a mitre.

Writing to Wadding on the same day Fr. O Hartigan commented that, while the nuncio had Ireland's best interests at heart and wished her well, he

> gives ear and access to every Irish busy brain and idle fellow. There is none here but assumes to be an agent and speaks here and there for the country producing some letters or others. Among these his lordship gives more access to one John Callaghane, a priest, native of Carbry, who troubled our affairs heretofore and is like this day to undo others. . . . Your reverence must procure that his lordship relies only upon such as will be preferred by the country to treat of their affairs. It may be he makes use of this fellow to interpret such letters as we send you or you send us.

A week later Fr. O Hartigan added: "I pray that what I wrote in my former be kept to your own self, touching the over much access my lord gives to Mr. Callaghane and the use he seems to make of him about our letters for, being published, his lordship's zeal for

les calomnies de ce Jesuite regardent ce royaume (24 December, 1651), in Antoine Arnauld, *Oeuvres*, vol. 30 (Paris and Lausanne: Sigismond Darnay, 1779), 391-401, no. 11, esp. 393-396; *Commentarius Rinuccinianus*, 5:232; Corish, "Irish in Paris," *ITQ* 21 (1954): 42; Ruth Clark, *Strangers and Sojourners at Port Royal* (Cambridge: Cambridge University Press, 1932), 35-39.

us should lessen." Still later on 5 December Fr. O Dwyer urged: "of Doctor Callaghan it were not amiss to barr him of the Nunce is [Nuncio's] frequentation. For he does more harm unto the country than ever he can do good under pretext to come to a private fortune or mitre, as your reverence, I believe, was informed of already."[58]

The Supreme Council's letters of August 1643 expressed their concern that Fr. Callaghan should try to set straight the nuncio's opinion of them, their loyalty, and the fact that they are faithful subjects of King Charles I:

> What we have a deeper sence of is the Cappuchin's [Fr. Michael Cullain] letter to Doctor Callaghan wherein he relates that the Lord Viscount Mountgarret should have conspired to betraye the cittie and countie of Kilkneey [Kilkenny] and that his sonn, Edmond, did discover the plott. That his letter was the same day it was receaved translated into french and delivered unto the nuntio by Doctor Kallaghan. This wicked invention and the whole circumstance of it is the worke of darkenes and it is to bee admyred how the divell amonge Christians could fynd out an instrument to invent it by. We pray you question with the Capuchin where he gathered that reporte and let Doctor Kallaghan know from us that hee mought have spared his paines and hee needed not to bee so hastie in presenting the Nuntio with so scandalous a fiction.[59]

In 1645 Fr. Callaghan returned to Ireland where Viscount Muskerry persuaded the Supreme Council of the Confederation to nominate him to fill the then vacant bishopric of Cork but the nuncio, Archbishop Rinuccini, rejected him, preferring instead Robert Barry. Whereas the nuncio acknowledged that Fr. Callaghan was "a man truly of upright habits," he was identified as an adherent of the Ormondist faction and so was unacceptable.[60]

Following the downfall of the Confederation and the advance of the Cromwellian forces in Ireland, Fr. Callaghan departed for France along with many other Irish Catholics. There he soon became embroiled in the polemics and recriminations among the defeated Irish. In December 1648, John Rowe, a Carmelite friar, deputed by the Supreme Council of the Confederation to persuade the Roman curia to overturn the the ecclesiastical censures imposed by Rinuccini, tried to enlist the theological faculty of the University of Paris in support of his position. Fr. Callaghan was his most vociferous advocate but the faculty opted not to become involved.[61]

In May of the following year Fr. Paul King, O.F.M., who strongly supported the legate's policy, attacked Richard Bellings, secretary of the Confederation of Kilkenny, in an anonymous pamphlet. Corish described it as such "an intemperate and misleading

[58] Report on Franciscan Manuscripts preserved at the Convent, Merchants' Quay, Dublin (Dublin: *Historical Manuscripts Commission*, 1906), 178 (22 August 1642), 197 (3 October 1642), 201 (10 October), 227 (5 December).

[59] Bellings, *History*, 2:332-333.

[60] Corish, "Irish in Paris," *ITQ* 21 (1954): 42, citing Rinuccini's letter of 1 June 1646: "e dottor di Sorbona, uomo veramente di retti costumi, ma . . . depende da Ormonia;" *Commentarius Rinuccinianus*, 3:620, 5:232; Burke, *Hibernia Dominicana*, 875.

[61] *Commentarius Rinucciniaus*, 3:581-586, and 4:133. Corish, "Irish in Paris," *ITQ* 21(1954): 34, n. 2 says the outcome must have been disastrous because Fr. MacCallaghan made no reference to it in his report of Rowe's mission.

account of what had happened in Ireland in 1648 that it invited reply."[62] Fr. Callaghan took up the challenge and published an anonymous volume bearing the title *Vindiciarum Catholicorum Hiberniae* at Paris in 1650. The complete title might be translated: "Two Books in Vindication of the Catholics of Ireland by Irenaeus, a Lover of his Country, [addressed] to Alitophilus. The First Book contains a true synopsis of the events in Ireland from 1641 to 1649 and the second contains a refutation of the famous libel against the Catholic nobles of Ireland. May you not hesitate to speak the truth (Ecclesiasticus, 4)." In effect, the first book relates the nunciature of Rinuccini and the second refutes Fr. King.[63]

Corish describes it as "by far the most comprehensive indictment of the nuncio's policy to be produced in the 1650's." Contemporaries wrongly assumed that Richard Bellings was the author. Rinuccini was so furious that when Richard O Ferrall began to write the *Commentarius Rinuccinianus* he urged him to refute the *Vindiciarum*. Rinuccini (who died in 1653) and his supporters were likely responsible for persuading the Congregation of the Index to condemn the book, identifying it as Bellings's work, and putting it on the Index of Forbidden Books on 10 June 1654.[64]

As the foundation for his work Fr. Callaghan could draw on his personal experiences with Lord Muskerry and other Irish leaders as well as the records of the Supreme Council and other documentary materials that he obtained from Fr. John Rowe and others. Although he asserted that the nuncio's opposition to his episcopal aspirations had no influence on his work, the *Vindiciarum* was not an objective history. His opponents accused him "not merely with errors of fact, but of deliberately tampering with the text of documents;" they denounced his work as "unworthy of any faith" and reflective of his "accustomed bad faith." The compiler of the *Commentarius Rinuccinianus* "had little respect for Callaghan's historical honesty, but he stubbornly retained a great measure of respect for him as a man."[65]

In the meantime Fr. Callaghan had gained a reputation as a Jansenist and seems to have associated himself with the convent of Port Royal, the center of Jansenism in Paris. Named parish priest of Cour-Cheverny, near Blois, in 1650, his Jansenist rigor and his encouragement of the practice of abstaining from reception of the Eucharist, out of a sense of unworthiness, aroused opposition. When the Jansenist controversy erupted among Irish priests and students at Paris in 1650 he upheld the Jansenist cause. He also attracted the ire of the Franciscan John Punch, not so much because of his interpretation of Irish affairs, but rather because he was a Jansenist. Although he did not respond, he remarked that the apothecaries found the pages of Punch's text on Scotist philosophy

[62] In *Contemporary History*, 2:211-215, John T. Gilbert published King's *Epistola nobilis Hiberni ad amicum belgam scripta ex castris catholicis eiusdem regni 4 Maii 1649*, according as Fr. MacCallaghan quoted it paragraph by paragraph; the original pamphlet is no longer extant. Corish, "Irish in Paris," *ITQ* 21 (1954): 35, 40-41.

[63] *Vindiciarum Catholicorum Hiberniae authore Philopatro Irenaeo ad Alithophilum Libri duo, quorum primus rerum in Hibiernia gestarum ab anno 1641 ad annum 1649 verissimam et actorum publicorum fide munitam synopsim, secundus libelli famosi in Catholicos Hiberniae proceres qui honestissimam cum regirum partium hominibus pacem inierunt confutationem continet. Ne confudaris dicere verum. Eccles. 4* (Paris: Vidua I. Camusat et Petrum le Petit, 1650).

[64] Corish, "Irish in Paris," *ITQ* 21(1954): 36.

[65] *Commentarius Rinuccinianus*, 3:70, 104, 156, 186, 242, 247, 261, 296, 414, 473-474, 498, 580-581, 610, 620; 4:147-148, 524; 5:233; Corish, "Irish in Paris," *ITQ* 21(1954): 43-44.

very useful as wrapping paper. In 1651 the Jesuit Jean Brisacier attacked Fr. Callaghan's Jansenist views and an anonymous satire, *Calaghanus an Satyrus? – Is Callaghan a Satyr?* – attacked the validity of his doctorate and condemned his family as swine. In the following year Fr. Callaghan issued a vigorous defense of his ideas and his origins. Thereafter he seems to have abandoned the field of political and theological polemic and died on 19 May 1664.[66]

Among those who defended Fr. Callaghan against the calumnies directed against him was Richard Bellings, the former Secretary of the Supreme Council of Kilkenny. While intending to defend Fr. Callaghan's family, he actually praised the O Callaghans of Duhallow:

> I can guarantee that the Calaghans have been a noble family, notoriously powerful in the province of Munster; and that ever since the kingdom of Ireland passed to the Crown of England, they have always lived as people of honor and great fortune in the same province; that Donat O Calaghan, who is still alive and is chief of that numerous family, possesses great estates even though the rebels have not yet been driven from his lands and his castles, and he has served his nation during these wars as a member of its Sovereign Council, and in other great affairs of the civil magistrature; and that his brother Colonel Calaghan O Calaghan is a brave and valiant gentleman and who on diverse occasions has given many signal proofs of his courage, his prudence, and his good conduct.[67]

While the exiles continued the battle of words, hurling recriminations at one another, the people left behind in Ireland had to contend with the territorial and religious adjustments consequent upon Cromwell's triumph.

---

[66] Jean Brisacier, S. J., *Le Jansenisme confundu dans l'advocat du Sr. Callaghan* (Paris 1651); "Lettre du M. Callaghan . . . touchant les principales impostures du P. Brisacier, Jésuite," in Arnauld, *Oeuvres* 30:391-401, no. 11; see his second and third letters in Arnauld, *Oeuvres* 30:405-421, nos. 13-14; Corish, "Irish in Paris," *ITQ* 21(1954): 37-39; Patrick Boyle, C. M., "A Jansenist Agent in Ireland n 1646. John Callaghan, D. D.," *Irish Ecclesiastical Record*, Series 5, 22 (1923): 1-9; Thomas Wall "Irish Enterprize in the University of Paris, 1651-1653," *Irish Ecclesiastical Record*, Series 5, 74 (1944): 94-106, 159-172; Joseph S. O Leary, "The Irish and Jansenism in the Seventeenth Century," in Liam Swords, ed., *The Irish-French Connection, 1578-1978* (Paris: The Irish College, 1978), 21-43, esp. 31-39.

[67] "Lettre de Monsieur Bellings . . . a Monsieur Calaghan," in Arnauld, *Oeuvres,* 30:402-404, no. 12, esp, 403.

CHAPTER 6

FROM CROMWELL TO THE WILD GEESE

Despite the transplantation to Clare, there was still the expectation that the settlement was not final. Opposition to the Commonwealth regime was steadily building in England and resulted in the restoration of the Stuart dynasty in the person of Charles II in 1660. Hopes were now high that the Cromwellian settlement would be undone and that civil and religious liberties would be extended to Catholics. In his "Declaration for the settlement of his kingdom of Ireland" in 1660, Charles II thanked Donough O Callaghan of Clonmeen along with thirty-eight others for their loyalty to the crown. The Act of Settlement passed by the parliament in 1662 included Donough among the king's nominees who ought to be restored to their estates. They were assured of the restoration of their principal seats and two thousand acres. The names of Donough O Callaghan of Dromaneen and Ellen his wife; Callaghan O Callaghane of Skarragh;[1] Teige of Roskeen; Dermot of Gortroe; Cahir of Kilpadder; Donough of Ballymacmurragh; Dermot McShane of Gortnawohy (near Garrymcowney); and Conoghor Reagh of Ballybahallagh were presented to the Duke of Ormond, as the king's representative, for possible restoration to their confiscated lands. In the following year, however, Donough was not included among the innocents whose lands would be restored to them. Among those enrolled in the Decrees of Innocents were Teige Callaghane, Cormack McCallaghane, and Callaghane and Connor Reghe O Callaghane or Conoghor Reagh, the agent for Sir Philip Perceval; and Teige McConoghor O Callaghan who recovered 233 acres in Dromalour in the Parish of Dromtariffe.[2]

The idea of restoring former proprietors to their estates was soon abandoned as the new government quickly realized that an attempt to uproot the adventurers who had occupied those

---

[1] Around 1700 William Taylor, Esq., claimed Kilcolman and other lands whose forfeiting proprietor was Callaghan O Callaghan. As Kilcolman was near Skarragh, I think he may be the same person. Taylor claimed to have a lease and release with a mortgage of £400 from Thady Callahane et alii, dated 7-8 February 1680. *A List of the Claims as they are entred with the Trustees at Chichester-House on College-Green Dublin, on or before the tenth of August, 1700* (Dublin: Joseph Ray 1701), no. 1966. I have not had access to Geraldine Tallon. *Court of Claims, Submissions and Evidence 1663* (Dublin: Irish Manuscripts Commission, 2006).

[2] *Statutes at Large*, 2:245-263 (30 November 1660), 264-348 (1662); Brendan Jennings, *Wild Geese in Spanish Flanders. Documents relating chiefly to Irish Regiments* (Dublin: Irish Manuscripts Commission, 1964), 510-512, no. 27 (30 November 1660); Edmund Curtis and R.B. McDowell, *Irish Historical Documents, 1172-1922* (London, 1943; reprint New York: Barnes and Noble, 1968), 158-169; E. G. More O Ferrall, "The Dispossessed Landowners of Ireland 1664. Part II. Munster and Ulster," *TIG* 4 (1972): 434-436; J. G. Simms, "The Restoration, 1660-85," *NHI*, 3:420-425; Foster, *Modern Ireland*, 117-137; O Hart, *Gentry*, 308, 312, 319, 321, 427, 434, 464; Ó Murchadha, *Names*, 70.

lands would stir renewed hostility toward the crown. In 1659, just before the Restoration, the government had given orders for the apprehension of the Earls of Clanricard and Westmeath and many others who were "conceived active or dangerous persons." Among those in County Clare to be apprehended were Callaghan O Callaghan and Charles O Callaghan, no doubt Donough's brothers. The intensity of feeling against the monarchy was revealed in testimony by Kennedy O Callaghan, probably Donough's nephew and a son of Callaghan O Callaghan. He testified that about a year before the king's return he heard Lieutenant John Chinnery (one of the Cromwellian soldiers who received a portion of O Callaghan lands) tell a group of gentlemen at a tavern called the Sign of the Bear in Mallow, that if he were in power he would make the sea red with blood before he would allow the king to enter the kingdom. Addressing Chinnery "in broken Irish", Captain Thomas Cosabone thanked God that "your father's son should speak such words of the great king of England." Given such sentiments it is not surprising that the government was reluctant to alter the Cromwellian settlement. Thus while Donough O Callaghan was one of fifty-four nominees mentioned in the Act of Explanation who were to be restored to their lands, the Act of Settlement of 1665 confirmed him in his estates at Mountallon in Clare.[3]

In view of the uncertainties of the settlement, Sir Richard Kyrle received a patent for Clonmeen, Dromaneen and other lands in Duhallow and Fermoy in 1659, agreeing to pay £43 s10 to the royal exchequer, but saving to Donough O Callaghan and his heirs, whatever right they might have to the lands in question, as determined by the commissioners appointed to execute the acts made for the settlement of Ireland. In that case, Kyrle would be provided with other forfeited lands of equal value. In 1667 he received a patent under the Act of Settlement for Dromaneen, Knocknamona, and Kilroe (866 acres); Kilvealaton (328 acres); Kilpadder (169 acres); Skarragh (502 profitable and 421 unprofitable acres); Oulert (Aldworth, 101 acres); Dromahane (194 acres); and Gortroe and Drompeesh (611 profitable and 98 unprofitable acres). He married Mary Jephson, perhaps the daughter of Colonel John Jephson resident at Dromaneen in 1650. As a knight of Dromaneen, Kyrle was returned as a member of parliament for Cork City on 30 April 1661. Two years later his tenants at Clonmeen, where he erected an iron works, complained of the excise tax being levied. In addition to cutting down extensive woodland, he reportedly destroyed Clonmeen castle. Again in 1678 he passed patent for Dromaneen, Clonmeen, and other lands "saving to Donogh O Callaghan and his heirs all such right, title and interest as the Commissioners shall adjudge to him as one of the 54 persons appointed to be restored in the Explanatory Act." In a letter to the earl of Orrery in August 1678 Donough's son Callaghan commented that it was only through Kyrle's generosity that he was able to "put bread into his mouth." Later Kyrle sold his interest in Dromaneen to Richard Newman and in 1667 was named governor of the American colony of Carolina where he died in 1684. Newman obtained a royal patent in 1686 establishing the manor of Newberry including the lands purchased from Kyrle, namely, Dromaneen, Knocknamona, Kilvealaton, Kilroe, Carrigolane or Dromore wood, Kilpadder, Skarragh, Oulert, Gortroe, and Drompeesh. The Newmans planted English families on these lands and in 1694 restored Dromaneen, but by 1739 it was reportedly in such bad condition that it was abandoned and ruined.[4] In 1805 William Barry restored the castle and it remained in his family's possession until the 1950s when it was sold to the Forestry Department.

---

[3] Dunlop, *Commonwealth*, 2:702-703 (6 August 1659); *Egmont MSS*, 2:33 (27 March 1674).

[4] Berry, "Kilshannig," *JCHAS* 11 (1905): 59-62, and "English Settlement," *JCHAS* 12 (1906): 4; Smith, *Cork*, 1:293, nn. 3, 6; Francis H. Tuckey, *The County and City of Cork Remembrancer or Annals of the County and City of Cork* (Cork: O. Savage & Son, 1837), 320. *Egmont MSS*, 2:6 (12 February 1663); Lewis, *Dictionary*, 1:368;

From Cromwell to the Wild Geese

In 1666 Roger Brettridge, another beneficiary of the confiscation of Donough O Callaghan's estates, was confirmed in possession of Kilbrin (148 acres), Rathmaher (73 acres), Ballyheen (224 acres), Dromcummer and Killrush (270 acres), and Kippagh (122 acres). He also sold Knockardsharriv, Coolaveen and Cloonteens near Roskeen and purchased Kippagh from Lord Kingston, who acquired it from Donough O Callaghan. When he disposed of those estates in his will of 1683, he provided that the income from East Dromcummer should be used to maintain seven poor Protestant veterans of the Cromwellian wars.[5]

The development of Mallow as an important urban center continued apace during the seventeenth century. Among the twenty-five free burgesses of Mallow on 29 August 1688 were John Callaghan, gentleman, and Anthony (Owney, an Anglicised form of Uaithne) Callaghan, innkeeper. Evidently, Anthony was the proprietor of the tavern known as the Sign of the Bear where Lieutenant Chinnery denounced Charles II in 1659. Cornelius Callaghan, gentleman, was the town clerk. In order to hold that position he likely had to be a Protestant. Other family members were settled in Cork City. Among them was Thady Callaghan, gentleman, who in 1688 claimed the right to seal leather there, but the municipal corporation argued that they had that right by "a more ancient grant" from the crown and "he was obliged to desist." I suspect that Thady may be the same person as Teige of Coolroe, one of the O Callaghans of Banteer mentioned below.[6]

Donough O Callaghan, meanwhile, was attempting to develop his new lands in Clare. His principal residence was "at Mountallon, near Kilkishen among the secluded lakes and rolling hills of East Clare." Located in the Parish of Clonlea, Mountallon, in Irish, *Min Thalun Flathuil*, meant "the hospitable and princely plain." Donough (and his three sons, Teige, Donough and Cahir) also held Kilgory in Kilnoe Parish and barony of Tulla Upper.[7] Even so, he remained hopeful of being able to return to his ancestral lands in Cork. So for example, in 1666, Daniel O Brien, Viscount Clare, leased Calluragh, Carrounacloghy and Poulglass in the parish of Inchicronan and Kilboggoon in the parish of Tulla to him at a pepper corn rent for a thousand years with the proviso that the lease would be void when Donough or his heirs was restored to his estates in "Pubbleocallaghan . . . previously possessed by him till he was transplanted by the late usurped powers." A pepper corn rent preserved Lord Clare's ownership, but did not create a significant financial burden for Donough.[8]

Grove-White, *Notes*, 2:235, 237, 3:62-63, 70-71, 4:129-130, 133; Ó Murchada, *Names*, 71; John Kavanagh, "Excerpts from the History of Kilshannig," *MFCJ* 2 (1984): 55-69; Con Tarrant, "How the Planting of Clonmeen Failed," *SD* 7 (1989): 39-40.

[5] Grove-White, "Notes," M. V. Conlon, "Will of Roger Brettridge, 1683," *JCHAS* 61 (1956):110-14; Niall O Brien, "Roger Brettridge, the 1662 Act of Settlement and Duhallow Affairs at the Court of Claims," *Seanchas Dúthalla* 25 (2011): 10-16.

[6] In 1711 Anthony's malt house was leased to Richard Beare; Berry, "English Settlement," *JCHAS* 12 (1906): 12, 25; Smith, *Cork*, 1:417; C. J. F. MacCarthy, "Seanchas," *MFCJ* 5 (1987): 152, and 8 (1990): 101.

[7] O'Donovan, "To Hell or to Clare," 73. John O Donovan had it as *Maidhm Talún*, "a breach or eruption of the earth." Other townlands that Donough held in whole or in part in the barony of Tulla were: Oughterarte and Ballymacdonell (Killuran parish); Ballynahinch, Coolready, Clonmoher, and Kilgory (Kilnoe parish); Kilboggoon, Liscullane, and Lahardaun (Tulla parish). In the barony of Bunratty: Calluragh (Doora parish); Caherculla (Quin parish); Ballyduff, Knockanaura, Ballyhoe, Cloonton, Ballymulqueeny, Cragaweelcross, Derry, Faunrusk, and Maghery (Templemaley parish).

[8] James Frost, *The History and Topography of the County of Clare from the Earliest Times to the Beginning of the Eighteenth Century* (Dublin: Sealy, Breyers and Walker, 1893), 385-386, 425, 431, 435-436, 508, 511-512, 520-521, 525. The proprietors in Kilcorney parish in 1641 included Conor Óg Callaghane and Melaghlin Roe

The poll tax evaluation carried out under the direction of Sir William Petty in 1659 identified nineteen O Callaghan families in the baronies of Tulla Upper and Tulla Lower and seven in the barony of Clonderalaw. All of them no doubt had accompanied Donough as he made the journey from their ancestral home in Cork to a new life in Clare. In addition to Donough, other exiled family members included:

Name	Place	Parish	Barony
Daniel	Inchilaghoge		Tulla Upper
Conor, Esq.	Ballyquin	Killokennedy	Tulla Lower
Callaghan	Dromanure	Kilmaley	
Israel	Ballygallin, Ballymayley	Templemaley	
Irrelagh	Licknaun, Reaskaun		

Daniel, Conor, and Callaghan were probably Donough's brothers. Israel and Irrelagh were likely the same person; Irrelagh, outlawed in 1642 while resident at Clonmeen, was probably the son of Dermot, son of Irrelagh, a brother of Conor of the Rock, and the father of two sons, Dermot and Callaghan.[9] Eve Campbell estimated that there were about 145 persons settled in O Callaghan lands. Aside from family members, there were others such as Anthony Garvane, whose fsmily had been O Callaghan tenants in Cork.[10]

When a new wave of anti-Catholic hostility broke, Donough O Callaghan, formerly lord of Clonmeen and Dromaneen, transplanted to Clare for his participation in the Confederation of Kilkenny and for his allegiance to Charles I and Charles II, was dead. Now known as Donough Mór, to distinguish him from his son and heir, he died intestate sometime before 1683, perhaps in the previous year. His burial place is not mentioned, though O Donovan suggested that he may have been interred "in the O Callaghan tomb in St. Mochulla's grave-yard in Tulla." More than likely his wife Ellen had predeceased him, as there is no mention of her after his death. Their children included Teige, who evidently died without children, and perhaps predeceased his father; Donough Óg or the Younger of Mountallon; Cahir of Leatherdon or Lahardaun (the ancestor of the O Callaghans in Spain); Callaghan; Murrough; Patrick; and Joan. At the time of his death Donough held Derrineveagh, Derrymore, Coolready, Ballydonaghan, Kilgoreyorterush, Ballymcdonell and Crevagh in County Clare. In 1673 he settled these lands in trust for himself and his sons (Donough Óg, the oldest and immediate heir, Cahir, Murrough, and Patrick). Although Donough Óg had an annual income of £250 from those lands, he neglected to pay £400 to his sister Joan and £300 each to his brothers Murrough and Patrick; the three siblings, claiming to be "in a distressed condition," brought suit against him and the trustees. Although

Callahane (O Cullinane) but they may not have been members of the O Callaghan family of Cork. *Ibid.*, 442. Donough was listed in 1661 among the tenants in Calluragh. In 1641 John and Conor MacNamara disposed Caherculla to Dr. Mara, Donough O'Callaghan, and John MacNamara. Frost, *Clare*, 336-337 (citing an inquisition of 2 July 1696, Ennis), 425, 431, 601 (MacNamara's petition of 1700). Donough leased lands in Ranna parish, barony of Tulla, to John MacNamara on 26 June 1675; NLI D 24014: Hayes, *Manuscript Sources, Supplement I*, D 24014.
[9] *A Census of Ireland circa 1659*, 165, 172, 174, 178; Frost, *Clare*, 386, 434, 499, 510 (n. 2), 521; *LM*, 162.
[10] Campbell, *Displacement*, 238-239.

Donough Óg agreed to mortgage several properties to meet these demands, he failed to do so and Murrough brought suit against him in 1685.[11] Meantime, in 1679, Donough Óg leased Mountallon, Cappalaheen, Coolistoonan, and Cunninagh to his uncle Connor for an annual rent of £26.[12] That signified Donough Óg's intention to establish a more permanent residence at Kilgory in Killnoe Parish.

The Court of Claims also entertained the petition of Thady MacNamara of Rannagh, who asserted that the Commissioners, then sitting at Loughrea, assigned Kilboggoone's 355 acres to Donough Mór as partial compensation for his confiscated estates in Cork. After his death, Donough Óg, in 1684, in consideration of £400, conveyed Rannagh, Knockmanistragh, Lacnegoologe, and Knockballykelly and a lease of Kilboggoone for 31 years to Thady's fafher, John MacNamara. Among the witnesses to the conveyance was Darby Callaghan. Thady also claimed that Donough Óg, on 19-20 March 1696 mortgaged Knockacloggin to him. Owen O Callaghan witnessed that document.[13]

The Popish Plot

In England, meanwhile, hostilities among the diverse religious and political forces compelled Charles II to follow a very wary path. When he issued the Declaration of Indulgence in 1672 suspending the penal laws against Catholics and Protestant nonconformists, parliament forced him to back down. Tensions flared again in 1678 when Titus Oates spread the story of a Catholic plot to murder the king and restore the Catholic religion. The Earl of Shaftesbury, the king's chief minister and leader of the Whig party, realized the value of the alleged conspiracy for the Protestant cause and tried to establish that the plot also had roots in Ireland. The Duke of Ormond, Lord Lieutenant in Ireland, discounted that suggestion.[14]

On the other hand, Roger Boyle, Earl of Orrery, one of the great landowners in Cork who had supported the Cromwellians and then returned to his allegiance to the crown, had long been active in seeking out plots in Ireland. As early as 1667 he expressed his suspicion to Ormond that Donough O Callaghan was in contact with the French. Captain Betagh, "thought to be the French correspondent in these parts," was reported to have "much resorted to one Donogh O Callaghan who lives two miles from the Broad Ford on the left hand as you go between Limerick and Galway. Betagh said that he often lay at the house of Callaghan who had formerly owned a great estate near the Blackwater." Orrery sent for Donough, promising to get out of him what he could. What came of this is unknown, but it seems unlikely that any significant action was taken against Donough as a potential collaborator with the French.[15]

Rumors of a Popish Plot served to fan anti-Catholic prejudice in Ireland. When Ormond prevented the Dublin Apprentices from pulling down the mass houses in the city, Lieutenant

---

[11] *LM*, 161; Dublin, GO, MS 177, p. 492 (Donough's genealogy), and 1-3, 78-80 (genealogy of Cahir of Leatherdon). MacNamara's petition of 1700 says that Donough died about twenty years ago; but a chancery bill of 4 February 1683 indicates that he was dead at that time; NLI, O Callaghan Papers at Lismehane, County Clare, Report on Private Collections, no. 110 (4 February 1683), (9 July 1685); O Donovan, "To Hell or to Clare," 73; *BIFR*, 888-889.

[12] Frost, *Clare*, 601-602.

[13] *A List of the Claims*, no. 1591; Shoosmith, *Settlement*, 99.

[14] Simms, *"The Restoration," NHI*, 3:432-433.

[15] *CSP Ireland. Charles II*, 7:478 (29 October 1667).

John Chinnery, a justice of the peace in County Cork, according to Teige Callaghan, condemned the duke and said that he would be called to account for it.[16] This was the same Chinnery who had said he would make blood run before he would accept the royalist restoration.

More seriously, several Irish priests were found to bring evidence against various persons in Ireland, including Oliver Plunkett, Archbishop of Armagh, who was supposedly involved in a Catholic conspiracy to assist in a French invasion. In responding to various charges brought against him in January 1680, Plunkett remarked that Friar Anthony Daly accused him of suborning "two false witnesses who planted the crime of lese majesty on Fathers James Callaghan and Denis Rafferty. I do not know these witnesses; I do not know who they were or what name or surname they have, nor what they look like. This is the truth as God is my witness and I lie not." Several months later he commented that Callaghan accused him of "exercising papal jurisdiction in this country, a charge that is glorious to me." Writing from London on 18 December 1680, James Callaghan, a parish priest of the Armagh archdiocese, reported that "the most part of the gentry of the west parts of Ireland is impeached with the Plot, but none out of the north." James asked his cousin Edmond to inquire about Neale Callaghan "who was in trouble concerning the Tories," probably an outlaw still in arms. He remarked that the archbishop, "Primate and Metropolitan of all Ireland heretofore so titulated, is upon the Newgate [prison] of London to his great woe," and asked that "my loving friend Mr. Denis Raverty [Rafferty]" be informed "that his worthy friend" Plunkett was in Newgate. "Let Mr. Denis be sure not to fear any suborned evidence against the next Assizes of Ardmagh, for there are as many priests, friars, and other chief members of the laity out of Munster, Leinster, Connaught, Italy, England and other parts as might hang him and a thousand more if they had been as much concerned as he is."[17] Given that James Callaghan belonged to the see of Armagh it is likely that he was not a member of the O Callaghan family of Cork, but rather of an entirely different Ulster family, the Irish form of whose name was Ó Ceileacháin. Plunkett was executed in 1681.

Witnesses purporting to have knowledge of the Popish Plot included Owen Callaghan, a priest, who, together with three others, Fathers Murphy, Moyer and Heron, was brought from Ireland to England in 1680. When Callaghan said that he could provide information about several persons having a hand in the Popish Plot in Ireland, the royal council ordered him sent to the duke of Ormond, who evidently did not regard him as a trustworthy witness. Callaghan and his fellow priests complained against the duke for "not using them well, but discouraging them . . . and treating them worse when they were sent back." In the fall of 1681 Callaghan, Murtagh Downey or Downing, Maurice FitzGerald, and John Arthur were sent back to Ireland to give testimony against several persons awaiting trial on the charge of high treason. The earl of Longford informed Ormond that this was essentially a ploy on the part of the earl of Shaftesbury to strengthen the Whig and Protestant faction. In 1683 Ormond revealed his impatience with Murtagh Downey and Owen Callaghan who "have been already whipped at Basing[stoke] for vagabonds." Perhaps they were Franciscan friars. Though Callaghan seemed to have disappeared, Ormond intended to send both men to Bridewell prison, commenting that this differed from their previous treatment in London, "but I take it to be suitable to their desert."[18]

---

[16] Richard Aldworth to Ormond, 3 March 1678/9; *Calendar Ormonde, 4:340-341.*

[17] *The Letters of Saint Oliver Plunkett, 1625-1681, Archbishop of Armagh and Primate of All Ireland,* ed. John Hanly (Dublin: Dolmen Press, 1979), 539-543, 552-557, nos. 206 (17 January 1680), 211 (15 July 1680); *Calendar Ormonde,* 5:531-533 (18 December 1680).

[18] *Calendar Ormonde,* 5:314 (8 May 1680), 318 (15 May), 349 (17 July), 490-491 (16 November), and

Although anti-Catholic feeling subsided in the last years of Charles II's reign, suspicion of Irishmen coming to England appears to be reflected in the examination of several travelers arriving by ship at Bristol from Cork in 1685. One of them, John Callahan, declared that he was a glover living in County Cork, on his way to London to see his uncle Owen Callahan and John MacKunny, "who do or did lately belong to" Mr. Patrick Trant; perhaps they were Trant's indentured servants. Once interrogated, John presumably was allowed to go on his way.[19]

Meantime Pierse Creagh, Catholic bishop of Cork and Cloyne, was arrested in 1680 on suspicion of his participation in the Plot. One of the potential witnesses against him was Daniel Callaghan who visited the priests held prisoner at Sir Richard Aldworth's house near Newmarket; strengthened by their exhortations Callaghan declared that "he would not hang his Bishopp and Priest for an hundred pound [pounds]." As other witnesses refused to testify against him Bishop Creagh was found not guilty.[20]

Writing in 1685, meanwhile, Sir Richard Cox expressed satisfaction at the successful imposition of a new order in Ireland. Not only had the number of English inhabitants increased, but the country was "improved daily after the English fashion." Moreover, "there remains noe considerable fastnesse to hyde Toryes or shelter rebels nor is there any part of the worlde more free from fear and disturbance than this kingdom. Tanishy [tanistry]. gavelkind, the Brehon law, cosherings [*cóisir*, feasting], coyne & livery & all other old barbarous customs and unreasonable exactions are obsolete or abolished & the English habit, language & manners altogether used except by the poorer sort."[21]

The Glorious Revolution

As the century drew to a close a new upheaval in England had disastrous consequences in Ireland, completing in some measure the destruction of the old order and the establishment of the Protestant Ascendancy on a firm foundation. When Charles II died in 1685 his brother, James II, a convert to Catholicism, succeeded to the thrones of England and Ireland. Quickly showing his favor to the Catholics, he permitted them to hold public office, even though the Test Acts enacted in 1673 and 1678, as a result of the Declaration of Indulgence of 1672, excluded them. He also encouraged Richard Talbot, Earl of Tyrconnell and Lord Lieutenant of Ireland, to build up the Catholic element in the army in Ireland.[22]

When James II issued a Declaration of Indulgence in 1687, suspending the laws against Catholics and Protestant nonconformists (Presbyterians and others who did not adhere to the Church of England or the Church of Ireland), he outraged many. Outrage gave way to downright rebellion when his Catholic queen gave birth to a son, James, in July 1688, thus seeming to

6:75 (4 June 1681), 217 (2 November), 219-220 (8 November), 262-263 (14 December), and 7:105 (14 August 1683).

[19] *Calendar of State Papers preserved in the Public Record Office, Domestic Series, 1547-1695*, 81 vols. (London: Public Record Office, 1856-1972), James II, 1:12-14, no. 56 (13 February 1685).

[20] William P. Burke, *The Irish Priests in the Penal Times (1660-1760). From the State Papers in H. M. Record Offices, Dublin and London, the Bodleian Library and British Museum* (Waterford, 1914; reprint Shannon: Irish University Press, 1969), 96.

[21] Swift Paine Johnson and T. A. Lanham, eds., "On a Manuscript Description of the City and County of Cork, cir. 1685," *JRSAI* 32 (1902): 361-362.

[22] J. G. Simms, "The War of the Two Kings, 1685-91," *NHI*, 3:478-508; Foster, *Modern Ireland*, 138-163.

assure the Catholic succession. The Protestants then invited William of Orange and his wife, Mary, James II's Protestant daughter, to accept the throne. After landing in England William crossed to Ireland in November, prompting James II to flee to France, but he returned in March 1689, intending to regain his crown from there.

Several O Callaghans, Callaghans, and MacCallaghans served in James II's Irish army:

Name	Regiment	Dates	Place
Charles, Ensign to Sir John Ivory; Lieutenant	Maj.Gen.Justin MacCarthy, Infantry	3/1685/6; 9/1685/6	Waterford
Callahan McCallahan, Ensign	Ormond; MacCarthy	3/1684/5; 1685/6	Carlow; Cork/ Kinsale
Callaghan McCallaghan, Cornet		2/1686/7	
Donough O Callaghan, Lt. Colonel	Brig. Thomas Maxwell, Dragoons		
Major Callaghan	Brig. Thomas Maxwells		
Captain Callahan	Lord Clare		Cork
Lieutenant Callaghan	Lord Clare		Cork
Dermot O Callaghan, Kilgory, Ensign	O Brien, Infantry	1689	
Callaghan O Callaghan, Kilgory, Ensign	O Brien, Infantry	1689	
John Callaghan, Ensign		1689	

The family of Donough Mór O Callaghan, exiled from Cork, was well represented. His son Donough Óg was a Lieutenant-Colonel of Dragoons. Ensign, and later Lieutenant, Charles Callaghan (Cahir, in Irish Cathaoir) may have been another son. Dermot and Callaghan O Callaghan of Kilgory were members of his family. Perhaps the same is true of John Callaghan who in 1689 wrote to Sir John FitzGerald at Limerick thanking him for continuing him as an ensign; though he expressed the hope of having his own company, he feared that he would have to resign, as he could not draw his sword and might not recover use of his hand. He conveyed to Sir John Colonel Dennis Callaghan's expression of gratitude. The latter was likely Donough Óg. Representing the MacCallaghans of Muskerry, Callahan McCallahan, listed as an ensign in 1684/5 is probably identical with Callaghan McCallaghan, a cornet in 1685/6. Major Callaghan, Captain Callahan, and the two Lieutenants Callaghan have not been identified.[23]

In addition to the foregoing, the following may be mentioned: Captain Cornelius Callaghan (Sutherland's Regiment); Ensign Auliff O Callaghan (Mountcashel's); Captain Cornelius O Callaghan (Clancarthy's); Lieutenant Denis O Callaghan (Antrim's); Ensign Callaghan (Kenmare's); Ensign O Callaghan (FitzGerald's); Captain Thady O Callaghan, Lieutenants Cornelius O Callaghan and Callaghan MacCallaghan, and Ensigns John and Owen O Callaghan (Browne's); Lieutenant Colonel Donough O Callaghan, Ensign John O Callaghan

[23] *Calendar Ormonde*, 1:403, 415, 428, 445; John D'Alton, *Illustrations Historical and Genealogical of King James' Irish Army List* (Dublin: The Author, 1855), 12, 408, 866-868; John T. Gilbert, *A Jacobite Narrative of the War in Ireland, 1688-1691* (Dublin, 1892; reprint New York: Barnes and Noble, 1971), 213; Frost, *Clare*, 566-567; O Hart, *Gentry*, 509 (Retinue of King James the Second in Ireland 1690); Appendix to 5th *RDK* 321.

(Barrett's); Captain Dermot O Callaghan and Ensign Callaghan O Callaghan (O Brien); Ensign O Callaghan (McEllicott's); and Captain O Callaghan and two Lieutenants O Callaghan (Clare's).[24]

In view of the threat posed by James II and the support given him by so many of the Irish, the following members of the family were indicted for high treason and outlawed in the Court of King's Bench in Ireland in 1689:

Name	Place	County
Donough, Esq.	Mountallon	Clare
Cornelius, Gent.	Carrogoure	Cork
Donough, Esq., alias O Callaghan of Clonmeen	Clonmeen	Cork
Thady, Esq.	Dromaneen	Cork
Thady, treasurer		Cork

There is some confusion of identities here. Donough, alias O Callaghan of Clonmeen, would seem to be Donough Mór, though he appears to have died about 1683. Donough of Mountallon must be his son Donough Óg. The authorities may also have identified him as of Clonmeen to be certain of his person. Diarmuid Ó Muchadha stated that Cornelius Callaghan of Carrogoure came from Carrigoon east of Mallow and Thady O Callaghane, Esq. of Dromaneen resided at Dromalour south of Kanturk. Smith reported that during the Williamite Wars the English maintained a garrision in Dromaneen castle.[25] The second Thady Callaghan was an agent for Dominick Sarsfield, Lord Killmallock, and served as treasurer for County Cork in 1689-1690.[26]

Several other O Callaghans were outlawed for treason beyond the seas:

Name	Place	County
Cornelius Callaghan, Gent.	Loughnane	Cork
John, Gent.	Loughnane	Cork
Owen, Gent.	Loughnane	Cork
Callaghan O Callaghan, Gent.	Clonmeen	Cork
Charles O Callaghan, Gent.	Clonmeen	Cork
Major Dermot Callaghan, Gent.	Curragh	
Patrick Callaghan	Mountallon	Clare
Morgan [Murrough] Callaghan	Mountallon	Clare
Callaghan O Callaghan, Gent.	Kilgory	Clare

Included in that group were Donough Óg's brothers Callaghan, Charles (Cahir of

---

[24] Charles Ffrench Blake-Forster, *The Irish Chieftains, or, a struggle for the Crown* (Dublin: McGlashran & Gill, 1872), 618, 630-632, 639, 643, 655, 659-661, 663, 668. Noting that D'Alton's list was for 1689 only, he presented a list for the three years 1689, 1690, and 1691.

[25] Ó Murchadha, *Names*, 72; Smith, *Cork*, 1:300.

[26] James Power, Esq., around 1700 claimed a "house and backside, called the Crown" in Cork City whose forfeiting proprietor following the treaty of Limerick was Thady Calloughan, perhaps the treasurer. *A List of the Claims*, no. 1848.

Leatherdon or Lahardaun), both identified as of Clonmeen; Patrick and Morgan of Mountallon; and his son Callaghan of Kilgory. The three gentlemen from Loughane (not Loughnane; probably Loughane East or West in Muskerry, north of Blarney) probably belonged to the MacCallaghan family of Muskerry. Major Dermot Callaghan of Curragh was a son of Cahir of Curragh. Most were probably serving in France in the army of James II.[27]

After James II's defeat at the Battle of the Boyne on 12 July 1690, he fled to France, leaving the Irish to continue the struggle on their own. In August they successfully withstood the siege of Limerick, but Cork and Kinsale surrendered in September. Not long afterward the O Callaghans joined MacDonough MacCarthy in submitting to the victors. In a letter addressed to the duke of Würtemberg on 29 October 1690, Lord Barrymore commented that he had received a petition from "Colonel McDonogh, Chief of the country called 'Dunhallow' between Mallow and the County of Kerry and of another Chieftain of a country called O Callaghan, in order to obtain the protection of their Majesties. It is of very great consequence to draw over people of their quality and interest, who will bring with them a thousand men and at least seven or eight thousand cows." The O Callaghan described as "Chieftain of a country called O Callaghan" must be Donough Óg, as his father had died several years before. The bloody battle of Aughrim, fought on 12 July 1691, was another defeat for the Jacobite cause. Limerick, besieged once again, surrendered at the beginning of October. The Treaty of Limerick signed on 3 October 1691 completed the downfall of the Gaelic Order, which disintegrated with the removal or departure of the chiefs, leaving a leaderless people behind. New confiscations followed, and the penal laws against Catholics were intensifed.[28]

Under the articles of Limerick and Galway the Board of Claims in 1694 determined that the following should be restored to their estates:

Name	Place	County	Date
Col. Donough O Callaghan	Kilgory	Clare	1694
Darby [Dermot] O Callaghan	Killurane	Clare	1694
Dennis Callaghan	Dublin	Dublin	1698
Callaghan McCallaghan	Caherlag		1698
Capt. John Callaghan	Dublin	Dublin	1699
Teige Callaghan	Mountallon	Clare	1699
Charles Callaghan	Rossline	Cork	1699
Teige Reagh Callaghan	Rossline	Cork	1699
Dennis Callaghan	Subulter	Cork	1699

In addition to Donough Óg, Darby of Killurane, and Teige of Mountallon represented the O Callaghans of Clare. Charles and Teige Reagh of Rossline and Dennis of Subulter were the sons of Conoghor Reagh, an agent of Sir Philip Perceval. The identity of Dennis and

---

[27] John T. Collins, "Extracts from the Caulfield MSS, University College, Cork, *JCHAS* 66 (1961): 51-54; Smith, *Cork,* 1:308; J. G. Simms, "Irish Jacobite Lists from TCD MS N.1.3," *AH* 22 (1960): 12, 48, 68-69, 74-75; Albert E. Casey and Thomas E. Dowling, *O Kief, Coshe Mang, Slieve Lougher and Upper Blackwater in Ireland,* 14 vols. (Birmingham, AL: Knocknagree Historical Fund, 1952-1968), 6:1396-1400.

[28] Ó Murchadha, *Names,* 71; J. G. Simms, "The Restoration and the Jacobite War," in T. W. Moody and F. X. Martin, eds., *The Course of Irish History* (Cork: Mercier, 1967), 204-216.

Captain John of Dublin is unclear.[29]

Callaghan McCallaghan of Caherlag in the barony of Barrymore north of Cork City may be the ensign and cornet mentioned in 1685-1686. He may also be Lieutenant Colonel Callaghan McCallaghan, who sought to recover his estates by petitioning the Court of Claims established to resolve these issues. He claimed by reversion in fee (that is, the right to reenter his estates) Castlehinchy (Caisleán na hInse) and Killneasly among other lands in the barony of Muskerry as recorded in a deed dated 5 October 1676, and witnessed by Dermot McCarthy, Cornelius Callaghan, and others. The proprietor of those lands was Justin MacCarthy, or the current earl of Clancarthy.[30] Cornelius Callaghan of Loughane, who was outlawed for treason, may have been Callaghan's brother. Justin MacCarthy, whom James II named viscount Mountcashel, died in 1694. The ambiguous reference to the earl of Clancarthy was prompted by the fact that Justin's nephew Donough, the fourth earl of Clancarthy, lost his title and his estates for supporting James II and was in exile in Germany where he died in 1734. In a petition presented by Lieutenant Colonel Callaghan McCallaghan to Queen Anne on 19 June 1707, he stated that he had served as a page to Callaghan (Justin's older brother), the third earl of Clancarthy, who at the time of his death in 1676 leased the lands at Laghane (probably Loughane in Muskerry) to him at an annual rent of £20 for a term of three lives, The property in question would likely bring him an annual income of £100. However, he lost those holdings when the earl was attainted of treason and his estates were confiscated. Lieutenant Colonel McCallaghan argued that according to the decree of the trustees for forfeited estates he should receive £20 yearly for life from the estates mentioned, which were then in the possession of Lord Woodstock.[31] His petition was probably approved. In 1713, while residing at Caherlag, he, among othrer Catholics, was licensed to carry a sword, a case of pistols, and a gun. That signified that the goverment did not consider him a threat.[32]

It seems unlikely, therefore, that he was the same person as that Callaghan McCallaghan, who, like many other dispossessed soldiers after the collapse of the Jacobite cause, turned to the career of a tory or rapparee, a highwayman. Perhaps he was Lieutenant Colonel's son.The Cork Grand Jury on 27 July 1702 awarded £20 to anyone who brought in or killed a proclaimed tory. One such was Callaghane McCallaghane, who was killed by Will Parker, though Parker lost his life in the process. His widow was rewarded, however, with £20 for his service. Another person was awarded £20 for bringing in a tory. As both tories were followers of Charles and Donough MacCarthy the sum of £40 was to be levied on their property. Charles (d. 1655) was the second earl of Clancarthy and his nephew Donough (d.1734) was the fourth earl.[33]

The Wild Geese

One of the more devastating consequences of the Treaty of Limerick was the departure of thousands of Irish soldiers to the continent. The treaty allowed them to go and provided for their Transport abroad. Most of those who chose to emigrate did so, no doubt, with the expectation

---

[29] Simms, "Irish Jacobite Lists," *AH* 22 (1960): 92, 108, dated 23 November and 6 December 1694; 25 February and 3 March1698, 3 June and 3 July, 5 July, and 20 August 1699; Casey, *O Kief*, 6:1402-1409.

[30] *A List of the Claims*, no. 1790.

[31] *Calendar of Treasury Papers*, Volume 3, 1702-1707 (London: (Her Majesty's Stationery Office,, 1874), 516.

[32] *Calendar Ormonde*, 2:479 (18 March 1713/4); Simms, "Irish Jacobite Lists," *AH* 22 (1960): 92, 108.

[33] Brady, *Records*. liii.

that, regrouped there in the service of the exiled monarch, James II, they would eventually be able to effect a Stuart Restoration. That was not to be, but as a result many Irish men (and women) made their careers on the continent in the service of French, German, Russian, and Spanish sovereigns. They came to be known as *na géanna fiadhaine*, the wild geese who had flown from their homes to a new world. If they expected ever to return in triumph to Ireland that hope quickly dissipated with the failure of the Stuart efforts to regain the British throne in 1715 and 1745. Gradually the exiles thrust down roots in their new homelands, married, and had children. For example, Honora Callaghan, daughter of Kennedy Callaghan, deceased, married Jean Baptiste O Mullane in the parish church of St. Benoît on 4 July 1697; John Callaghan, perhaps her brother, was a witness. Kennedy, her father, may have been a son of Callaghan O Callaghan, a brother of the chieftain Donough, and a lawyer active in the Confederation of Kilkenny. Similarly, Denis Callaghan wed Catherine Mirabeau at St. Germain-en-Laye on 23 February 1699; Jean Baptiste O Mullane, doctor of medicine, witnessed the marriage. The two families shared common roots in Cork, as the O Mullanes came from Brittas near Lombardstown.[34]

In France the Irish exiles soon discovered many opportunities to wage war against the English and their allies. Louis XIV, king of France, engaged in a series of wars directed against the ascendancy in continental Europe of the Habsburg dynasty of Spain and the Holy Roman Empire. In addition, he attempted to extend his frontiers by expansion into the Spanish Netherlands and the Rhineland. As a consequence, the Holy Roman Empire, the United Provinces of the Netherlands, Spain, England, and other countries, were often found allied in opposition to him.

Irish soldiers emigrating to France after the Treaty of Limerick were organized in the military regiments of Dillon, Roth, Clare, and FitzJames. The following O Callaghans were officers from the close of the seventeenth century until the middle of the eighteenth:[35]

Name	Regiment	Date
Capt. Denis	Dillon	1698
Capt. Denis	Dorrington	1717
Capt. Denis	Rothe	1722
Capt. O Callaghan	Clare	1719
Capt. O Callaghan	Dillon	1746
Capt. O Callaghan	FitzJames	1756

Captain Denis O Callaghan in Dillon's Regiment in 1698 may perhaps be identified with

---

[34] Maurice N. Hennessy, *The Wild Geese: The Irish Soldier in Exile* (London: Sedwick and Jackson, 1973); Mark McLaughlin, *The Wild Geese: The Irish Brigades of France and Spain* (London: Osprey, 1980); Richard F. Hayes, *Irish Swordsmen of France* (Dublin: Gill, 1934); Basil O Connell, "Catherine O Mullane, Mrs. O Connell, mother of Daniel O Connell, the Liberator," *TIG* 2:10 (1953): 311-316.

[35] John O Hart, *Irish Pedigrees or the Origin and Stem of the Irish Nation,* 2 vols. (New York: Murphy and McCarthy, 1923), 2:798, appendix 2; John Cornelius O Callaghan, *A History of the Irish Brigades in the Service of France from the Revolution in Great Britain and Ireland under James II to the Revolution in France under Louis XVI,* Cameron and Ferguson Edition (Glasgow: R. & T. Washbourne, 1870).

Donnchadh or Denis O Callaghan of Kilcranathan, son of Domhnall Mór na Pálach or Donal More of the Paal (Páil, southwest of Kanturk), who was wounded in the battle of Knocknanuss in 1647. Donnchadh's brother Eoghan or Owen, a cornet in the cavalry, was one of the many who "did great deeds at the battle of Aughrim." A Lieutenant-Colonel in the Yellow Dragoons in James II's Irish army, Donnchadh was one of the Irish soldiers who went to France, where he became a captain in the French army. He married Rebecca Dawson of County Cork by whom he had three daughters: Oiléan or Ellen, Máire or Mary, and another whose name is not known. Oiléan married Colonel Arthur of Meath, whose mother was a daughter of Richard Talbot, duke of Tyrconnell, James II's lieutenant in Ireland. Colonel Arthur may have been that Captain Arthur of Hackettstown who opted to go to France after the treaty was signed. Máire, the second daughter, married Colonel William Dorrington, an Englishman and one of the notable military officers of the later seventeenth century. After Limerick he went abroad where he was appointed Lieutenant-General of the royal armies in 1704; he died at Paris in 1718. In 1841 the Count and the Chevalier Macclesfield Dorrington, brothers aged eighty-five and seventy-four respectively, descended from Colonel Dorrington and Máire Ní Cheallacháin, died within a few days of one another. Siobhán or Joan, the sister of Donnchadh, and daughter of Domhnall Mór na Pálach, married Murchadh Ó Briain or Murrough O Brien, Major-General in France, who commanded the Regiment of O Brien until his death in 1720. His son by Siobhán, Domhnall or Donal O Brien, O Brien, Colonel of Lord Clare's regiment, was made earl of Lismore for his service to the Stuarts and died in Rome in 1759. Siobhán's grandson, Séamas Domhnall Ó Briain served as Captain in Ruth's Regiment in 1766. During an inquiry in 1761 into the relationship between Murrough O Brien's family and the O Briens of Clare, Donough O Callaghan of Kilgory, the chief of his name, affirmed that Murrough had married "Julian Callaghan of Pale," that is Siobhán or Joan. The investigators concluded that the O Callaghans of Clare "will not willingly lessen the name and character of Lord Lismore, whose father was married to their relation Julian Callaghan."[36]

The O Callaghans of Baden-Baden

The descendants of Donough O Callaghan, transplanted to County Clare, eventually established branches of the family in Germany and Spain. Donough's third son, Cahir O Callaghan of Leatherdon (Lahardaun), County Clare, and his wife Ellen FitzGerald (daughter of Maurice FitzGerald of Inchinacrannagh) had two sons. The eldest, John, "late Captain in O Brien's Regiment," died in the service of Louis XIV; a declaration of his nobility was issued on 17 March 1712 at Saint-Germain-en-Laye and presented to his widow. From Cahir's second son, Cornelius, a Captain in the Regiment of Ultonia in Spain, are descended the Spanish O Callaghans; more will be said of him later.[37]

Captain John O Callaghan, just mentioned, was the father of two young men who found service with the margrave of Baden-Baden, a territory situated a few miles east of the Rhine in

---

[36] See the testimony of Síle Ní Cheallacháin given in 1762 in Joseph F. O Callaghan, "The O Callaghans of Kilcranathan, County Cork," *JCHAS* 92 (1987): 106-112; John Ainsworth, *The Inchiquin Manuscripts* (Dublin: Irish Manuscripts Commission, 1961), 169, 171, 173-181, 186, nos. 570, 572, 581, 583, 592-594, 606.

[37] *Calendar of the Stuart Papers belonging to his Majesty the King preserved at Windsor Castle*, 6 vols., ed. F. H. B. Daniell (London: Historical Manuscripts Commission, 1902), 1:244; *BIFR*, 889.

the Black Forest in southwestern Germany. The elder of the two brothers, James Louis O Callaghan, apparently was named for the two sovereigns his father served, namely, James II of England and Louis XIV of France. William Hawkins, Ulster King of Arms, on 26 August 1765 recorded his genealogy and arms (a wolf exiting from a wood) as a descendant of Cahir Modarta of Dromaneen. At that date James Louis bore the title of Baron and *Magnus Venator* or Chief Huntsman of the margrave of Baden-Baden. Thus far no further information about him or his possible descendants has come to light.

His brother, Louis Denis O Callaghan, was probably named for Louis XIV and his paternal grandfather, Donough, as well as the patron saint of France. Again William Hawkins testified on 3 September 1768 to his genealogy and arms. At that time Louis Denis also had the title of Baron and *Magnus Venator* of Baden-Baden, perhaps in succession to his brother, who may have died. According to records of the margravate, Louis Denis, known by his German name, Ludwig Dionysius, transformed the family name O Callaghan into the more Germanic form von Gallahan or von Gallahann. As early as 1730-1731 he received funds for his maintenance from the margrave. He was Chief Bailiff (*Oberamtmann*) in Rastatt (a few miles north of Baden-Baden and south of Karlsruhe) and Kuppenheim, and Chief Master of the Hunt (*Oberjägermeister*), as well as a member of the Secret Council. On 20 September 1736 he was admitted to the *Ordre de la Fidelité* or Order of Fidelity, a noble association founded in 1715 by the Margrave Karl Wilhelm of Baden-Durlach. He married Maria Josepha, Baroness von Russenstein.

When the Catholic line of the margraves of Baden-Baden died out in 1771, their lands were united to those of the Evangelical Lutheran branch of the family known as Baden-Durlach. As a consequence, Karl Friedrich, the new margrave, in 1772 gave Louis Denis, now retired, a pension and an estate at Lahr (south of Baden-Baden in the so-called Morburgerhofes). He lived with his daughters at Strassbourg (on the Rhine directly west of Baden-Baden and Lahr), where he died on 1 February 1784. His daughter Maria Anna, lady-in-waiting to the marchioness, in 1769 married Baron Julius von Hornstein. She died after a long illness, aged 59, on 29 April 1798, and was buried in the church of Bietingen. Her sister Maria Louisa in 1776 wedded Baron Franz Karl von Weitersheim. At that point we lose sight of this family, whose history illustrates the process whereby Irish exiles were integrated into the society where they found themselves. In the case of Louis Denis, the process of acculturation led to an alteration of his family name so that it no longer appeared Irish. By the further process of intermarriage, his daughters, known by the name of von Gallahan, were fully assimilated into German society. Whether they had children is unknown; one can only speculate how long remembrance of the Irish connection persisted in this family.[38]

The O Callaghans in Spain

At the outset of the seventeenth century, when Spain controlled the Netherlands and was viewed as England's archenemy, many Irishmen entered Spanish service. In 1638 the Spanish government, with the consent of Charles I of England, surely pleased to be rid of potential troublemakers, organized the *Regimiento de Irlanda*.[39] Composed of Irish troops, the Regiment

---

[38] Dublin, GO, MS 165, pp. 1-3, 78-80; Karlsruhe, Badische Generallandesarchiv, 173, nos. 40, 42, 220/513, 2575-2576, 2685-2686; Edward Freiherr v. Hornstein–Grüningen, *Die von Hornstein und von Hertenstein Erlebnisse aus 700 Jahren* (Konstanz: Pressverein, 1811), 614-616; *BIFR*, 889.

took part in the long war between Spain and France that evolved from the Thirty Years' War, but in 1659 the Treaty of the Pyrenees brought hostilities to a close. When Louis XIV then tried to extend his frontiers by claiming the Spanish Netherlands as his wife's inheritance, he provoked the opposition of the Dutch, the English, and the Holy Roman Empire who regarded French expansion with alarm.[40]

In these circumstances various O Callaghans served in the Spanish army in the Netherlands. The earliest recorded individual was Denis Callaghan, who had participated in the Irish wars in defense of the Catholic cause; in 1605 he received a grant of six crowns monthly from King Philip III of Spain to serve in the Irish Infantry. In 1658 Charles Callaghan, an ensign with the troops in Lorraine, was commissioned as an ensign in the Irish infantry company of Captain Florence Carty in the Regiment of Colonel van der Clussen. In addition to the soldiers, John Callaghan was a military chaplain in the regiment of Colonel Owen O Neill - the famous Owen Roe - stationed in the Spanish Netherlands, and received a monthly wage of twelve crowns in 1638. Six years later he was transferred from the Spanish infantry regiment of Colonel de Velardia to the infantry company of Captain Roque Negrete, governor of the royal fortress at St. Philip at Gravelines. Licensed to go to Spain on business in 1662, he was described as licentiate (an academic degree either in theology or canon law) and senior chaplain of the royal hospital of Malines in present-day Belgium.[41]

Captain Malachy O Calan, whose company in Colonel John Morfi (Murphy)'s regiment was disbanded in 1656, was likely another O Callaghan in the Spanish army in the Netherlands. Two years later Malachy Calahan, no doubt the same person, was commissioned as captain of a company of Irish infantry in Colonel Murphy's Regiment. Other O Callaghans in the Spanish army included Lieutenant Daniel O Kalechane serving in the regiment of Colonel Theodore de Meara (O Meara) in the army of the French Prince Condé. The regiment was disbanded when the Treaty of the Pyrenees in 1659 ended the war between France and Spain and Lieutenant Daniel, along with others, in 1660 received a special grant of six crowns in addition to his pay.[42]

Irish soldiers appeared in Spain in large numbers as a result of the War of the Spanish Succession (1701-1713). The war followed the death of Charles II of Spain, who, lacking immediate heirs, designated as his successor the grandson of Louis XIV of France, namely, the future Philip V. Wary of this expansion of Bourbon power, the Holy Roman Empire, England, and the Netherlands formed an alliance in opposition. In order to uphold his rights, Philip V brought Irish troops from France to Spain and organized them in five Spanish regiments:

---

[39] O Callaghan, *Brigades,* 293. The "Marcha del Regimiento de Irlanda" was a musical celebration of the regiment.

[40] Hugo O'Donnell, ed., *Presencia irlandesa en la Milicia española. The Irish Presence in the Spanish Military – 16th to 20th Centuries* (Madrid: 2014).

[41] Jennings, *Geese,* 81, 305, 362, 414, 450, nos. 168 (4 November 1605), 1544 (16 November 1638), 1858 (12 May 1644), 2235 (25 April 1658) 2606 (12 September 1662); O Hart, *Gentry,* 495.

[42] Jennings, *Geese,* 401-402, 415, nos. 2122 (15 January 1656), 2132 (20 Janaury 1656), 2240 (28 July 1658); Captain Walter Cahalan of O Neill's Regiment in 1642 (referred to as Captain Walter Calan in 1651) and Art O Calan, adjutant in the O Donnell's Regiment in 1644 probably did not belong to the O Callaghans of Cork; *ibid.,* 356-357, 362, 385, 428, nos. 1796-1797, 1799, 1861, 2004, 2381. Nor was Daniel O Callaghan, born in County Cavan, Ireland and sponsor for Raymond O Brady in 1667, one of the Cork O Callaghans; Micheline Walsh, *Spanish Knights of Irish Origin: Documents from Continental Archives,* 3 vols. (Dublin: Irish Manuscripts Commission, 1970), 3:10, no. 337; O Hart, *Gentry,* 495.

Hibernia, Ultonia (Ulster), Irlanda, Limerick and Waterford. He stipulated that they should be recruited from young Irishmen of noble families. When the French and Spanish forces won a victory over the imperial army at Luzzara on the Po River in Northern Italy on 15 August 1702, Lieutenant John O Callaghan was mortally wounded.[43]

Another O Callaghan who survived wounds received in the war, though enlisted on the other side, was Captain Ferdinand O Callaghan, an officer in the Regiment of Count Reventlow, then in Catalonia in the service of the Holy Roman Emperor Joseph I. According to a report issued by the regimental commander, General Anthony Dwyer, at Barcelona in March 1710, Captain O Callaghan "acquitted himself in all places and occasions in storms, sieges and battles as behoveth a brave, honourable, and trusty officer, but being by many wounds, bruises, and other infirmities rendered incapable of his post and having in due manner requested of me his discharge to return to his own country which I could not nor would refuse him, I request all military and civil magistrates to aid and assist him to pass securely and without molestation." Three years later General James Stanhope certified that O Callaghan was wounded while serving in Catalonia as a captain in General Reventlow's ("Ravenclough's") regiment. Doctor J. Lecann, director of Queen Anne's Hospital in Catalonia, certified that O Callaghan was "dangerously wounded . . . and, the climate being so contrary, was obliged to quit the country." Captain Ferdinand may perhaps be the same as Ferdinando Callahan [or Ferdinand O Callahan] who petitioned the Duke of Ormond in 1713 seeking some military employment:

> If your Grace be pleased to inform yourself, from Sir William Windham, about the list of the Roman Catholic officers, that was sent into France, the necessary directions I gave in the matter, and the search that was made in the offices there, 'tis then your Grace will be thoroughly satisfied of the truth of what I gave in evidence to your Grace and the Comittee against them, &c., which proceedings has put a stop to forty officers more of the same stamp, that would be put in (if they succeeded) to be on the same establishment. My negotiations in these matters oblige me now to complain to your Grace of the continual danger I am in of my life, being attacked two or three times at night by some gangue and very narrowly escaped, besides am attacked otherwise with false actions and a hundred other villanies by them, and others by their procurement.[44]

It would seem that Ferdinando found himself unwelcome among his fellow Irish soldiers because he was not on the French and Spanish side. Nevertheless, his appeal to Ormonde apparently was successful because in 1715 he received a pension of £80 from George I. He may have used that money to acquire land in Maryland where "Ferdinando Callaghan's plantation" was mentioned in June 1748 in a proposed division of St. Paul's Parish.[45]

---

[43] Marquess MacSwiney of Mashanaglass, "The Casualty List of the Infantry Regiment of Albemarle in the Battle of Luzzara, 15th August 1702," *JRSAI* 60 (1930): 84-90; O Callaghan, *Brigades*, 217-218, 274-279, 293D'Alton, *Army List*, 868; Walsh, *Knights*, 3:67, no. 111; Anthony MacDermott, "The Irish Regiments in the Spanish Service," *TIG* 2:9 (1952): 259-268.

[44] *The Manuscripts of his Grace the Duke of Portland preserved at Welbeck Abbey*, 10 vols. (London: Historical Manuscripts Commision, 1891-1931), 10:91 (15-16 September 1713); *Ormonde MSS*, 216-217 (20 March 1713/1714).

[45] *The Journals of the House of Commons of the Kingdom of Ireland from the Second to the Tenth Year of King George the First, viz., From 1715 to 1723, vol. IV* (Dublin: Abraham Bradley, 1763), 78; Thomas Bacon, *Laws of Maryland* (Annapolis: Jonas Green, 1765), June 1748.

Among the O Callaghans serving in the Irish regiments in eighteenth-century Spain were:

Name	Regiment	Date
Morgan, Lieutenant	Irlanda	1715
Cornelius, Sergeant-Major	Ultonia	1718
Callaghan, Cadet	Waterford	1719
Julian, Cadet	Ultonia	1725
Denis, Cadet	Waterford	1731
John, Sergeant	Waterford	1731
Denis, Cadet; Sublieutenant; Captain; Lieutenant Colonel	Irlanda	1733 1734, 1737 1741, 1752, 1761, 1766
John, Sergeant	Irlanda	1733
Denis, Cadet	Hibernia	1741
Thady (Tadhg, Tadeo)	Ultonia	1772

Lieutenant Morgan was described as *teniente reformado*, that is, either on half pay or unemployed. He may have been a son of the chieftain Donough Mór. Sergeant-Major Cornelius held a rank just below Lieutenant Colonel. The Regiment of Waterford, organized in 1709, was disbanded in 1734. As late as 1782, there were as many as 2,400 Irish soldiers in the three regiments of Irlanda, Hibernia and Ultonia.[46]

Cornelius O Callaghan (1693-1741), a son of Cahir of Leatherdon (Lahardaun) and grandson of Donough Mór, became the progenitor of the O Callaghan family of Barcelona, whose head, Juan O Callaghan Casas, was recognized in 1944 as chief of his name. Identified as a native of Ardan, County Clare, Cornelius, a captain in the Regiment of Ultonia, in 1729 wed Paula de Dameto of Benisanet in the the province of Tarragona, by whom he had four children: Carlos, Dionisio, Francisca, and Elena. The first two names are reminiscent of the names of his father and grandfather: Cahir or Charles and Donough or Denis; Elena of course was also an Irish name, Ellen or Oiléan. Cornelius served in Algeria where the Spaniards had long controlled Oran and he died there in 1741. More will be said of his family in the following chapters.[47]

O Callaghans in the Spanish Military Orders

Many Irishmen settled in Spain in the service of the crown sought admission to the Military Orders of Santiago, Calatrava, and Alcántara, once major elements in the Christian Defense of medieval Spain against the Moors, but now essentially honorary associations of noblemen. Perhaps the earliest O Callaghan descendant to be admitted to one of the Orders was Domingo O Morough MacCarthy O Daly y O Callaghan, born in La Guardia, Portugal, the son

[46] Herbert Gallwey, "Irish Officers in the Spanish Service: III. The Regiment of Waterford," and "IV: The Regiment of Irlanda," and "VI. The Regiment of Hibernia," *TIG* 6:1 (1980): 18-21, and 6:2 (1981): 204-211, and 6:4 (1983): 461-468; John Oakland, "Irish Officers in the Spanish Service: V. The Regiment of Irlanda (concluded)," *TIG* 6:2 (1982): 328-333; O Hart, *Pedigrees,* 2:659, Appendix I; O Callaghan, *Brigades,* 293.
[47] Dublin, GO, MS 182, p. 569; *BIFR,* 889.

of Teige O Morough O Daly of Ross and Mariana, the daughter of Manuel (or Michael?) MacCarthy of Manch, and Mary O Callaghan. Mary and her sister Ellen were the daughters of the chieftain Callaghan O Callaghan of Clonmeen and Joanna Butler. Domingo applied for admission to the Military Order of Calatrava in 1657, submitting his genealogy, and received the habit of the Order in 1663.[48]

More than three hundred pages of documentation preserved in the archives of the Military Orders of Santiago and Alcántara in the Archivo Histórico Nacional in Madrid present the proofs of nobility and Catholicity required for the admission to the Orders of two members of the O Callaghan family of Muskerry. Although the name MacCallaghan had been used there in the previous century by the eighteenth O Callaghan had become common, making difficult any distinction from the O Callaghans of Duhallow. In addition to recording genealogies to the fourth generation, the proofs include the testimony of numerous Irishmen in Spain, soldiers, merchants, and bankers, who knew the candidates. This material is useful not only in tracing the family history of the candidates, but it also throws some light upon the fairly numerous Irish colony in Madrid, as well as the attempts of the exiles and their relatives in Ireland to maintain contact.

In 1722 Mathew O Callaghan, Captain of Dragoons, applied for admission to the Spanish Military Order of Santiago and achieved that goal two years later. According to his own account he had come to Spain twenty-eight years before, that is, in 1694. Military records show that in 1709 Mateo Calakam (a tortured Spanish rendering of his surname) was Ayudante Mayor of Alcira and was appointed Colonel of Dragoons *reformado.*[49] His documentation showed him to be the son of Eugene O Callaghan of Carrigadrohid, Barony of Muskerry, County Cork, and of Catherine Power of Torbeagh, Barony of Imokilly, County Cork. His paternal grandparents were Cornelius O Callaghan of Carrigadrohid and Ellen MacCarthy of Macroom; David Power and Joanna Condon, both of Torbeagh, were his maternal grandparents. He was baptized on 21 September 1666 by Fr. Denis O Callaghan, pastor of the parish of Carrigadrohid. His godparents were Eugene MacCarthy and Mary Egan.

Matthew stipulated that his family were known as lords of Carrigadrohid and the adjacent villages from the coming of the Spanish Milesians to Ireland until the reign of Queen Elizabeth when they were dispossessed because of their adherence to the Catholic religion. Carrigadrohid castle, lying to the west of Coachford, stands on an island in the middle of the river Sullane; a bridge of three arches serves to connect it to the mainland. Built apparently by MacCarthy of Muskerry to protect this ford on the river Lee, the castle was seized by Lord Broghill in 1650. With his three brothers, Matthew entered the Irish army in the service of James II about 1684. His brothers reportedly died in defense of "our sacred religion," but Mathew survived. After Limerick he sailed for France and first came to Catalonia in Spain probably in 1696 (when he was about thirty), as a cadet in a Company of Guards and as interpreter to Lieutenant-General Arthur O Brien, commander of Irish soldiers dispatched to Spain by Louis XIV. General O Brien was related to him in the fourth degree, and, as the witnesses testified, "esteemed him greatly."[50]

[48] Marquesa de Ciadoncha, *Los caballeros portugueses en las Ordenes militares españolas* (Lisbon: Sociedade Cestíoria, 1946), 57. Maria O Callaghan was born in the Castle of Clermien, obviously a misspelling for Clonmeen. Manuel, the name given her husband, seems highly unlikely and is probably a misspelling, perhaps for Michael. Teige O Morough O Daly was the son of Edmund O Morough of Ross and Joanna O Daly of Dromsicane.

[49] Emilio de Cárdenas Piera, *Indice onomástico de la colección de libros de registro del Archivo General Militar de Madrid* (Madrid: Ministerio de Defensa, 2005), 105.

[50] Madrid, Archivo Histórico Nacional, Ordenes Militares, Santiago, Expediente 5795; James Cooney,

For twenty-eight years Matthew resided in Spain in the king's service and was known as a faithful Catholic. While witnesses testified to his ancestry, conduct and religious beliefs, the interrogators were hesitant to propose his admission to the Order because he lacked a baptismal certificate and any other documents. To meet this objection, he explained that the soldiers who went into exile in 1691 were unable to carry documents with them and would have difficulty obtaining them from Ireland. Under the persistence of the interrogators, he finally secured a Latin letter from Bishop Denis MacCarthy of Cork and Denis MacSweeney, the parish priest of Carrigdrohid, testifying to his baptism in 1666. The bishop's letter was dated 12 July 1723 "*in loco nostro refugii*" – "in the place of our refuge" - an expression that caused some consternation among the Spanish commissioners until it was explained to them that the bishop's failure to identify his residence was intended to protect him and his people from the harassment of the Penal Laws. Twenty-eight witnesses, chiefly Irish soldiers in Spanish service, but also a banker, a priest, and a Franciscan friar, testified in Matthew's behalf. One of them, Captain Thady O Callaghan from County Cork, was not related to him, but may have belonged to the O Callaghans of Clonmeen and Dromaneen.[51]

Besides the evidence of his baptism, Matthew was also able to produce a letter from James, duke of Ormond, dated 7 December 1722, to the effect that the O Callaghans were known to be Roman Catholics of noble rank. As further evidence of his nobility, Matthew presented a certificate dated 28 May 1723 from James Terry, King of Arms to the Old Pretender, James III, describing the arms of the O Callaghan family as follows: "on a silver shield, issuing on the left from a green wood, a wolf, in its own colors." When Terry recorded the death in 1707 of Robert Cusack, who had been married to a daughter of O Callaghan, he gave the same description of the family arms: "d'argent au loup contrepassant de sable, sortant d'une foret de sinople." To my knowledge, this is the earliest description of the O Callaghan arms. The same arms were depicted In eighteenth-century genealogical documents of the O Callaghans of Duhallow. In addition, Terry affirmed that the family was descended from Ailill Alum, king of Munster, of the race of Milesius the Spaniard. Ailill Alum, said to be the progenitor of the Eoghanact from whom the O Callaghans and MacCarthys descended, reigned around one hundred sixty years before the coming of Christ.[52] King Philip V formally approved Matthew's acceptance as a knight of Santiago in 1724. He was then about fifty-eight years of age.

We hear no more about Matthew until twenty years later when, as Don Mateo O Callaghan, Captain of Dragoons and knight of Santiago, he testified on behalf of his cousin, Dionisio O Callaghan y White, who applied for admission to the Order of Alcántara in 1744. As there is no evidence of another Matthew O Callaghan, knight of Santiago, then he would have been about seventy-eight years old. Dionisio's family came from Carrignavar (Carraig na

---

Macroom People and Places: A Brief Historical Sketch (Macroom: Macroom and District Literary, Historical and Archaeological Society, 1976), 11-12; O Murchadha, *Names,* 59.

[51] Walsh, *Knights,* 3:63-70, nos. 115-126, One of the witnesses, David Power, who was probably Mathew's cousin, offered three letters from his cousin, Fr. Denis MacSweeney, to James Power dated 6 June 1721, 16 May 1722, and 9 August 1723, as evidence of the priest's handwriting and the authenticity of the baptismal certificate that he had signed. James FitzJames Stuart, duke of Liria, and son of the duke of Berwick, testified to Mathew's conduct while living in France.

[52] Walsh, *Knights,* 3:68, no. 124 (28 May 1723, Versailles); *The Pedigrees and Papers of James Terry, Athlone Herald at the Court of James II in France 1725,* ed. Charles E. Lart (Exeter: William Pollard, 1938), 46, no. 14.

Bhfear) in County Cork and his genealogy offers some interesting information.[53]

    Dionisio's great-grandparents were Teige O Callaghan and Margaret MacCarthy, both of Carrignavar. Perhaps born about 1619, Teige was said to be a native of Cashel (probably Castle Inch, Caisleán na hInsí) and Margaret came from Cork. The MacCarthys appear to have acquired Carrignavar following the overthrow of the earl of Desmond about 1588. Daniel MacCarthy, an Irish Papist, was recorded as proprietor in the Civil Survey of 1654-1656. CastleInch stood on the southern bank of the River Lee between Macroom on the west and Ballincollig on the east.[54] Teige was also described as *"conde de Clanscarti,"* or earl of Clancarthy, and according to one witness was reported to have "had many tasks by sea and land in the service of King Charles I of England in the parliaments of Ireland." Thus his career would coincide with the regnal years of Charles I from 1625 to 1649. Two parliaments were held in the king's name in Ireland in 1634 and 1640, but I have not been able to discover any information concerning Teige's involvement in them. The basis of his claim to be earl of Clancarthy is uncertain. In 1658 the exiled Charles II first bestowed that title on Donough MacCarthy, viscount Muskerry, who died in 1665. The death of Donough's son Charles in 1665 and his infant son of the same name in 1666 may have prompted Teige to put forward a claim in the name of his wife Margaret. I believe she was Donough's daughter, who is recorded as the wife of Luke Plunkett, third earl of Fingall. She may have married him after the death of her first husband Teige O Callaghan. Meanwhile, the title of earl of Clancarthy eventually passed to Donough's son Callaghan MacCarthy (d. 1676). His son Donough forfeited the title for supporting James II against William of Orange.[55]

    Dionisio's genealogy tells us that Teige's son, Denis (perhaps born circa 1652) of Carrignavar, married Mary MacCarthy; the daughter of Patrick MacCarthy of Muskerry and Winifred White, both of Cork. Denis was described, in his son Julian's will, as "head of the ancient and illustrious house of O Callaghan in the kingdom of Ireland." - *"Caveza de la antigua y ilustre casa de O Callaghan en el reyno de Irlanda."* Denis or Donough O Callaghan, then resident in Castle Inch (Castle ne Hensy), purchased the castle, town and farm of Carrignavar, to hold for one year at a pepper corn rent, from Charles (Cormac) MacCarthy of Carrignavar, a first cousin of Donough, the first earl of Clancarthy, and Theobald Matthew of Annfield, County Tipperary, on 14 September 1683.[56]

    Dionisio's father, Julian O Callaghan, a native of Carrignavar, born perhaps around 1685, served both in James II's army and later in the Spanish army. In a letter of recommendation, written at Versailles on 14 April 1708, Lieutenant General William Dorrington, colonel of the Regiment of Lifeguards of James III, the Stuart claimant to the English throne, related something of Julian's career. He was "the first-born heir of one of the most ancient and most illustrious houses of Ireland," a family that had lost most of its estates in faithful service to their legitimate

[53] Madrid, Archivo Histórico Nacional, Ordenes Militares, Pruebas de Caballeros, Alcántara, Expediente 1080; Walsh, *Knights*, 3:

[54] "The late 15th century tower house of Castle Inch (now demolished as a result of the Iniscarra hydro-electric scheme) was long in contention between the Barretts and the MacCarthys of Muskerry." Ó Murchadha, *Names*, 16, 18.59, 61.

[55] R. C. Simington, ed., *The Civil Survey, A. D. 1654-1656*, 10 vols. (Dublin: Stationery Office, 1936-1961) 6:161-162. Sir Cormac mac Teige MacCarthy, the Fourteenth Lord of Muskerry, took initial possession of Carrignavar. In 1641 Cormac or Charles MacCarthy, the son of Donal (Daniel), a son of Sir Cormac mac Dermod, the Sixteenth Lord of Muskerry, held Carrignavar. Donal's brother Cormac was the first Viscount Muskerry. In 1688 Donal's son Cormac or Charles was in possession. Butler, *Gleanings*, 126; O Hart, *Pedigrees*, 1:135.

[56] John T. Collins, "Some Cork Wills, Deeds and Indentures," *JCHAS* 64 (1959): 107-108.

kings. For seventeen years he had served in Dorrington's Regiment as *alférez* (ensign), lieutenant, captain, and aide-de-camp, fulfilling his duties with honor and valor. Given the date of Dorrington's letter and his reference to Julian's seventeen years of service, Julian likely came to France in 1691, after the Treaty of Limerick. Dorrington detailed Julian's participation in all the Regiment's sieges, battles, and military actions, suffering wounds, and having his horse killed under him. Now that Julian wished to enter the service of the king of Spain, Dorrington gave him a well-merited commendation.

Dorrington's letter, written in French, was translated into Spanish and included in a memorial composed by the marquess of Castellar on 14 April 1726. Upon coming to Spain in 1709, Julian was named *Coronel Agregado* in Count Mahony's Regiment of Dragoons, and later in the same year he was given the same rank in the Regiment of Milan. As it was commonplace to refer to a regiment by the name of its commanding officer, the *Regimiento de O Calahane* cited in 1711, was likely the Regiment of Milan. After notable service in several engagements, and being wounded in the battle of Zaragoza, he was given command of the Regiment of Milan. At the battle of Villaviciosa on 10 December 1719, despite being wounded in his body, he rallied his troops, scattering the enemy cavalry and ravaging the infantry. His wise counsel during the night saved the king from grave danger, prompting him to praise Julian before the entire court. Another witness reported: "The Sieur Ockalagan, being for the 3rd time, in the thick of the fight, where he defended the standards of Milan with a proud intrepidity, received a sword thrust through his body, and many wounds, by which he was for some time disfigured . . . . His Catholic Majesty then honored him with the Regiment of Dragoons of Killmalock, vacant because of the death of its colonel."[57] When Castellar wrote his memorial, Julian had already given nineteen years of honorable service to the king of Spain and had been advanced to the rank of Brigadier. He was also appointed Governor of Balaguer in Catalonia and of other places.[58]

Julian married Anna Christina White, a native of Dublin, the daughter of Ignatius White, marquess of Albeville and Count of Albi, and Maria Warren, in the chapel of the royal palace at Madrid on 8 January 1716.[59] Jacinto Muñoz Castilblanque, chaplain of honor and preacher to King Philip V and curate of the royal palace, witnessed their union at four p.m. in the chambers of the countess of Attarnina, lady-in-waiting (*camarera mayor*) to the queen. The marriage record identified the groom as "Julian O Callaghan y Laze, native of Carignavar in the diocese of Cork," the son of "Dionisio O Callaghan y Laze and Maria Mccarthy." The name "Dionisio O Callaghan y Laze" indicates that Julian's grandmother (Denis's mother) was a member of the Lacy or de Lacy family. The families were also connected by the marriage of Colonel William de Lacy to Theresa White, Julian's sister-in-law. Colonel de Lacy was among those who testified in support of Dionisio's application for admission to the Order of Alcántara.

[57] Chevalier de Bellerive, *Histoire des campagnes de Monseigneur le Duc de Vendosome* (Paris: Pierre Prault 1715), 226-227; O Callaghan, *Brigades*, 279.

[58] Oscar Hernanz Elvira, "Documents concerning an Irish soldier in Spanish Service, Julian O'Callaghan MacCarthy (d. 1727)," *Archivium Hibernicum* 67 (2014): 313-318, no. 1; Emilio de Cárdenas Piera, *Indice onomástico de la colección de libros de registro del Archivo General Militar de Madrid* (Madrid: Ministerio de Defensa, 2005), 443, records that Julian was appointed Captain of Dragoons in 1709; Colonel, named Capitán de la Compañía del Regimiento de Caballería de Jaén, 1711; and Colonel of the Regimiento de Dragones del Visconde de Killmallock, 1711.

[59] John J. Silke, "The Irish Abroad, 1534-1691," *NHI*, 3:607, 623-624; Bellings, *History,* 4:189-210; Walsh, *Knights*, 3:13; Jennings, *Geese*, 384, 456; *Commentarius Rinuccinianus*, 4:411-413.

The marriage of Julian and Anna Christina was blessed by the birth on 8 July 1718, in Madrid, of a son Dionisio, named no doubt for his paternal grandfather Denis or Donough. Perhaps one of the first children born to Irish exiles in Spain, he was baptized in the parish church of San Juan Bautista on 20 July by the parish priest Manuel González de Artoaza. His parents, residing in the houses of the Count of Villa Alonso, opposite the Church, were members of the parish. The child's aunt, Winifred White, acted as proxy godmother for Maria Warren, marchioness of Albeville, Anna Christina's mother. In addition to the name Dionisio, he received as patrons Saints John, Joseph and Francis Xavier.[60]

The death of Maria Warren, the marchioness of Albeville, probably prompted Julian, together with Don Antonio Sartine, Don Antonio Álvarez de Bohorque,[61] Don Simon Connock and Don Guillermo Lacy (William de Lacy), to petition for use of the imperial titles of count of Albi and marquess of Albeville. All of them were married to the daughters of Ignatius White, who originally held these titles. The royal response given in 1725, however, was "se les atenderá," that is, no decision was made at that time. Nevertheless as Anna Christina White was identified in the documents of 1744 as marchioness of Albeville, it would appear that a decision was made in her favor, though it probably occurred after her husband's death.[62]

In his will of 22 July 1726, Julian and Anna Christina named Dionisio their only and universal heir. Julian unfortunately died suddenly in an accident on 11 January 1727. "Having always lived as a faithful Catholic, Christian, Apostolic, and Roman, and having frequented the sacraments as such," he received the sacrament of extreme unction before he died. On the next day his widow made a statement to the effect that he allowed her to appoint executors of his estate, naming Dionisio as his heir. Julian chose to be buried in the church where he had been a parishioner for life, San Juan Bautista, as he had lived in the adjacent *alcázar* or royal palace. He was buried in the church in one of the niches below the main altar on 13 January 1727. Seven years later a fire destroyed the *alcázar*. When the king ordered the construction of a new *Palacio real* in the Plaza de Oriente, the parish church of San Juan Bautista was torn down. As a consequence, Julian's grave has disappeared. After his death, his widow, Anna Christina, petitioned Philip V for a pension that would enable her to settle his debts and also to educate their young son Dionisio. The king responded on 14 March 1727 by giving Dionisio a pension of 1,000 ducats for his upbringing and education. As lady-in-waiting (*señora de honor*) to Queen Isabel of Spain and governess (*aya*) to the Infanta María Theresa, Anna Christina had received a pension of 1,000 ducats on 4 February 1724. She died in 1732 and was buried on Wednesday, 23

---

[60] Madrid, Archivo Histórico Nacional, Ordenes Militares, Pruebas de Caballeros, Alcántara, Expediente 1080, fol. 237v: Baptismal certificate, 20 July 1718.

[61] Anna Christina's third sister, Winifred White, born in The Hague, married Antonio José Álvarez de Bohorque, knight of Santiago and Lieutenant-General in the Spanish army. Their son, José Álvarez de Bohorque, born in Cádiz, was admitted to the Order of Santiago on 3 December 1741. Eusebio Bohorque, named as one of the executors of Anna Christina's will, was perhaps a brother or son of Antonio José. Simon Connock and Maria White de Albeville were identified as natives of Carrignavar; Walsh, *Knights,* 2:12-19, nos. 25-39.

[62] Madrid, Archivo Histórico Nacional, Asiento de consulta sobre que se permite a D. Julián O Callaghan, don Antonio Sartine, don Antonio Álvarez de Bohorque, don Simón Connock, y don Guillermo Lacy el uso del título de Conde de Albi y Marqués de Albiville, mercedes imperiales. Se les atenderá. 1725. [Está en consultas del año 1740 al núm. 120]. Libro 2757, año 1725, núm. 4, fols. 136v-137r. *Catálogo alfabético de los documentos referentes a Títulos del Reino y Grandezas de España conservados en la Sección de Consejos suprimidos*, 3 vols. (Madrid: Archivo Histórico Nacional, 1952), 2:570. Walsh, *Knights,* 2:40, no. 70 cites Don Julian O Calaghan as resident in Madrid on 28 May 1725.

January, in the convent of Santiago, outside the walls of Seville.[63]

Given the family connections among the O Callaghans, Connocks, and Lacys, it seems possible that Dionisio, Julian's and Anna Christina's son, may be identified with that Dionisio O Callaghan who was a baptismal sponsor, together with Maria Connock, for Maria Francisca Lacy in the parish of San Martín, Madrid on 27 December 1729. If that were true, he would only have been eleven years old, so it is possible that there was another Dionisio. Nevertheless, Philip V, on 15 April 1744, admitted Dionisio, then aged twenty-six, and holding the rank of Ayudante-Mayor in the Guardias de Infantería Española, to the Order of Alcántara. The propensity of the O Callaghans to use certain personal names repeatedly can lead to confusion. Thus Captain Dionisio O Callaghan, born in Ireland, who sponsored Joseph Comerford's application to the Military Order of Calatrava in 1747, is probably not the same person as the Ayudante-Mayor just mentioned. Identified in his will drawn up in Barcelona in 1755 as colonel of infantry, and captain in the Regiment of Royal Guards of Spain, and Commander of Esparragal in the Order of Alcántara, Dionisio expressed his wish to be buried in the church of the Discalced Trinitarian Fathers of Barcelona in the pantheon of his regiment. His heirs were his three aunts, Winifred, Maria, and Theresa White y Albeville, the last two being *señoras de honor* to the queen. His papers were to be entrusted to his aunt Winifred, marchioness of Ruchena.[64]

Another O Callaghan in the Spanish service, Captain Thady (Thadeo), a character witness in 1726 for Matthew O Callaghan, whose application for admission to the Order of Santiago has already been considered, emphasized that they were not related. Thady, born around 1694 at Ermenen (probably a scribe's error for Clonmeen), seven leagues from Carrigadrohid, was a Captain of Dragoons in the *Regimiento de Suezia* (the Regiment of Switzerland), and resided in 1726 in the Calle de los Tedescos in Madrid. Possibly he was the same Captain Thady who formed part of the entourage accompanying the Spanish Ambassador La Mina to the court of Louis XIV of France at Versailles in 1739. The purpose of the embassy was to complete the arrangements for the hapter When the ambassador presented her with a picture of the prince on 23 August 1739 and again two days later, "Thadee O Chalagan, Capitaine de Dragones," was present. He probably also joined her when she departed for Spain at the end of the month. More likely, he can be also identified with that Captain Thady O Callaghan born in Cork, who was a sponsor in 1741 for José Alvarez de Bohorque who sought admission to the Military Order of Santiago.[65]

As one reads of the exploits of these and the other anonymous Irish soldiers in the service of France, Germany, Spain, and other continental countries, one can only be struck by the

[63] Statement of Anna Christina White, January 12, 1727, Madrid. Copy, May 19, 1744, Madrid; nformation from copy May 18, 1744; Information from copy of April 28, 1744. King Philip V on 4 February 1724 granted a pension of 1,000 ducats to Anna Christina and on 14 March 1727 another pension of 1,000 ducats to Dionisio for his upbringing and education. Madrid, Archivo General de Palacio, caja 32, expediente, 2. Hernanz Elvira, "Documents," 318, no. 2, published Anna's request for a pension.

[64] Madrid, Archivo Histórico Nacional, Ordenes Militares, Pruebas de Caballeros, Calatrava, Expediente 614; Walsh, *Knights,* 3:44, nos. 77-78; "Irish Wills from Barcelona. Second Series," *TIG* 6:4 (1983): 473-474. Francisco O Callaghan y de Gournay served in Cuba in the nineteenth century. Madrid, Biblioteca Nacional, 807: Datos para escribir la historia de la isla de Cuba durante el mando de los Generales Dulce y Caballero de Rodas, Ano 1869.

[65] Madrid, Archivo Histórico Nacional, Ordenes Militares, Santiago, Expediente 5795; Alfred Baudrillart, *Philippe V et la cour de France*, 5 vols. (Paris: Firmin-Didot, 1870), 4:503-505; Walsh, *Knights,* 2:14-15, no. 30.

tremendous loss of talent to Ireland at a crucial stage in her history. Like their nineteenth-century relatives these men had little choice but to emigrate. As Catholics they could not serve in the English army or in any of the professions. Military service abroad was the only viable option open to them.

CHAPTER 7

THE PENAL LAWS

In the eighteenth century members of the O Callaghan family followed diverse paths. While Donough O Callaghan and his descendants began a new life as landlords in County Clare, remaining steadfast in their allegiance to Catholicism, others in County Cork apparently conformed to the Established Church. By so doing they were able to secure landed property and access to the professions. An act of 1703 required converts to renounce their Catholic faith publicly before a Protestant cleric and congregation and to obtain a certificate from a bishop attesting to their conversion. The names of several O Callaghans who abjured Catholicism were recorded on the convert rolls. Other young aristocrats went abroad to the service of the exiled Stuart kings, but eventually found themselves in the employ of most of the European monarchs until the French Revolution. The majority of O Callaghans, as was no doubt true for other families, remained firm in their allegiance to the Catholic religion and consequently suffered the brunt of the Penal Laws enacted after the Glorious Revolution. Aside from a few aristocrats, most of the O Callaghans were peasants likely still settled on ancestral lands in County Cork, but now as tenants of the Cromwellian planters. Like the peasantry in general the planters, other than the more well-to-do, apparently lived in makeshift cabins with few of the amenities of life.[1]

The Penal Laws excluded Catholics, or Papists as they were called, from voting and from sitting in parliament; they were forbidden to bear arms; to own a horse worth more than five pounds; to travel overseas to be educated; to maintain schools; to receive degrees from Trinity College, the only university in the country; or to practice law. In accordance with an act passed to disarm the Catholics, circa 1692, "only those protected by the Treaty of Limerick were allowed to carry the arms of a gentleman for self-defense and fowling." As noted above, Lieutenant Colonel Callaghan McCallaghan of Caherlag was among those so licensed.[2]

During the same period the English parliament enacted laws intended to inhibit Irish trade except to England itself. As a consequence, exports were severely limited and

---

[1] Eileen O Byrne, ed., *The Convert Rolls* (Dublin: Irish Manuscripts Commission, 1981); Maureen Wall, "The Age of the Penal Laws (1691-1778)," and R. B. McDowell, "The Protestant Nation (1775-1800)," in Moody and Martin, *Course*, 217-247; Foster, *Modern Ireland*, 168-240; Edith Mary Johnston, *Ireland in the Eighteenth Century* (Dublin: Gill, 1974).

[2] Edmund Curtis, *A History of Ireland* (London: Methuen, 1961), 279-280.

the wool trade was practically obliterated. From time to time famine and pestilence also visited the country, with especially grievous consequences for the peasantry. In the middle of the eighteenth century, Smith reflected on economic conditions in Duhallow:

> The northern part of this barony though far from being barren is yet thinly inhabited, and the farmers are the only consumers of what corn [wheat] grows upon the premises. The roads in winter time, are, for the most part, deep and very bad; and there being no navigable river, it is very hard to get off the tenant's corn, but at such a price of carriage, as must greatly increase the value when it is sent to Cork market. There is plenty of turf and coal; but for want of water carriage, if quantities of this last material were dug, it would be of little value. There seems to be no other remedy for those evils, as there are but little hopes of making the Black-water navigable so far from its exit, but by finding out means of bringing markets to the goods. Artists and manufacturers have, and may be, with care and some expence, encouraged and brought together; people thus living close, must cause a consumption, and small market towns may be easily, especially by persons of extensive fortunes, founded, by degrees at an inconsiderable expence. Those people will cultivate and improve the adjacent places, add soil to the land, increase the value of an estate where they settle, and bring riches into the country by their labor.[3]

The Gaelic language, spoken for ages in Ireland and known even to some degree by the planters, came under an ever-stronger challenge from English in the eighteenth and early nineteenth centuries. Despite that, numerous Irish manuscripts from this era are extant containing poems commenting not only on Irish issues but also on the affairs of the outside world. Rural people settling in the towns brought their language with them, reciting their poems and singing their songs in the taverns; Humphrey O Sullivan, for example, described a night of singing and cheering in Ó Ceallacháin's tavern in Callan, Kilkenny in 1827. Perhaps the the tavernkeeper was Pádraig Ó Ceallacháin whose funeral in 1834 is noted in O Sullivan's diary. The prevalence of Irish was such that Protestant clergymen used the language in the early nineteenth century in a concerted effort to convert the Irish-speaking population. The onward march of English was inexorable, however, and by the time of the famine, Irish was in retreat in much of County Cork. While attending mass in the Mallow chapel in 1844, an officer and soldiers from the 33d Regiment, billeted in the town, listened as the priest informed his congregation that the bishop would soon administer the Sacrament of Confirmation. When the priest then spoke in Irish to the country people, "who generally occupy the aisle of the chapel," the officer demanded that his men follow him out of the chapel. The incident suggests that while Irish was still in daily use in rural areas, townspeople were more accustomed to English.[4]

---

[3] Smith, *Cork*, 1:302-303; Jim Meagher, "Duhallow's Hidden Coal Wealth," *SD* 2 (1976-77): 25-28; John J. Kavanagh, "Kilshannig: The Changing Times," *MFCJ* 8 (1990): 82-94.
[4] Cornelius G. Buttimer, "Gaelic Literature and Contemporary Life in Cork, 1700-1840," in O Flanagan and Buttimer, *Cork*, 585-654; *The Diary of Humphrey O Sullivan, 1827-1835*, trans. by Tomás de Bhaldraithe (Cork: Mercier, 1979), 33-34, 132; *CE*, 15 July 1844.

Tories, Rapparees and Peasants

The unsettled times following the overthrow of James II resulted not only in the departure of thousands of soldiers for the continent, but in the continuance of guerilla activities by many, now known as tories (*toiridhe* - a pursued person) and rapparees (*ropaire*, robber), who had served in the recent wars. Some Catholics, dispossessed by the Cromwellian confiscations, became tories and attempted to harass the Protestants who supplanted them. Often viewed as heroes by the defeated populace, they were regarded as criminals by the authorities. In 1619 the Lord Deputy St. John described tories in this way: "the younger sons of gentlemen who have no means of living and will not work go into the woods to maintain themselves by the spoil of the quiet subjects" of the king. The Earl of Orrery made the same point in 1664: "Would to God we had some vent for the many loose people who having served abroad will not work at home and therefore live upon robbery to the great detriment of the public." Major-General Kirke in 1690/1 personally killed a rapparee officer and two others and took several prisoners, including a Captain Callahan. In 1702 the Cork Grand Jury accused Callaghan MacAuliffe Callaghan and Owen MacCallaghan, yeomen, "both late of Killcorny" (south of Banteer), of several robberies, "and are now tories and robbers in arms, upon their keeping." In the following year, the Grand Jury charged Dermod Callaghan, yeoman, "late of Cappanagawl [Cappanagoul west of Liscarroll] in the Barony of Duhallow" and several others, as tories, rapparees and robbers, "out in arms upon their keeping and traitors to the government."[5] As noted in the previous chapter, in 1702 the Grand Jury awarded a bounty of £20 to the widow of Will Parker, who killed the rapparee Callaghane McCallaghane but died in the attempt.[6] In 1732 the Grand Jury accused of being tories, robbers, and rapparees several persons including Callaghan McCallaghan, another member of thsat family.[7]

Over the course of the century the lot of the peasantry became increasingly onerous. As many landlords were absentees living in Dublin or in England, they leased their lands to middlemen who in turn sublet plots to small farmers often at exorbitant rents, called rack rents, a word reminiscent of the rack used to torture people. The tenant lacked any security in his holding and could be evicted at will. Should he make any improvement on the property his rent would be increased. Meantime, landlords, concluding that there was more profit to be had by turning their land over to pasture for cattle and sheep, began to expel their tenants and to enclose the land (including common lands) for pasturage. Peasants who tried to eke out a living from wasteland and bogland were subjected to excessive rents and, should they protest, could be fined or whipped publicly. Moreover, Catholics as well as Protestants (including non-conformists) were required to pay tithes – theoretically a tenth of their income - to support the Established

---

[5] *The Manuscripts of S. H. Le Fleming, Esq. of Rydal Hall* (London: Historical Manuscripts Commission, 1890), 310, no. 4148 (24 February 1690/1); *Calendar Ormonde*, 2:465 (26 March 1702), 471 (21 April 1703).

[6] Brady, *Records*. liii.

[7] https://durrushistory.com/2014/09/01/proclamation-of-11th-november-1732-23rd-march-1732-arising-from-grand-jury-at-general-assizes-and-gaol-delivry-sittting-at-the-kings-old-castle-cork-whereby-murtough-mcowen-sullivan-john-sullivan/

Church of Ireland. Tithe proctors who received a percentage of their collections attempted to extort as much as possible from the peasants.

The strains of landlord-tenant relations are illustrated in the case of the O Callaghans living on the Perceval estate north of Kanturk. Dennis and Teige Reagh O Callaghan, probably sons of Conoghor Reagh, an agent for Sir Philip Perceval, previously mentioned, respectively held Ballybahallagh, and the plowlands of Rossline, Meelaherragh, and Rathranna in the parish of Clonfert about a mile and a half west of Coolageela. Tensions between Teige Reagh and the Percevals eventually led to the ejection of his family. In 1681 he leased from Sir John Perceval the three plowlands mentioned during the lives of his sons, Callaghan, John, and Cahir at an annual rent of £37 10s. Sir John complained that Teige made no attempt to improve the land, and lived off the rents of his subtenants and thus was enabled to pay his creditors. During the Williamite wars, Teige Reagh took the oath of fidelity to the king and queen and joined the garrison at Ballyclough on 3 October 1691. As a consequence, in 1699, then identified as resident at Rossline, he was restored to his estates, together with Charles of Rossline (perhaps his son Cahir), and Dennis of Subulter, probably his brother. Despite Teige's profession of loyalty to the crown, his three sons were in the French service in 1713. When Teige died two years later Perceval, contrary to Teige's widow, Margaret, argued that, as the sons had died, the lease was terminated. In 1720, Perceval, complaining of Margaret's "litigiousness," "made it appear" that her sons were dead and leased the land to another tenant. Two years later Margaret appealed "for some charitable relief for herself, her son George and his six motherless children." What came of that we do not know, but the O Callaghans were ejected from their father's lands. However, in 1743 Denny Callaghan, a likely member of this family, was a tenant at Ballybahallagh.[8]

The plight of the very poor is suggested by a decision of the inhabitants of Kilshannig (probably the gentry) in May 1745 to license beggars, who received badges authorizing them to seek alms in the parish. "Foreign beggars" from other parishes were prohibited. A "brass badge marked Parish of Kilshannig was given to be publickly worn" by twenty-four persons who were strictly forbidden to give or lend it to anyone else. The fact that twenty of the beggars were women, including Joan Callaghan of Kilcolman, and at least two were widows indicates the precarious situation of poor women in eighteenth-century society. At the fall harvest the beggars had to surrender their badges, probably because they could expect to find work then. Early in the following century Croker commented that "beggars crowd around strangers at every town or village . . . always urging their demands in the imperative mood. . . . The eloquence of an Irish mendicant is very peculiar and sometimes incredible." The parish also had its own stocks and whipping post for the punishment of petty offenses. More serious crimes merited more serious penalties. Timothy Callaghan of Laharan (south of Lombardstown) in 1762 offered a reward of five guineas (about £5) to anyone who could recover his stolen horse and apprehend the thief. In 1753 Matthew Callaghane was sentenced to death in the Cork municipal court for the robbery of Captain Capel, but "leaped out of the docks with his bolts on" and escaped, though he was soon retaken and hanged. The mob cut off the ear of the person who informed on him. Thirty-two years later John Callaghan, known as

---

[8] RIA MS 23, L 49; Simms, "Irish Jacobite Lists," *AH* 22 (1960): 92, 108; Ó Murchadha, *Names*, 72; Denis O Mullane, "Ballybahallow," *SD* 3 (1978-1979): 37-40; P. S. O Sullivan, "Papist and Protestant in Wild Goose Time," *SD* 4 (1980-81): 96-97.

Jack-a-boy, "a most notorious offender," joined others in escaping from gaol.[9]

As a means of defending themselves the peasants (farmers and tradesmen) began to form secret societies such as the Whiteboys (they wore white coats or sheets so they could identify one another) who appeared in Tipperary, Cork, and Limerick around 1761-1765 and again about 1769-1775. Raiding the property of landlords, they threw down fences enclosing common pastures and tore up land previously cultivated but now turned into pasture. Troops were employed to suppress them and within a few years their activities were curtailed, though their grievances were not resolved. For his participation in the violence Owen O Callaghan of Clogheen in Tipperary (near the O Callaghan estates) was sentenced to a year in prison in 1762. Fr. Nicholas Sheehy, parish priest of Shanrahan in Tipperary, was accused of encouraging insurrection in 1764, but after a period of hiding out, he surrendered to Cornelius O Callaghan of Shanbally, the future Baron Lismore, who sent him under escort to Dublin because he did not believe that he would receive a fair trial in Tipperary. Early in 1766 he was declared innocent, but in a second trial he was convicted and executed. The Coercion Act of 1765 convinced the peasantry that they could expect no redress from the Irish parliament dominated by the Protestant landowning ascendancy. Toward the end of the century the Whiteboys reappeared as the Rightboys, a sign that conflicts between landlord and peasant were not really settled. Nor would they be until the end of the next century. The move for political independence by the United Irishmen in 1798 found an echo in O Callaghan's country when a band of men, including John O Callaghan from Nagle's Mountains east of Mallow, decided to attack the town. The North Cork Militia, raised by the Protestant gentry to maintain good order, intercepted John and his fellow pikemen at Oliver's Cross a mile east of the town and routed them. Those who had the misfortune to be captured were flogged and hanged.[10]

The Religious Situation

In order to suppress the Catholic religion the bishops were driven into exile, although about a dozen of them remained in hiding. With the bishops gone, it was expected that the parish clergy would soon conform to the Established Church or abandon their posts altogether. Catholic churches were in ruins or had been taken over by the Protestants. Priests said mass in the open air or in private homes. Young men received some elementary education in the hedge schools, but to gain the necessary training for priestly service one had to go abroad to France or Spain to the Irish Colleges of Louvain,

[9] Robert Day, "Licensed Beggars," *JCHAS* 4 (1898): 318-320; Thomas Crofton Croker, *Researches in the South of Ireland* (London, 1824; reprint New York: Barnes and Noble, 1969), 237; *Cork Journal*, 5 April 1762; Tuckey, *Cork Remembrancer*, 134, 191; Colman O Mahony, *In The Shadows: Life in Cork, 1750-1930* (Cork: Tower, 1997), 332.

[10] James S. Donnelly, "The Whiteboy Movement, 1761-5," *Irish Historical Studies* 21 (1978): 20-54, and "The Rightboy Movement, 1785-88," *Studia Hibernica* 18 (1977-78): 120-202; Thomas P. Power, *Land, Politics, and Society in Eighteenth-Century Tipperary* (Oxford: Clarendon Press, 1993) 259-263; A. J. Coughlan, "The Whiteboys' Origins," *MFCJ* 17 (1999): 63-79; Michael Beames, *Peasants and Power: The Whiteboy Movements and their Control in Pre-Famine Ireland* (New York: St. Martin's, 1983); Patrick C. Power, *History of South Tipperary* (Cork: Mercier, 1989), 97; Seán O Callaghan, *Down by the Glenside: Memoirs of an Irish Boyhood* (Cork: Mercier, 1992), 13.

Douai, Bordeaux, or Salamanca.

Priests studying or teaching at the Lombard College in Paris included John Callahan (1716), Cajetan O Callahan (1726), Morgan Callahan (1734), and Fr. Donat Callaghan of Cork, recipient of a scholarship there in 1776. Simon O Callaghan and Andrew O Callaghan were seminarians at Douai in Belgium (then the Spanish Netherlands) in 1786-1788 and 1789-1791 respectively; the former left in 1789 and the latter in October 1792 because of the revolution in France.[11]

Just as Catholics were denied entry to Trinity College, so too did the government attempt to prevent them from obtaining even the rudiments of education, especially as preparation for the priesthood or the legal profession. In 1656 a law proscribing Popish schoolmasters ordered that they be arrested and sent to the continent and then to Barbados. Despite the law many schoolmasters taught their pupils in the open air under the shelter of the hedges. One hedge schoolmaster was Mártan Ó Ceallacháin, a scribe, who in 1755 compiled a manuscript containing the oldest known copy of a poem in 176 lines composed by Donnchadh MacCaochlaoich (Coakley) around 1641.[12]

The life of a priest was a hazardous one, as they were subjected to harassment from time to time, although the situation eased toward the end of the eighteenth century. An Act of 1703 banished Catholic bishops, regulars (that is members of religious orders such as Franciscans and Jesuits), and vicars general. A Registration Act, in force until 1780, allowed any secular priest who took a simple oath of allegiance to be registered and to perform priestly functions. Over 1,000 priests did so. Unregistered priests were subject to the penalties of treason. By 1750 twenty-four Catholic bishops, under the authority of the papal internuncio at Brussels, administered the affairs of the church in Ireland. In the absence of the bishops the priests assumed a position as the natural leaders of the Catholic Irish peasantry. As many of the clergy were educated in French seminaries they also inculcated a Jansenist or puritanical code of morality among Irish Catholics.[13]

One of the more notable members of the family was Ambrose O Callaghan, a Franciscan, recorded among the Order's personnel in Ireland in 1700. He taught philosophy and theology and was active in efforts to restore the Stuart dynasty. Though he was not native to the diocese of Ferns in Wexford, he became bishop there on 26 September 1729 and died about 18 August 1744 in Dublin. He used the name Dr. or Mr. Walker to conceal his identity from the civil authorities. When the clergy of Ferns submitted their postulation to Rome for a new bishop they expressed their discontent with Bishop Ambrose's tenure. They complained of the

> serious and irreparable crimes, evils and scandals experienced in the diocese among clergy and people, among Catholics and Protestants, during the last thirty years or so; they are convinced that these evils were

---

[11] Liam Swords, "Calendar of Irish Material in the Files of Jean Fromont, notary at Paris, May 1701-24 January 1730 in the Archives Nationales, Paris: Part 2, 1716-1730," CH 36-37 (1994-95): 89, 117, 134, nos. 584, 645, 681; Patrick Boyle, The Irish College in Paris from 1578 to 1901 (London: Benziger, 1901), 199; P. R. Harris, Douai College Documents, 1639-1794 (Dublin: Catholic Record Society Publications, 1972), 152, 311, 314, 318-319, 322, 326, 330, 333.

[12] Bolster, Cork, 2:226; P. J. Dowling, The Hedge Schools of Ireland (Cork: Mercier, 1968). I must thank Ruairí Ó hÍci of Seandrom, Westfields, North Circular Road, Limerick, for the notice of Mártan Ó Ceallacháin.

[13] Curtis, History, 284.

due to the fact that their last two bishops came from outside the diocese and province and were promoted without any letters of commendation from the diocese itself. This is borne out by the great numbers of appeals, summonses and complaints as yet undecided which were lodged by both clergy and people with the archbishop of Dublin, their metropolitan, against the last two bishops. It is known that the chief cause of all these evils is that the last two bishops, though they were men of great merit, were not acceptable to the clergy and people of the diocese.

In his recommendation to Rome, the archbishop of Dublin noted the lack of prudence in Dr. O Callaghan. He seems to have spent much of his time away from his diocese on the continent, so much so that the papal nuncio in 1735 remarked that he was a prelate in perpetual motion.[14]

A report giving information on priests and schoolmasters in 1712 recorded Derby (i.e., Diarmuid or Dermot) Callaghan, "popish priest, registered for Aglis parish, but officiates in the parishes of Aglismagh and Ahobullog [Aghabulloge] and suplyed Aglis with a curate." The Grand Jury in 1714 listed Dermod Callaghan of Aghinagh, Aglish, and Ovens among the priests who refused to take the oath of abjuration, rejecting the claims of James II to the throne; Cornelius Murphy of Burren and James Egan of Skart went surety for him to £50. Because of his refusal to take the oath he was indicted but was said to be extra, presumably out of the county or perhaps even out of Ireland. John Callaghan was the parish priest of Monadeen, Carrick and Clonourt; Donough Callaghan, priest of Castletown, Ballyhooly and Kilathy, took the oath. Daniel O Callaghan, registered priest of Kilbrogan, Murrogh and Templemartin, near Bandon, succeeded Owen O Cahill in the parish of Clonmeen and was succeeded there by Charles Carthy. Both were indicted but extra. Owen O Cahill may be the same person as Owen O Connell, recorded as the parish priest of Clonmeen, Kilshannig and part of Castlemagner in 1704; then sixty-six, he lived at Kilcaskan. Denis Callaghan of Lismeelcunnin and Manus O Keeffe of Knocknagehy went surety for him to the sum of £50 each. Owen O Callaghan of Lottsy put up £50 as surety for William Sheehan, parish priest of Kilbrin, Castlemagner and Ballyclough. Teige Callaghan, parish priest of Skull and Kilmoo, refused to take the oath. John Callaghan alias Jones, a name he probably used to disguise his profession from the authorities, was the parish priest in Carrigaline.[15]

[14] Konrad Eubel, et alii, eds. *Hierarchia Catholica Medii et Recentioris Aevi*, 8 vols. (Padua: San Antonio, 1910-1968), 5:200; Cathaldus Giblin, "A List of the Personnel of the Franciscan Province of Ireland, 1700," *CH* 8 (1965): 53, and "Catalogue of Material of Irish Interest in the Collection Nunziatura di Fiandra, Vatican Archives, Part 6, vols.133-135 Gg," *CH* 10 (1967): 99-101, and "Miscellaneous Papers," *Archivium Hibernicum* 16 (1915): 73, nos. 6-8; Pádraig Ó Suilleabháin, O.F.M., "Documents relating to Wexford Friary and Parish, 1733-1798," *CH* 8 (1965):112-113, and *Wexford Friary* (Wexford, 1950), 74; Benignus Millett, "Copies of some Decisions from the Missing Discretorial Registers of St. Isidore's College, Rome, 1652-1739," *CH* 43 (2001): 86-111; Canice Mooney, *Irish Franciscans and France* (Dublin: Clonmore and Reynolds, 1964), 48; William Carrigan, "Catholic Episcopal Wills in the Public Record Office, Dublin 1683-1812," *Archivium Hibernicum* 4 (1915): 66, no. 53; Eamonn Ó Ciardha, *Ireland and the Jacobite Cause, 1685-1766: A Fatal Attachment* (Dublin: Four Courts Press, 2002), 147, 207, 219-220, 233, 242-243, 248, 263, 305; Thomas Walsh, *History of the Irish Hierarchy* (New York: Sadleir, 1854), 187; S. J. Connolly, *Priests and People in Pre-Famine Ireland, 1780-1845* (New York: St. Martin's, 1982), 64.
[15] Burke, *Priests*, 374-375 (22 June 1712), 377 (9 April 1714); Grove-White, *Notes*, 2:222.

The Penal Laws

The Grand Jury in 1715 reported that Daniel Calahan, a schoolmaster and a reputed Protestant, was seen at mass. Daniel's situation probably reflects the ambiguity that many persons felt with regard to the competing claims of the Catholic Church and the Church of Ireland. In 1726 a popish priest named O Calahan was reported. Calahanus O Callahane, vice-pastor of the church of St. Mary, Monegea, subscribed in June 1737 as one of the petitioners to Pope Clement XII for the appointment of Robert Lacy as bishop of Limerick in June 1737. Rev. John O Callaghan, parish priest of Carrigaline, probably the same priest cited above who went by the alias of Jones, in his will dated 6 December 1730, included Fr. Callaghane O Callaghane (probably the Calahanus O Callaghane mentioned above) among those receiving bequests. Fr. John left his chalice, oil stocks, and other priestly accoutrements to his brother Fr. Kennedy O Callaghane of the diocese of Cork. Fr. John's expressed desire to be buried in Barnehely church was evidently fulfilled, as a tombstone in the churchyard indicates that he was interred in his family's sepulchre. Another Rev. John O Callaghan, D. D., whose ministry extended from the close of the eighteenth century into the beginning of the nineteenth, died on 1 July 1814 at Cloghroe, County Cork. A contemporary account described him as "The Rev. Dr. O Callaghan, Doctor of the Sorbonne, universally regretted by his numerous friends, acquaintances and parishioners." His doctorate in divinity from the Sorbonne, the University of Paris, distinguished him among the many priests of his age.[16] This barebones record of names suggests the continued effort of the ecclesiastical authorities to maintain a Catholic presence under hostile conditions. Parish priests such as those mentioned above evidently went about the business of ministering to their people both in the extraordinary and the ordinary events of life.

The physical and statistical status of the church is revealed to some extent in a "Report on the State of Popery in Ireland 1731" issued by Henry, Bishop of Cloyne, Church of Ireland. The Report stated that "mass houses (in County Cork) are generally mean thatched cabbins; many or most of them open at one end." For the diocese of Cloyne, in the rural deanery of Muskerry, in the parish of Kilshannig, there is "no publick mass house, one reputed parish priest, no convent of friars or nuns, two reputed popish schools in the extream parts of this large parish." In the rural deanery of Buttevant in the parish of Clonmeen is "one mass house, one popish priest, no convent of friars or nuns, no popish school." In the parish of Castlemagner, there is "one old mass house, two officiating popish priests, no convent, no school." The Augustinian priory of Clonmeen founded by the O Callaghans and regarded as a family burial ground had likely disappeared in the course of the religious wars and the church itself had probably been taken over by the Church of Ireland. Though it apparently was still used in the eighteenth century, a description of the church of Clonmeen in the following century tells us that "The church is closed and the graveyard overgrown with rank vegetation. A small portion of a ruin is in the churchyard probably that of a former church. The communion plate is in the possession of the rector of Castlemagner." Overgrowth now threatens to cause the collapse of the walls that remain.[17]

Some further data concerning t he religious situation is provided by the return of

---

[16] Burke, *Priests*, 395-397; William Carrigan, "The Old Priests. Part II. Gleanings from Documents in the Public Record Office," *JCHAS* 4 (1898): 214, 216. *JAPMD* 6:16 (4 June 1779).

[17] "Report on the State of Popery in Ireland 1731," *Archivium Hibernicum* 1 (1912) 10-27; 2 (1913) 108-156, especially 121, 127; *JAPMD* 2: 463-464; Grove White, *Notes*, 2:222-223, 228.

the collectors of hearth money (a property tax) in the diocese of Cloyne in 1764-1765. According to this document, there was a Protestant church and 255 parishioners in the parish of Kilshannig, a church and 78 parishioners in Clonmeen, but no church and 60 parishioners in Castlemagner. The Catholics, on the other hand, in the parish of Kilshannig numbered 1,561, with a chapel in good order. The 1,259 Catholics in the parish of Clonmeen also had a chapel in good order; although there were 845 Catholics in the parish of Castlemagner, there was no chapel.[18]

In the Census of Parishes of 1766, Rev. John Hingston, the Protestant Rector, reported the following Protestant families in the parish of Clonmeen, Roskeen, and Kilcorny: Cornelius O Callaghan, Esquire, and Cornelius Magrath O Callaghan, both of Banteer, and Robert O Callaghan of Clonmeen. They were the descendants of Cornelius Senior O Callaghan of Banteer, of whom more below. All told there were 20 Protestant families, but 359 Catholic families, and three "reputed popish priests," two of whom were "said to be under suspension from their superior for irregularities." Twenty-eight male Catholic Callaghan householders were located in these townlands:

Name	Place	Name	Place
Anthony	Glynn	Owen	Clonmeen
Cornelius	Fermoyle	Cornelius	Dromcummer
Timothy	Fermoyle	Patrick	Dromcummer
Denis	Banteer	Charles	Gurteencloona
Cornelius	Banteer	Timothy	Pallas
John	Banteer	Timothy	Pallas
Darby	Banteer	Owen	Roskeen
John	Banteer	Darby McCallaghan	Glaunleaghmore
John	Banteer	Daniel	Shanakill
John	Banteer	Denis McCallaghan	Knockacappul
John	Banteer	Timothy McCallaghan	Knockacappul
Cornelius	Curraghrour	Daniel McCallaghan	Knockacappul
Simon	Killarush	Denis McCallaghan	Knockacappul
Cornelius	Clonmeen	Darby	Crinnaloo
Timothy	Clonmeen		

Most of the places mentioned are familiar. Glynn or Glen lies south of Mount Hillary on both sides of the Glen River. South of Banteer are Fermoyle, Glaunleaghmore (Glenleigh), Shanakill, Crinnaloo, and Knockacappul. Curraghrour is east of Clonmeen. North of the Blackwater are Killarush near Dromcummer, and Gurteennacloona east of Roskeen and northeast of Pallas. My own family is likely related to Cornelius and Patrick then resident in Dromcummer.

In the parish of Kilshannig there were 61 Protestant families and 409 Papist families. Thirty-two male Catholic Callaghan householders were settled in these townlands:

---

[18] Dublin, PRO, The Return of the Hearth Money Collectors in the Different Portions of the Diocese of Cloyne, A.D. 1764-1765, p. 533.

Name	Place	Name	Place
John	Dromore	John	Glantane
John	Dromore	Darby	Glantane
Darby	Kilvealaton	Daniel	Lackendarragh
Owen	Dromaneen	John	Brittas
John	Dromaneen	Timothy	Kilknockagaur
Darby	Kilpadder	Daniel	Mohereen
Daniel	Carrigcleena	Daniel	Lombardstown
Cornelius	Carrigcleena	Cornelius	Gortroe
Owen	Carrigcleena	Darby	Gortroe
Daniel	Kilcolman	Darby	Gortroe
Cornelius	Kilcolman	Daniel	Gortroe
Denis	Ballysimon	Timothy	Gortroe
Denis	Aldworth	Darby	Gortavoher
Joseph	Skarragh	Patrick	Gortavoher
John	Glantane	John	Gortavoher
Owen	Glantane	Cornelius	Glanminane
Callaghan O Callaghan	Glantane		

Most of these placenames have previously appeared in the documentation. From east to west were Dromore, Kilvealaton, Dromaneen, Mohereen, Kilknockagaur, Brittas, and Lombardstown. Gortavoher is just west, and Gortroe and Glanminane are southwest of Lombardstown. Glantane and Lackendarragh are southeast. Turning southward we find Kilpadder, Skarragh and Aldworth. Ballysimon is located near the Lyre Rriver south of Kilpadder and Kilcolman, and Carrigcleena is still farther south. A "popish priest" served the parish but no friar was known to be active in either Clonmeen or Kilshannig.[19]

One is struck again both by the traditionalism of the names and by the substitution of more obviously English names for the Irish ones of a previous generation. Among the Catholics the most frequently used names were John (12), Cornelius (9), Darby (9), Daniel (7), Timothy (7), Denis (5), Owen (5), Patrick (2), and one each for Anthony, Charles, Joseph, Simon, and Callaghan. John (Seán) does not seem to have been used in the previous century but now it was the most common name. Cornelius now replaced Connor; Darby replaced Dermot; Daniel, Donal; Timothy, Teige; Denis, Donough; Anthony, Owney; and Charles, Cahir. Joseph and Simon evidently were new usages. While most individuals were identified as Callaghan, five were called McCallaghan. Perhaps the most traditional of all was Callaghan O Callaghan. Not only was his first name distinctive but the use of O Callaghan rather than Callaghan sets him apart from the rest. Perhaps he was more closely connected to the chieftain's family as the Protestant

[19] Dublin, PRO, VII B/2/21. IA 41 657, pp. 93-103, 107-119. Records of the Diocese of Cloyne. Religious Census 1766. Copy of Transcripts by Rev. Bartholomew O'Keeffe. The census was compiled by rectors of the Church of Ireland on the orders of the government. The original records were destroyed in the fire in the Four Courts in 1922. See the data for Clonmeen and Kilshannig at **www.rootsweb.com**, County Cork-L Archives or www.sci.net.au/mgrogan/cork/clonmeen.nun.

landowners were also identified as O Callaghan. There seems to have been some sense that only members of that family were entitled to be called O Callaghan. Lastly, it ought to be emphasized that no women were mentioned by name in this census.

A comparison of the number of parishioners given by the hearth money collectors in 1764-1765 with Hingston's number of families in 1766 is instructive. Thus while Hingston cited 61 Protestant families and 409 Catholic families in Kilshannig (32 of whom were Callaghans), for a total of 470 families, the hearth money figures show 255 Protestants and 1,561 Catholics, or a total of 1,816 persons in Kilshannig. This gives an average of 4.18 persons in each Protestant family and 3.81 in a Catholic family. For Clonmeen, Hingston recorded 20 Protestant families and 359 Catholics (28 of whom were Callaghans), or a total of 379; the hearth money figures are 78 Protestants and 1,259 Catholics, or a total of 1,337 persons. In this case, the average Protestant family consisted of 3.9 persons and the Catholic one of 3.5. The total population for the two parishes was 3,153, of whom 333 were Protestants and 2,820 Catholics. In both parishes the Catholic family was slightly smaller than the Protestant one. If one multiplies the number of Catholic Callaghans recorded by Hingston in Clonmeen (28) and Kilshannig (32) by the average family size (3.5 and 3.81) the totals would be 72.8 and 118.92, or approximately 192 Catholic Callaghans in both parishes.

In Kilshannig parish John and Timothy Callaghan of Dromore, gentlemen, perhaps brothers, abjured the Catholic faith in 1735. John's offer of a reward of a crown in 1756 for the return a scarlet cloak attests to his prosperity. From 1741 to 1784 the offspring of John and Katherine of Dromore, Owen and Anne of Glauntane, John and Joanna of Keale, and John Boulster and his wife Jane Callaghan of Glauntane were baptized there. John and Katherine's daughters were married there and their son was buried in the graveyard.[20]

The O Callaghans of Clare

The main branch of the O Callaghans, the family of the chieftain, Donough O Callaghan, or Donough Mór, was transplanted to Clare following the Cromwellian wars. Succeeding his father around 1683, Donough Óg, the Younger, with whom the family pedigree begins in the Book of Munster, held lands in the baronies of Tulla and Bunratty, including Mountallon, Liscullane, Kilgory, Derrymore, Ballymcdonnell, Dromod, Inchilahoge, Clerida, Clonmoher, Ballyhenry, Lisbarren, Ballydonoghane, Killboggoon, Derryfanrushe, Gortenalla, Ballymulquiry, and Mahery. Kilcolman and half a ploughland in Mohereen were the last remnant of the family estate in the barony of Duhallow. By 1679 he seems to have established his principal residence at Kilgory, nearly three miles north of Mountallon. Situated close to Lough Kilgory, the two-and-a-half-storey house is now in ruins. Eve Campbell suggested that Donough Óg may have financed construction in the 1680s by mortgaging lands to John MacNamara and Ambrose Perry for the respective sums of £400 and £130. Donough Óg and perhaps his father may have been interred in a private graveyard to the rear the house.[21]

[20] O Byrne, *Convert Rolls*, 39; *Cork Journal*, 5 January 1756; Dublin, PRO, The Church of Ireland Parish of Kilshannick, Cork, Register of Baptisms, Deaths, and Marriages, 6-9, 12, 14-15, 31-32, 54, 149, 211, 229, 232, 251, 253, 272, 274.

[21] For a detailed description of the property, see Campbell, *Displacement*, 230-257.

Donough Óg married Mary, daughter of Cormac Spáinneach (the Spaniard) MacCarthy (Charles MacCarthy of Thresherstown). In 1686 he was a justice of the peace. After the surrender of Limerick in 1691 he sent his sons Callaghan and Charles, at the tender ages of four and two respectively, to France to be educated. After the Williamite victory, they were outlawed and indicted for high treason overseas. Lest that charge be used to dispossess his family, Donough Óg, by his will of 31 March 1698, left his estate in tail male to his younger sons, Donough, Michael, Daniel, Teige and Conor, and appointed Captain Thady O Callaghan as their guardian and executor of his will. No mention was made of Callaghan or Charles. Witnesses to the will included Owen O Callaghan, yeoman. Tail male restricted the inheritance to Donough Óg's direct male descendants. [22] Donough Óg's executor, Captain Thady O Callaghan (d. circa 1716), the son of Connor O Callaghan, gentleman, of Coolroe, County Cork, married Mary, Donough's widow in 1701.[23]

Some objection to the exclusion of Callaghan and Charles from Donough Óg's will was voiced at an early date. In 1700, for example, it was reported that Donough "being comprehended in the articles of Limerick and his eldest son having gone away to France, the second son is the heir and successor to his estates." That would imply that Callaghan was abroad but Charles was still at home and entitled to his share of the inheritance. A brief submitted on Thady's behalf, as guardian of Donough's minor children, in a suit to be heard on 3 November 1701, affirmed that, following the Treaty of Limerick, Callaghan (then not more than four) and Charles had been sent to France for their education. Both were subsequently outlawed for treason. In 1725 it was claimed that Callaghan was forced "by absolute necessity" to enter the French service in 1694-1695; but if he were born in 1687 he would have been only seven or eight at that time. In any case he never reversed his outlawry. On 18 June 1722 Owen O Callaghan of Mountallon, yeoman, aged about seventy, who had witnessed the will in 1698, swore an affidavit in support of its validity.[24]

Nevertheless, in 1728 Charles O Callaghan of Liscullane, gentleman, "being sick and weake & likely to depart this life in a few hours," stated that when Donough Óg made his will he knew that his two oldest sons, Callaghan and Charles, were attainted because they served in the French army and so excluded them from their inheritance. He later revoked that will and, making a new one, bequeathed his property to Callaghan and Charles and then to his younger sons. Charles did not have a copy of the second will but asserted that Captain Thady O Callaghan had had it and that it had then come into the possession of Daniel O Callaghan (d. 1724), both of whom were deceased.[25] The identity of Charles O Callaghan who made this declaration is uncertain, but perhaps he was

---

[22] O Callaghan-Lismehane Papers (31 March 1698). A chancery bill of 4 February 1683 indicates that Donough Mór was deceased. Burke, *Gentry*, 2:519-520; Dublin, GO MS, p. 492. For Donough's many leases (witnessed by Darby Callaghan and Owen O'Callaghan, among others) see Frost, *Clare*, 596, 601-602, 616; Edward MacLysaght, ed., *The Kenmare Manuscripts* (Dublin: Irish Manuscripts Commission, 1942), 145 (22 April 1685, witnessed by Charles and Thady O Callaghan, and Anthony Callaghan).

[23] O Callaghan-Lismehane Papers (1701). See Thady's leases in Frost, *Clare*, 54-55, 601-602 (to Connor of Coolroe, witnessed by Mor, Con, and Darby Callaghan, 11 November 1679; to Thady of Liscullane, 16 December 1695, and 16 April 1696).

[24] Dublin, PRO Court of Claims Petitions, 1700; O Callaghan-Lismehane Papers (1700, 1701, 1722, 1725); Frost, *Clare*, 601-602.

[25] O Callaghan-Lismehane Papers (1728).

Donough Óg's son, now returned from France to claim his inheritance.

In the meantime, when the Court of Trustees was established in 1700 to dispose of forfeited estates following the downfall of James II, Captain Thady O Callaghan, as executor of Donough Óg's estate put forward several claims. First, he asked that Mountallon, Liscullane and other lands should be restored to his wards Donough, Michael, Daniel, Teige and Conor in accordance with Donough Óg's will of 1698 naming them as his heirs. The petition did not include Donough Óg's older sons Callaghan and Charles who had been sent to France for their education and were then outlawed for treason. However, in another petition Thady claimed for Teige, Charles, Donough, Callaghan, and Daniel, all minors, Clonmoyle, Carrignamuck, and other lands in the barony of Muskerry formerly held by the earl of Clancarthy; and, citing a deed of 1 July 1684, he claimed Knockmorduff in Muskerry for Catherine McCarthy, perhaps his sister in law.[26]

Furthermore, Thady petitioned for the restoration of Mountallon and other lands as the dowry of his wife Mary, Donough Óg's widow. In his own name, he asserted that Donogh O'Callaghan of Kilgorey (Donough Mór), on 11 November 1679 leased Mountallon, Cappalaheen, Coolistoonan, and Cunninagh, for a term of forty-one years, at the yearly rent of £26, to his father Connor O'Callaghan, who conveyed them to him five days later. Witnesses to the original lease included Mor[rough], Conor, and Darby, Donough Mór's younger sons; Patrick, still another son, witnessed the conveyance. In addition, Donough Óg on 16 November 1695 leased Liscullane to him for nineteen years and Kealderry and Knocknasilly on 15 April 1696 for twenty-one years.[27] Thady's claims were dismissed, however, and as a consequence the right of Daniel, Donough Óg's son and heir, to Mountallon and the other lands cited was preserved.

Several other persons made their own claims to lands held by the O Callaghans of Clare. For example, John MacNamara of Creevagh, Esq., alleged that Donough Mór in 1670 conveyed Calluragh and other lands to him in mortgage for £60. Lord Clare in 1666 had leased those lands to Donough in 1666. Donough Óg's widow Mary and her new husband Thady O'Callaghan in 1699 conveyed to MacNamara the equity of redemption of the mortgage, in consideration of eight pounds.[28] Thady MacNamara of Rannagh claimed that on 16 August 1683 Donough O Callaghan leased Kilboggoone for thirty-one years to his father John. Morrough O Callaghan, Donough Mór's son, witnessed the deed. Then, after Donough Mór died, his son Donough Óg, on 20-21 January 1684, for £400, conveyed to John MacNamara, the lands of Rannagh, Knockmanistra, Lacnegoologe, and Knockballykelly. Darby O'Callaghan, Donough Óg's brother, witnessed the deed. Donough Óg also mortgaged Knockacloggin for £44 on 19-20 March 1696. Owen O Callaghan was a witness.[29]

Among other petitioners, Thomas Dalton stated that Donough Óg on 1 June 1688 mortgaged Ballydonoghan, in the parish of Kilnoe for £130 to Ambrose Perry who assigned it to Dalton the next day. In 1696 Dalton made other leases of this property. Donough Óg similarly mortgaged Coolready and Inchilahoge to John Grady for £60 on 7 November 1687. John Wate, Doctor of Physick, obtained a lease of Lisbarren for £360 on

---

[26] *A List of the Claims*, nos. 1978-1979.

[27] *A List of the Claims*, nos. 1980-1981; Frost, *Clare*, 602; Shoosmith, *Settlement*, 101-102

[28] Frost, *Clare* 601-602.

[29] *A List of the Claims*, no. 1591; Frost, *Clare*, 596; Shoosmith, *Settlement*, 99.

x22 April 1685. Callaghan and Charles O Callaghan (perhaps Donough Óg's sons?) were listed as proprietors of Culishill (perhaps Culausheeda near Kilgory) which they leased to Connell O Connell on 9 February 1694. Thady O Callaghan (probably Captain Thady) witnessed that document.[30]

Meanwhile, Captain Thady and Mary's son Thady, a captain in the Hibernia Regiment in Spain, made his will in 1736 and asked to be buried in Quin Abbey, a few miles west of Kilgory, near his father and grandfather. He named his brother-in-law, Daniel MacNamara, as executor and left to his sister Mary all the money, plate, jewels, arrears of pay and subsistence that he was entitled to from his Spanish service, all the money and plate in the hands of his good friend, Captain Thomas Kindellane, and all his right to a portion of his father's estate. "In consideration of his care and tenderness of me and his faithfull service to me," he left his grey suit (except for the silver buttons) six coarse shirts, two pair of stockings, his shoes, and six pistols to his servant Dominick Savelli to defray his expenses to Spain, and asked Captain Kindellane to grant him on arrival there a "full and absolute congee or discharge." When his effects were remitted from Spain his debts were to be paid.[31]

Donough Óg's son Donough, born probably in 1691, seems not to have been legally capable, because the Killaloe Diocesan Court in 1716 granted administration of his affairs to his mother Mary and his stepfather Thady, and to Mary alone, then a widow, in 1722. His brother Michael died in 1708 and the youngest brothers, Teige and Connor, apparently had no descendants.[32]

As a consequence, Donough Óg's fifth son, Daniel (c. 1695-1724) inherited the estate of Mountallon. He is likely to be identified with that Daniel Callaghan, gent., of Mountallon admitted to the study of law at Gray's Inn in London in January 1702/3.[33] He married Catherine Purcell of Loughmoe who died in 1731. No doubt he lived much like other landlords, collecting rents from his tenants, letting his lands to lease, and enjoying the hunt. Documentary references of 1720 and 1725 to O Callaghan's Mills, three miles southwest of Tulla, suggest that it may have been about this time, if not before, that the mill or mills were erected that led to the development of the village.[34]

After Daniel's death at Thresherstown on 24 August 1724 and burial at Kilcrea Abbey in Cork (the burial place of the MacCarthys), the last great Gaelic poet of the age, Egan O'Rahilly, celebrated his life in two lengthy elegies. The news of Daniel's death sent "a wounding, venomous dart through the brain of Fodla [Ireland],/ A blast of the

---

[30] *A List of the Claims*, nos. 2941, 2160, 1982-1983; Frost, *Clare*, 601.

[31] O Callaghan-Lismehane Papers (1725, 1736). Administration of the effects of Thady O Callaghan late of Mountallon was granted to his grandson Daniel MacNamara in 1772; Dublin, GO MS 143, p. 26. His daughter Mary married Daniel MacNamara and died on 23 June 1756 and was buried at Quin Abbey; Frost, *Clare*, 54-55.

[32] O Callaghan-Lismehane Papers (14 April 1716). Dublin, PRO, Testaments; Dublin, GO MS p. 492; *BIFR*, 889.

[33] Joseph Foster, *The Register of Admissions to Gray's Inn, 1521-1889, together with the Register of Marriages in Gray's Inn Chapel, 1695-1754* (London: Hansard Publishing Union, 1889), 353, fol. 1374.

[34] Dublin, GO MS, p. 492; Dublin, PRO Testaments (Daniel's will, 28 September 1724; proved 20 November 1724); Thrift Abstracts, 2867, 2870, 2891. See Daniel's leases of Kilcolman and Mohereen in the barony of Duhallow in Casey, *O Kief*, 6:1991-1992, 1996, nos. 16.122.6941 (30 July 1715), 19.17.9358 (5-6 December 1716), 26.109.74796 (18-19 January 1719); Burke, *Gentry*, 2:519-520. On O Callaghan's Mills see Camobell, *Displacement*, 259-268.

plague through her inmost breast." All the rivers and great seas lamented with loud groaning and weeping. Dinneen commented that the "slow continuous and mournful" [moan] heard among the rocks of Glandore harbor as the prelude to an approaching storm was Cliodhna's wail on the death of a chieftain. It was called Tonn Cliodhna or Cliodhna's wave. The clergy and the friars, whom Daniel no doubt sheltered from persecution, were distressed, but his death, said the poet, was "the signal for the ruin of the bards" (XV, ll. 1, 9-11, 29-40).

In earlier times poets such as O Rahilly, journeying from mansion to mansion, expected to share in the largesse of a great lord, but that time was rapidly coming to an end. He exalted Daniel's virtues of "hospitality, and courage, and brightness, and fame without sorrow" (XV, ll. 269). Invoking the voice of the fairy Cliodhna, the protector of the O Callaghans, symbolizing their land, O Rahilly depicted in an idyllic way the festivities in his house in Clare, thereby also giving us a glimpse into the courtly life of Clonmeen and Dromaneen in the previous century:

> I beheld, said she, in his musical, princely mansion
> Speckled silks and garments of pure satin,
> Swords being whetted, invalids quaffing mead,
> And warriors playing at chess noisily.
>
> Coverlets being prepared, morn and even,
> Young maidens engaged in arranging down,
> Wines, newly opened, being drunk, and jollity,
> Viands on spits and usquebagh [whisky] on tables . . .
>
> Airs being played harmoniously on harps,
> The wise and learned reading histories
> In which an account was faultlessly given of the clergy
> And of each great family that arose in Europe.
>
> The doors not closed on enclosures bright as amber,
> Waxlights blazing from every wall and chamber
> Every moment fresh casks being opened for the multitude
> While there was no ebb in the liquid thst came into that drinking feast.
>
> Steeds being presented on the *ollamhs* [learned men] of Fodla,
> Strong steeds in teams prancing on the hillside,
> Footsoldiers contending, abundance of *beoir* [beer]
> In goblets of wrought silver, of great purity (XV, ll. 65-92).

Cliodhna also described the pleasure of the hunt:

> Often in that plain was heard the clamour of sportsmen,
> The loud uproar of the chase on the sides of the misty mountains,
> Foxes and red-bucks were being wakened for them
> Hares from the mead, water-hens and thrushes.
>
> Oh! The rapture of the chase, as it presses onward with great force,

With pheasants wide-scattered and wildly screaming;
The princes's hounds and his men fatigued
From their pursuit up the slopes of the misty mountains.

Oh pain without relief! A great evil do I deem it
That the vale is given over without reserve to the screams of the jackdaws.
Loud is the voice of foreigners in the golden mansion,
Where there was wont to be the play and the chatter of chessplayers (XV, ll. 93-105).

Daniel Corkery commented that O Rahilly

> scarcely took even poetic licence with the facts, as is the manner of Irish poets. He invented nothing; he hardly even heightened the tints: the clear vision in his mind of the house at Clonmeen was, if anything, already too full and too rich. The whetting of the swords, the invalids drinking mead, the young girls stripping the feathers with their slender fingers, the laden tables, the heavy drinking, the harpers, the scanning of the genealogies, the crowds coming and going, the rewarding of the poets, the racing on the hillsides, the fox-chase along the misty slopes, the fowling - it is all flung out at us, as it were, with swiftness, with energy, as if the reason for thus recalling the glories of Clonmeen was all the time so urgent in the poet'sthoughts, that hastening toward it, he could not bear to dally on the arranging of his picture or to linger on its choicest features. The theme was a favourite with him; he was of the old order and held that a poet's trade was to sing the deeds of a patron while living and to keen him when dead.[35]

Still using the voice of Cliodhna, O Rahilly praised Daniel in extravagant language. After describing his coat of arms "drawn in golden colours" on his gravestone ("A wolf, fierce, violent, impetuous/ Issuing from the wood's border in rapid race/ And going forth to hunt in the plains of Fodla") (XV, ll. 22-24) he traced his descent from Adam, giving a lengthy genealogy that compares well with the contemporary version in the Book of Munster. Addressing his hero's gravestone, he exhorted: "Should anyone inquire what chieftain is this . . . / reply readily . . . the true O Callaghan and the son of the O Callaghan is he" (XVI, ll. 50-52). Those lines emphasized that even though the O Callaghan clan had been dispossessed of Pobul Uí Cheallacháin, the chieftainship of the family continued and was personified in Daniel.

Corkery cited O Rahilly's poem to illustrate the function of the big house or aristocratic mansion in eighteenth-century Ireland. A notable landmark, the big house was the center of an active economic and social life for the surrounding area. A large number of live-in servants were employed in tending to the needs of the family, cooking their meals, doing their laundry and tailoring, while others cared for the grounds, the

---

[35] Daniel Corkery, *The Hidden Ireland: A Study of Gaelic Munster in the Eighteenth Century* (Dublin: Gill and Macmillan, 1967), 51-53; Seán Ó Faoláin, *King of the Beggars: A Life of Daniel O Connell, the Irish Liberator in a Study of the Rise of Modern Irish Democracy (1775-1847)* (New York: Viking, 1938), 26-27.

farms, and the pastures. The house also offered welcome hospitality to weary travelers. Poets and minstrels roaming about the countryside could expect comfortable lodging and sustenance in return for entertaining the household with their poems, music, and songs. O Rahilly's depiction of the hospitality provided in O Callaghan's house merely masked the fact that the old order was rapidly changing. In many houses, especially those of the Cromwellian planters, the poets discovered that they were not welcome. O Rahilly grieved: "Loud is the voice of the foreigners in the golden mansion,/ Where there was wont to be the play and chatter of chessplayers" (XV, ll. 103-104). In the previous century the priest-poet Brian MacGiollaPhádraig expressed his contempt for the planters who had dispossessed the Gaelic aristocracy, describing them as "beggarwomen's sons" and "slaveys" surrounded by servants "with grimy English, but no regard for one of the poet class, save 'Out! and take your precious Gaelic with you!'"[36]

The O Callaghan line in Clare would soon suffer the fate of the poets. Daniel's oldest son Donough of Kilgory Castle inherited his property and in 1743, together with his wife Hannah, appeared on the convert rolls, that is, he was identified as a convert to the Church or Ireland. Like many others he probably gave outward adherence to the Established Church to preserve the family estates against any Protestant claim.[37] Acknowledging the importance of having a mastery of the law in order to defend the family property, his son Daniel was admitted to the Middle Temple in 1770; but described as "late of Skillgarry, Co. Clare," he died two years later at the age of twenty-two, leaving as his heir, his younger brother Edmond.[38]

Edmond married Ellen, the daughter of Denis O Brien of Dublin, in 1785; her marriage portion of £5,000 was quite subtantial.[39] Though trained as a barrister, Edmond evidently lacked the financial skills to manage his inheritance which ultimately passed into the hands of Cornelius O Callaghan of Liscullane, as will be described below. Edmond had no sons and was killed in a duel on 8 September 1791. Though his sharp tongue apparently provoked the duel, John Lloyd commented that Edmond was descended from Donough, who had been transplanted from Duhallow and was himself a descendant of "the renown'd CALLAGHAN CASHILL." Edmond was "a respectable Young Gentleman, Senior and Chief of that Heroic, Eugenian Sept."[40]

---

[36] *Poems of Egan O Rahilly*, 66-91, nos. XV-XVI, and p. liv; Corkery, *Hidden Ireland*, chapter 2: The Big House; Seán Ó Tuama and Thomas Kinsella, *An Duanaire: An Irish Anthology, 1600-1900: Poems of the Dispossessed* (Philadelphia: University of Pennsylvania, 1981), 90-91, no. 25. Grady McWhiney, *Cracker Culture: Celtic Ways in the Old South* (Tuscaloosa: University of Alabama Press, 1988), 98, cited O'Rahilly's poem as an example of gentry life in the antebellum American South.

[37] Dublin, GO MS, p. 492; O Byrne, *Convert Rolls*, 220; Frost, *Clare*, 634; Burke, *Gentry*, 2:519-520; Sir Henry Blackall, "The Memorandum Book of David Rochfort," *JCHAS* 67 (1962): 54-56. See litigation concerning Lisbarren, Kilboogoon, and Kilroe in O Callaghan-Lismehane Papers (1728, 1730, 1745); Ainsworth, *Inchiquin Manuscripts*, 499, no. 1476).

[38] Dublin, PRO Testaments (Daniel's will, 12 May 1772; probated 28 October 1772); Thrift Abstracts 1808, 2896; Betham Abstracts; O Callaghan-Lismehane Papers (1772); Frost, *Clare*, 634; Henry Macgeagh and H. A. C. Sturgess, eds., *Register of Admissions to the Honourable Society of the Middle Temple: From the Fifteenth Century to the Year 1944*, 3 vols. (London: Middle Temple, 1949), 1:370 (17 February 1770).

[39] O Callaghan-Lismehane Papers (1785).

[40] John Lloyd, *A Short Tour; or, an Impartial and Accurate Description of the County of Clare with Some Particular and Historical Observations* (Ennis: John Busteed and George Trinder, 1780), 13.

Edmond O Callaghan of Kilgory

(Portrait in Longueville House)

Noting that Edmond was "the lineal descendant of Callaghan Cashell," *The Ennis Chronicle* spoke of his "most refined manners and accomplishments" and his "most exalted ideas of honour and probity." "His premature and untimely death" was cause for sorrow, made even more so by "the extinction of the male line of that ancient and illustrious family, as he died without a son." Although he had been listed as a convert to

See https://celt.ucc.ie/published/E780004-001/. Edmond was one of the executors of James Butler of Cragnagour (20 May 1789); Sir Henry Blackall, "The Butlers of County Clare," *North Munster Antiquarian Journal* 7:2 (1955): 19-45, esp. 35-36.

the Established Church in 1772, he received the last rites of the Catholic Church. His portrait hangs in Longueville House overlooking the Blackwater. *The Ennis Chronicle* erred, however, as it failed to reckon with the descendants of Donough Mór who had settled in Spain. More will be said of them later. Kilgory House, the family's mansion, was in ruins by 1845.[41]

The O Callaghans of Liscullane/Lismehane

As Edmond had five daughters but no sons, his estates were acquired by a branch of the family descended from Denis O Callaghan of Liscullane. Aged thirty-nine in 1732, his precise relationship with the Kilgory house is unclear. Perhaps he was a grandson of Donough Mór or of Donough Mór's brother Cornelius and a son of another Cornelius. He leased Liscullane from the Kilgory family and witnessed their legal documents, even having power of attorney. In 1744 Matthew Robnett, a Dublin shoemaker, charging that Denis was a papist and the "grandson of an outlaw," tried to use the Penal Laws to dispossess him of lands at Doone that he leased from Donough O Callaghan. In response Denis threatened Robnett "with instant death if he ever came again to his house at Liscullane." Was Denis a son of Captain Thady and a grandson of Connor of Coolroe? Was the latter the outlaw?[42]

Donough O Callaghan of Kilgory, "who had a great regard and friendship" for Denis's son, Cornelius, leased Coolready to him in 1749 and Ballydonoghane in 1765. Successively resident at Coolready, Clonloum, and Liscullane, Cornelius was listed among eligible voters in 1768, 1776, and 1783. In 1768 his name was crossed out, but a marginal note indicated that objection was made because he was "a Convert and took the Converts oath in Court. Vote allowed." Cornelius seems to have had a close relationship with Edmond O Callaghan of Kilgory. A lawsuit brought in 1821 by Edmond's eldest daughter Brigid O Reilly recounts something of the family history. As Edmond was under age at the time of his father's death in 1772 and grew up to be "extravagant and indolent, and in constant state of pecuniary distress and embarrassment" he supposedly fell "prey and dupe to the schemes and designs of the said Cornelius and his sons." He allowed himself, so it was charged, to be controlled by Cornelius, who took advantage of that relationship to obtain Edmond's property. Nevertheless, the court denied Brigid's claim. The fortunes of the family of Liscullane in the nineteenth and twentieth centuries will be discussed in later chapters.[43]

The O Callaghan Restoration in Clonmeen and Dromaneen

Meanwhile, as a consequence of Donough Mór's forfeiture of his estates in County Cork and transplantation to Clare, several Protestant adventurers acquired the family lands in Duhallow. What is most interesting is that within forty to fifty years of

---

[41] Dublin, GO MS, p. 492; O Callaghan-Lismehane Papers; Burke, *Gentry*, 2:519-520; Dinneen, *Poems of Egan O Rahilly*, 66-67; Frost, *Clare*, 634; O Donovan, "To Hell or to Clare," 73; *BIFR*, 889.

[42] O Callaghan-Lismehane Papers (1744, 1772). See the deposition by Dionysius O Callaghan on 14 July 1732 at www.limerickcorp.ie/appplications/generalmuseum_details.aspx?RowID=27282.

[43] O Callaghan-Lismehane Papers (1821). Brigid married Thomas O Reilly, Esq. in 1809; their son Edmund O Reilly, S. J., a distinguished theologian, died in 1878.

the initial confiscation Cornelius O Callaghan Senior was able to recover a portion of those lands in Banteer, Clonmeen, and Dromaneen. Cornelius's descendants retained possession through the eighteenth century and in the early nineteenth century the same lands passed into the hands of Viscount Lismore, representing another branch of the family. The recovery of O Callaghan estates was likely made possible when the persons in question opted to conform to the Church of Ireland. If they had not done so, they would not have been able to regain possession and transmit these ancestral lands to their heirs. The process by which they accomplished this is uncertain but it emphasizes the continuing attraction of the ancient clan holdings for later generations. This may rightly be described as a restoration in the sense that, whereas the O Callaghan lordship seemingly had been effectively terminated by Donough Mór's transplantation, some of the ancient clan lands were once again in O Callaghan possession early in the eighteenth century if not before.[44]

Dromaneen with Longueville in the Background

In a previous chapter it was pointed out that a branch of the family descended from Teige McConoghor, the third son of the chieftain, Conor of the Rock, held lands in Banteer and Inchidaly about a mile west of Clonmeen at the close of the reign of Queen Elizabeth. After Teige's death in 1624 his son Conoghor McTeige (Conor or Cornelius) succeeded to his property, receiving livery of possession in 1631. An inquisition of 1638 identified him as holding lands in Banteer and Inchidaly, apparently in dependence on the chieftain Donough Mór, recorded as the forfeiting proprietor in 1641. Following confiscation, Banteer came into the possession of Peter Courthorpe who transferred it to Richard Nagle who in turn disposed of it to Abraham Dixon.[45]

Although the date of Conoghor's death is uncertain (probably around 1638), it is

---

[44] Joseph F. O Callaghan, "The O Callaghans of Banteer in the Eighteenth Century," *JCHAS* 115 (2010): 115-134.

[45] Dublin, PRO Books of Survey and Distribution, Cork, Parish of Clonmeen, 163. See above chapter 4. Gillman, "Chieftains," *JCHAS*, Series 2, 3 (1897): pedigree; *CPCRC Charles I*, 590; Dublin, RIA Ordinance Survey, Inquisitions, Cork.

reasonable to surmise that he had a son Teige. He was likely that Teige O Callaghan who acquired Dromalour near Kanturk in the Cromwellian confiscation and was enrolled among the innocents. As I suggested in the previous chapter, he may be the same person as Thady Callaghan, gentleman, who in 1688 claimed that he had a royal grant authorizing him to seal leather in Cork City. Perhaps he or his son Cornelius Senior acquired Banteer from Abraham Dixon. In addition to Cornelius Senior he was also probably the father of Teige of Coolroe More south of Clonmeen and of Sheila O Callaghan of Banteer, whose husband Owen O Callaghan of Kilcranathan fought at the battle of Aughrim 1691. Whereas the O Callaghans of Kilcranathan threw in their lot with James II, Cornelius and Teige apparently opted to remain neutral or to support William of Orange. Besides seeking to expand their landed property, they apparently also participated in commercial ventures in Cork City and intermarried with Protestant families.[46]

In 1672 when Cornelius Senior married Joanna Williams, likely the daughter of Robert Williams who held various properties in Cork City, he may have already conformed to the Church of Ireland. Cornelius and his brother Teige probably are identical to the Teige and Connor Callaghan who appeared at Sir John Perceval's house at Burton in March 1686. A month later "a fowling piece, a musket and a brass carbine" stolen from Abraham Dixon of Clonmeen were recovered, one at Richard Gesse's house at Clonmeen, "the other two at Connor Callaghans;" but there was no hint that Connor was responsible for the theft. Also related to this family, though it is not clear how, was Captain Thady O Callaghan, a son of Connor O Callaghan, gentleman, of Coolroe, who was named executor of the will of Donough Óg O Callaghan of Clare in 1698.[47]

In addition to his holdings in Banteer, Cornelius Senior also acquired other O Callaghan lands. In 1696 he leased Dromcummer from the Cork City Council (the administrators of Brettidge's trust) for twenty-one years at £25 for the first three years and £30 for the remainder. He was charged with erecting a house there and planting an orchard. Though he fell in arrears, after inspection of the property the lease was renewed in 1718 at £66 *per annum*.[48] Lord Kingston, on 13 December 1702, leased several properties to him for 999 years at a rent of £200 payable semi-annually on 1 May and 1 November. In addition to Clonmeen (two ploughlands and three gneeves, about 270 acres; a gneeve was a twelfth of a ploughland or ten acres), the following were included:

[46] Dublin, PRO Books of Survey and Distribution 1657, Parish of Clonmeen; Smith, *Cork*, 1:417. See leases involving Teige of Coolroe More and his son Dermot in Casey, *O Kief*, 6:1992-1993, 1997 (10 March 1713, 15 August 1716, 3 April 1717, 30 December 1718). Joseph F. O Callaghan, "The O Callaghans of Kilcranathan, County Cork," *JCHAS* 92 (1987): 106-112; Grove-White, *Notes*, 3:60.

[47] Egmont MSS, 3:371, 373 (18, 23 March 1686, 6 April); Herbert W. Gillman, *Index to the Marriage Licence Bonds of the Diocese of Cork and Ross, Ireland for the years from 1623 to 1750 preserved in the Public Record Office of Ireland* (Cork: Guy & Co. 1896-1897), 22-23; Simington, *Survey*, 6:409, 436, 487; Casey, *O Kief*, 5:533. Dublin, GO, MS 177, pp. 458-459 lists Cornelius Senior, Denis, and Timothy (with the notation that he is the ancestor of the Viscounts Lismore) among the sons of Donough Óg and grandsons of Donough Mór. However that is uncertain. Margaret O Callaghan of Banteer who married Teige O Brien of Kilcor was probably Conoghor McTeige's sister; Donough O Brien, *History of the O Briens from Brian Boroimhe, A.D. 1000 to A.D. 1945* (London: Batsford, 1949), 184; J. G. Simms, *War and Politics in Ireland, 1649-1730* (London: Hambledon Press, 1986), 279, 286.

[48] Richard Caulfield, *The Council Book of the Corporation of the City of Cork from 1609 to 1643 and from 1690 to 1800* (Guildford, Surrey: J. Billing, 1876), 253 (27 April 1696). See also, *ibid.*, 254, 278, 313, 354, 385, 389, 392-393, 396, 401, 403, 627, 652, 862, 1061, 1603.

Gortmore (nine gneeves, about 90 acres); Roskeen (three ploughlands, about 360 acres); Little Dromcummer or Dromcummer Beag (three gneeves, about 30 acres); Kilcaskan (four gneeves, about 40 acres); Coolnahane, and Gurteenbeha (nine gneeves each or about 90 acres each). The total was about 880 acres.[49] As a principal beneficiary of the Cromwellian confiscation, Dame Elizabeth Fenton, known as the Dowager Baroness of Shelburne after Sir William Petty's death in 1687, obtained Clonmeen (880 acres), Gortmore (458), Dromcummer (59), Kilcaskan (129), Roskeen (370), and Gurteenbeha (343). Kingston had received 96 acres in Dromcummer and 122 in Kilcaskan. Cornelius Callaghan, the lessee, was resident at that time at Monkstown lying to the east of Cork harbor opposite Cobh. In 1699 Bishop Dive Downes of Cork reported that "Mr O'Callaghan, a Protestant, lives in Monkstown, in a good square castle with flankers." The Archdeacon family erected the castle, a four storey fortified house, earlier in the seventeenth century, but were dispossessed by Cromwell, and again by William of Orange. Cornelius probably acquired the castle before the end of the century. It manifested to all his wealth and his connections with the mercantile establishment in Cork City.[50]

A deed of gift dated 28 January 1705 throws additional light on the above transaction. Cornelius explained that the Lady Baroness Dowager of Shelburne had leased three ploughlands of Clonmeen to William Hovell, a merchant of Cork City, whose executors subsequently assigned them to Cornelius in return "for valuable consideration." In addition, Hovell's executors "sold and conveyed" to Cornelius lands leased by Robert, Lord Baron of Kingston, to Sir Richard Kyrle who "sold and assigned" them to Hovell. As already mentioned, in 1702 Lord Kingstion leased to Cornelius "three plowlands of Clonmeen *inter alia* for a valuable consideration for 999 years to commence immediately after the determination of Lady Shelburne's right to the premises." Both barons of Kingston were important planters, as was Kyrle, who gave up his interests in Ireland about 1680 to become governor in Carolina. Thus Cornelius purchased or leased permanently the ploughlands of Clonmeen that had once formed part of the patrimony of Donough O Callaghan, the chieftain exiled to Clare. As he styled himself Cornelius Callaghan of Dromaneen, Gentleman, he may have also acquired some portion of Dromaneen from Sir Richard Kyrle or Richard Newman, the beneficiaries of the confiscation.[51]

In accord with the deed just cited, Cornelius granted to his son Robert (probably named for his maternal grandfather) the three ploughlands of Clonmeen together with their stock, namely, 99 dairy cows and four bulls; a plow of eight horses plowing at Curraghrour, part of the lands of Clonmeen; all the corn (wheat) in haggard and on the ground; 40 fat wethers (castrated rams) grazing at Inchidaly; two breeding mares and two colts grazing on the castle lands. He also handed over to Robert "all the writings, leases, counterpart of leases, and escripts touching and concerning the premises" as outlined above. Robert was required to pay Lady Shelburne, during the continuance of her interest

---

[49] Cork, University College, Boole Library, Grehan Papers, A, 1, 1.1 no. 1 (copy dated 18 October 1722), 1.20, 1.33, 1.99, 100, 229; Casey, *O Kief*, 5:378.

[50] *Bishop Dive Downes Visitation of his Diocese 1699*, ed. T. A. Lunham Gibson (n.p. n.pub., 1900): Smith, *Cork*, 1:208.

[51] Mrs. Riordan of Clonmeen, who had the original, gave me a copy of this deed in 1988. I deposited a copy in the Boole Library, University College, Cork.

in the premises, the annual rent of £100 sterling and a yearly quit rent as stipulated in her lease to Hovell. After her interest ceased, the same amounts were payable to John, Baron of Kingston, as stipulated in his lease to Cornelius. All this was to go to Robert on 1 May 1705 and thereafter to whatever issue he might have by "any wife that he shall hereafter be married to." In default of children the lands would pass to Robert's brothers, as Robert thought fit, "it being the intent and meaning of the said Cornelius and Robert Callaghan that the said lands shall still remain in their family and not be sold or conveyed from them by the said Robert Callaghan or his heirs." In other words, they wished to preserve these ancestral lands in the O Callaghan family.

Robert agreed to confirm all the leases made by his father and by Hovell. In addition to the foregoing, Teige Callaghan of Coolroe More, Gentleman, apparently Cornelius's brother, had leased "part of the premises" of Coolroe More (south of Clonmeen) from Hovell at an annual rent of £18. Daniel Connell leased Coolroe Beg for £15 annually; James Brooke and Dennis Callaghan leased the iron work (that Kyrle had started) and Philip Nagle the grist mill, each for £10 annually. John Dore, one of the Cromwellian planters, leased Curraghour, east of Clonmeen, for £45 the first year and £50 thereafter. Roger Fahy and his wife were confirmed in their copyhold of Clonmeen during their lives for "two couple of capons" yearly. Cornelius fixed his seal to this document, but it is missing from the copy made years later. In return for this substantial gift Robert had to pay an annual rent of £100 to Lady Shelburne and a quit rent to Hovell. Cornelius's other leases mentioned in the document brought him a total of £80 annually.

Either as Connor or Cornelius Callaghan of Dromaneen, Cornelius Senior made additional leases (usually of 99 years) of Roskeen and Lower Gortmore situated south of the Blackwater, east of Clonmeen, and Kilcaskan on the opposite side of the river, bringing in £88 annually. By leasing various segments of the O Callaghan estates, he assured himself that those lands would be profitably exploited and that he would receive a steady income from them.[52]

Perhaps he resided chiefly at Banteer though it is possible, if the castles of Dromaneen and Clonmeen had not fallen entirely to ruin, that he may have spent some time there as well. More than likely his principal residence was Clonmeen Old Court reportedly built by Sir Richard Kyrle, lying about 330 feet southwest of Clonmeen Church. His contemporary, Charles Smith remarked: "Clonmene is a good house of Cornelius O Callaghan, Esq. Near it is the parish church and east are the remains of the castle of Clonmeen ruined in the wars of 1641." Clonmeen house may have been situated where the modern Clonmeen Lodge (built by the Grehans about 1841) and Clonmeen House (built in 1893) stand opposite the churchyard.[53]

Cornelius donated a chalice to Clonmeen church (now held at Castlemagner) inscribed as follows: "The gift of Cornelius Calleghane, Esquire, to ye Church of Clonmeene, anno dom. 1718."[54] He also erected a monument in the church with this inscription:

---

[52] Casey, *O Kief,* 6:1989-1990, 1996, nos. 16.27.5677 (30 August 1712), 9.308.3708 (10 October 1710), 25.527.15762 (1 November 1718).

[53] Smith, *Cork,* 1:30; Grove-White, *Notes,* 2:219, 238, citing the Field Books of 1838 and 1840.

[54] Day, "Kilmallock Chalice," *JRSAI* 9 (4th series 1889): 218; *JAPMD,* 3:403. His daughter Mary, the wife of Francis Power, made a bequest of a silver paten to the church of Clonmeen. Grove-White, *Notes,* 2:227.

In the yeare of our
Lord God 1735
the underneath monument was erected by Mr. Cornelius O
Callaghan Sen[r] of
Banetyre for him-
self his wife and Children.

The monument (no longer visible) was surmounted by the family coat of arms and the motto, *fidus et audax*, faithful and bold. This is the first evidence that I know of that O Callaghan motto. Grove-White described the monument as follows: "Arms - Arg. In base a mount vert, on the sinister side, a hurst of oak trees, therefrom issuant a wolf passant, towards the dexter ppr. Crest - A bare dexter arm, embowed, holding bendwise a sword, entwined with a small snake all ppr. Motto - Fidus et Audax." In plain English this means that the arms were depicted on a silver shield. At the base was a green hill with a grove of oak trees on the left, from which a wolf emerged toward the right. The crest displayed a bare right arm, bent, holding a sword around which a snake was entwined. Decorations included a skull and crossbones, a cherub, a head and wings and another skull and crossbones. The lettering was in gilt on black and the armorial bearings were also gilded. The colors were well-preserved when Grove-White described them more than a century ago. Cornelius Senior probably died in the fall of 1739, leaving two sons Timothy and Cornelius; his three daughters Margaret, Mary, and Eleanor were married respectively to Nicholas Chinnery of Dromsecane (a son of Lieutenant John Chinnery, a Cromwellian officer mentioned previously), Francis Power of Roskeen, and Robert Holmes.[55]

Cornelius's oldest son, Robert O Callaghan, Esquire of Clonmeen, who served as justice of the peace in 1709, predeceased his father. Dying sometime in late 1727, he provided for his burial in Clonmeen Church. In addition to a legacy of £100 and another £100 *per annum* he left his wife Mary "the furniture of the best room in my house at Clonmeen, the plate and china dishes belonging to my tea table, my chair, and two of my best horses." He bequeathed Clonmeen to his oldest son Cornelius and Bannagh (144 acres) to his second son Robert, both of whom were under age. Cornelius died in 1731 while still a minor. Robert also provided for the education of his four daughters, Meliah or Mildred, Margaret, Mary, and Joan, and mentioned his brothers Cornelius of Dublin, Timothy, and Cornelius's son Cornelius. Among his executors he named Cornelius Callaghan, Esq. of Dublin, likely his first cousin, the son of Teige of Coolroe More, the brother of Cornelius Senior.

After Robert died in October 1737, his widow, Mary Towgood, who stressed that she and her husband were always Protestants and born of Protestant parents, was appointed guardian for her surviving son Robert. When Mary died in 1750 an auction of her household goods suggests that Clonmeen, a typical house of the landed gentry, was

---

[55] *JAPMD* 2:464; Grove-White, *Notes*, 2:228. Cornelius's will, dated at Banteer on 7 August 1739, was proved on 1 December. Dublin, PRO, Testaments, Prerogative Commission; Prerogative Grants 1738-1741, 42, 52, 64; Thrift Abstracts, 1691, 2873; Grehan Papers, A 1, 1.1, no. 4 (two copies of his will dated 14 October 1737); Dublin, GO MS 143, p. 17 (summary of will dated 1736, proved 18 December 1739).

comfortably, but not luxuriously, furnished. The house included a parlour, common hall, little parlour, green room (bed room), middle room (bedroom), Mrs. Callaghan's room (bedroom), Miss Milly's (Meliah's) room (bedroom), nursery, upper room (bedroom), and kitchen. Sold were chairs, chests, beds, bedclothes, bedcurtains, mirrors, desks, an escritoire, a writing table belonging to Cornelius Senior, old broken guns and pistols, a fowling piece and a musket out of repair, dishes, pots and pans, and kitchen utensils, as well as "an old book of philosophy," a bible, "3 vol. of Clarendon," perhaps his account of the wars of the past century, and Dunstan's Horace. The most costly items were silver candlesticks and other silver objects. Among the properties cited were East Drumcummer north of the Blackwater, Curraghrour, Parkmore, Gortroe, Gougane, Loughleagh, Gurteentamagh, Parkruddery, Inchidaly. Coolkilty, Duinche, Shanour, Coolroemore, Loughlane (Lackloun), Munaduff, and Coolroebeg. Parkmore, Loughleagh, Gurteentamagh, Parkruddery, and Munaduff are unidentified.[56]

Clonmeen Church I

(O'Flanagan, *The Blackwater in Munster*)

---

[56] Grehan Papers, A 1, 1.1, nos. 1.2 (Robert's will dated 8 August 1727; proved 26 February 1728); 1.33 (2 November 1706, marriage settlement between Robert and Mary); 1.34 (death of Cornelius 1731); 1.5 (21 March 1737, Mary's appointment as guardian); A 1, 1.1.2, no. 38 (8 January 1755, auction). See Robert's leases in Casey, *O'Kief*, 6:1989, 1995, 1996, nos. 6.108.1392 (1 May 1710), 22.532.12704 (1 May 1710), 22.533.12765 (22 May 1717), 19.17.9357, 24.14.12766 (18 November 1718). John Callaghan of Mitchelstown and Cornelius Callaghan of Dublin witnessed the deeds of 1710 and 1717 respectively.

The younger Robert held office as justice of the peace in 1738, as a member of the Irish parliament for Clonmeen in 1740, and as a commissioner of the peace in 1750. Daniel O Callaghan, Esq., whose connection to the family is unknown, also served as a commissioner of the peace in 1750 and as justice of the peace in 1768. Appearing in 1757 before the Commissioners of Array (including another Cornelius Callaghan), Robert swore allegiance to the crown and displayed his readiness for military service; though he had a horse he had no weapons. Numerous leases and other documents relating to his properties at Clonmeen have survived. For example, in 1759 he leased lands in Dromcummer to Timothy Lehane for 31 years at a yearly rent of £93.29.25 and two fat pigs, 2 fat turkeys, 2 dozen fat ducks, and 2 dozen fat chickens; the animal payments could be made in cash.[57]

In the census of 1766 Robert was listed among the Protestant parishioners of Clonmeen. In the last two years of his life at least he was blind and had to make his mark and affix his wax seal on legal documents. The Hibernian Chronicle on 6 March 1778 recorded Robert's death in Cork City. As he had no sons to succeed him, he was described as "the last of the ancient family of O'Callaghan of Clonmeen." Though he made a bequest of £2,000 to "my dear wife Ann, otherwise Brady," he left his lands in Bannagh, Clonmeen, and Dromcummer in trust for his nephew Crosbie Morgell of Rathkeale, County Limerick. Ann, who died intestate in 1779 or 1780, was harshly criticized in litigation initiated by John Craggs, the husband of Robert's sister Margaret, who alleged that Robert failed to surrender the legacy left by her father. In the course of the legal wrangling Robert's wife Ann was described as a woman of "low extraction" who lived with him for many years as his housekeeper. Moreover it was charged that they had never been married and that she was a papist and so her legacy of £2,000 should be given to a Protestant. The list of Ann's goods sold at auction after her death included a dining room table and side board, mahogany chairs, French pictures, sconces, brackets, a carpet, copper coal box, kettle, plate warmer, cistern, coffee mill, frying pan, tongs, pots and pans, a clock, an Indian cabinet, glassware, assorted tables, "a bible and a parcell of books," china, several bedsteads, hangings, bolsters and pillows, a salver, spoons, knives, and forks, candlesticks, an old book case, a desk, a chest of drawers, chamber pots, and family pictures. In the Field Book of 1838-1840 it was reported that "the late Robert O Callaghan, was the last person that resided in" Clonmeen Old Court, southwest of Clonmeen Church. His estate there passed through several hands until the Grehan family acquired it early in the nineteenth century.[58]

Cornelius Senior's second son, Cornelius Junior, was his father's principal legatee but apparently died sometime in 1737. His son Cornelius O Callaghan III, Esquire of Banteer, justice of the peace in 1755, was listed in 1766 as one of the Protestant parishioners of Clonmeen and died in 1772. He held lands in fee farm (requiring payment of an annual rent) from Daniel O Callaghan of Mountallon, County Clare, Esq. He is also

[57] *Edwards Cork Remembrancer or Tablet of Memory* (Cork: Anthony Edwards, 1792), 106; H. F. Berry, "Justices of the Peace for the County Cork," *JCHAS* 3 (1897): 64, 107; Denham-Jephson, *Miscellany,* 371; Grehan Papers, A 1, 1.1, nos. 1.7-19; no. 15 (10 August 1759). The Lehanes were my father's cousns.

[58] Grehan Papers, A 1, 1.1, nos. 21 (Robert's will dated 10 January 1778), 23 (28 May 1780, auction), 1.2, nos. 35-46 (1748-1792). The charge against Ann appears in 1.1.2, no. 46. Dublin, PRO, Prerogative Will (10 January 1778); Thrift Abstracts, 1835. *The Hibernian Chronicle* cited by Ó Murchadha, *Names,* 72 listed Robert's death on 6 March 1778.

noteworthy for having taken part with Edmund Blake in the world's first steeplechase (or or so it was reported) over four and a half miles along the Awbeg River eastward from St. John Church in Buttevant to the steeple of St. Mary Church in Doneraile in 1752. History did not record the winner. The event, sponsored by the Duhallow Hunt, an association of landed gentry, gained fame as the beginning of steeplechase racing.

While Cornelius III left his estate to his wife, he designated Robert O Callaghan of Clonmeen (who died in 1778) and his cousin Cornelius O Callaghan the Younger of Shanbally, County Tipperary as his heirs after her decease. Cornelius Senior's third son Timothy probably should be identified with Timothy O Callaghan of Bregoge (a few miles west of Buttevant), justice of the peace in 1730, whose will was proved in 1759. The male line descended from Cornelius Senior seems to have died out by the end of the eighteenth century and most of the family's lands eventually passed into the possession of the O Callaghans of Tipperary. In 1814 the village of Clonmeen was said to belong to Viscount Lismore and the Field Book of 1840 reported that Banteer was also his property.[59]

The O Callaghans of Glynn, Dromskehy, Derrygallon, and Cahirduggan

According to family tradition, the O Callaghans of Glynn, Dromskehy, Derrygallon, and Cahirduggan descend from Conor, a son of Cahir Modarta, outlawed in 1642, who acquired possession of Dromskehy (Drom Sceiche, about four miles west of Banteer in the parish of Dromtarrif) and died around 1660. However, that is not certain. Denis O Callaghan, the known progenitor of this family, may perhaps be identified with that Denis Callaghan of Lismeelcunnin (Lios Maol Coinín, about two miles west of Kanturk) who went surety for the parish priest of Clonmeen and Kilshannig in 1704.[60] How the family came into possession of Glynn, Dromskehy, Derrygallon, and Cahirduggan is unclear. Glynn or Glen is about three miles south of Clonmeen straddling the Glen River. Either Denis or his sons, Cornelius of Dromskehy and Roger of Derrygallon (Doire Ghealbhan, three miles west of Kanturk) likely conformed to the Established Church in order to retain their lands and their status.

In 1712 Cornelius (1679-1748/9) acquired a life interest in Dromskehy and Dromahoe (Drom Dhá Thuath. less than a mile to the south) for himself, his wife, and his younger brother Roger of Lismeelcunnin at £70 per annum. Five years later he and Roger (now of Derrygallon) took a lease for 99 years at a yearly rent of £105. In the following year Francis Edwards of Dublin released them from their obligation to pay £70 annually for Dromahoe and Dromskehy.[61] Cornelius's son, Denis (1708-1792), destined for the

[59] Wills of Cornelius Junior (Banteer, 10 February 1737), Timothy of Bregoge (2 November 1758, proved 28 April 1759), in Dublin, PRO, Testaments; Thrift Abstracts, 1684, 1835; Betham Abstracts; Berry, "Justices", *JCHAS* 3 (1897): 62-65; Grove-White, *Notes*, 1:279, 2:219-220, 238; *Great and Direct Roads*, col. 499.

[60] Burke, *Priests*, 374-375 (22 June 1712), 377 (9 April 1714); Grove-White, *Notes*, 2:222; David G. Collingwood, "O'Callaghan Family Documents," www.angelfire.com/folk/trotman/ocal.htm.

[61] Casey, *O'Kief*, 6:1992-1993,1994, 1995, nos. 17.173.8478 (9 August 1712), 18.50.9648 (8 August 1717), 21.342.11721 (18-19 August 1718), 22.170.11706 (15 August 1718); Dublin, PRO, Testaments (Cornelius's will, dated 20 March 1708/9; probated 30 September 1749); Betham Abstracts; Marriage License Bonds; *14 RDK*, 253.

law, was admitted to the Middle Temple in 1729; his son, Cornelius of Dromskehy (1756-1831), acquired Cahirduggan (Cathair Dhúgáin, near Doneraile) by marriage in 1781.[62]

Like many younger sons, Roger of Derrygallon (d. 1747/8) was trained as an attorney, an occupation that the O Callaghans valued for defending property claims in court. His son Denis of Glynn (d. 1760), also an attorney, married Mary, the daughter of Robert O Callaghan Senior of Clonmeen.[63] Upon the extinction of the male line of the O Callaghans of Clare in 1791, Denis and Mary's grandson, another Denis, claimed the chieftainship. This was clearly an error because the link between his great-greatgrandfather Denis and the principal branch of the family settled at Clonmeen and Dromaneen has never been established.[64]

The family was well connected through marriage with the landed Protestant gentry, namely, Gillman, Dore, Foott, Holmes, Davies, and Pyne. Several young widows, still of child-bearing age, whose husbands died in their prime, married O Callaghan men and likely brought the property of their deceased spouses into their new family. Arthur Pyne O Callaghan (1837-1930) of Cahirduggan, ordained in the Church of Ireland, emigrated to New Zealand where his numerous progeny live today.[65]

His grandson, Denis Richard O Callaghan (1825-1902), established a branch of the family at Killeenleigh (An Cillín Liath, about two and a half miles southwest of Kanturk). In 1863, he was accused of urging Catherine Connell to abandon her baby outside the gates of the Kanturk workhouse. Moreover, he was charged with seducing a maid in Kanturk who gave birth to a child in 1873 and in the next year he was again accused of seducing another young woman. In 1877 he married Adelaide Mathilda Grainger, a wealthy Englishwoman by whom he had two sons, Richard Grainger and Cornelius Leslie. An enthusiastic horseman, in 1887 for £6,600 he purchased Brackenstown, an estate of 207 acres outside Dublin noted as a place to breed fine horses. His son Richard Grainger Denis O Callaghan achieved distinction as a Major in the British army during the Boer War and World War I. However, in 1903, he was sentenced to three months in Mountjoy Jail for manslaughter of a boy as he sped away from the Phoenix Park races in his new car.[66] His brother Cornelius Leslie was an avid huntsman who served as Master of The Fingal Harriers Hunt and was awarded seven silver cigar ashtrays engraved wth the family crest and the motto *Fidus et Audax*.[67] In 1922 Richard sold Brackenstown and moved to Australia. Cornelius also seems to have left Ireland.

[62] Macgeagh and Sturgess, *Register*, 1:307 (8 October 1729); Dublin, PRO Marriage License Bonds (20 August 1781); Testaments; Thrift Abstracts, 2141; Dublin, GO MS 805.

[63] N.M. (Norman Moore, M.D.), in the *Dictionary of National Biography* 9 (1887): 393, s.v. Ceallachan, stated that Denis was believed to be "the last chief in direct line of the chief branch of his race." He cited the "genealogical manuscripts of the late B. C. Fisher."

[64] MacLysaght, *Kenmare Manuscripts*, 302 (8 May 1724); Dublin PRO Marriage License Bonds (Roger, 14 October 1713; Denis, 24 June 1747); Testaments (Roger's will, 10 October 1747; probated 5 March 1747/8; Denis's will, April 1754; probated 26 September 1768); Thrift Abstracts, 2141.

[65] Dublin, GO MS 177, pp. 460-463, MS 179, p. 178, and MS 289, p. 170; Burke, *Gentry*, 2:520; Grove-White, *Notes*, 3:14. Mrs. Veronica McLernon, Bishopstown, Co. Cork, kindly sent me a genealogy comparable to that in the Genealogical Office.

[66] https://www.historyeye.ie/brackenstown-house-part-2 citing Dublin, Registry of Deeds 1887, book 32, p. 90; The Irish Times, 8 May 1878, and 25 July 1903.

[67]https://www.the-saleroom.com/en-gb/auction-catalogues/jacobs-and-hunt/catalogue-id-2769102/lot-6832163.

The Penal Laws

The O Callaghans in Tipperary

Another important arm of the O Callaghans settled in Tipperary. Like those of Banteer and Dromskehy their connection to the main family of Dromaneen and Clonmeen is not entirely certain. Nevertheless, they seem to have been descended from Teige or Timothy O Callaghan, gentleman, variously identified as of Clonmeen and Coolroe More, a brother of Cornelius Senior of Banteer.[68]

Teige had several sons, the third of whom, Cornelius O Callaghan (b. c. 1682-1740/1), founded the family fortune in Tipperary. Given the ever-present threat to family lands, the O Callaghans realized the value of having one of their own trained in the legal profession. Thus, "Cornelius Callaghan eldest son of Timothy C. of Bantry, Co. Cork, gent." was admitted as a student at Gray's Inn in London on 24 December 1700-1701.[69] Cornelius was Timothy's third son, not the eldest and their residence was Banteer, not Bantry. The eldest son would normally inherit his father's estates and Cornelius did not. If the family needed a lawyer, a younger son would be sent to acquire a legal education. The O Callaghans, like most Gaelic families, tended to repeat personal names from one generation to the next, but it is likely that Cornelius may be identified with Conor O Callaghan who witnessed the will of Daniel O Keeffe of Dromagh Castle on 10 March 1699 and with Cornelius O Callaghan of Dromaneen named as one of his executors by Dermot O Mullane in 1705 and as a witness to the will of his cousin, Dermot's son John; more than likely because he was an attorney he was entrusted with custody of the will.[70]

Most notably, Cornelius Callaghan, Esq., of Dublin, abjured the Catholic faith on Christmas Eve, 24 December 1709. Whether the O Callaghans of Banteer and Clonmeen had already done so is uncertain, but many families recognized that conversion to the Established Church of Ireland helped to guarantee the security of their estates and to facilitate their participation in the dominant society. The one who renounced his faith was expected to do so publicly in a Church of Ireland parish and his action was also reported in the press. No doubt Cornelius did so in order to advance his career as a barrister, but he may also have taken marital considerations into account.[71]

In 1709, the very year of his conversion, he married Maria Jolly, the daughter of Robert Jolly and Elinor Meagher of Knockelly Castle, near Fethard in Tipperary. Maria Jolly was heir to her parents' estates. When Cornelius came courting, his future mother-in-law asked where his estates were and he pointed to his tongue as the sum and substance of his wealth.[72] He and Maria were probably married in Holy Trinity Church in Fethard in 1709, perhaps after her father's death in August and just before the groom's

---

[68] Leslie G. Pine, *The New Extinct Peerage, 1884-1971* (London: Heraldry Today, 1972), 180, identified Timothy as of Blantyre, an obvious error for Banteer. Teige leased "part of the premises" of Coolroe More from William Hovell at an annual rent of £18.

[69] Foster, *Register of Admissions to Gray's Inn*, 352, fol. 1371.

[70] Dublin, GO, MS 143, p. 17; Collins, "Extracts," *JCHAS* 66 (1961): 51-54, esp. 52

[71] Eileen O'Byrne and Anne Chamney, *The Convert Rolls: The Calendar of the Convert Rolls, 1703-1838 with Fr Wallace Clare's Annotated List of Converts, 1703-78* (Dublin: Irish Manuscripts Commission, 1981), 303; Michael Brown, Charles I. McGrath, and Thomas P. Power, eds., *Converts and Conversion in Ireland, 1650–1850* (Dublin: Four Courts Press, 2005)..

[72] For a different version of this story see *The London and Paris Observer* (Paris: A. and W. Galignani, 1828), 4:427, and the *Clare Journal*, 16 May 1872, cited by Charles Ffrench Blake-Forster, *The Irish Chieftains, or, a struggle for the Crown* (Dublin: McGlashran & Gill, 1872), 611.

abjuration of the Catholic faith.[73] He apparently made good on his promise to Mrs. Jolly and earned a lot of money as a lawyer in the service of the landed gentry in Tipperary, Cork, and Kerry. It was reported that Sir Theobald (or Toby) Butler, Solicitor-General of Ireland under James II, became his patron and helped to make his fortune.[74] For example, Cornelius was one of the arbiters in disputes involving Lord Kenmare at Killarney in August 1732.[75] In his will of 1739 Cornelius Senior of Clonmeen referred to his nephew Cornelius Callaghan, counselor-at-law. His political base was the borough of Fethard (about ten miles southwest of Cashel) where he was elected a freeman in 1710 and served as recorder (or town clerk) from 1712 to 1734. Together with Sir Redmond Everard, he was elected to the Irish parliament for Fethard in 1713, but a defeated candidate protested their election.[76] As the Everards encountered financial difficulties, Cornelius arranged loans and mortgages for them and ultimately acquired their property around Clogheen. In 1721 he purchased their holdings in the baronies of Iffa and Offa for £11,500. Thereafter he and his descendants vied for political ascendancy in Fethard with the Bartons, a merchant family. Cornelius and his heirs fostered the development of Clogheen by encouraging artisans, mostly Protestant, to settle there. They also endeavored to improve the land by insisting that tenants build houses, plant orchards, enclose fields for pasturage, and exploit the land wisely. He established his residence at Shanbally (An Seanbhaile) about four miles from the village of Clogheen (about eight miles south of Cahir) in the parish of Shanrahan, where he built a mansion around 1735. His library there included a copy of Keating's *History of Ireland* as well as another anonymous work with the same name.[77]

His death "at an advanced age" was reported in the *Dublin Journal*, 3/6 January 1740/1. *Pue's Occurences* recorded the death at his residence on Nicholas Street in Dublin of "one of the most eminent lawyers in the kingdom" on Saturday evening 6 January 1740/1. His last will and testament was proved and administration of his estate was granted to his widow, Mary O Callaghan, as sole executrix on 15 January 1740. She died on 6 June 1757.[78] Cornelius was buried in the family mausoleum in the churchyard

---

[73] Jolly died on 20 August 1709. *Journal of the Association for the Preservation of the Memorials of the Dead in Ireland* 7 (1907-1909): 176-77.

[74] Ffrench Blake-Forster, *The Irish Chieftains*, 611.

[75] Edward MacLysaght, *Kenmare Manuscripts* (Dublin: Stationery Office, 1942), 54, 87, and 15, 148, 269.

[76] W. G. Skehan, "Extracts from the Minutes of the Corporation of Fethard, Co. Tipperary," *The Irish Genealogist* 4 (1971): 305-22.

[77] Henry F. Macgeagh and H. A. C. Sturgess, *Register of Admissions to the Honourable Society of the Middle Temple, from the Fifteenth Century to the Year 1944*, 3 vols. (London : Honourable Society of the Middle Temple, 1949), 1:295 (30 May 1724); *Journals of the House of the Commons of the Kingdom of Ireland from the Eleventh Year of King James the First to the Twenty-fifth Year of the Reign of his Majesty King George the Second Inclusive*, 9 vols. (Dublin: Abraham Bradley, 1753-1757), 3:941, 949, 956, 958; Mary Johnston-Liik, ed., *History of the Irish Parliament 1692-1800*, 6 vols. (Belfast: Ulster Historical Foundation, 2002-2003), 2:54, 5:377-78, no. 1560; Thomas Laffan, "Fethard, County Tipperary. Its Charters and Corporation Records, with some Notice of the Fethard Everards," *JRSAI* 36 (1906) 143-153; T. P. Power, *Land*, 41, 53, 84, 88, 149-150, 168-172, 236-237; Toby Barnard, "Histories of the 1640s," in Micheál Ó Siochrú, ed., *Kingdoms in Crisis: Ireland in the 1640s: Essays in Honour of Donal Cregan* (Dublin: Four Courts Press, 2001), 33; Irish Georgian Society, *Newsletter, Spring 1985*, 5. I want to thank my colleague, Professor Maurice O'Connell, for bringing this *Newsletter* to my attention.

[78] *Debrett's Peerage of the United Kingdom of Great Britain and Ireland*, 2 vols. (London: J. Moyes, 1825), 2:1068-69.

of Shanrahan, a mile west of Clogheen. The mausoleum is in need of repair as vandals have damaged it. The building contains "a finely-executed marble memorial to Cornelius O Callaghan by David Sheehan, signed and dated 1742. The tympanum contains a vivid portrait of O Callaghan reading a book, with putti [cherubs] and an urn on top of the pediment."[79]

Memorial of Cornelius O Callaghan, Shanrahan

An eighteenth-century mezzotint portrait of Cornelius Callaghan or O Callaghan in the National Portrait Gallery in Dublin is, to my knowledge, the earliest pictorial representation of a member of the O Callaghan family.[80] The portrait was done by John Brooks around 1740 or after. The black and white engraving depicts a middle-aged gentleman wearing a white wig, a black cloak or pleader's gown over a black buttoned jacket with a side pocket. About his neck he wears a white divided bib. The white sleeves of his shirt protrude from the sleeves of his waistcoat. His right hand rests on his breast and in his left hand he holds a document, but it is difficult to read it. His face is full and he appears to have a jowly neck, a prominent nose, eyes directed toward the viewer. A bag sits on a table to his left. Below the portrait is a Latin inscription divided by the O'Callaghan coat of arms. A wolf comes out from a wood on the right. This differs from the usual depiction showing the wolf emerging from the left. Atop the shield is a flexed arm holding a sword around which a snake is entwined.

The inscription consists of twelve verses taken from his tomb at Clogheen celebrating Cornelius's career as a legal advocate. They read as follows:

Rostri dulce Decus Legum Tutamen et Aequi,
Cui toties Dubii Credita Jura Fori?
Veridice Hibernum qui Regerat ore Tribunal
Huncse tibi Lector Pieta Tabella Refert
Quid Nomen Referam Scis tam Callaghan ille est
Cui Cessit Rostrum, Cessit et omne Forum,

---

[79] www.buildingsofireland.ie › Surveys.

[80] The measurements are 14 in. x 10 in. (356 mm x 255 mm) plate size; 15 3/8 in. x 10 3/8 in. (391 mm x 263 mm) paper size. John Brooks was an engraver working in Dublin in the second and third quarters of the eighteenth century. His earliest known engraving is dated 1740.

Quid Pietas, quid Lingua tibi, Quid profuit Aetas
Quid tibi Virtutum Splendida tota Cohors,
Mens tibi Vocis Iter properavit Candere vestra
Ne Possit Diras flectere Lingua Deas,
Cognatos Animus Petiit Coetusque Beatos
Erectum ad Clogheen Caeterea Marmor habet.

The anonymous poet praised him as "the sweet ornament of the bar, the defender of the laws and justice," a man who brought certitude to doubt, and "with his tongue truly ruled the Irish tribunal," his "spirit now seeks the company of his happy relatives" in the monument erected at Clogheen.

Cornelius and Maria had numerous progeny, fifteen in all, as he recorded their names and birthdates: Robert, b. 10 July 1710; Cornelius, b. 27 August 1711; Donal, b. 28 July 1712; Thomas, b. 15 August 1713; Mary, b. 14 August 1714; William, b. 10 July 1715; Matthew, b. 11 July 1716; Ellenor, b. 25 July 1717; Mary, b. 10 July 1718; Margaret, b. 18 January 1719; Penelope, b. 29 January 172(?); Leonora, b. 28 May 1723; Timothy, 20 June 1725; Lucretia, b. 19 November 1728; Mariamne, b. 14 September 1730.. Most of them were baptized in Dublin at St. Nicholas Within, Nicholas St. and Christ Church Place. Located in the center of the city, the family residence, as one might expect, was not far from the Inns of Court.[81]

Most of Cornelius and Maria's chlldren died in childbirth, infancy, or early childhood. Their three sons, Robert (1710-1761), Cornelius (1712-1781), and Thomas (1713-?), after attending school in Dublin, were then admitted to Trinity College: Robert on 30 March 1725/6, Cornelius, 4 June 1728, and Thomas, 17 November 1730. As was typical of the landed gentry they were trained in the law and were admitted to the Middle Temple, Robert in 1728 and Cornelius in 1732. All were active in Tipperary politics.[82]

Robert served as Recorder, an officer of the town corporation of Fethard in 1742-1754, and petitioned parliament in 1753 concerning the construction of a highway from Clonmel through Clogheen and Mitchelstown to Doneraile. In 1755 he was elected to parliament and took his seat in January 1756, serving until his death. The Commons journal recorded that he took the required oaths, including the oath of abjuration, rejecting the dethroned Stuart kings. Meantime the family continued to prosper. Whereas the rental income from the family estates was £477 in 1743, it was £6,000 in 1760. The marriage portion for members of the family could range from £2,000 to £6,000. After mid-century that amount could approach £20,000. Alicia Worth Callaghan, whom Robert married in 1735, was reportedly worth £10,000. When Dr. Thomas Sheridan, a friend of Jonathan Swift, whose school Robert and Cornelius had attended, fell ill, Robert took him into his home at Rathfarnham, where he died in 1738.[83] Dying childless late in 1760 or

---

[81] The Parish register records the death of eight O Callaghan children without naming them, on 5 August 1713; 7 October 1715; 6 August 1717; 22 December 1718; 12 September 1723; 27 September 1723; 20 June 1725; 20 February 1732. The death of Penelope, his only surviving daughter, was recorded on 6 April 1736. W.R. "The Church of St. Nicholas Within," *The Irish Builder* (July 1, 1890), 158-159.

[82] *Alumni Dublinenses : a register of the students, graduates, professors and provosts of Trinity College in the University of Dublin (1593-1860)*, ed. George Dames Burtchaell and Thomas Ulick Sadleir, 2d ed. (Dublin: A. Thom 1935), 127-128.

[83] Thomas Sheridan, *The Life of the Rev. Dr. Jonathan Swift* (London: J. R. Rivington et al., 1787), 338-339.

early 1761, Robert stipulated that he should be buried with his parents in a vault in the church of Shanrahan.

Cornelius O Callaghan of Shanbally, County Tippperary

(National Gallery of Ireland, NGI 10187)

In 1748 Rev. John K'eogh, chaplain to Lord Kingston, dedicated his *Vindication of the Antiquities of Ireland* to "Robert Callaghan, Esq., One of the Governors of the County of Tipperary, and Captain of an Independent Company of Foot." After lauding his virtues and his family, K'eogh noted his "great loyalty and steady adherence to the present government" and his support for "the Protestant interest, which you have always at heart, against Popery and arbitrary power." As was his custom, K'eogh also wrote a separate dedication to Robert's wife, Alicia. In the appendix to his work, he included a genealogy tracing the descent of Cellachán of Cashel, the ancestor of the O Callaghans, from Adam. Among the numerous subscribers to his book were the following members of the family: Robert Callaghan, Esq. (the dedicatee); Donato O Callaghan, Esq. (perhaps Donough of Kilgory, County Clare; Dr. Cornelius O Callaghan; Cornelius O Callaghan of Banteer (probably Cornelius III, d. 1772); Tho[mas] Callaghan (probably Robert's brother); Robert Callaghan of Clonmeen (grandson of Cornelius Senior, d. 1778); Dennis Callaghan, attorney (perhaps Denis of Dromskehy); Mrs. Callaghan (Alicia?); Mrs. Mary Callaghan (perhaps Mary Towgood, widow of Robert, son of Cornelius Senior of Clonmeen, d. 1750); Miss Callaghan of Banteer; Tim[othy]. Callaghan, Esq. (perhaps Timothy of Bregoge, d. 1759). The list reveals the continuing connection between the O Callaghans of Tipperary and their cousins in Cork.[84]

Robert's brother Cornelius married Elinor Ford of Limerick who brought him £10,000. Besides service in the municipal corporation of Fethard (Portreeve 1738; Recorder, 1754-1755; Sovereign 1751-1752, 1761-1762, 1764, 1766), he was elected to the Irish parliament for Fethard in 1761 and was succeeded by his nephew, another Cornelius, in 1768. Elected again for Newtownards in 1775, his annual income at that time was £5,000. He died in England in 1782 without children to inherit his estates. Both he and his brother Robert were active Freemasons. Robert served as Senior Grand Warden in 1738 and Cornelius in 1737 and then as Deputy Grand Master from 1738 to 1746.[85]

There seems reason to believe that one or the other of the brothers found a place in the *Memoirs* of Laetitia Pilkington (d. 1750), the wife of Rev. Matthew Pilkington, whose extramarital affairs prompted her infidelity and led to their divorce.[86] Thinking that she was secure "from any farther Attacks from the Male World," she endured "a furious onset from 'A Tinsel Babler Blunderbuss of Law.'" That was "One C——n, a person not otherwise known, than by his being acquainted with all the tricks and roguery

---

[84] John K'eogh, *A Vindication of the Antiquities of Ireland* (Dublin: S. Powell, 1748). T. C. Barnard, "Writing and Publishing Histories in Eighteenth Century Ireland," in Mark Williams and, Stephen Paul Forrest, eds., *Constructing the Past: Writing Irish History, 1600-1800* (Woodbridge: Boydell, 2010), 95-112, esp. 105-106.

[85] *Journals of the House of the Commons of the Kingdom of Ireland*, 9:182, 219, 247, 636, 646; Dublin, PRO Testaments; Thrift Abstracts, 1765, 1846, 1941, 2891-2892 (Robert's will, 26 December 1758; proved 13 January 1761; Cornelius's will, 6 March 1782, proved 2 July 1782); Betham Abstracts; Skehan, "Extracts," *TIG* 4 (1969): 81-92, and 4 (1970): 183-193; Johnston-Liik, *Irish Parliament*, 2:54, 330, 5:378-379, 381, nos. 1561, 1563; John T. Collins, "Gleanings from Old Irish Newspapers," *JCHAS* 69 (1964): 56-59, citing *The Cork Journal* of 22 January 1756; Casey, *O Kief*, 6:2403; T. P. Power, *Land*, 88, 93, 227; William Nolan and Thomas McGrath, eds., *Tipperary History and Society: Interdisciplinary Essays on the History of an Irish County* (Templeogue, Dublin: Geography Publications, 1985), 297.

[86] *Memoirs of Mrs. Laetitia Pilkington Wife to the Rev. Mr. Matthew Pilkington*, 3 vols. Dublin: Privately Printed, 1748-54). Also see *Memoirs of Laetitia Pilkington*, ed. A. C. Elias, Jr. (Athens: University of Georgia Press, 2016), 486-87.

of the courts; who, because I treated him with the contempt he deserved, railed at me wherever he went, insomuch that I was obliged to compliment him with the following lines." In a poem addressed to "Counsellor C——N," she "looked through all the vile deceit, . . . and knew the CHEAT." Dismissing him as a "dull imposter," who thought "to purchase me with gold or drink," she demanded that he cease his suit and threatened otherwise "or in a print, I swear to show you,// So like, that all mankind shall know you." Despite that, he told "all the lawyers at the Rose Club, that I made love to him," prompting her to assail him in vulgar verses and to demand that they be read aloud "for the amusement of the company of lawyers." She heard that even though "this song made C——n blush," "he promised to publish" it; but when he did not she decided do so herself. Whoever "C——n" may have been, Mrs. Pilkington's *Memoirs* convey something of the character of social life among the Anglo-Irish aristocracy in eighteenth century Dublin.

The youngest of the three brothers, Thomas of Shanbally had only one son, Cornelius (1740/1-1797) who, at the age of twenty-nine, occupied the family seat in the Irish House of Commons in 1768. Succeeding his uncle Cornelius "who is much connected with the Speaker," John Ponsonby, he represented Fethard in four parliaments from 1768 to 1785. In 1772 in a duel over control of local government in Fethard he wounded William Barton in the thigh. He voted in favor of the Catholic Relief Act of 1775 permitting Catholics to take a simple oath of allegiance to the king. In that year he was described as "a gentleman that requires great caution to talk with - has always been in opposition - he asked and got from Lord Harcourt a living of £150 - gave at that time thro' Mr. Scott some expectation of his support - he lately married Mr. Ponsonby's daughter [1774]." The marriage alliance with the Speaker of the House obviously advanced his political and social ambitions and in 1785 King George II appointed him "Lord Baron Lismore of Shanbally in the Co. Tipperary" in the Irish peerage.

Relinquishing his seat in the Commons to a relative, he took his seat in the Irish House of Lords on 30 June. His arms were the same as those of Cornelius Senior of Banteer mentioned above: "Argent in base, a mount vert, on the sinister side a hurst of oak trees, therefrom issuant a wolf passant towards the dexter ppr." The crest was "a naked dexter arm embowed, holding a sword bendwise, entwined with a snake all ppr." His motto was *Fidus et Audax*. Meanwhile he maintained his political base in Fethard where he held the post of Sovereign, that is, head of the municipal council in 1786 and 1790.[87]

Communication between the O Callaghans of Tipperary and Clare, as deriving from a common ancestry in Cork, is illustrated by a letter from Richard O Connell of Clare to his cousin Maurice O Connell of Derrynane in Kerry on 29 December 1781. He commented that

a Mr. O Callaghan, of Shanbally, in the County of Tipperary [Cornelius], a grandson of old Counsellor O Callaghan, had my Grand Father's Papers,

---

[87] Pine, *Extinct Peerage*, 180; Lascelles, *Liber Munerum*, 2:47, 61 (Lodge's Baronetage); Berry, "English Settlement," *JCHAS* 12 (1906): 7; Grove-White, *Notes*, 4:61; T. N. Sadleir, "The Register of Kilkenny School (1685-1800)," *JRSAI* 54 (1924): 152-169; Johnston-Liik, *Irish Parliament*, 2:54, 5:379-380, no. 1562; David Large, "Irish House of Commons in 1769," *Irish Historical Studies* 11 (1958-1959):38-39; *The Irish Parliament of 1775 from an Official and Contemporary Manuscript*, ed. William Hunt (Dublin: Hodges Figgis, 1907), 39; T. P. Power. *Land*, 273-274, 283-291, 294; Art Kavanagh and William Hayes, *O'Callaghan & Otway of Tipperary* (Create Space. 2013), 5-8.

---

and when I began to mend, I went to enquire for them. If I had not been a fool, all I could do was to apply to one of the O Callaghans of Kilgory [Donough or Daniel] to write to O Callaghan of Shanbally, his intimate Acquaintance. He excused himself by telling me he would go to that County last October and do my Business, but he is not yet gone, nor in truth do I expect much from him.

Cornelius O Callaghan, Baron Lismore[88]

Whatever the outcome of that matter, Cornelius died on 12 July 1797 at the age of fifty-six.[89] The further history of the O Callaghans of Tipperary will be told in the following chapter.

---

[88] Painting by Hugh Douglas Hamilton in 1769. Provenance: Lord Lismore; Marsh Auction House, Cork, Shanbally Castle Sale, September 1935, lot 191 with Arthur Tooth & Sons, London. https://www.christies.com/lotfinder/Lot/hugh-douglas-hamilton-1739-1808-portrait-of-197656-details.aspx

[89] Mary Anne Bianconi O Connell, *The Last Colonel of the Irish Brigade: Count O Connell and Old Irish Life at Home and Abroad*, 2 vols. (London: Kegan, Paul, Trench, 1892), 2:275-276; Pine, *Extinct Peerage*, 180-181; George E. Cokayne, *The Complete Peerage of England, Scotland, Ireland, Great Britain and the United Kingdom*, new ed., 13 vols. (London: St. Catherine, 1910-1959), 8:81. Dublin, PRO, Prerogative Court in 1797; Brady, *Records*, 3:317.

Although several branches of the O Callaghan family enjoyed the prestige of belonging to the landed gentry, it is likely that many of them lived well beyond their means and incurred heavy debts. Landlords as a whole became more concerned than ever to extort the highest possible rents from their tenants with unfortunate consequences for the latter. The eighteenth century was perhaps the most brutal for Irish Catholics because of the severity of the Penal Laws. In the belief that they would be able to enjoy the full benefits of society, especially in the cities of Dublin, Cork, and Limerick, only by conforming to the Established Church several O Callaghans renounced the Catholic faith. In addition to those already mentioned the converts included:[90]

Name	Place	Date
Cornelius, Esq.	Dublin	4 June 1728
John, gentleman	Dublin	26 May 1735
Timothy, servant	Prospect Hall, Tipperary	15 October 1747
John	Carrigrohane	18 March 1748
Darby, gentleman	Dromtariff	25 January 1748
James	Skull	15 January 1748
Charles	Dublin	7 March 1754
Cornelius	Dublin	19 November 1759
Timothy	Mallow	12 April 1762
Charles	Diocese of Cloyne	6 December 1762
Ellen	Cork	9 October 1764
Thomas	Kilgobbun, Co. Dublin	7 December 1764
Robert	Dublin	20 May 1766
Daniel, gentleman	Aghadown	21 July 1766
Dennis	Cashel	16 April 1771
Daniel O Callaghan, Esq.	Limerick	11 May 1772
Edmond, gentleman	Limerick, now of Dublin	14 November 1772
Hellen		1 August 1779
Andrew O Callaghan	Dublin	4 April 1790
Michael	Currans, Co. Kerry	18 April 1790

Toward the latter part of the century, however, the harshness of the laws was ameliorated and Catholics began to gain some measure of civil rights. Full emancipation had to wait, however, until the following century.

[90] O Byrne, *Convert Rolls*, 38-39, 220, 284, 294.

CHAPTER 8

CATHOLIC EMANCIPATION, THE FAMINE, AND THE LAND LEAGUE

The nineteenth century opened with the Act of Union and the abolition of the Irish parliament and ended with agitation for Home Rule. In the intervening years Catholics gained civil rights, but relationships between landlords and tenants deteriorated even more. As the Great Famine decimated the population, thousands fled the country seeking a new life abroad. While the Fenians plotted to overthrow the government the Land League sought to give tenants a real right to their land. At the same time a new Irish nationalism, sparked in part by the Gaelic revival, that tried to recover the ancient literature and encourage the use of the language, fueled the drive toward independence.[1]

The Act of Union and Catholic Emancipation

The outbreak of the French Revolution, an abortive French invasion of Ireland in 1798, and Napoleon's attempt to dominate Europe frightened the English government, which recognized that a foreign power might use Ireland to threaten England. In order to quell dissent the government proposed to abolish the Irish parliament and to declare the union of the crowns of England and Ireland, a plan that did not meet with universal acceptance. Early in 1799 Cornelius O Callaghan, the second Baron Lismore, subscribed to a petition by the people of Tipperary protesting the proposed union. Lord Lismore's younger brother, Sir Robert William O Callaghan (1777-1840), a member of parliament for Bandon Bridge (1797-1800), who later pursued a military career, voted against the union in 1799 and 1800. Others, however, were prepared to give their votes in return for honors or other compensation. At last the government had its way and the Act of Union of 1800 united the crowns of England, Scotland, and Ireland and abolished the Irish parliament. In the future Ireland would send its representatives to Westminster. As the the parliamentary borough of Fethard was dissolved, the O Callaghans of Tipperary and

---

[1] K. Theodore Hoppen, *Ireland since 1800: Conflict and Conformity* (London: Longman, 1989); Foster, *Modern Ireland*, 293-318, and R. F. Foster, "Ascendancy and Union," in *The Oxford History of Ireland*, ed. R. F. Foster (Oxford: Oxford University Press, 1992), 134-173; James S. Donnelly, Jr., *The Land and the People of Nineteenth-Century Cork: The Rural Economy and the Land Question* (London: Routledge & Kegan Paul, 1975).

their rivals, the Bartons, each received £7,500 in compensation.[2]

After the overthrow of Napoleon the French threat no longer seemed quite so important, but the winds of change were stirring. Under the leadership of Daniel O Connell, a movement was set afoot to gain emancipation for Catholics from all the civil restraints they had labored under for the last century. The Catholic Emancipation Act of 1829 allowed Catholics to worship freely, build churches (called chapels to distinguish them from the churches of the Church of Ireland), enter the legal and medical professions, own property, and sit in parliament. As a consequence several Catholic churches were erected in O Callaghan's Country, e.g., at Banteer, Glantane, Kilpadder, and Bweeng.[3] Subsequently O Connell turned his attention to the repeal of the legislative union of Ireland and Britain, but without success. A story suggesting O Connell's skill as a lawyer concerned Callaghan O Callaghan of Kerry, who was accused of a crime; though he knew English, he would only speak Irish. When O Callaghan was brought to trial and denied that he understood English, an interpreter was appointed. O Connell, representing the plaintiff, crossexamined him in English; but then, noting that O Callaghan was a fat man and was probably tired of standing, he invited him in English to sit down. When he did so, O Connell pounced and charged him with perjury![4]

The Family of Daniel Callaghan Sr.

In Cork City two members of the family played significant roles in municipal politics as well as serving in the parliament at Westminster. Both were the sons of Daniel Callaghan (1760-1824). The family genealogy identified as C traced his descent from Cornelius or Conoghor Reagh who lived in the seventeeth century and his son Jeremiah or Dermot Reagh. The latter's son Daniel held land in Skagh, Clonbannin, Coolalougher, and Island (townlands west of Kanturk). Daniel's son John, after settling in Cork in 1758, dropped the O from the family name. Though it is not clear how he did so, in the 1770s he came into possession of Monkstown Castle, the residence at the beginning of the century of his cousin Cornelius O Callaghan of Banteer. Perhaps Cornelius sold it to him.[5] John was the father of Daniel Sr. who married Mary Barry of Lyre, by whom he had ten children, six sons and four daughters. Daniel and Mary's portraits currently are preserved at Fota House in Cork City.[6]

---

[2] Jonah Barrington, *Rise and Fall of the Irish Nation* (New York: Sadlier, 1833), 464; Tuckey, *Cork Remembrancer*, 321, 323; Brian Walker, *Parliamentary Election Results in Ireland, 1801-1922* (Dublin: RIA, 1978), 205-206, 313-314; Skehan, "Extracts," *TIG* 4 (1960): 191; P. C. Power, *South Tipperary*, 110; T. P. Power, *Land*, 319-320; Johnston-Liik, *Irish Parliament*, 2:54, 5:381-382, no. 1564; G. C. Bolton, *The Passing of the Irish Act of Union: Study in Parliamentary Politics* (Oxford: Oxford University Press, 1966), 149.

[3] O Flanagan, *Blackwater*, 154; Grove-White, *Notes*, 2:222, 3:5, 339; Donogh McCarthy, "Mass Rocks and Altar Sites in Duhallow," *SD* 8 (1991): 83-97.

[4] https://doras.gaois.ie/cbes/CBES_0364/CBES_0364_211.jpg?width=1600&quality=85. This story was taken down from Liam Mullane as part of an oral history project sponsoedd by Dúchas.ie.

[5] https://www.castles.nl/monkstown-castle; https://www.formerglory.ie/period-property-for-sale-in-ireland/monkstown-castle-monkstown-cork/; Lewis, *Topographical Dictionary*, 2:389-390.

[6] The genealogy, hereafter cited as *C*, was compiled in 1844 by Daniel Callaghan Jnr. of Lotabeg House, Cork City. Subsequently a member of Sir George Astley Callaghan's family extended it into the twentieth century. Stella Callaghan who presented the scrapbook containing the genealogy to Chris Callaghan in 1960, is, in his judgment, the most likely author of this latter part. Although *C* begins in the

Daniel Callaghan Sr.

(Fota House, Cork and Irish Heritage Trust)

late seventeenth century there is no indication that it was compiled contemporaneously; rather it seems to represent the oral memory of this branch of the family, finally given written form early in the nineteenth century. I want to thank Chris Callaghan for his kind permission to use it.

"One of the most enterprising and successful merchants of Cork," Daniel Sr. acquired great wealth by supplying victuals for the English navy during the Napoleonic wars. In addition to substantial real estate holdings in the city, his family also owned the largest distillery. While butter and beef were the principal markets there, tanning, brewing, and distilling were the chief industries. At the end of the eighteenth century Daniel was among a significant number of wealthy Catholics admitted as freemen of the city; but he soon challenged the Cork Corporation, a Protestant oligarchy that controlled municipal patronage. Daniel's fourth son, Patrick, fought a duel with Christopher Hely-Hutchinson, M. P. for Cork in 1820, though both men survived the encounter. Daniel's fifth son Richard, intended for a career in law, was admitted to the Middle Temple in 1816.[7]

Daniel's third son Gerard, who converted to Protestantism while being educated in England, initially supported Catholic emancipation, but after his election as M. P. for Dundalk from 1818 to1820 he emerged as a staunch proponent of the Protestant cause.[8] The *Dublin Evening Post* denounced him as a "kiln-dried and medicated mongrel," who sought only his own profit by turning away from the Catholic religion. He lived at "Monkstown in a good square castle with flankers," words used by Bishop Downes in 1699 to describe the castle. In 1831 together with his brother Daniel (a Catholic) he granted land for the erection of a church there. While Catholics generally detested Gerard as an apostate, Protestants were never quite sure of him. After losing his seat two years later he attempted to develop a strong Protestant party with the intention of overthrowing the aristocracy who had long dominated Cork politics and of gaining greater power and influence for the mercantile class. Though proposed for parliament in 1820 and again in 1826 he failed to garner sufficient votes for election. Now opposing Catholic emancipation, he expressed his views quite bluntly in 1829:

> I value Protestantism, connecting religion with our form of civil polity – I value the constitution as settled in 1688, which secures to me my religion, and a proper degree of well-regulated liberty and I will not surrender those advantages.

Despite those words, when the Tories, in protest against the passage of Catholic Emancipation, again proposed Gerard for parliament, he indicated that he would not seek to overturn the law. Although he was elected, the Catholic liberals, with O Connell's support, alleged that his government contracts invalidated the election and secured his ouster. His older brother Daniel, "a reputed Roman Catholic," was proposed in his stead and was duly elected in 1830, but he chose not to step down in Gerard's favor as most people expected him to do. Gerard opted not to oppose him but remained a force in Cork politics until his accidental death in 1833. Daniel, who had a long parliamentary career, died of cholera at his residence at Lotabeg on 29 September 1849, aged 63. Lotabeg House at Lower Glanmire Road on a hill overlooking the river, has been described as "a

---

[7] Maurice O Connell, ed., *The Correspondence of Daniel O Connell*, 8 vols. (Dublin: Irish Manuscripts Commission, 1972-1980), 2:256-257, no. 836 (10 April 1820); Macgeagh, *Register*, 2:438 (5 November 1816); Casey, *O Kief*, 6:1419.

[8] He expressed his views in his campaign against John Hely Hutchinson in *A History of the Rise, Progress and Termination of the Election for the City of Cork* (Cork: John Hennessy, 1827).

good example of early 19th-century domestic design. At the entrance is a fine stone gateway, known as 'Callaghan's Gate,' surmounted by the figure of a dog. According to legend a dog saved a Callaghan child from drowning and consequently the dog became the basis of their family crest." The animal in the family crest, however, is not a dog but a wolf. Several campaign ballads were written about him including "Callaghan and Cork," "Callaghan and Repeal," and "Callaghan forever."[9]

The Fate of the Peasantry

Despite gains in the political sphere, the condition of the majority of the population, the peasantry, small farmers and tenants cultivating the land of others - and that included the O Callaghans of Cork - became increasingly harsh. The rapid increase in population in the first half of the century made it more and more difficult to eke out a living from holdings that grew smaller and smaller and had to support more and more people. Families were dependent on the potato crop as their primary means of sustenance. Relations with their landlords, many of whom were absentees, were never worse. Tenants, often living in mud cabins and holding year-to-year at the will of the landlord or middleman, were subject to arbitrary increases in rent should they make any improvements and the possibility of eviction if they failed to pay. As the number of those wandering the countryside increased, the Poor Law Act of 1838 tried to alleviate their condition by dividing the county into unions and requiring each union to establish a work house where the poor could find refuge as well as coarse food. A board of guardians, some elected, others appointed, was responsible for administering the system. Work houses were erected for the unions of Kanturk (for 800 persins) and Mallow (for 700).[10] One of the guardians for Mallow, Jeremiah H. O Callaghan, Esq., was hailed for "his zealous exertions in behalf of the poor of the district [and] won the respect and gratitude of the poor." When he died in 1864 The Cork Examiner, recognizing his encouragement of the sport of horseracing, commented that "twenty years ago there was no more popular name in the county than that of the dashing, handsome young horseman from Mallow." When he was buried in the cemetery of Kanturk chapel all the shops in town closed out of respect for him.[11]

` Even before the Great Famine some peasants emigrated to the New World. As part of a group of settlers bound for Ontario, Canada, Jeremiah Callaghan of Mallow, aged thirty-five, his wife Kitty, a year younger, and their five children aged two to fourteen sailed on the Regulus from Cobh in 1825. Connell Callaghan, a forty-year-old

---

[9] Ian D'Alton, *Protestant Society and Politics in Cork, 1812-1844* (Cork: Cork University Press, 1980), 32-33, 100, 112, 132-151, 159-162, 165, 162, 168, 225-226, 234; and "Keeping the Faith: An Evocation of the Cork Protestant Character, 1820-1920," in O Flanagan and Buttimer, *Cork*, 759-792, esp. 765-767; Fergus O Ferrall, *Catholic Emancipation: Daniel O Connell and the Birth of Irish Democracy, 1820-1830* (Dublin: Gill and Macmillan, 1985), 171; "Distinguished Corkmen," *JCHAS* 11 (1905); 194; Brady, *Records*, 1:215-216; Tuckey, *Cork Remembrancer*, 321, 323; Denham-Jephson, *Miscellany*, 396 (letter of Daniel Callaghan, M. P. for Cork, 27 April 1832 to C. D. O. Jephson); Walker, *Election Results*, 205-206, 313-314; "Daniel Callaghan, M. P.," *JCHAS* 11, 2d Series (1905): 194; *Co. Cork, North and East, Cork City* (Naas: Irish Tourist Board, 1982), 10; *A Catalogue of the Bradshaw Collection of Irish Books in the University Library*, 3 vols. (Cambridge: Cambridge University, 1916).

[10] http://www.workhouses.org.uk/Kanturk/ **and** http://www.workhouses.org.uk/Mallow/

[11] Con Tarrant, "House Building: Its Art and Culture in Duhallow over the past 150 Years," *SD* 4 (1980-81): 64-66; *CE*, 8 April 1846, 28 October 1864.

laborer from Mallow with his wife, son and three daughters, and James Callaghan, aged thirty-five, described as a "reduced farmer" from Mallow, also sailed from Cobh with his wife and five children. Prior to their departure David Callaghan of Mallow, a mason, approached the organizers of the Canadian migration looking for his son Jeremiah who still owed him two years of apprenticeship but intended to join the emigrants. What happened to him is unknown. A Mrs. Callaghan delivered a baby girl on the John Barry.[12]

Based on his personal observations from 1812 to 1822, Thomas Crofton Croker commented that the peasantry, no matter how poor, retained an inordinate sense of pride in their ancestry, claiming descent from the kings of Ireland. They were also well aware that the lands they now cultivated for the benefit of Anglo-Irish or English landlords had once belonged to the Irish clans. The women were "generally short and plump" and the men were "well-proportioned, tall and rather handsome." Both men and women dressed in coarse clothing, the latter wearing "a brown stuff gown and green petticoat . . . with stockings of the brightest blue," topped off by a cloak. Men usually wore blue, black, or gray. Shoes and stockings were ordinarily reserved for special occasions.

The old tradition of hospitality was maintained even if it meant giving the guest the largest potato and the chair closest to the fire. Passersby greeted one another with blessings and good wishes for the journey. An enemy, however, might be charged with a curse such as this example cited by Croker, perhaps one of the mildest: "May you stand friendless and alone in this world." The annual average rent of a cabin was about 40 shillings or 50 with a patch of ground. Men from surrounding villages collaborated with one another in the tasks of husbandry such as turf cutting. Weddings were joyous occasions made more so by the presence of a piper and free-flowing ale and wine. Among annual religious rituals was the pattern (*pátrún*) usually marked on the feastday of the patron saint of the parish. It was often celebrated by visiting holy wells, such as those of St. Fursey north of Clonmeen churchyard and of St. Latiaran at Cullen in the barony of Duhallow. Fr. John O Callaghan, D. D., parish priest of Inishcarra from 1787 to 1814, was a noted healer and his grave near the ruins of the eighteenth-century church of Aghinagh, was "one of the 'stations' during the rounds which take place on certain Sundays of the year."[13] After making the rounds of the well its healing waters or a little earth from the grave were applied to sores or other afflicted parts of the body. Gatherings of people from different communities were not only occasions for renewing family ties and friendships, dancing in the night air, and courtship, but also for drinking, and in some instances, fighting. Faction fights were common as people from different families came to battle one another with cudgels and stones and whatever other weapons were at hand. Paddy Callaghan, "an itinerant spalpeen, the lowest form of labour," known as Captain Cutter, led one fighting band of Caravats in Waterford. At times fights occurred at fairs, such as those of Kanturk and Mallow or even during patterns. Although the causes of such battles probably went back several generations they still provided justification for contemporaries to assail one another.[14] In the years following the famine, the bishops

---

[12] Christy Roche, "Mallow and the Robinson Setlements," and Carol Bennett McCuaig, "Farewell to Old Ireland: The Voyage of the 'John Barry,'" *MFCJ* 8 (1990): 52-59, and 13 (1995): 137-150; Denham-Jephson, *Miscellany*, 380-381.

[13] See the oral account of Fr. O Callaghan's healings by Eugene Lane of Berrings in duchas.ie.

[14] Croker, *Researches*, 220-237; P. J. Hartnett, "Holy Wells of East Muskerry, Co. Cork," *JCHAS* 52 (1947): 9-10; John J. Ó Riordáin, "Investigating St. Latiaran of Cullen," *SD* 6 (1986): 31-35; Richard

and clergy discouraged the popular belief in the healing powers of holy wells and the appropriate behavior often associated with the patterns.

The Tithe War

Tenants were especially aggravated by the tithe, a tax for the maintenance of the clergy of the Established Church, payable by everyone, Catholics (the majority of the population), Protestant Dissenters, and members of the Church of Ireland. Among the clergy was Robert O Callaghan appointed to the curacy of St. Nicholas in the Diocese of Cork about 1826. The tithe, initially a levy of one-tenth on income from land, livestock, and labor, became a monetary payment in the seventeenth century, but given that pasturage controlled by the landlords was exempt until 1824, it fell heaviest on tillers of the soil, mostly peasants, the poorest of all. Landlords, in addition to having the right to name the rectors of Protestant churches, often secured control of tithes as well. The Longfields of Longueville, for example, purchased the tithes of the parishes of Kilbrin, Kilroe, Clonfert, Ballyclough, Castlemagner, Dromdowney, and Rahan around the end of the seventeenth century. In 1834 Jeremiah Callaghan had a lease of the tithes of Castlemagner from John Longfield; Callaghan, who may have been a Catholic, earned a living by collecting tithes in Longfield's name.[15] Opposition to the tithe was one of the motivations behind the Whiteboy movement in the late eighteenth century. As resistance to the tithe stiffened after Catholic Emancipation, the government employed police and soldiers to seize the livestock and property of those in arrears; confrontations of this sort often ended in violence. In September 1832, for example, two tithe proctors, whose task was to assess the amount of the tithe in Castlepook in the Doneraile area, were stoned to death by local people. The government, solely on the evidence of two small children, indicted 24 people, both men and women. Several, including one woman, were hanged and others were sentenced to transportation overseas.[16] Then in November 1833, when Rev. Edmond Lombard attempted to seize a horse belonging to Denis O Connell of Gortroe, for failure to pay the tithe, the local people stoned him and chased him off. He blamed this unrest on the harangues of the recently appointed Catholic curate of Kilshannig, Rev. Murray. Among his assailants were tenants on Owen O Callaghan's estate and Lord Lismore's estates. In response to his plea for help, the government dispatched a combined military and police force in late December to seize cattle and other animals and impound them until the tenants paid their tithes. Rev. Joseph O Keeffe, the Catholic rector of Glantane, as the Catholics named the parish of Kilshannig (1811-1842), blamed Rev. Lombard for stirring up the crowd by acting in "the most wanton and

---

Henchion, "The Gravestone Inscriptions of Cork. I. Aghinagh Burial Ground," *JCHAS* 73 (1967): 104; Con Tarrant, "Matchmaking in Duhallow at the Turn of the Century," *SD* 4 (1980-81): 14-16, noted that Murray O Callaghan of Banteer provided a coach and four horses to transport the bride and groom to the church and to the railroad station if they were going away on a honeymoon. Patrick O Donnell, *The Irish Faction Fighters in the Nineteenth Century* (Dublin: Anvil, 1975), 31, 84, 171; Paul E. W. Roberts, "Caravats and Shanavests: Whiteboyism and Faction Fighting in East Munster 1802-11," in Samuel Clark and James S. Donnelly, *Irish Peasants, Violence and Poltical Unrest, 1780-1914* (Madison: University of Wisconsin Press, 1983), 80.

[15] Lascelles, *Liber Munerum*, 2:231, 235; Grove-White, *Notes*, 4:58; Brady, *Records*, 102-103, 142-144, 287-290.

[16] Michael Shine, "The Castlepook Tithe Proctor Murders," *MFCJ* 5 (1987): 62-78.

---

outrageous manner," threatening "physical violence," and firing a pistol, though no one was hit. By the beginning of the new year the agitation died down and the people resumed payment of their tithes.[17] The so-called Tithe War came to an end only after the Tithe Rent Charge Act of 1838 converted the tithe into a payment by landlords. Not until the Disestablishment of the Church of Ireland Act of 1869, however, was the tithe finally abolished.

As the Compensation Act of 1823 required tithes to be paid in coin a record of landholding had to be compiled. The resulting tithe applotment books for 1824, 1825, 1827, 1829, and 1834 provide the names of numerous Callaghans and O Callaghans in County Cork and point up some of the characteristics of rural society just described.

Parish of Clonmeen in 1825[18]

Name	Place	Acres	Name	Place	Acres
Widow	Clonmeen	3	Owen	Gougane	10
Widow	Coolacheesker		Michael	Inchidaly	19
John	Coolroe Beg	4	Cornelius	Inchidaly	3
Cornelius	Coolroe Beg	1	Timothy	Inchidaly	23
Denis	Coolroe More	8	Jeremiah	Inchidaly	?
John	E. Corrough	1	John	Kilmacrana	7
Denis	E. Corrough	1	Thomas	Kilmacurrane	18
Denis	W. Corrough	1	Denis	Lough Gloun	?
Jeremiah	Derry	5	Patrick	Lough Leagh	8
John	Derry	8	Jeremiah	Lough Leagh	8
Daniel	Derry	4	Jeremiah	Lough Leagh	4
John	Dromcummer	26	Owen	Lough Leagh	3
Matthew	Dromcummer	26	Jeremiah	Lyre	3
Widow	Duinche	1	Andrew	Nadmore	63
Patrick	Duinche	8	Thomas	Shanour	17
John	Garrane	3	Timothy	Shanour	8
Cornelius	N. Glen	46	Michael	Shronebeha	1
Denis O Callaghan	N. Glen	22	Jeremiah	Tincoora	26
Patrick	W. Gortmore	6	Callaghan	Tooreen	65
Thomas	Gortmore, Upper	5	Peter	Tooreen	64

Many of these place names have been cited before but their location may be plotted again. North of the Blackwater lie Dromcummer and Coolacheesker; south of the river the road runs eastward from Clonmeen to Gortmore. Gougane and Corrough Bridge

---

[17] See "Correspondence relating to Glanntane and Kilshannick Tithes," in *Accounts and Papers relating to Church; Clergy; Tithes; Poor; Elections, Session 4 February – 14 August 1834*, 43 (1834): 363-378; ; A. J. Coughlan, "A Riot in Kilshannig and Glantane," *MFCJ* 28 (2010): 101-114.

[18] TAB Parish of Clonmeen, 1825; www.sci.net.au/userpages/mgrogan/cork/clonmeen.htm. orhttp://titheapplotmentbooks.nationalarchives.ie/pagestab/Cork/Clonmeen

are between Clonmeen and Curraghrour. South of Mount Hillary are Coolroe Beg, Coolroe More, Glen, Tincoora, Lyre, Nadmore, and Shanour. Inchidaly lies northeast of Banteer; Duinche, Shronebeha, Toureen, and Kilmacurrane are to the south, and Garrane and Derry to the west. Lough Gloun is likely Lackloun south of Coolroe More, but the location of Lough Leagh is uncertain.

Only three places, Clonmeen, Glen, and Dromcummer, were recorded in both Hingston's report of the inhabitants of Clonmeen in 1766 and the tithe applotment of 1825 as having Callaghan residents. Many of the places where Callaghans lived in 1766 do not appear in 1825. Conversely in 1825 there are Callaghans in places not mentioned in 1766. Both reports were probably incomplete, but it also seems that many Callaghans changed residence in the interval of fifty-nine years.

No one of the O Callaghans held as many as 100 acres in the parish of Clonmeen. The few who did included Edward Foott, Esq., who held 361 acres in Glentaneatnagh; and Pierce Power, Esq., who, with John Stack, had 103 acres in Roskeen; Power built Roskeen House in 1837. Both Foott and Power were descendants of Cornelius Senior O Callaghan of Banteer. There were no O Callaghans in Banteer other than Lord Lismore who held five acres there and two parcels of 17 and 26 acres in nearby Knockeenathuder. Most family members (27) held tiny plots under 10 acres. Six persons had only 1 acre; five had 3; three each had 4 and 5; two each had 6 and 7; six had 8. Six others had mid-size holdings of 10, 17, 18, 19, 22, and 23 acres, and three had 26 acres. The larger plots included 46, 63, 64, and 65 acres each held by one person. The number of family members is not recorded, nor is there any mention of animals. Some of the smallest holdings must have provided little more than a mere subsistence.

The landed gentry probably included: Denis O Callaghan and Cornelius Callaghan (perhaps brothers), representing the O Callaghans of Glen or Glynn cited in the previous chapter; they held 22 and 46 acres respectively in North Glen. Callaghan and Peter O Callaghan (perhaps brothers) of Tooreen holding 65 and 64 acres respectively also belonged to the gentry, as did Andrew Callaghan with 63 acres in Nadmore. My own family is descended from John and Matthew Callaghan each of whom held 26 acres in Dromcummer.

The tithe applotment for the parish of Kilshannig in 1834 provides information concerning Callaghans comparable to that for Clonmeen:

Parish of Kilshannig in 1834[19]

Name	Place	Acres	Name	Place	Acres
Timothy	Kilvealaton	19	John, William	Lackendarragh	33
Owen	Knockansweeney	13	John	Lackendarragh	33
Widow, Son	Cryan, Upper	9	Widow	Lackendarragh	7
Cornelius, Patrick, John, Richard; one other	Glandine	455	Denis; one other	Beenalaght	74

[19] TAB Parish of Kilshannig, 1834; www.sci.net.au/userpages/mgrogan/cork/kilshannig.htm.

Name	Place	Acres	Name	Place	Acres
John	Beenamweel	36	Jeremiah	Mohereen	4
Michael; sons	Knockdrislagh	35	Callaghan O Callaghan	Mohereen	11
Widow	Kilcolman	18	William	Mohereen	2
John; seven others	Glashalive Keeffe	58	Owen O Callaghan	Brittas, Upper	19
Laurence; four others	Glashalive Ard	144	David; sons	Skarragh/Aldworth	56
Michael; six others	Carrigcleena More	140	Patrick; two others	Boola	24
Patrick	Lackendarragh	36			

Most of these placenames are familiar. Lying southwest of Mallow is Kilvealaton; Mohereen and Brittas are west and southwest of Dromaneen. Knockansweeney, Skarragh, Aldworth, Kilcolman and Lackendarragh are south of Dromaneen. Still farther south are Knockdrislagh, Carrigcleena More, Beenamweel, Boola, Beenalaght, and Glandine. Cryan, Glashalive Keeffe, and Glashalive Ard are all located near Glashaboy and the Glashaboy River. A comparison with the 1766 record indicates that Callaghans continued to reside in Kilvealaton, Carrigcleena, Kilcolman, Skarragh, Aldworth, Lackendarragh, Brittas, and Mohereen; but others lived in places not mentioned in 1766.

The smallest individual holding recorded was 2 acres, but most were in double digits. However, as there were several instances of multiple occupiers, it is impossible to determine how many acres any one person held. Thus four Callaghans (perhaps brothers) and Patrick Walsh held 455 acres in Glandine, the largest holding of all; John and seven others held 58 acres in Glashalive Keeffe; Laurence and four others, 144 acres in Glashalive Ard; Michael and six others, 140 acres in Carrigcleena More; Patrick and two others, 24 acres in Boula. Owen of Brittas and Callaghan of Mohereen were the only ones with the surname O Callaghan.

In the neighboring parish of Roskeen north of the Blackwater there were no Callaghan occupiers in 1834, but there were several in the parish of Ballyclough north and east of Roskeen:

Parish of Ballyclough in 1831[20]

Name	Place	Acres		Name	Place	Acres
Eugene	Ballyclough	11		John	Ballythomas	1
John; one other	Ballykitt	73		Denis	Gortnagross	1
John	Ballyneeker	?		John	Kilcranathan	14
Cornelius	Ballyneeker	?		Owen	Lisleagh	9
Timothy	Ballythomas	7				

---

[20] TAB Parishes of Ballyclogh & Dromdowney, Diocese of Cloyne, Baronies of Duhallow and Orrery, 1831; www.sci.net.au/userpages/mgrogan/cork/ballyclogh.htm.

On the north bank of the Blackwater, Gortnagross, Kilcranathan and Ballythomas lie south of Ballyclough; Lisleagh, Ballykitt. and Ballyneeker (or Ballynuchiery) are to the north. The largest holding was 73 acres, followed by 14, 11, 9, and 1. The acreage of two holdings was not recorded.

Other Callaghans were resident in the parish of Castlemagner, the ancient territory of the Magners, situated north of O Callaghan's Country:

Parish of Castlemagner 1834[21]

Name	Place	Acres		Name	Place	Acres
Jeremiah, Esq.	Ballintubber	95		Charles	Cecilstown	2 rods
John	Castlemagner	14		John	Knockardsharriv	12
Jeremiah	Cecilstown	9		John	Knockardsharriv	1 rod
John	Cecilstown	24		Jeremiah	Two Gneeves	15

Ballintubber is west of Castlemagner; Two Gneeves is north; Knockardsharriv is southeast and Cecilstown is farther east. Aside from Jeremiah, Esq. who, with 95 acres, was obviously gentry, the other Callaghans in this parish were hardly well off. Holdings of 24, 15, 14, 12, or 9 acres were large in comparison to 2 rods or 1 rod, a fraction of an acre.

As before, traditional family names recur in the four parishes cited: John, the most popular (20); Jeremiah (10); Denis, Owen, and Patrick (6); Cornelius (5); Timothy and Michael (4); Thomas (3); Callaghan and William (2); Andrew, Charles, Daniel, David, Laurence, Matthew, Peter, and Richard (1). Some were likely fathers, sons and brothers. The personal names of five widows were not mentioned. Perhaps that was simply a reflection of the fact that their existence was forever linked to that of their deceased husbands.

The tithe listings for 1824, 1827, and 1829 also record numerous Callaghans in the more southerly parishes of Aghabulloge, Aghinagh, Inchigeelagh, and Desertserges. Most were probably descendants of the MacCallaghans or O Callaghans of Muskerry.[22]

Jeremiah O Callaghan, Opponent of Usury

In addition to the burden of the tithe, small tenant farmers suffered from the growth of capitalism in the nineteenth century and some of its unfortunate consequences. Often tenants were at the mercy of the gombeen men (*Fear gaimbín*, usurer), mostly merchants and shopkeepers who lent money at high rates of interest; tenants used the money to subsist and to pay their rent, but when they failed in their payments the gombeen men seized their stock and produce. As many peasants were ruined in this way, the people, not surprisingly, hated them.

They found a champion in Fr. Jeremiah O Callaghan (1780-1861), who condmned the practice of taking interest or usury as contrary to Church teaching. Jeremiah, one of fifteen children raised by his parents in Dooneen, Aghinagh Parish near Macroom, was

---

[21] TAB Parish of Castlemagner, Diocese of Cloyne, Barony of Duhallow, 1834; www.sci.net.au/userpages/mgrogan/cork/castlemagner.htm.

[22] TAB Parishes of Aghabulloge, Aghinagh, Inchigeelagh, and Desertserges.

ordained for the diocese of Cloyne in 1805. He became aware of interest at a priestly conference in 1819. Over many centuries the Church had frequently condemned interest-taking or usury as it was known; in modern parlance the word has come to mean excessive interest. When Fr. O Callaghan refused absolution to a corn-dealer until he made restitution of the interest he had taken, complaints were made to Bishop William Coppinger of Cloyne. He ousted Jeremiah from his parish and demanded that he never refuse absolution to a usurer in the future. After briefly conducting a classical school at Ross Carbery in 1820, Jeremiah visited France but his continued insistence that usury was contrary to the teachings of the Church did not sit well with the bishop who eventually prohibited him from saying mass. When his appeal to Rome received no response, he went to America in 1823, but neither the bishop of New York, the archbishop of Baltimore, nor the bishop of Quebec would accept him. Living off the charity of a fellow priest in Montreal, he penned his book *Usury or Lending at Interest* which was published in New York in 1824. Meantime the Roman curia recommended that he seek reconciliation with Bishop Coppinger but the latter accused him of slander and refused to meet him when he returned to Ireland. Determined to go to Rome to lay his case before the pope, Fr. O Callaghan traveled to London where he deposited a copy of his book with the populist reformer William Cobbett, who republished it in 1825 and again in 1828.[23] After five months of investigation the Roman curia decided to be done with him and terminated the allowance given for his sustenance. In effect, while Jeremiah insisted that the orthodox teaching of the Church based on the Fathers and Church Councils prohibited interest-taking in any manner, the curia preferred to acquiesce silently to the reality of nineteenth-century capitalism.

As Bishop Coppinger would not allow Fr. O Callaghan to resume his priestly ministry unless he repudiated his stand on usury, he emigrated to the United States in 1830. Bishop Benedict Fenwick of Boston accepted him and sent him as a missionary to Vermont. Renowned as the "Apostle of Vermont," he traveled widely ministering to French Canadians and Irish immigrants. In 1832 he built St. Mary's, the first Catholic church in Vermont at Burlington, but nativists (Protestants), determined to carry Fr. O Callaghan out of town on a rail and to drive out all Irishmen, burned the church to the ground in 1838. Rebuilding it in 1841, he dedicated it to St. Peter. He also brought the sacraments to Catholics in western Massachusetts and eastern New York and established many other churches, all the while continuing to denounce interest-taking and pamphleteering against the Protestants. While carrying out his ministry he often preached in Irish, the language of most of his congregants. Insisting that seating should be free and open to all, he inveighed against the custom of demanding pew rent. He died in 1861 at St. Jerome's Church in Holyoke, Massachusetts, another of his foundations. "As a tribute of respect and love" his parishioners erected a monument commemorating his "cheerful fidelity" in discharging "the duties of his laborious mission."[24] In the woods of Vermont a

---

[23] *Usury or Interest proved to be repugnant to the Divine and Ecclesiastical Laws and Destructive to Civil Society* (London, C. Clement, 1825).

[24] R. J. P.[urcell], "Jeremiah O Callaghan," *Dictionary of American Biography* 13:613-614; *History of St. Jerome's Parish, Holyoke, Massachusetts, Diocese of Springfield, issued in Connection with its Diamond Jubilee, 1931* (Holyoke: M. J., Doyle, 1931), 29-36, 116-124; John Michell, *Eccentric Lives and Peculiar Notions* (Secaucus, NJ: Citadel Press, 1989), 51-56; C. P. Hyland, "Father Jeremiah O Callaghan, A Man of Principle," *MFCJ* 17 (1999): 135-140. See Molly Gallaher Boddy's doctoral dissertation "Beyond Boston: Catholicism in the Northern New Borderlands in the Nineteenth Century,"

rock bearing the inscription "In Memory of Rev. Father O'Callaghan who said mass on this stone in 1853" stands as a reminder of the Penal Days when priests had to say mass on rocks hidden from prying eyes.[25]

On the Eve of the Famine

In the fifteen years following Fr. O Callaghan's departure for America, Ireland unwittingly was moving toward disaster. As a measure of reform, a system of national schools was established in 1831 to provide public education for the mass of the people. Some 250 students attended the primary school held in the cottage adjacent to Clonmeen cemetery. In 1824 Callaghan O Callaghan continued the earlier educational tradition by offering instruction in a stone house at Glenn in Clonmeen Parish to fifty-four children whose families were able to pay a small tuition. Eleven years later J. O Callaghan held a day school for sixty-seven students who paid 1s to 2s 6d every quarter. Schoolmasters in the new national schools included Cornelius O Callaghan, Bweeng, 1846; John O Callaghan, Kilpadder, 1848; Callaghan O Callaghan, Listowel in Kerry, 1870; and Denis and Mary O Callaghan, Dromore, 1890. National schools were open to students of every faith, but religious instruction was left to the pastors, both Catholic and Protestant. There was some opposition to the schools because it was believed that the children attending them would lose both their Gaelic heritage and their Catholic religion. Instruction was given only in English and poems and other stories were borrowed from English literature. As a consequence use of the Irish language and knowledge of the ancient Irish tales was severely limited.[26] As a deterrent to the use of Irish, schoolmasters hung a *bata scoir* or tally stick round the students' necks; for every time that they spoke Irish the master made a notch in the stick and punished them accordingly at the end of the day. Indeed, the intent was to encourage Irish children to think of themselves as English, as this verse hung in every school suggested:

> I thank the goodness and the grace
> That on my birth have smiled,
> And made me in these Christian days
> A happy English child.[27]

When Fr. Peter O Leary was stationed in Bweeng in 1868 most of his parishioners spoke Gaelic; he gave a sermon in English at one Sunday mass and in Irish at the other. However, when my father attended the national schools at Bweeng and Banteer toward the end of the century he learned by heart such poems as Oliver Goldsmith's *Deserted*

(University of New Hampshire, 2015), chapter 4: Frontier Missionary in a Catholic Borderland: Jeremiah O'Callaghan and The Vermont Church, 1830-1853; Thomas Moriarty, "From the Cork Gaeltacht to Holyoke, Massachusetts: The Turbulent Career of Reverent Jeremiah O Callaghan, 1780-1861." I want to thank Rev. Daniel Foley, pastor of St. Jerome Parish, and Sr. Joan, pastoral associate, for their warm hospitality and for giving me copies of the parish diamond jubilee volume and Professor Moriarty's unpublished paper. I have not seen John Joseph Cadden, *Father Jeremiah O'Callaghan: Economist and Pioneer Missionary (1780-1861)* (Washington, D.C.: Catholic University of America, 1936).

[25] Patrick J. Mahoney "An raibh tú ag an gCarraig? Deep in Vermont's woods lies the story of West Cork's Rev. Jeremiah O'Callaghan," http://www.westcorkpeople.ie.

[26] Edmond Curtis, *A History of Ireland* (London: Methuen, 1961), 362.

[27] Cyril Ó Ceirín,"The National Schools," Appendix IX to his translation of O'Leary, *My Story*.

Village, but nothing of the Fenian tales. The national school erected in 1841 at Shronebeha was transformed in 1994 into The Banteer Old School Heritage Center.[28]

Some family members, hoping to improve their situation, joined the British army. Among them were Jeremiah Callaghan of Newmarket who served in the 96th Foot Regiment from 1824 to 1850 and was discharged at age 45. Denis Callaghan of Kanturk, aged 23, after seven years in the 17th Foot, was discharged in 1850.[29] Many more, seeking better opportunities in the towns, formed part of a growing Catholic middle class. In 1824, for example, Daniel Callaghan, Esq., of Lotabeg was listed among the gentry in Cork City. Others included:

Name	Status/Occupation	Residence
Cornelius O Callaghan, Esq.	Gentry, Attorney	Dean Square
Mrs. O Callaghan	Gentry	Dyke Parade
Rev. Denis O Callaghan	Curate	St. Mary's Chapel
C. Callaghan	Gentry, Barrister	St. Finn Barr's

Kanturk, once the seat of MacDonough MacCarthy, passed into the hands of the Percevals following the rebellion of 1641, and the first sporadic steps were taken to create a town. In the second quarter of the nineteenth century, Kanturk was transformed into a modern urban center with a main street, a bridge over the Dalua River, a court house, a hotel, and a market house. Its older houses were thatched cabins but were now replaced by. more solidly constructed homes. The population came to number more than 4,000 before the famine. Among the householders resident there in 1824 were thirteen O Callaghans:

Name	Status	Residence	Name	Status	Residence
Anthony	Stonemason	Peacock Lane	Eugene	Physician	Kanturk
Cornelius	Nailmaker	Sradeen	Mary	Gentry	Kanturk
Crosby, Esq.	Gentry	Kanturk	Mrs.	Gentry	Kanturk
Denis, Esq.	Gentry	Sunlodge	Roger, Esq.	Gentry	Baunoulagh
Denis	Nailmaker	Greenane	Thomas	Stonemason	Peacock Lane
Eliza	Gentry	Kanturk	Timothy	Gentry	
Eugene, Esq.	Gentry	Kanturk			

The population declined rapidly after the famine, but in 1846 there were twelve Callaghan families in Kanturk: [30]

Name	Status	Residence	Name	Status	Residence
Mrs. Ann	Gentry	Main St.	Owen	Shoemaker	Chapel La.

---

[28] J. Anthony Gaughan, *Listowel and its Vicinity* (Cork: Mercier, 1973), 227, no. 80; Peter O Leary, *My Story*, tr. Cyril Ó Céirín (Oxford: Oxford University Press, 1987), 86-87; John Kavanagh, "Kilshannig: The Changing Times," *MFCJ* 8 (1990); 90, and *Kilshannig*, 120-130; Jim Eldridge, "Banteer History Project, 1995," *SD* 10 (1996): 74-77.

[29] London, Public Record Office, TNA; www.catalogue.pro.gov.uk.

[30] Patrick O Sullivan, *Where Dalua Rolls Its Flood Along: An Historical Profile of Kanturk, 1550-1900* (Kanturk: Kanturk District Community Council, 2011).

Name	Status	Residence	Name	Status	Residence
Callaghan O Callaghan, Esq.	Gentry, Attorney	Watergate Lane	Cornelius O Callaghan	Carpenter	Main St.
Denis O Callaghan, Esq.	Gentry, Attorney	Garraun-Awarrig	John O Callaghan	Coaldealer	The Square
Richard O Callaghan, Esq.	Gentry, Attorney	Killeen-leigh	Cornelius	Grocer	Main Street
Thomas	School-master	Blue Pool	Roger Cornelius O Callaghan	Draper	The Square
Thaddeus O Callaghan	Gentry, Attorney	Egmont Place	Cornelius O Callaghan	Nailmaker	Egmont Place
Thaddeus O Callaghan	Clerk, Union Work-house	Peacock Lane			

The town of Mallow, just east of O Callaghan's Country was also growing. A sketch map of Mallow dated 1780-1810 identified nine Callaghan householders (Daniel, Timothy, William, Owen, David, Andrew, Cornelius, a cooper). Living there in 1824 were Daniel, a cooper, and Elizabeth, a draper. A map of Mallow in 1831 recorded twelve Callaghan householders (John, Cornelius, Michael, George, Daniel, Jeremiah, six widows). Other Callaghans were buried in Mallow cemeteries:[31]

Name	Cemetery	Date	Name	Cemetery	Date
Mary, d. of John	St. James	1724	James	St. James	1818
Ellen	St. James	1735	James	St. James	1822
Eleanor	St. James	1745	Denis	St. James	
Daniel	St. James	1761	Timothy	St. James	1851
Edmond	St. James	1787	Bridget	St. Mary	1820
John	St. James	1778	Daniel	St. Mary	1847
Charles	St. James	1804	Mary Ann, d. of Owen O Callaghan	St. Mary	1865
Cornelius O Callaghan	St. James	1811			

On the eve of the famine, Samuel Lewis remarked on the houses of various members of the family ranking among the gentry. On the road from Midleton to Fermoy was "Cadogan [Cahirduggan], the elegant residence of Dennis O Callaghan, Esq., . . .

---

[31] *Pigot & Co.'s Directory 1824 – Cork City, Co. Cork; Pigot & Co.'s Directory 1824 – Kanturk; Slater's National Commercial Directory of Ireland 1846 – Kanturk;* "Pigott's Directory 1824," and "St. James's Cemetery, Mallow," and St. Mary's Cemetery, Mallow," *MFCJ* 8 (1990): 137-140, 141-162, and 13 (1995): 151-168; Seamus Crowley, "An Old Ground Sketch of Mallow," and "Mallow Map: 1831," *MFCJ* 5 (1987): 6-17, and 9 (1991): 85-98.

situated in grounds carefully laid out. The rhododendron planted in clusters in its native soil flourishes in great luxuriance and beauty, and in the lower grounds is an arbor vitae of great size, also some laurels of large growth." J. O Callaghan, Esq., of Rock Cottage, in the parish of Skull, H. O Callaghan, Esq., of Nadrid in Muskerry, and H. O Callaghan, Esq., of Castle Connell House near Stradbally in Tipperary, also merited comment.[32]

Members of the family also participated in the Repeal Association founded by O Connell in 1840 to achieve repeal of the Act of Union and to restore the Irish parliament. At a great repeal meeting at Kanturk in September 1841 attended by some 20,000 people - "the honest frize-coated peasantry from the surrounding districts of Newmarket, Dromtariffe, and Clonmeen" - Eugene O Callaghan of Kanturk was nominated to be a repeal warden. Cornelius O Callaghan was a repeal warden in Mallow and George Callaghan was one of the subscribers to the repeal rent. The task of repeal wardens was to persuade people to join the Repeal Association and to support its activities financially by paying a repeal rent. A shilling a year gained membership in the Association.[33] The parish priest often encouraged his parishioners to contribute. In the parish of Clonmeen and Kilcorney Father E. J. Murphy collected some £28 in 1843 and £21.8.0 in the following year. Among the Callaghan contributors were the following:

Name	1843	1844	Name	1843	1844
Andy	2s	2s	J. Owen	2s	
Cornelius		1s 6d	Mick	2s	
Edmond	2s 6d	2s 6d	Thade		5s
Jerry	2s	2s 6d	Tim	2s	
John		2 s 6d	T., Messrs.	2s 6d	

In 1843 contributors in Kanturk Parish included Mr. O Callaghan (5s); Cornelius Richard O Callaghan. Esq. (£1), who gave 10s in 1844; Eugene O Callaghan (2s 6d), and Thaddeus O Callaghan, Esq., Solicitor (£1). Denis O Callaghan gave 5s in 1844 and again in 1845. In Castlemagner Parish John Callaghan contributed 5s in 1843 and 1844, while in Dromtarriff Parish Simon Callaghan gave 1s in 1843; Jeremiah O Callaghan and John O Callaghan each gave 5s in 1843 and 1844, and T. Callaghan 2s 6d in 1844. In Mallow Parish William O Callaghan (elected as one of the town commissioners in 1846) contributed £1 and Daniel Callaghan 2s 6d in 1843.[34]

However, O Connell's announcement of a monster meeting at Clontarf on 8 October 1843, a frightened government, worried that as million people might attend, banned it as a threat to the constitution of the empire. O Connell, who always favored peaceful means rather than violence, acquiesced, lest the people be slaughtered. As a consequence the agitation for repeal came to an end. Not until late in the century was the cry for home rule and the restoration the Irish parliament taken up again.

---

[32] Lewis, *Dictionary*, 1:293, 2:335, 560, 600.

[33] *Instructions for the Appointment of Repeal Wardens and Collectors of the Repeal Fund* (Dublin: J. Browne, 1843).

[34] *CE*, 15, 17 September 1841; 8, 14 April 1843; 17 January, 2, 5 February, 11 June 1844; 12 March 1845; 29 April 1846; 10 July 1846.

Catholic Emancipation, the Famine and The Land League

The Great Famine

Not long after the collapse of the repeal movement Ireland was visited by one of the greatest tragedies in her history, the Great Famine. The population had grown steadily during the eighteenth century and as a consequence holdings were subdivided among sons, so that many held plots of an acre or less. Laborers got by with even less. Mountain and bog land, described as unprofitable by Petty after the Cromwellian confiscation, was reclaimed and settled. Appearing before the Devon Commission appointed to investigate the land question, George O Callaghan of Tulla in Clare emphasized that both large and small farmers were doing well, but laborers receiving only a subsistence wage were in dangerous straits. The population was estimated at about 5 million in 1800 but more than 8 million in 1841. Although there was an abundance of grain to feed the people, farmers, rather than consume it themselves, raised grain as a cash crop to pay their rent, and depended for their daily sustenance on a diet of potatoes and milk. Most of the grain was shipped overseas to Britain and the English government, faced with famine in Ireland, chose not to check the forces of a free market, and refused to relieve the famine from that home-grown supply of grain. Partial failures of the potato crop in the early 1840s followed by a general failure in 1845 and 1846 brought on the Great Famine and resulted in a terrible loss of life. 1847 was a particularly disastrous year

Inability to pay rents often resulted in eviction as was the case with Tim Callaghan, head of a family of six, in Boolymore in Dromtarriff Parish. To alleviate the situation the government set up soup kitchens and workhouses. Starving people flocked to workhouses in search of some means of sustaining themselves and their families. Unable to survive on the fixed starvation wage of 7 pence per day, 218 laborers demanded admittance to the Mallow Poor House in 1846. When the government raised the wage a penny, the Mallow Relief Committee protested that as "arbitrary cruelty." Among the contributors to the Dromtarriff Relief Committee in 1847 were John Callaghan of Carragraigue (£1), Mrs. Callaghan of Knockaneroe (10s), Denis O Callaghan Esq. of Cahirduggan (£5) and Richard O Callaghan of Kileenleigh (£1). In Kanturk contributors included Daniel Callaghan, Esq. of Dromalour (£2); Mrs. Callaghan, widow (10s); Cornelius Richard O Callaghan, shopkeeper (£2), and Denis C. O Callaghan, Esq. of Garraunawarrig (£1); Patrick Callaghan, Tuorard (£1); and M. O Callaghan (5s). Hospitals filled beyond capacity with the sick and dying. Food riots occurred, such as the fracas at Kanturk in October 1847 over the distribution of meal. Soup and Indian meal (or corn meal) were distributed three days a week at a house near Clonmeen graveyard. Some landlords such as Lord Lismore tried to ease the hunger by providing a soup kitchen at the gates of Shanbally Castle, dispensing Indian meal throughout the area, and reducing the rents of his tenants; but he also had to secure dragoons to protect ten mills at Clogheen. In 1846 Daniel Callaghan, M. P., mentioned above, was commended for canceling the rent owed by his tenants. As the specter of starvation spread across the land, thousands died. A report from Mallow in January indicated that "the coffin trade is the most flourishing one at present here;" but even the courtesy of a coffin soon began to disappear. Many people were left unburied for days at a time or their bodies were thrown into mass graves.[35]

---

[35] *CE*, 27 April, 6 May, 21 July, 5 October 1846; 8, 15 January, 8 February, 10 October, and 15 October 1847; Patrick S. O Sullivan, "The 1847 Crisis within Kanturk Union," *SD* 11 (1997): 37-46;

Writing from Ballydehob in West Carbery on 10 January 1847, Jeremiah O Callaghan described the terrible loss of life and the despair afflicting those still alive. Numbed of any human feeling by this tragedy, they likely had little expectation of escaping the fate of their friends and family:

> Deaths are fearfully on the increase in this locality. Four have died in the immediate vicinity of this village within the last few days. In the mountain districts they die unknown, unpitied and in most instances unburied for weeks. . . . Death has taken forcible possession of every cabin. . . . They have in most cases forgotten the usual ceremony of interment. The living are so consumed by famine they are unable to remove the dead.[36]

Fr. Michael Lane, pastor of Donoughmore, recorded the extent of the tragedy in the parish baptismal register on 29 December 1847:

> This was the Famine Year. There died of famine and fever from Nov. 1846 to Sept. 1847 over fourteen hundred of the people and one priest, Rev. Dan. Horgan. Requiescant in pace. Numbers remained unburied for over a fortnight, many were buried in ditches near their houses, many without coffins, tho' there were four men employed to bury the dead and make graves and two and sometimes four carpenters to make coffins. On this year also we were visited by cholera. Five only died of it in this parish.

A plaque containing Fr. Lane's note was erected on the wall of the Old Cemetery by the people of Donoughmore in September 1995, with the prayer: "I bhFlaitheas Dé go rabhadar. [May they be in God's mercy]. Please pray for them."

John Kavanagh noted that many in Kilshannig Parish were buried in Abby's Well and Newberry Cemeteries, at Cill Chuilling in Lackendarragh and in Rollig Phádraig in Dromore. Legend has it that a lone piper in Kilcolman played a lament all day and all night for the dying and the dead until he died of a broken heart. There was also a famine graveyard at Killavoy in the Parish of Clonmeen.[37] About a million died of the famine and another million fled the country. By various estimates the population declined by a third to a half. Holdings of less than 5 acres were reduced to 15% and those over 30 acres rose from 7% to 26%.[38]

Statistics for the parishes in O Callaghan's Country in the years 1831, 1841, 1851 clearly illustrate the population increase and precipitous decline:

Gerard Moran, *Sending out Ireland's Poor: Assisted Emigration to North America in the 19th Century* (Dublin: Four Courts Press, 2004), 68; P. C. Power, *South Tipperary*, 142, 149; Cecil Woodham-Smith, *The Great Hunger: Ireland 1845-49* (London: NEL 1970), 122; Foster, *Modern Ireland*, 318-344.

[36] *CE*, 18 January, 8 October 1847; Also see Jeremiah's reports *ibid.*, 2 September, 2 October 1846; 15-17 February, 14-16 June; 9, 27 August; 10 September 1847; Laura Sweeney, "Shanbally Castle," www.tipperary.local.ie.

[37] John J. Kavanagh's comments are recorded on a plaque at Bweeng Church; Kavanagh, *Kilshannig*, 63-72.

[38] E. R. R. Green, "The Great Famine, 1845-1850," in Moody and Martin, *Course*, 263-274; Donnelly, *Land*, 73-131; Thomas Gallagher, *Paddy's Lament: Ireland 1846-1947. Prelude to Hatred* (San Diego: Harcourt, 1982).

Parish	1831	1841	1851
Clonmeen	5,334	6,361	4,040
Kilshannig	8,057	9,348	5,473
Roskeen	591	691	279
Totals	13,982	16,400	9,792

In the ten years from 1831 to 1841 the population of the three parishes rose by 2,418, but declined by 6,608 in the decade from 1841 to 1851. Comparable figures for the northern parishes show the same results: Castlemagner (2,853, 3,007, 2,098), Kilbrin (4,292, 4,855, 2,900), Kilroe (1,291, 1,798, 701), and Subulter (268, 273, 135).[39]

The Protestant population in the parishes of Clonmeen and Roskeen, Kilshannig, and Castlemagner, also declined steadily (F=Families; P=Persons):

Parish	1785	1805	1830	1834	1860
Clonmeen/Roskeen	60 P	8 F	117 P		50 P
Kilshannig	111 P	75 F		559 P	335 P
Castlemagner		6 F	106 P		60 P

In 1837 Protestants constituted .019% of the population in Clonmeen and Roskeen; .06 in Kilshannig; and .037 in Castlemagner, but their numbers declined from 1830 to 1860 by 57% in Clonmeen and Roskeen; 40% in Kilshannig; and 43% in Castlemagner. Kilshannig had the largest number of families and persons. The parish church of Clonmeen was said to be in need of repairs in 1860 when the number of Protestants was recorded as 65; when Clonmeen and Roskeen were united to Castlemagner in 1879, the rector, Rev. Henry Swanzy, gave the bell of Clonmeen church as well as the O Callaghan chalice to Castlemagner.[40]

Clonmeen Church II

[39] Bowman, *Place Names*, 16, 100, 175, 266, 268, 344, 348; Lewis, *Dictionary*, 1:368, 2:208.

[40] Rev. R. H. V. Brougham of Castlemagner and Clonmeen (1913) to Grove-White, *Notes*, 2:225-228, 3:342-343; D'Alton, *Protestant Society*, 5-13.

Catholic Emancipation, the Famine and The Land League

During the years 1851-1853 Richard Griffith carried out his valuation of tenements or holdings in County Cork. Listed are the householders and occupiers of land, the townland, the acreage, its estimated value, and the person from whom it was leased. Hundreds of Callaghans, including many women, are listed in the index to Griffith's valuation; the names of many northern Callaghans, who have no connection to the Cork family are also included.[41] Griffith also conducted a survey of counties and townlands in preparation for drafting the Ordnance Survey maps. The following table illustrates the number of Callaghans and O Callaghans in the principal parishes where they were settled:

Parish	Number of Occupiers	Callaghans	O Callaghans	% Callaghans
Clonmeen	754	46	3	.065%
Kilshannig	1,081	46	3	.045
Kilcorney	180	9		.05
Rosskeen	57	2		.035
Kilbrin	471	10		.021
Ballyclough	518	28	3	.059
Castlemagner	402	11		.027
Donaghmore	722	31		.043
Totals	**4,195**	**183**	**9**	**.045**

From the foregoing it is apparent that the Callaghan/O Callaghan population of these parishes was a mere fraction of the whole, not even reaching as high as 7%. If we divide the census figures of 1851 by the number of occupiers we have the following average household size: Clonmeen, 5.36; Kilshannig, 5.06; Roskeen, 4.89; Kilbrin, 6.15; Castlemagner, 5.22. If we multiply the number of Callaghans/O Callaghans by the average household size we have: Clonmeen, 262.64; Kilshannig, 247.94; Roskeen, 9.78; Kilbrin, 61.5, Castlemagner, 57.42 or approximately 640 Callaghans/O Callaghans in these parishes.

For the most part the occupiers were male, but many women were also listed, perhaps most of them widows. Male names were much the same as before: Cornelius, Daniel, Denis, Eugene, James, Jeremiah, John, Michael, Owen, Patrick, Thomas, Timothy, and William. Andrew, Bartholomew, David, Edmond, Edward, Francis, Maurice, Richard, Robert, Roger, and Silvester were the exceptions. Female names (with their Irish equivalents were: Anne (Áine), Catherine (Caitlín), Elizabeth, Ellen (Oiléan), Honoria (Nóra), Johanna (Siobhán), Julia (Síle), Margaret (Mairead), and Mary (Máire).

While the population of the parishes cited was largely rural, there were at least nine Callaghan (and one O Callaghan) householders in the town of Mallow and an additional sixteen in the villages belonging to the parish of Mallow.[42]

---

[41] Dublin, PRO, Richard Griffith, Primary Valuation of Tenements, 1848-864, 200 vols.; Richard Griffith, *Primary Valuation of that Portion of the Barony of Duhallow comprised in the Union of Kanturk*, Parts I-III (Dublin, 1852); Kavanagh, *Kilshannig*, 140-168 (text for Kilshannig Parish); *Index to Griffith's Valuation of Ireland, 1848-1864*, CD No.188, Family Tree Maker, Family Archives, Broderbund Software 1997.

[42] Dennis J. Ahern, "Index of Occupiers in Griffith's Valuation for Mallow in the Barony of Fermoy," *MFCJ* 17 (1999): 164-165, 180.

As a result of the famine subdivision of farms became less and less common and the size of rural tenements increased. In order to maintain the substance of the family farm late marriage became common and consequently there were fewer children. Younger sons, with no prospect of a share in the family farm, were obliged to emigrate. As the size of farms grew so also was there a notable rise in the standard of living.

Landlords seized the opportunity provided by the famine to clear their lands of tenants, thereby heightening resentment. Patrick Murphy charged that the Grehans bought up all the land around Banteer and Clonmeen and compelled the tenants to withdraw to the nearby mountainous area. Thousands of Irish abandoned their homeland in the hope of finding a better life abroad. Many departed for England but even more for Canada and the United States. The so-called coffin ships witnessed the deaths of countless persons fleeing the disaster in Ireland.[43]

The Land League

In the years following the famine the land question achieved paramount importance. Landlord-tenant relations became more acrimonious. A fight between the ribbonmen, a secret society, and the English, for example, began at Glenpike in Shronebeha townland (about a mile and a quarter south of Banteer) and the English were driven westward to the townland of Derry. As a reminder of their victory the ribbonmen erected a gallaun or standing stone there.[44]

Property owners of one acre or more in 1870 and 1876 included several Callaghans, both Protestants and Catholics, who had achieved the status of gentry and as landlords had tenants of their own.[45] Area is given in acres, roods, and perches:

Owner	Date	Residence	Area	Value
Catherine	1870	Carhue	105	
Charlotte	1870	Superior, Midleton Convent	899	
Capt. Frederick	1870	Bath, England	1,025	
John	1870	Curraghraigue	39	
John	1870	Old Abbey, Ballinhassig	65	
John	1870	Cleanrath, Inchigeelah	155	

---

[43] Green, "The Great Famine, 1845-1850," in Moody and Martin, *Course*, 263-274; Foster, *Modern Ireland*, 345-371; Pat Murphy, *The View from Mount Hillary: A Chronicle History of Banteer, Lyre and Duhallow from 1886 to 2003* (Banteer: Pat and Eileen Murphy, 2003), 607-608; Jo Good, "The Grehans of Clonmeen: Portrait of an Irish Catholic Unionist Family," *SD* 12 (2000): 46-52. Many Callaghans and O Callaghans appear in Ira Glazier and Michael Tepper, eds., *The Famine Immigrants: Lists of Irish Immigrants arriving at the Port of New York, 1846-1851*, 7 vols. (Baltimore: Genealogical Publishing Co., 1983).

[44] James Twohig of Tooreen as told to Grove-White, *Notes*, 2:223.

[45] *Landowners in Ireland. Return of Owners of Land of One Acre and Upwards in the Several Counties, Counties of Cities and Counties of Towns in Ireland . . . Presented to both Houses of Parliament by Command of her Her Majesty 1876* (Reprint: Baltimore: Genealogical Publishing Co. 1988).

Owner	Date	Residence	Area	Value
Maria	1870, 1876	Millstreet	70.0.15	£ 41 5s
Patrick	1870	Curraghraigue	1	
Richard	1870, 1876	Ballydoyle, Castletownroche	68.3.5	£73 5s
Timothy	1870	Curraghraigue	87	
Cornelius O Callaghan	1870	Brookville, Glanmire	117	
Cornelius O Callaghan	1870, 1876	Gortmore	458.1.10	£143 10s
Denis O Callaghan	1870	Queenstown	984	
Denis C.O Callaghan	1870, 1876	Kanturk	326.0.0	£62 10s
Denis R. O Callaghan	1870, 1876	Killeenleigh	515.0.20	£331
Edward M. O Callaghan	1870, 1876	Kanturk	331.1.30	£68 15s
Edward O Callaghan	1870	Tralee	190	
Ellen O Callaghan	1870	Cork	99	
Francis O Callaghan	1870	North Mall, Cork	57	
Henry O Callaghan	1870	Queenstown	373	
Rev. James O Callaghan	1870	Cathedral House, Rosscarbery	9	
James O Callaghan	1870	Rock Cottage	466	
John O Callaghan	1870	Tralee	675	
Mary O Callaghan	1870, 1876	Gortmore	120.2.30	£25 10s
Minnie O Callaghan	1870, 1876	Kanturk	524.1.30	£79 15
Richard O Callaghan	1870	Rockvale	430	
Robert O Callaghan	1870	Cork	113	
Roger O Callaghan	1870, 1876	Knocknanagh	108.0.15	£18 5

Only twenty-eight members of the family were recorded, including a nun and a priest. If we discount the 899 acres held by Charlotte Callaghan as superior of the convent at Midleton, the individual holdings ranged from a high of 1,025 acres to a low of 1 acre. Among those resident in O Callaghan's Country were Cornelius and Mary of Gortmore with 458 and 120 acres respectively. Denis C. of Kanturk (326) and Denis Richard of Killeenleigh (515) represented the Dromskehy family. Richard O Callaghan succeeded to Rockvale in the parish of Castletownroche, after the death of his uncle Leslie in 1860.[46]

The principal landowners in what was once O Callaghan's Country included George Grehan, a Catholic, with 7,319 acres in Clonmeen, Banteer, and Kanturk; Edward Foott with 1,498 acres in Gortmore; Henry Foott in Kilvealaton (371); several members of the Hunt family in Danesfort, formerly Kilpadder (2,120, 832, 782, 280, 191); Daniel Bastable, Gurteenard (880); Charles Coote, Ballyclough Castle (4,500); Richard Hutch, Bannagh (251); Richard Longfield, Longueville, formerly Garrymcowney (9,410); Daniel McCarthy, Banteer (296); John Newman, Dromore House (6,146); John Power, Roskeen

---

[46] *Francis Guy's County and City of Cork Driectory for the Years 1875-1876* (Cork: Francis Guy, 1875), 1, listed among the gentry of Banteer: Michael O Callaghan of Dromahoe, Patrick of Crinaloo, Timothy of Curraghraigue, and Timothy of Banteer.

(773); Pierce Purcell, Dromore (1,942); Rev. Henry Swanzy, Newberry near Dromaneen (685); and Robert Walpole, Rathmaher (106). Edward Foott, who built Gortmore House in 1771, Henry Foott of Kilvealaton, and John Power of Roskeen were descended from Cornelius O Callaghan Senior of Clonmeen.[47]

In 1878 several Callaghans or O Callaghans owned nore than 500 acres. Most notable among them was Viscount Lismore whose holdings of more than 42,000 acres valued at more than £16,000 in Cork, Limerick, and Tipperary made him one of the wealthiest men in Ireland. Also included were representatives of the O Callaghans of Killeenleigh near Kanturk and the O Callaghans of Clare.[48]

Name	Residence	Location	Acreage	Value
Charlotte Callaghan	Midleton Convent	Cork	899	659
Mrs. Elizabeth Callaghan	Dublin	Galway	561	65
Frederick Marcus Callaghan	Bath, England	Clare Cork	4318 1025 5343	996 492 1488
Charles George O Callaghan	Ballinahinch, Tulla, Clare	Clare	8735	3745
Denis O Callaghan	Queenstown	Cork	984	491
Denis Richard O Callaghan	Killeenleigh, Kanturk	Cork	515	331
Frederick O Callaghan	Clonsilla, Dublin	Dublin Louth	47 1166 1213	88 540 628
John O Callaghan	Tralee, Kerry	Cork	675	309
Lt. Col. John O Callaghan	Maryfort, Tulla, Clare	Clare	4842	1919
Mrs. Minnie O Callaghan	Kanturk	Cork	524	70

Meanwhile the Tenant Right League of 1850 and then the Land League, founded in 1879 under the leadership of Michael Davitt and Charles Stewart Parnell, stepped up agitation for land reform. The reformers demanded a fair rent established by a land court in accord with the extent and fertility of the tenement; fixity of tenure that protected the tenant against eviction so long as he paid the rent; and free sale that guaranteed his right to sell his interest. The League hoped to end landlordism entirely and to secure for the peasantry a true right of ownership. Nevertheless, for three years, Ireland endured the

---

[47] Grove-White, *Notes*, 2:237-238, 3:3-13, 81, 151-152.

[48] U. H. Hussey de Burgh, *The Landowners of Ireland. An Alphabetical List of the Owners of Estates of 500 Acres or £500 Valuation and Upwards* (Dublin: Hodges, Foster, and Figgis, 1878), 68, 272-272-273, 344-345.

so-called "Land War" as tenants demanded a reduction in rents and an end to arbitrary evictions. Standing up for their rights, tenant farmers demonstrated against evictions, supported the families of those evicted, and used the boycott so that no one would take up a farm from which another family had been evicted. Others turned to more violent measures as in February 1881 when the land of Denis Richard O Callaghan of Killeenleigh was put to the torch. The Cork Defence Union, an association of landlords and merchants condemned boycotting and listed individuals subject to the boycott. For example, because E. O Callaghan, a shopkeeper of Killavullen, had carted bricks for the erection of a police station and had supplied the police with provisions, no one would purchase anything in his shop. Similarly when Lord Lismore evicted forty-eight families at Shanbally in Tipperary in March 1882, no one would assume their tenancies.[49] In 1886 the Plan of Campaign targeted landlords in economic difficulty and attempted to persuade their tenants to withhold rents until reductions were granted.[50]

Over the next quarter century parliament enacted successive measures enabling tenants to buy their farms. The Wyndham Land Purchase Act of 1903 permitted nearly every tenant to purchase his holding cheaply while the government also compensated the landlords. For example, Leslie O Callaghan, nephew of Denis Richard O Callaghan, J. P. of Killeenleigh, took advantage of the act to acquire Derrygallon west of Kanturk from R. E. Longfield, Esq. Derrygallon had long been in O Callaghan hands. Longfield also sold part of his holdings at Dromrastill to the tenants. Similarly the property of the Foott family of Gortmore was sold to the tenants.[51] In the past tenants were derided as shiftless and lazy because they did not work to improve their holdings. Any development, however, meant an increase in rent that only benefited the landlord. As tenants became proprietors, they improved their homes and ancillary structures; built new homes, and repaired old ones. Despite this progress, the Land League had its own internal difficulties and the scandal of Parnell's adulterous behavior destroyed his career.

The Bodyke Evictions

Two examples from O Callaghan history, one from the landlord's stance and the other from the tenant's, illustrate the battle over the land. Colonel John O Callaghan of Bodyke, County Clare was the protagonist of a bitter struggle with his tenants.

As we have seen, his great-grandfather, Cornelius (d. 1793), upon Edmond's death in 1791, acquired the estate of the principal branch of the family at Kilgory. Cornelius's descendants married well among the Clare gentry, acquiring additional wealth, pursuing careers in the military, and holding public office. His second son John (1754-1818) of Kilgory, Coolready, and Lismehane (later called Maryfort), for example, was High Sheriff in 1807, and his grandson Charles George was High Sheriff in 1855. In 1878 he held 8,735 acres.[52] John's son George (1788-1849) was the defendant in a suit brought in 1821 by Edmond's daughter Brigid O Reilly for the recovery of her father's

[49] Patrick O Sullivan, "Out of Darkness 2: The Fight for the Land 1850-1882: Tenant Right and Land League," *SD* 13 (2003): 63-71; The Cork Defence Union, *Boycotting in the County Cork: What Boycotting Means* (Cork: Purcell, 1886), 15; P. C. Power, *South Tipperary*, 189.
[50] Foster, *Modern Ireland*, 373-399; Donnelly, *Land and People*, 173-376, esp. 350-353.
[51] Grove-White, *Notes*, 3:14, 85, 152.
[52] O Callaghan-Lismehane Papers (John's marriage 1784; will and codicils, 1814, 1816, 1818); Ainsworth, *Inchiquin Manuscripts*, 534, no. 1533; *BIFR*, 890; T. J. Westropp, "The Colpoys of Ballycarn,"

lands wrongfully occupied by Cornelius, so she alleged. The suit was protracted for many years but the court, perhaps because George was a Protestant, denied her claim.[53] In 1838 as treasurer of County Clare George was found to be in default for the payment of sums owed to the County and a statute was enacted to recover the funds involved.[54]

Colonel John O Callaghan of Bodyke

(Clare County Library)

In 1878 George's eldest son, Lieutenant Colonel John of Maryfort (1829- 1912), owned 4,842 acres stretching from Tulla eastward to Bodyke. The family mansion at Maryfort, built in the eighteenth century, had three-storeys, five gables, and a pillared portico; a reporter described it in 1887:

> Mary Fort is a splendid modern residence, which might have been transplanted from the most aristocratic West-end square of London. A square flight of stone steps, seven yards wide, leads up to the door under its four handsome columns, and the visitor finds himself in a large and magnificently furnished hall, typical of the lavishness with which the whole mansion has been constructed and furnished.

JRSAI 28 (1898): 71-72.

[53] O Callaghan-Lismehane Papers (O Reilly vs. O Callaghan, 1821); O Donovan, "To Hell or to Clare," 74; *BIFR*, 890.

[54] *The Statutes of the United Kingdom of Great Britain and Ireland 1 & 2 Victoria 1838* (London: Her Majesty's Printers, 1838), 447-449.

Maryfort

(Clare County Library)

Nevertheless, when Colonel John inherited the property from his father it was saddled with a mortgage and other obligations. According to another reporter, John, "although a black Protestant . . . was ambitious of Catholic good-will. He wanted to have the tenants blessing him. He coveted the good name which is better than rubies. He wished to make things comfortable, to be a general benefactor of his species." His tenants were £6,000 in arrears but he agreed to accept £300. Over time he increased rents to the level of his father's time, but fluctuations in the price of agricultural produce made it difficult if not impossible for his tenants to pay. Even when he conceded an abatement of rent in 1879, some tenants still could not pay. In November 1880 when an estimated 10,000 people participated in a demonstration at Scariff organized by the Land League the parish priest of Tuamgraney, Fr. Peter Murphy, argued for full tenant ownership. Angered, John denounced the attempt to organize the peasantry as a crime and chastised the government for "allowing stump orators and agitators to preach at public meetings a most dishonest gospel to the hoodwinked and misguided peasants."

A violent confrontation, later known as the Battle of Bodyke, ensued on 1 June 1881 when Colonel O Callaghan, supported by 150 policemen, set out to evict twenty-six tenants at Bodyke and a crowd attempted to impede them. A commemorative plaque was later erected at Bodyke. The enactment of the Land Act of 1881 brought a period of calm and, by judicial arbitration, also resulted in a reduction of rents. Nevertheless in the next several years even those reductions were deemed too high. In 1887 the Bodyke tenants joined the Plan of Campaign and formed a "Combination" or union to further their demand for reductions, but Colonel John refused to back down.

Then on 2 June and continuing for two weeks thereafter he dispatched the sheriff, his agent, a resident magistrate, police, soldiers, and bailiffs to evict recalcitrant tenants.

Alerted by church bells and horns, a crowd estimated at 5,000 protested. While emergency men armed with crowbars tried to break in, tenants barricaded their houses and threw boiling water, cow dung and other unsavory materials at them. Once the "Crowbar Brigade" seized the house, household goods and livestock were moved out to the road. Every evening orators protested the evictions while local bands stirred the assembled crowds with appropriate music. By 15 June twenty-eight of fifty-seven tenants in the Combination had been ejected, but in each case they reoccupied their houses in the evening. The *Pall Mall Gazette*, one of the numerous newspapers reporting the evictions, commented: "after the forces had gone, however, the crowd rushed in, forced the door, relighted the fire, replaced the furniture, and a score of willing hands rebuilt the wall. So much for O Callaghan's victory and the supremacy of the English law." Three days later twenty-two women and four men were tried at Ennis for attempting to prevent the evictions and several were sentenced to hard labor for three months. Bridget Callaghan, mother and daughter, were sentenced to a month's hard labor, while Hannah and Ellen Callaghan were bound to the peace. Meantime, the colonel's son George complained that the press had distorted and sensationalized the story of the evictions.

When the colonel agreed to accept a third of arrears as full payment and granted a further abatement of rents, a period of relative peace ensued. Hard-pressed for cash, however, in November 1891 he stopped the abatements and many tenants were again unable to meet their obligations. This time Colonel O Callaghan opted to seize the goods and livestock of those in arrears and to sell the animals at auction. Bailiffs sometimes were deceived into seizing animals belonging to tenants not being evicted, and so left the colonel open to litigation for wrongful seizure. To prevent seizure sixteen cattle were poisoned at Clonmoher. In November 1893 eight tenants were evicted and caretakers occupied their farms to prevent their return.

The process took a toll on Colonel O Callaghan both personally and financially. A contemporary described him as "a soldierly-looking man of sixty, with iron grey hair and moustache, exhibiting, and to such an extent as to provoke immediate sympathy, in the deep lines of his face and his haggard and worn look, the strain which his truly unenviable position has imposed upon him." In addition to having to pay all those employed in evicting his tenants, he also suffered the loss of rent and any good will that he might ever have enjoyed. This impasse continued until 1909 when the Land Commission took over the O Callaghan estate and permitted the tenants to purchase their farms.[55]

The Example of the Dromcummer O Callaghans

By contrast, the O Callaghans of Dromcummer More, a townland in the barony of

[55] John S. Kelly, *The Bodyke Evictions* (Scariff, Co. Clare: Fossabeg Press, 1987); Jessie Craigen, "A Visit to Bodyke," and Robert John Buckley, in Brian Ó Dálaigh, *The Stranger's Gaze: Travels in County Clare, 1534-1950* (Ennis: Clasp Press, 1998), 291-294, 308-313; Dublin, NLI, National Library Report on Private Collections, no. 205: John F. Ainsworth, Interim Report on the O Callaghan-Westropp Papers (from 1727) the property of Mr. C. J. O Callaghan-Westropp, Lismehane, O Callaghan's Mills, Co. Clare, deposited in the National Library of Ireland. L. P. Curtis, Jr., *Coercion and Conciliation in Ireland, 1880-1892* (Princeton: Princeton University Press, 1963), 155,167-168, 243, 345; Mary Mullins, "Colonel John O Callaghan, Landlord of Bodyke," Local Ireland: Clare: Bodyke; www.clarelibrary.ie/eolas/coclarehistory/bodyke.

Duhallow, north of the Blackwater, represented the other side of the coin. Dromcummer (*Dromchomair*), meaning the ridge of the confluence of the Blackwater and Allow Rivers, comprises Dromcummer More (Great Dromcummer, 375 acres) and Dromcummer Beag (Little Dromcummer, 249 acres). The earliest historical reference that I have found concerning it dates from 1297 when Tadhg MacCarthaigh, heir to the king of Desmond, died of illness in his stronghold at Drom Chomair. In the sixteenth and seventeenth centuries Dromcummer was cited among O Callaghan lands, but was then allotted to Cromwellian planters. Roger Brettridge, the principal beneficiary, in his will of 1683 devised the lands of East Dromcummer to his wife and after her death to the "Mayor, Sheriffs and Commonalty" of the City of Cork in a perpetual trust to provide a weekly sum of 10s 6d to seven poor Protestant veterans of the Cromwellian wars. If there were a surplus it would be used to apprentice poor Protestant children in the city. The income of this trust in 1837 was £258 yearly. He also bequeathed three gneeves (about 30 acres) in West Dromcummer and Horse Island (a small island in the River Allow) to his nephew Roger Brettridge.[56] In 1696 Cornelius O Callaghan Senior leased Dromcummer from the Cork City Council for twenty-one years at £25 for the first three years and £30 for the remainder. He was charged with erecting a house there and planting an orchard. Though he fell in arrears, after inspection of the property the lease was renewed in 1718 at £66 *per annum.*[57]

Although several persons owned different segments of Dromcummer over time, O Callaghans were there at least from 1662, when the subsidy rolls recorded that Dan Liegh Callaghan (Donal Liath - Grey Donal) held property valued at £11 13s 11.5d. In the following year the value was £4. A century later, in 1766, Cornelius and Patrick Callaghan, perhaps brothers sharing acreage, were listed among the Catholics there. According to the Tithe Applotment Books of 1825, 1834, and 1836 John and Matthew Callaghan (perhaps the sons of Cornelius and Patrick) each held 26 acres in Dromcummer or 52 acres all told, a fairly large holding. In 1825 the price per acre was 10s; each man paid a composition for the tithe of £1 2s 3d; the composition in 1834 was 10s 3.5d and in 1836 £1 7s 3.5d.[58]

John Callaghan was the father of Denis, my great-grandfather, who, when he was about thirty, married Mary Carroll (about twenty-five or twenty-seven) in the Catholic Church at Donoughmore on 31 January 1837. William Carroll and John Callaghan, probably the fathers of the bride and groom, witnessed the marriage. Fr. Michael Lane, the pastor of Donoughmore, likely presided. The village of Donoughmore (*Domhnach mór*, the great church or house) is situated on R619 about fourteen miles southwest of Mallow and about eight miles northeast of Coachford. St. Lachtín who lived in the sixth century is the patron of Donoughmore. The small church standing in the midst of gravestones is now in ruins. Taking up residence in the townland of Dromcummer More, Denis and Mary had their first child, who was baptized in Castlemagner, the local parish,

---

[56] P. W. Joyce, *The Origin and History of Irish Names of Places*, 3 vols. (Dublin: 1901-1913; reprint New York: Blom, 1968), 3:414-415; *AI*, 391. See Brettridge's will in *JCHAS* 48 (1943): 110-114; Lewis, *Dictionary*, 1:428; Smith, *Cork*, 1:388-389; Tuckey, *Cork Remembrancer*, 109.

[57] Caulfield, *Council Book*, 253 (27 April 1696). See also, *ibid.*, 254, 278, 313, 354, 385, 389, 392-393, 396, 401, 403, 627, 652, 862, 1061, 1603.

[58] Dublin, PRO, VII B/2/21. IA 41 657, pp. 93-103, 107-119; Records of the Diocese of Cloyne. Religious Census 1766; National Archives of Ireland, TAB, 6N/13:51-52, 55-56; IA 41 657, pp. 93-103. TAB Parish of Clonmeen, 1825; Grove-White, *Notes*, 3:73.

---

on 12 December 1837. They named him John, in accordance with the custom of naming the oldest son after the paternal grandfather.[59] Four other children followed: William (1838), Matthew (1840), Denis (1842), and Ellen (1844). In the circumstances of the time, all the younger sons eventually emigrated to the United States. Denis and Mary and their children were no doubt counted in the Census of 1841:

Census of 1841

Place	Population	Gender	Families	Houses	Acreage	Value
Dromcummer More	156	79 M 77 F	23	20	373.1.35	£238 7s
Dromcummer Beag	44	28 M 16 F	9	8	249.2.25	£170 11s
Totals	**200**	**107 M 93 F**	**32**	**28**	**995**	**£409**

The average family size in Dromcummer More was 6.78 persons, for a density of 2.39 persons per acre. In Dromcummer Beag the average was 4.88 persons and the density was 5.65 persons. It seems likely that Dromcummer was overpopulated and that 2568some of the people there were subsisting on very small plots.[60]

The effects of the Great Famine are evident in the population changes that took place in the thirty years following 1841. Griffith's Valuation, carried out between 1851 and 1853, recorded 12 householders in Dromcummer More, or 11 fewer than in 1841; but the number in Dromcummer Beag (9) remained the same. The only Callaghan in Dromcummer was Timothy, who held less than an acre of land (1 r, 10 p) and a house and garden valued at 15s from Jeremiah Lane; he in turn held 84 acres from Lord Lismore (himself an O Callaghan). Lord Lismore also held 13 acres in Dromcummer More, but the largest landholders there were William and Daniel Flynn, who held 333 acres from the Cork Corporation. By 1871 the population of Dromcummer More had dropped from 156 in 1841 to 57; ten years later it was down to 32. The population of Dromcummer Beag was halved from 44 in 1841 to 22 in 1871, but it rose slightly to 28 in 1881.[61]

A great crisis in the family fortunes occurred around 1846 when Denis died in the midst of the famine. His oldest son John was nine years of age, but there were at least four other children, William (8), Matthew (6), Denis (4), and Ellen (2), all born at Dromcummer and baptized at Castlemagner. Five days after Denis's death, his widow Mary (then about thirty-four or thirty-six) was evicted from Dromcummer for failure to pay the rent and put out on the road with her children and her movable goods. Denis's brother Matthew apparently was responsible for the eviction because he failed to pay his

---

[59] I would estimate that Denis was born between 1797 and 1807 and may have married between the ages of 30 and 40. Mary Carroll was probably born in 1810 or 1812. According to the Census of 1901 she was eighty-nine years of age but her death certificate records that she died on 22 April 1905 at the age of 95 at Dromcummer. Death Certificate registered in the District of Kanturk in the Superintendent Registrar's District of Kanturk by the Registrar P. J. O'Leary.

[60] *Addenda to the Census of Ireland for the Year 1841*, 13; Lewis, *Dictionary*, 1:368.

[61] Griffith's Primary Valuation, Part I, p. 76; Guy, *Cork 1875-6*, 60.

share of the rent; for this he earned the lifelong enmity of his sister-in-law.[62]

Evictions in the early nineteenth century were common and were effected on the slightest pretext. The process was not pleasant. The landlord's agent, accompanied by police and sometimes by soldiery arrived at the house and ordered the occupants to leave. Peasants from the neighborhood often gathered to protest vociferously and sometimes threw stones and other missiles at the agent and the police. Rather than submit meekly, the inhabitants attempted to resist by barricading themselves within. The police then used force, including battering rams, to break in and to expel the family. No matter their age or health, men, women and children, weeping and wailing, were thrown out by the side of the road. Lest they try to regain entrance, the thatched roof was ripped off and sometimes the walls were knocked down, reducing the house to rubble. There is no record that I know of that related the eviction of Mary Carroll and her family, but it may have occurred as just described. Scarcely having time to grieve for her husband, who died five days before, and to give him a proper burial, Mary Carroll, a young widow, was put out on the Killarney Road. How could she explain what was happening to her five children, John, William, Matthew, Denis, and Ellen, ranging in age from nine to two, all bewildered and probably sobbing and screaming. Whatever personal treasures she possessed were likely thrown out on the road as well and the thatched roof may have been torn off to make the house uninhabitable. I got a sense of the grievous hurt inflicted on her when I listened to my mother tell the story.

My great-grandmother Mary, an indomitable woman, solemnly swore to recover possession of Dromcummer at the earliest date. Her return came about in this way. While living at Bweeng in 1891 or 1892, her grandson, my father William, then about eight or nine years of age, read a notice in the newspaper inquiring about heirs of the Carrolls who had gone off to Texas where they made money as horsetraders. When he called that to her attention she praised him highly for his perceptivity and apparently used that inheritance to regain possession of Dromcummer, when its most recent tenants, the Flynns, were evicted. In doing so, she, having been once in possession of Dromcummer, defied the strictures of the Land League against occupying farms whose tenants had been evicted.

Thus nearly fifty years after being evicted she was able to return with her son John and his family to a farm of 117 acres in Dromcummer More. John held it from the City of Cork Church School Board at the yearly rent of £56 11s payable semi-annually. The Church School Board was set up in 1890 to manage the charity created by Roger Brettridge in 1683. The house had two-storeys built around a central hearth with a thatched roof. One night my father awoke to find the straw burning above him, and so the thatch was replaced by slate. In addition to standing stones, and a double limekiln used to break down limestone so that it could be used to fertilize the soil, there is an old fort on the property. Sometime in the 1920s Michael Bowman located it on Mrs. O Callaghan's farm (John's daughter-in-law, Mary Barrett). The fort had a double rampart, but half the outer wall was leveled; the rest was about five feet high. An eighteen-foot ditch separated the outer and inner walls; the inner wall rose thirteen feet. The interior was saucer-shaped with a diameter of forty-five yards. Family tradition held that stones from the fort were used to build the house, thereby offending the fairies, who were thought to dwell therein.

---

[62] My mother, Helen O Sullivan, related the story of the Dromcummer O Callaghans to me, as she had received it from my grandmother, Margaret Leonard O Callaghan.

As a consequence, the O Callaghans never had any luck and eventually lost the farm. The family also hid a priest there during penal times. However that may be, my great-grandmother Mary lived at Dromcummer until her death at the age of ninety-five in 1905. Her son John died seven years later, leaving six adult children. Until 1888 public documents identified him as John Callaghan, but thereafter his name was recorded as O Callaghan, a change attributable to the influence of the Gaelic revival.[63] The vicissitudes of this branch of the O Callaghan family were likely typical of the alterations of fortune experienced by so many of their relatives and neighbors.

Despite substantial gains in civil rights, the nineteenth century was an especially troublesome one as the lot of the peasantry became more difficult to bear, due to overpopulation, tiny holdings, the famine, and the struggle for landownership. By the end of the century some of those obstacles had been removed and the condition of the rural population improved significantly.

---

[63] Bowman, *Place Names*, 104-105; *AICC*, 4:1, nos. 9967-9968, 10752-10753, 12441-12443, 15011. In 1913 J. Callaghan was listed as one of the farmers at Dromcummer; Grove-White, *Notes*, 3:74; Mary Sleeman, "A Lost Tradition: The Forgotten Kiln," *MFCJ* 8 (1990): 95-100.

CHAPTER 9

THE O CALLAGHAN DIASPORA

In the latter half of the nineteenth century the rising tide of nationalism accompanied an intensified agitation for Home Rule that eventually became a push for independence. After World War I Britain agreed to the establishment of the Irish Free State, a decision unacceptable to staunch republicans who turned to violent opposition. After peace was restored all ties to Britain were gradually severed and Ireland became a truly independent state. The bitter conflict over the six counties of Ulster, nevertheless, continues to the present day. In the meantime, although O Callaghans had been emigrating for many years, the Famine spurred a great diaspora as Irishmen spread around the globe, not only in Europe, but also in the United States, Canada, Australia, Africa, South America, and Asia.

The Fenians

The upsurge of nationalism on the European continent found an echo in nineteenth-century Ireland. In order to emphasize the distinctiveness of Irish culture, the Gaelic League was founded to encourage the study and use of the Irish language. Simultaneously efforts were made to reestablish the Irish parliament and thus to secure Home Rule. Wilfrid O Callaghan (d. 1877), son of Viscount Lismore, elected to parliament in 1874 as a member of the Liberal Party, was also active in the Home Rule League. While constitutionalists sought to achieve that goal by swaying votes in the British parliament, the Irish Republican Brotherhood, more commonly known as the Fenians, tried to effect change by revolution. Among literary agitators was Thomas O Donnell O Callaghan, born in 1845 the son of Innocent O Callaghan and Ellen O Donnell. A schoolteacher from Kilmallock, County Limerick, he wrote for the *Irish People*, a Fenian newspaper published in Dublin, using the pen name *Libertas*. He also contributed poetry to *The Irishman*. After emigrating to the United States in 1866 he continued his journalistic career. John and James Callaghan were imprisoned with oither Fenians after an attempted insurrection in Cork in March 1867. Also in Clonmeen the Fenians apparently burned hay and oats belonging to George Grehan, one of the principal landlords there. James O Callaghan from Cork, who worked in a draper's shop in Dublin helped to bring the drapers and others into the Fenian organization. John O Callaghan, the American correspondent for the *Irish Daily Independent* between 1893 and 1896, and later Secretary of the United Irish League of America, seems not to have impressed John Devoy, one of the founders of the Fenian movement. Meeting him in Boston in 1907, Devoy remarked: "their organization fitted easily into the corner of a small tap-room. But what a figure they cut on paper!" Two years later John accompanied the Fenian Edward Condon, who planned the rescue of the Manchester martyrs in 1867, on a visit to Millstreet. Cornelius O Callaghan J. P., of Altamount House, Millstreet, welcomed them and praised John's work in America for Irish unity. Despite the failure of the Fenian uprising in 1867, republicans continued to keep the idea of revolution alive.[1]

Bishop Thomas Alphonsus O Callaghan

As the century drew to a close perhaps the most distinguished member of the family was Thomas Alphonsus O Callaghan, O. P., bishop of Cork (1839-1916). Ordained in Rome for the Dominican Order, he was provided as coadjutor with right of succession to the aged Bishop Delany in 1884. Intrigue and political maneuvering, however, surrounded his selection. Bishop Delany preferred Msgr. Neville, the dean of the cathedral, with whom he had worked for many years. Neville, however, was regarded as too accommodating to the government and his support of Queen's College recently opened in Cork - described as godless by some - was held against him. Fr. O Callaghan, Prior of the Dominican Order, then resident in Rome, was the candidate of the bishops and clergy who favored an expansion of Roman influence and a firmer attitude toward the government, especially in the matter of providing support for Catholic schools. The rector of the Irish College in Rome stressed that Fr. O Callaghan "is a pious and learned and prudent man, sincerely devoted to religion and the salvation of souls, and at the same time humble and unassuming in his bearing and deportment." According to Neville, the priests of the diocese gave each of them the same number of votes, but the younger ones, all "professed Land Leaguers," favored O Callaghan. When the bishops of the province met at Thurles in Tipperary seven voted for O Callaghan and three for Neville. Archbishop Croke described Neville as a "desperate West Briton, a Castle hack, and, probably the most unpopular man in Ireland. O Callaghan is a Cork man born, a good man, a humble man, and no party man - just the sort of head or boss cleric, now required in Cork." He also affirmed that "O Callaghan will be a great blessing to Cork, distracted as it is, by rival ecclesiastical and other factions. The old regime must die out."

On the contrary, Bishop Delany complained to Pope Leo XIII that O Callaghan's selection would encourage factionalism and insubordination especially among the younger clergy. Nevertheless, O Callaghan was appointed as coadjutor on 13 June 1884

---

[1] James O Shea, *Priests, Politics and Society in Post-Famine Ireland: A Study of County Tipperary, 1850-1891* (Dublin: Wolfhound Press, 1983), 158, 209; *CE*, March 8-9, 1867; John O Leary, *Recollections of Fenians and Fenianism*, 2 vols. (London, 1896; reprint New York: Barnes and Noble, 1969), 1:131; William O Brien and Desmond Ryan, eds., *Devoy's Post Bag, 1871-1928*, 2 vols. (Dublin: Academy Press, 1948), 2:358, 360, 364; M. Murray O Callaghan, "A Fenian Officer: Captain Edward O Meagher Condon and his American Envoy Visit Millstreet," *SD* 2 (1976-77): 53-58; T. W. Moody, "Fenianism, Home Rule and the Land War (1850-1901)," and Donal McCartney, "From Parnell to Pearse (1891-1921)," in Moody and Martin, *Course*, 275-312; Foster, *Modern Ireland*, 431-460.

and consecrated in Rome two weeks later. His opponents were still hopeful of being rid of him, however; Cardinal McCabe proposed that he be transferred to Ossory and Neville installed in Cork. Bishop Delany was hardly welcoming and failed to provide his new coadjutor with a residence or income; above all he did not intend to give him any authority. O Callaghan stayed with Delany for a month before moving in with his sister in Cork. Even in the next year (5 January 1885) Delany plaintively inquired "is there any chance of [O Callaghan's] promotion to Trinidad which is a Dominican Mission?" After Delany's death O Callaghan succeeded as bishop in his own right on 13 November 1886 and died on 14 June 1916. Emmet Larkin, the preeminent historian of the nineteenth-century Irish Church, emphasized that O Callaghan's appointment helped to end the estrangement between the Irish Church and the papacy and to facilitate the "political reconciliation of the Irish Church and the Irish people."[2]

Bishop Thomas Alphonsus O Callaghan

(Journal of the Cork Historical & Archaeological Society)

---

[2] Emmet Larkin, *The Roman Catholic Church and the Creation of the Modern Irish State 1878-1886* (Philadelphia: University of Pennsylvania Press, 1975), 208-212, 223, 225-227, 232-235, 246; *JCHAS* 2 (1896): 101 (photograph of Bishop O Callaghan); Mark Tierney, "A Short Title Calendar of the Papers of Archbishop Thomas William Croke in Archbishop's House, Thurles, Part 2, 1886-1890," *CH* 16 (1973): 107 (23 January 1888); Patrick J. Corish, "Irish College, Rome. Kirby Papers. Guide to Material of Public and Political Interest 1884-1894 with Addenda 1852-1878," *AH* 32 (1974): 14-15, 17, 21, 26-27, 31, 34, 38; Bernard J. Canning, *Bishops of Ireland, 1870-1987* (Ballyharrow, Donegal: Donegal Democrat, n.d.), 252; Bolster, *Cork*, 1:13 (n. 36), 415 (n. 37), 462.

The bishops had roundly condemned the Fenians and had been lukewarm toward the Land League, but Parnell succeeded in persuading them to support Home Rule. However, when Parnell was accused of adultery with Kitty O Shea in 1890, the bishops and clergy withdrew their support and condemned him. His former enthusiastic supporters now became virulent opponents; when he visited Listowel in Kerry in 1890, for example, he encountered a hostile crowd led Fr. J. O Callaghan, the parish priest of Duagh. Fr. O Callaghan asked: "Were Irish Catholics to set up an avowed and unblushing adulterer as if he were a kind of god?" After Parnell was ousted as leader of the Irish Parliamentary Party, Bishop O Callaghan wrote in December of trouble in Cork: "The mob is for Parnell and the priests were insulted and hooted lately in the streets. . . . An attack was made on me some time ago in Cork. Fortunately the man in rushing at me slipped and fell at my feet, receiving a wound on his forehead." Thereafter Bishop O Callaghan strongly opposed Parnell's followers, denouncing their planned gathering in Cork on St. Patrick's Day 1891. Attributing the election of a Parnellite as one of the Poor Law Guardians to the "indifference of the priests," he promised that "this will be efficaciously remedied and it is not likely to occur again." Presumably he intended to instruct his priests to be more active in opposing the Parnellites. When John Redmond, the new leader the Irish Parliamentary Party, stood for Parnell's seat in Cork, vacated by his death, Bishop O Callaghan threw his support to Redmond's opponent. He described him as a good Catholic and Vice-President of the Confraternity of the Sacred Heart who was on a religious retreat when he was nominated for the seat. Redmond's brother William attributed the defeat to "clerical intimidation."[3]

Toward An Independent Ireland

Meanwhile the Irish Parliamentary Party could claim a measure of success when, in 1914 just before the outbreak of the First World War, the British parliament enacted Home Rule. Implementation, however, was suspended until the conclusion of the conflict. In Tipperary Michael O Callaghan was one of the delegates to a county convention of the Irish volunteers held at Cashel in July 1914 to discuss the possibility of partition and the need to obtain weapons. The postponement of Home Rule exhausted the patience of Irish nationalists who demanded complete independence and proclaimed the Irish Republic at Easter 1916. Although the planned rising throughout the country failed to materialize, the police attempted to arrest Michael O Callaghan of Tipperary; both policemen were shot and Michael fled to America. In the turbulent years of the War of Independence the British irregulars known as Black and Tans from the color of their uniforms gained notoriety for their viciousness in suppressing all signs of opposition. Among their victims was Fr. James O Callaghan, an ardent nationalist attached to St. Mary's Cathedral in Cork, who was killed in a raid on Pentecost Sunday 1921. A band of Irish volunteers including Jerry and Leo O Callaghan ambushed a column of Black and Tans at Nad on 10 March 1921. Christy O Callaghan of Tincoora celebrated the struggle

---

[3] Emmet Larkin, *The Roman Catholic Church in Ireland and the Fall of Parnell, 1888-1891* (Chapel Hill, NC: University of North Carolina Press, 1979), 236-237, 241, 260, 269, 287 n. 87; Mark Tierney, "Dr. Croke, the Irish Bishops and the Parnell Crisis, 18 November 1890-21 April 1891: Some Unpublished Correspondence," *CH* 11 (1969): 127, no. 19 (27 December 1890).

in his poem "My Home in Killavoy":

> There the lads are brave and daring and the girls are all true.
> How well they helped the flying column when they fought for Roisín Dubh.
> And when before the black and tans our heroes had to fly,
> They came and they found shelter in our homes in Killavoy.[4]

The aftermath of a planned ambush by the Irish Republican Army on 28 January 1921 near Dripsey revealed the brutality of the conflict. The British foiled the ambush when they received advance word of it from Mrs. Mary Lindsay, a loyalist. Among those captured and tried were Jeremiah and Daniel O Callaghan, both about twenty-one years of age. As the former claimed that he was not a member of the IRA and had been compelled to participate in the ambush, he was acquitted and released; but Daniel and four others were convicted and sentenced to death. To avert that, the IRA kidnapped Mrs. Lindsay and her servant and threatened to kill them if the five prisoners were executed. Doubting that the IRA would kill a woman, the British authorities carried out the execution of the five men on 28 February. In retaliation the IRA killed several soldiers in Cork City and executed Mrs. Lindsay and her servant on March 9. A monument at Godfrey's Cross on the road between Dripsey and Coachford commemorates the attempted ambush. The journalist Seán O Callaghan chronicled this and other violent episodes of that terrible period.[5]

Eventually negotiations resulted in the Treaty of Westminister in 1921 that established the Irish Free State. That was an anomaly of sorts, because it was not an independent republic, and six of the nine counties of Ulster, severed from the rest of Ireland, continued to be linked to Great Britain. Eamon De Valera and other hardliners refused to accept the treaty, however, and plunged the country into civil war.[6]

The Lord Mayors of Limerick and Cork

Two members of the O Callaghan family distinguished themselves in the struggle to establish a republic. In January 1920 Michael O Callaghan (1879-1921), a member of the executive of Sinn Fein in Limerick, was elected Lord Mayor of Limerick, the first republican to hold that position. His grandfather Eugene (d. 1885) had served as Lord Mayor in 1864. Originally from Cork, Eugene established O Callaghan Shoes and the City Tannery in Limerick in 1830.[7] Following his one-year term Michael continued to sit on the municipal council. On the night of 7 March 1921, about 1:20 a.m. he was murdered at his home in North Strand in the presence of his wife by the Black and Tans, British irregular forces who had previously threatened him and raided his home. On the same night they also murdered George Clancy, his successor as mayor, and the Volunteer

---

[4] P. C. Power, *South Tipperary*, 202-203; Dan Breen, *My Fight for Irish Freedom* (Dublin: Anvil, 1981), 74-75; Con Tarrant, "Terror and Counter-Terror," *SD* 7 (1989): 81-84; Murphy, *Mount Hillary*, 74, 87.

[5] Seán O Callaghan, *Execution* (London: Muller 1974), *The Easter Lily: Story of the IRA* (London: Wingate, 1956), and *The Jack Boot in Ireland* (London: Wingate, 1958).

[6] Foster, *Modern Ireland*, 461-567.

[7] Hugh Oram, *Bygone Limerick: The City and County in Days Gone By* (Cork: Mercier Press, 2010) 41.

Joseph O Donoghue. The funerals of the three men so brutally assassinated were celebrated in St. John's cathedral. Michael's widow, Kathleen O Callaghan, subsequently wrote an account of his murder and served as one of six republican women deputies elected to the Dáil Eireann, the de facto Irish parliament.[8]

Michael O Callaghan, Lord Mayor of Limerick

(Limerick Athenaeum)

Michael's contemporary, Donal Óg O Callaghan (1892-1962), a native of Cork City, served on the municipal council and as Deputy Lord Mayor to Terence MacSwiney. After the latter's death as a result of a hunger strike in October 1920, his good friend Donal succeeded to his office. In his youth he had distinguished himself for his ability to speak Irish. He was also Chairman of the Cork County Council and was elected to the Dáil in 1920, 1921, 1922, and 1923. The brutality of the Black and Tans drew the attention of 150 prominent Americans who organized the American Commission on Conditions in Ireland. Among those who testified before the Commission were the sister of Terence MacSwiney and Donal O Callaghan, then twenty-nine years of age. Fearful of what he might say, the British government denied him a passport, and wanted to imprison him, but in 1920 he stowed away on a ship bound for the United States. After much wrangling among American authorities, he was permitted to bear witness before the Commission. He presented an especially vivid description of the nightly raids, looting and destruction of property by the Black and Tans and British soldiers. Returning home, he became Minister for Home Affairs in the Dáil and was elected Lord Mayor again in 1922. As an opponent of the treaty Donal went into hiding, but in 1923 as one of three

---

[8] Kathleen O Callaghan, *The Limerick Curfew Murders of 7 March 1921: The Case of Michael O Callaghan, Councilor and ex-Mayor presented by his Widow* (n.p.n.d.); *Michael O Callaghan, 1879-1921: First Republican Mayor of Limerick 1920. Requiescat* (Dublin: Dun Emer Press, 1921). See an account of the 75th anniversary commemoration in *An Phoblacht/ Republican News,* 21 March 1996; Maedhbh McNamara and Paschal Mooney, *Women in Parliament, 1918-2000* (Dublin: Wolfhound Press, 2000), 81-83; Alvin Jackson, *Ireland 1798-1998: Politics and War* (Oxford: Blackwell, 1999), 262.

members of the Republican cabinet he joined De Valera and others in calling for a cessation of hostilities. After resigning as Lord Mayor in January 1924, he retired from public life. In 1995 another Lord Mayor, Joe O Callaghan, organized a commemoration of the 75th anniversary of MacSwiney's death and led a peace march following the IRA's declaration of a cease fire.[9]

Donal O Callaghan, Lord Mayor of Cork

(Cork Corporation)

After renouncing the use of violence De Valera formed a political party, Fianna Fáil, which captured control of the Dáil in 1932. One of his supporters, William O Callaghan (1881-1967), originally of Skarragh near Lombardstown, served in Seanad Eireann, the Irish Senate, from 1938 to 1943, and again from 1944 to 1961. He purchased Longueville House in 1938.[10] In the eighteenth century John Longfield had acquired an estate on O Callaghan lands on the north bank of the Blackwater just west of Mallow and changed the name from Garrymcowney to Longueville. A typical eighteenth century mansion, Longueville House faces the ruins of Dromaneen castle, the ancestral seat of the O Callaghans, on the opposite bank of the river. Under the ownership of

---

[9] Antóin O Callaghan, *The Lord Mayors of Cork, 1900 to 2000* (Cork: Inversnaid Publications, 2000), 45, 49, 51-56, 163-164; Charles Callan Tansill, *America and the Fight for Irish Freedom: An Old Story based on New Data* (New York: Devin-Adair, 1957), 410-414; Tim Pat Coogan, *The IRA: A History* (Niwot, CO: Roberts Rinehart, 1994), 26.

[10] https://www.longuevillehouse.ie/history.html; https://en.wikipedia.org/wiki/William_O%27Callaghan_(politician)

William's son Michael O Callaghan, Longueville House became a distinguished country residence. Michael hosted the first O Callaghan Clan reunion there in 1988.

The center portion of this beautiful Georgian mansion was built in 1720, while its two wings were added in 1800, and the beautiful Victorian Turner Conservatory in 1862. The drawing room at Longueville has been described as one of Ireland's grandest rooms, its atmosphere enhanced by the eternally burning log fire. The dining room is a fitting venue to serve the exquisite cuisine prepared by Michael's son William O Callaghan.

Dr. Pat O Callaghan, Olympic Athlete

The economic situation in Ireland in the years following the Irish Civil War was quite bleak, but the drabness of the time was relieved to some extent by triumphant news from the sporting world. Dr. Pat O Callaghan (1905-1991) of Derrygallon just west of Kanturk won the gold medal for the hammer throw (168'7") in the 1928 Olympics held at Amsterdam and repeated that feat four years later at the Los Angeles Olympic Games (176'11"). His brother Con competed in the long jump.

Patrick O Callaghan, Olympic Gold Medalist

(Castlemagner Historical Society)

Prior to the medal presentation in 1928 the British government argued that the Union Jack should be displayed as Pat was a British subject; he rejected that argument, insisting that the Irish flag be flown and the Irish national anthem, "The Soldier's Song" be played. He stated "I am glad of my victory, not for the victory itself, but for the fact that the world has been shown that Ireland has a flag, that Ireland has a National Anthem, and, in fact, that we have a nationality." Not only was he Ireland's first representative to win a gold medal, but also the first to win two gold medals. A poem entitled "Boy from Duhallow" exhorted: "Rejoice every Corkman from Youghal to Mallow/ He the joy and the glory of far famed Duhallow." Pat also won numerous Irish championships while practicing medicine at Clonmel, Tipperary. Many other O Callaghans, including Daniel of Lyre and Michael of Inchidaly, achieved distinction for their athletic prowess in Banteer and its vicinity.[11]

The Informer and the General

Meantime, the persistent hostility between nationalists and unionists in Northern Ireland continued to distress the country. One participant in that conflict was Seán O Callaghan, a native of Tralee, in County Kerry, the son of an old IRA man. Joining the Provisional IRA when he was fifteen, he took part in terrorist activities, bombing, robbing, and murdering two security officers. According to his own account he became sickened by this horror and resigned six years later, but rejoined when he was twenty-four. Eventually he became officer commanding the IRA Southern Command and a member of the executive council of Sinn Féin. Sentenced in 1990 to 539 years in prison, he was released after six years and then revealed that he had been an agent working for the government of the Irish Republic and British intelligence. In 1999 he published his book, *The Informer*, in which he claimed to have foiled a plot to assassinate Prince Charles and Princess Diana in 1983 and an arms shipment from the United States in 1984. Many have questioned his motives and his former associates despise him. Traditionally informers have been held in contempt because they were seen as collaborating with the ascendancy who held the people in subjection. Nevertheless, O Callaghan declared that he is proud to be an informer: "There are people alive and well today who would otherwise be dead or maimed had I not gone down that road." A television producer in 2004 described him as "a very strange man. He's very charming and seems to be incredibly warm and kind and insightful, but there's always something in the back of your head saying 'he did kill people.'" Asserting that he is now opposed to "political/terrorist violence" in Ireland, Seán also claimed that he could not live in Ireland for fear of being murdered by the Provos. He died in 2017.[12]

Lieutenant-General William Callaghan pursued an entirely different career, achieving distinction on the international scene. Born in Buttevant in 1921 he was commissioned in the Irish Defence Forces in 1940 and rose steadily in the ranks. He was deployed with Irish soldiers under United Nations auspices to the Congo in 1961, Cyprus in 1964, 1967, and 1971; he was also a member of the Truce Observation Organization in

[11] Henry Boylan, *A Dictionary of Irish Biography,* 3d ed. (Niwot, Colorado: Roberts Rinehart, 1998), 303; David Guiney, "Once a Duhallow Man – Always a Duhallow Man," *SD* 4 (1980-1981): 89-92; "Salute to a Sporting Legend: Dr. Pat O Callaghan," *SD* 9 (1993): 7; Tadhg Ó Muimneacháin and Mícheál Ó Léanacháin, "The Athletic and Historical Triangle," *SD* 10 (1996): 27-28; Murphy, *Mount Hillary*, 40, 53, 56, 58, 91-92, 146; Kavanagh, *Kilshannig*, 97, 110-113; www.Olympic.org/uk/athletes/heroes/bio.
[12] Seán O Callaghan, *The Informer: The Real Life Story of One Man's War against Terrorism* (London: Corgi, 1999); *Irish Examiner*, 19 April 2000, 28 January 2002; *The Observer*, 28 September 2003; Confessions of an IRA Informer, BBC 6 July 2004.

Jerusalem from 1976 to 1979. Promoted to Major-General in 1980 and Lieutenant-General in 1981, he was commander of United Nations forces in Lebanon until 1987 when he was appointed Chief of Staff of the United Nations Observer Corps in the Middle East. He .was commended for making "a significant contribution to establishing stability in the area, thus contributing generally to world peace."[13]

General William Callaghan

(Mallow Field Club Journal)

In the Dáil on the 23rd May 1986 the Minister of State for the Dept of Defence stated:

I also wish to pay a well deserved tribute to Lieutenant-General Callaghan, on the relinquishment of his appointment after more than five years service as Force Commander UNIFIL. Through his distinguished service with UNIFIL, Lieutenant-General Callaghan has brought honour to the

---

[13] Rev. Robert Forde, "Lieutenant General William Callaghan," *MFCJ* 5 (1987): 18-21; John P. Duggan, *A History of the Irish Army* (Dublin: Gill and Macmillan, 1991), 254.

Defence Forces and to our nation. I wish him every success in his new appointment as Chief of Staff, UNTSO.

A week later, the Minister for Defence, Mr. Barry, voiced his appreciation of the work done by the Lieutenant-General. He stated:

In addition to expressing appreciation to the members of theDefence Forces for the discharge of their tasks in a manner which brought great credit to their country, I want to pay a particular tribute to Lieutenant-General Callaghan, who has recently relinquished his post as Force Commander of UNIFIL after a long and distinguished period of service in that taxing position. We wish him well in his new appointment as Chief of Staff of the Truce Supervision Organisation.

The End of the House of Lismore

In the midst of those unsettling times the fortunes of the O Callaghan gentry rose and fell. After the termination of the principal male line in Clare in 1791, the O Callaghans of Dromskehy in Cork, Maryfort in Clare, and Spain put forward their claims to the chieftainship, but, as we shall see, the issue was not resolved until the twentieth century.

Meantime, the O Callaghans of Tipperary achieved even greater honor than before. Cornelius O Callaghan (1775-1857), who in 1797 succeeded his father as second Baron Lismore, was created Viscount Lismore of Shanbally on 30 May 1806, and Baron Lismore of Shanbally Castle in the peerage of the United Kingdom on 6 July 1838. The latter was one of the peerages created on the occasion of Queen Victoria's coronation. Cornelius also served as Lord Lieutenant of Tipperary from 1851 to 1857. His presence at a dinner for the Friends of Religious Liberty in 1811 and again at a provincial meeting called by O Connell at Limerick in 1825 suggests his liberal inclinations. According to Griffith's Valuation he possessed extensive estates in the Parish of Shanrahan (Ballynalona, Boolakennedy, Burncourt, Carrigmore, a house on Cockpit Lane in the village of Clogheen, Coolantallagh, Crannagh, Cullenagh South, Flemingstown, Glencallaghan, and Toormoor), as well as in County Cork. Twenty-one other Callaghans were listed as householders in Tipperary. The rental income from the Lismore estates in 1808 was £15,000 and in 1822 £17,120 and was enhanced by further acquisitions. Nevertheless, the viscount was financially strapped for many years. In 1808 he married the daughter of the earl of Ormond, but, on the grounds of her adultery, they were divorced in 1826. His second son, George Ponsonby O Callaghan (1815-1898), succeeded as Viscount Lismore. Like his father he served as Lord Lieutenant of Tipperary (1851-1885) and as High Sheriff in 1853; initially a liberal in politics, after 1886 he was a unionist. In 1883 he owned 34,949 acres in Tipperary, 6,067 in Cork, and 1,194 in Limerick, or 42,206 acres in all with a yearly income of £16,354. When he died on 29 October 1898 his estate was valued at £20,000. As his sons predeceased him the title became extinct.[14]

[14] Lascelles, *Liber Munerum*, 2:70, 79-80 (Lodge's Peerage); Cokayne, *Complete Peerage*, 8: 81-82; Pine, *Extinct Peerage*, 180-181; O Connell, *Correspondence of Daniel O Connell*, 1:307, no. 392 (12 September 1812), 3:191-192, no. 1253 (25 October 1825); Dublin, NLI, National Library Report on

Cornelius O Callaghan, Viscount Lismore[15]

In 1908 Leslie O Callaghan, a Cork farmer, claiming to be a grandson of Richard O Callaghan, a son of an earlier viscount, asserted his right of succession to the title and property of the deceased viscount. He stated that about 100 years ago Richard had married Nellie O Connor, the penniless daughter of a village bootmaker; though she was a Catholic, they were married in a Protestant church. Although he intended to pursue his claims, he obviously did not succeed.[16]

During this period family members dominated local politics and represented their community and the interests of their class in the British parliament. Cornelius O Callaghan, for example, as a member of the Liberal Party, represented Tipperary (1832-1835) and Dungarvan (1837-1841) in the House of Commons. Col. Wilfred O Callaghan,

Private Collections, no. 343: J. F. Ainsworth, Report on the Shanbally Estate Office Papers (from 1736) Clogheen, Co. Tipperary, relating to the O Callaghan family, Lords Lismore, and to lands in Co. Tipperary; T. P. Power, *Land*, 88, 91, 95; Kavanagh and Hayes, *O'Callaghan & Otway of Tipperary*, 1-4,

[15] https://blouinartsalesindex.com/auctions/Lowes-Cato-Dickinson-4883871/Cornelius-O'Callaghan-(1775-1857),-1st-Viscount-Lismore-and-3rd-Baron-Dunalley,-bust-length,-in-a-black-jacket,-white-shirt-and-black-cravat-

[16] Evening Expresss and Evening Mail, 24 July 1908.

a son of Viscount Lismore, a Liberal and a supporter of Home Rule, sat for Tipperary from 1874 until his death three years later.[17]

Among the most eminent military representatives of the name was Sir Robert William O Callaghan (1777-1840), second son of the first Baron Lismore, who served in the British army for nearly fifty years from 1794 until he died unmarried in London. After achieving distinction during the Napoleonic Wars and attaining the rank of Major-General in 1814, he was commander-in-chief of British forces in Scotland and India. Made a Knight Commander of the Bath in 1815, he also received the Military Cross. John Cornelius O Callaghan remarked that "his private character as a man was not less esteemed than his professional one as a soldier."[18]

General Sir Robert William O Callaghan

(Sotheby's)

The sons of the first Viscount Lismore also pursued military careers. Cornelius (1809-1849), a bachelor, served in the 12th Lancers, and George, the second Viscount, in the 17th Lancers. The youngest brother, William Frederick, a captain in the 44th Foot, died unmarried in India in 1836.

The symbol of the power and influence of the O Callaghans of Tipperary was Shanbally Castle near Clogheen. Erected about 1810 for the first Viscount Lismore, it was "the largest house built in Ireland by the famous English architect, John Nash." In

---

[17] Walker, *Election Results*, 313-314; O Shea, *Priests,* 158, 209; Tierney, "Croke Papers," *CH* 13 (71): 12, 112, no. 7.

[18] *Dictionary of National Biography* 14 (1917): 791-792; John C. O Callaghan, ed., Charles O Kelly, *Macariae Excidium*, in *Narratives Illustrative of the Contests in Ireland in 1641 and 1690*, ed. Thomas Crofton Croker, Camden Society, 14 (London: J. B. Nichols, 1841); *Report on the Manuscripts of the Earl of Bathurst preserved at Cirencester Park* (London: Historical Manuscripts Commission, 1923), 228; *Report on the Laing Manuscripts preserved in the University of Edinburgh*, 2 vols. (London: Historical Manuscripts Commission, 1914-1925), 2:774-775; Kavanagh and Hayes, *O'Callaghan & Otway*, 9-10.

addition to drawing rooms, a dining room, and a library, it had twenty bedrooms, marble fireplaces, and a mahogany staircase. After the death of the second Viscount in 1898 the house was gradually abandoned. The Irish Land Commission purchased the estate in 1954. Three years later, concluding that the castle, though "one of the most graceful and original examples in Ireland of later Georgian architecture," was in poor condition and had not been occupied for forty years, the Commission decided to demolish it. Describing this decision as "an act of vandalism," Professor Denis Gwynn protested to the *Cork Examiner*: "Shanbally Castle has been well known for years as one of the most graceful and original examples in Ireland of late Georgian architecture." In 1960 the last vestiges of the structure were blown up. Another relic of the grandeur of Lord Lismore's family is a sauce tureen with the arms of O Callaghan that was exhibited at the Philadelphia Antiques Show some years ago.[19]

Shanbally Castle

(National Library of Ireland)

[19] Laffan, *"Fethard,"* JRSAI 36 (1906) 152; Collins, "Gleanings," JCHAS 69 (1964): 56-59; Mark Bence Jones, *A Guide to Irish Country Houses* (London: Burke's Peerage, 1988); Bill Power, www.ocallaghan/shanbally.htm; Laura Sweeney, "Shanbally Castle," www.tipperary.local.ie. The tureen was illustrated in an advertisement by Elinor Gordon, an antiques dealer, in *Antique Monthly*. The Timothy Looney Papers in the University of Limerick include rent rolls, ledgers, and othed records relating to the estste at Shanbally. https://www.ul.ie/library/sites/default/files/documents/P43_Looney_0.pdf

The O Callaghans in Spain

The O Callaghans in Spain enjoyed greater longevity than their Tipperary counterparts. As we have seen, Cornelius O Callaghan (1693-1741), a grandson of Donough Mór, served in the Spanish army until his death at Oran. After Edmond O Callaghan died in 1791, Ramón (1765-1833), Cornelius's grandson, claimed the O Callaghan estates in Clare as well as the chieftainship, though that had long ceased to have any substance. As already noted Denis O Callaghan of Glynn also put in his claim, but his descent from the main branch of the family was never clear. Ramón, who was described in legal documents as a "French gentleman," was equally unsuccessful. Nevertheless, his descendants achieved great distinction in Spanish affairs in the nineteenth century.[20]

His third son, Ramón O Callaghan y Tarragó (1798-1844), played a significant role in the Carlist wars, a dynastic conflict precipitated by King Fernando VII's recognition of his daughter Isabel II as heir to the Spanish throne. By ignoring the Salic Law restricting the succession to males, he overrode the claims of his brother, Infante Don Carlos. Ramón had initially gained attention by opposing the liberal supporters of the Constitution of 1812 and headed an uprising in favor of Fernando VII in Benisanet, his native place. Nevertheless, he was compelled to emigrate to France in 1827. After the king's death in 1833 Ramón placed himself squarely on the side of Infante Don Carlos and organized and commanded the First Battalion of Mora de Ebro; he shortly attained the rank of colonel and was decorated with the Cross of San Fernando.

Ramón O Callaghan y Tarragó[21]

---

[20] Dublin, GO, MS 182, p. 569, MS 177, pp. 460-463, MS 179, p. 178, and MS 289, p. 170; *BIFR*, 889.

[21] From B. de Artágan, *Carlistas de antaño* (Barcelona: La Bandera Regional. 1910), 238.

Ramón acted as military governor of Cantavieja in Aragón before assuming the same responsibility in Morella, the Carlist headquarters, a post he held until the royalists captured it in 1839. For his defense of Morella he was promoted to brigadier. In the closing years of the conflict he displayed similar tenacity but joined other Carlists in seeking refuge in France. He died at Montpellier. His brothers, Salvador (1801-1844), Pedro (1803-1869), José (1806-1881), and Carlos (1812-1836) were respectively a captain in the army, a Benedictine monk, a notary, and a law student.[22]

The sons of the notary, José, pursued careers as priests, physicians, and advocates. Among the most notable was the historian, Ramón O Callaghan y Forcadell (1834-1911), a native of Ulldecona in the province of Tarragona. After obtaining his doctorate in Sacred Theology at Valencia and being ordained to the priesthood, he served as military vicar general of Tortosa and later as a canon of the cathedral of Tortosa. In that capacity he organized the cathedral archives and published several important volumes, including: the *Anales de Tortosa* (1890), a history of the city; *Derecho y práctica parroquial* (1892), a manual of pastoral practice; *Episcopologio de la Santa Iglesia de Tortosa* (1896), a biographical study of the bishops of Tortosa; *Los códices de la catedral de Tortosa* (1901), a description of manuscript volumes in the cathedral archive; and *Historia de la Santa Cinta que se venera en la Seo de Tortosa* (1910), an account of a cincture said to belong to the Virgin Mary. His labors gained him appointment as Chronicler of the City of Tortosa, election to the Real Academia de Buenas Letras of Barcelona, and as a Corresponding Member of the Real Academia de la Historia in Madrid. The municipality of Tortosa dedicated the Plaza O Callaghan in the vicinity of the cathedral in his honor. It is now known as the Plaça dels Estudis.[23]

In the twentieth century still another priest of this family, José O Callaghan, S. J. (1922-2001), gained renown for his contributions to biblical studies. After directing a seminar on papyrology at the Theological Faculty of San Cugat del Valls near Barcelona, and founding the journal *Studia Papyrologica* he was appointed to teach at the Pontifical Biblical Institute in Rome. Although he contributed interesting insights into the life of early Christians in his book *La vida en los primeros siglos según las cartas cristianas* (1964), he received worldwide attention in 1972 for his discovery concerning the Gospel of St. Mark. He argued that a scrap of the recently discovered Dead Sea Scrolls contains a portion of Mark's Gospel (6:52-53); that being the case he concluded that the Gospel was probably written about 50 A. D. rather than 70 A. D., the usually accepted date. That would mean that Mark was written less than twenty years after the death of Christ. In addition, he identified passages from the epistle of St. James, traditionally dated around 60 A. D. Though not all biblical scholars were convinced, Fr. O Callaghan's work was hailed as the discovery of the century in biblical studies.[24]

---

[22] Dublin, GO, MS 182, p. 569; *Enciclopedia Universal Ilustrada* 39 (1920): 485; *BIFR*, 889. Spaniards customarily used the names of both parents. Tarragó was the surname of Ramon's mother.

[23] Dublin, GO, MS 182, p. 569; *Enciclopedia Universal Ilustrada* 39 (1920): 485; *BIFR*, 889.

[24] José O Callaghan, S.J., "¿Papiros neotestamentarios en la cueva 7 de Qumran?" *Biblica* 53 (1972): 91-100; *New York Times*, 19 March 1972, 2 April 1972. See also his books *La vida en los primeros siglos según las cartas cristianas* (San Cugat del Vallés: Papyrologica Castrooctaviana, 1964; *El nuevo testamento en las versiones españolas* (Rome: Biblical Institute, 1982). See Simone Venturini's appreciation of José O Callaghan at simoneventurini.com/en/great-men-and-women/ 13 August 2016.

.

José O Callaghan, S.J., Biblical Scholar

(Pontifical Biblical Institute, Rome)

The claims of this family to the chieftainship of the O Callaghans will be discussed below.

O Callaghans in the New World

While the O Callaghans of Spain represented an earlier strand of emigration from Ireland, principally as a consequence of the Treaty of Limerick in 1691, other O Callaghans departed from their ancestral homes in the eighteenth century and in ever increasing numbers in the nineteenth. At the time of leaving most of them were known simply as Callaghan or Callahan, so that once they left Ireland it became almost impossible to distinguish the Duhallow and Muskerry families, to say nothing of the Callaghans from the northern counties. Indeed, many of the Callaghans sailing from Liverpool were probably from Northern Ireland. The reader should keep in mind this uncertainty about the origin of many O Callaghans or Callaghans mentioned below. Here only a few examples, mostly of emigrants who settled in the United States, can be cited. Perhaps the earliest was Charles Callahan who settled in Virginia in 1637. Two John Callahans arrived in Boston on 11 September 1764 aboard the schooner Hannah, sailing from Cork; another John arrived in 1765 and Mary Callahane, embarking on the brig Ann and Margaret, landed in Boston on 17 October 1767.[25]

Representative of an earlier phase of emigration is James Hughes Callahan (1814-1856), a native of Georgia, who served with the Georgia Battalion during the American war with Mexico. In 1855 as an officer in the Texas Rangers he led the Callahan Expedition against the Lipan-Apache and Kickapoo Indians, pursuing them into Mexico. Defeated by the Mexicans, he retreated, burning Piedras Negras, and in consequence was dismissed from the Rangers. In 1856 he was killed in conflict with the Woodson-Blassengame family. Callahan County, Texas, and The Callahan Divide, a mountain range separating the Colorado and the Brazos Rivers, both named for him, commemorate his exploits. Another branch of the family headed by Charles Callaghan, a Confederate veteran, achieved great wealth when the Callaghan Ranch, originally 80 acres devoted to sheepraisng, grew into one of the great ranches of Texas, consisting in 1946 of 250,500 acres, with herds of about 20,000 Hereford cattle under the Swinging Eleven brand.[26]

In the nineteenth century, especially following the famine, waves of emigrants abandoned Ireland, some for England, others for Canada, Australia, and New Zealand, but perhaps most for the United States. Until the United States declared independence in 1776 the English government treated it as a penal colony, sending some 13,000 Irish convicts there. From 1787 to 1868 about 39,000 Irish convicts were sent to Australia. Male and female, teenagers, and young people in their twenties and thirties, often married with small children, they poured into the ports of Boston, New York, and Philadelphia. Coming mostly from rural communities where they had gained their livelihood from the soil, they settled in the cities and towns where the men found employment as laborers, and the women as servants to the wealthy. Others who journeyed westward often were able to acquire land to farm. Still others joined the army, particularly during the American Civil War. In 1862, for example, William O Callaghan enlisted in the 155th or Second Regiment of Corcoran's Irish Legion, New York State Volunteers. John O Callaghan, born in New York, serving as a sergeant in Company 8, the 8th United States Cavalry, was awarded the Congressional Medal of Honor in 1869 for his bravery in the Indian wars in Arizona in the previous year. After the Civil War many participated in the Indian Wars while others helped to build the railroads that opened the west to settlement.[27]

Edmund Bailey O Callaghan, Historian

Among the emigrants who achieved great distinction was Edmund Bailey O Callaghan (1797-1880), born in Mallow, the youngest son of a merchant. Of his three older brothers, Theodore held a commission in the British army, gaining notoriety as a

---

[25] Michael Tepper, ed., *New World Immigrants: A Consolidation of Ship Passenger Lists and Associated Data from Periodical Literature*, 2 vols. (Baltimore: Genealogical Publishing Co., 1979), 1:72, 467-468, 470; Lawrence J. McCaffrey, *The Irish Diaspora in America* (Bloomington, IN: Indiana University Press, 1976).

[26] *The Handbook of Texas*, 1 (1952): 271-272.

[27] Thomas F. Magner, "Irish Convicts in America and Australia," *MFCJ* 13 (1995): 116-131; P. William Filby and Mary K. Meyer, *Passenger and Immigration Lists 11:01 AM10/14/2020: A Guide to Published Archival Records of about 500,000 Passengers who came to the United States and Canada in the Seventeenth, Eighteenth and Nineteenth Centuries* (Detroit: Gale, 1981); www.Callahans Ship List. Ships to the USA from 1764 to 1898; O'Hart, *Pedigrees,* 2:822; Foster, *Modern Ireland*, 345-371.

duelist (the eventual cause of his death), and Eugene and David were priests. After studying medicine at Paris for two years (1820-1822) Edmund completed his studies at Quebec and was licensed to practice in 1827. While living in Montreal he became active in Canadian politics, editing the *Vindicator*, a liberal newspaper. Elected to the assembly of Upper Canada in 1835, he initially opposed revolutionary action, but in 1837 he participated in the uprising against an inflexible colonial government. For his pains he was branded as a traitor on 29 November 1837 and fled to the United States where he remained, despite a later amnesty.

Edmund Bailey O Callaghan, Historian

(Nash E.W., ed. Catalogue of the Library of the Late E.B.O'Callaghan, M.D., LL.D., Historian of New York. New York: Douglas Taylor, Printer 1882, illustration preceding title page. Courtesy of the Albany Institute of History & Art.)

After settling in Albany, New York in 1838, he practiced medicine and edited *The Northern Light,* but also began to study the records of the Dutch colony in New York. His two-volume *History of New Netherland,* published in 1846-1849, was the first real history of New York State. As a consequence, he was called upon to edit Dutch colonial records, a task at which he labored for more than twenty years. The resulting four-volume

The Documentary History of the State of New York and the eleven-volume *Documents relative to the Colonial History of the State of New York* are a monument to his skill, breadth of knowledge, and attention to accurate detail. In recognition of his labors he received the honorary degrees of doctor of medicine from St. Louis University and doctor of laws from St. John's College, now Fordham University. In 1870 he moved to New York City to organize the municipal archives; but after suffering an accident in 1877 he was confined to his home where he died. *The O Callaghan Papers* containing his correspondence and other materials are located in the Manuscript Department of the Library of Congress. A physician turned historian, he helped to lay the groundwork for serious historical study in the United States.[28]

Eugene O Callaghan, Champion of Priests

A somewhat younger contemporary was Eugene O Callaghan (1831-1901), one of six children of Timothy, a woolspinner from Kanturk. Prompted by the famine, Eugene emigrated in 1847. The eight-week journey in steerage by sailing ship cost $37; like other passengers, he had to remain by day and night in the cargo hold and to bring his own food. He worked for a year helping to dig the canal from Miami, Ohio to Erie, Pennsylvania, and used his wages to bring the rest of his family to Ohio. After attending the University of Notre Dame (1849-1853), he entered the seminary and was ordained for the Cleveland diocese in 1859. As a missionary priest, he was sent by his bishop to establish or direct more than fifteen parishes and to build churches, rectories, and schools. After visiting Rome during the First Vatican Council, he returned to Kanturk in 1870, only to express his dismay: "You would not recognize the place of our birth. The land is empty; the West and South are deserted. Ireland is no longer alive. Our only hope is in America."

Aside from his extraordinary ministerial career, his principal achievement was to champion the rights of priests, who were often ignored or treated harshly by their bishops. He urged bishops to make provision for the care of aged and infirm priests. He also argued that priests were entitled to a firm tenure and due process of law before being summarily removed at the whim of the bishop. Under the pen name, *Jus* (law, right), he set forth his positions in twelve articles on "The Status of the Clergy" printed between 1868 and 1870 in the *Freeman's Journal*, a national Catholic newspaper published in New York. His challenge to episcopal authority aggravated his superiors, some of whom

---

[28] Francis Guy Shaw, *Edmund Bailey O Callaghan: A Study in American Historiography (1797-1880)* (Washington: Catholic University of America, 1934); Jack Verney, "Edmund Bailey O Callaghan, Rebel and Writer," *MFCJ* 5 (1987): 79-101, and *O Callaghan: The Making and Unmaking of a Rebel* (Ottowa: Carleton University 1994); *Dictionary of National Biography* 14 (1917): 790; *Dictionary of American Biography*, 13:613; Maureen Slattery, "Irish Radicalism and the Roman Catholic Church in Quebec and Ireland, 1833-1834: O'Callaghan and O'Connell Compared," *CCHA, Historical Studies* 63 (1997: 29-58, and "Dr. Edmund Bailey O'Callaghan, His Early Years in Medicine, Montreal, 1823-1828," CCHA, *Study Sessions*, 47 (1980): 23-40.

regarded him as a troublemaker and others even as a heretic. Nevertheless, his stand on behalf of his fellow priests eventually won greater security for them.[29]

**Fr. Eugene O Callaghan
December 1870**

(Callahan, *A Case for Due Process*)

The O Callaghans of Philadelphia and Dromcummer

Typical of many other emigrants were my great-uncles, William, Denis, and Matthew Callaghan, younger sons who left Ireland, probably around 1855 when they were in their teens. They probably sailed from Queenstown (now Cobh) for Philadelphia and apparently worked as sutlers provisioning the Union Army during the American Civil War. Until his death in 1916 in Philadelphia, William maintained his own bakery, a trade he may have learned in Ireland. His son Denis, and his grandson Robert, both graduates of the University of Pennsylvania, became distinguished lawyers. William's brother Matthew worked in the steel mills in Steelton, Pennsylvania.[30]

Although William was not rich, his sons bought him a first class ticket to Ireland in 1907. Making his way to Dromcummer, he visited his brother John and his family. As he was preparing his journey home, my father's sister Mary said she wanted to accompany him. Lest she be lonely and left without friends in Philadelphia, my father, William O Callaghan, who had been managing a store in Waterville in County Kerry,

---

[29] Nelson Callahan, *A ase for Due Process in the Church: Father Eugene O Callaghan, American Pioneer of Dissent* (Staten Island, NY: Alba House, 1971). Fr. O Callaghan's papers are in the University of Notre Dame Archives.

[30] Dennis Clark, *The Irish in Philadelphia: Ten Generations of Urban Experience* (Philadelphia: Temple University Press, 1973), 138, 161.

agreed to go with her; before he left home he scratched the date of his departure in the built-in china closet in his father's house. They likely took the train from Banteer to Cork and then boarded the Haverford at Queenstown for the voyage to Philadelphia. Soon after their arrival Mary declared that she wished to enter the Sisters of St. Joseph at Chestnut Hill, Philadelphia where she took the name, Sister John Edmond. That caught my father entirely by surprise; he was quite upset and probably would not have come to the United States if he had known her intention. After his father's death in 1912, he returned to Ireland but came back to Philadelphia.

Dromcummer in 2014

As his father died intestate, his six living children were entitled to a share of his estate; but his oldest son Denis persuaded his siblings to give up their claims to Dromcummer in 1914. One aspect of the settlement sheds an interesting light on contemporary customs and the fate of widows. Denis agreed that his mother, Margaret Leonard, "should have for life use of the room in the dwelling house . . . she now occupies and the furniture in the same. . . . He shall during her life clothe, support, and maintain her in the same manner as she has heretofore enjoyed and supply her with a horse and spring car and guide to bring her to mass on all Sundays and holidays and such other places as she shall require at all reasonable times." She was also entitled to a life annuity of £5. Sadly, the world-wide flu epidemic carried off my uncles John and Timothy, neither of whom had married, in November 1918. Denis died in 1917, the victim of a farm accident, leaving a widow and two minor children, John and Nora. When their mother, Mary Barrett, died in 1925 they were reared by her family and in 1941 sold Dromcummer. Young John told the purchasers that should my father ever return, they should be hospitable to him because he had always had great affection for Dromcummer.

My father never returned to Ireland. In 1916 he married Helen O Sullivan, the daughter of Irish immigrants, Michael O Sullivan from Ardnagashel near Bantry Bay and Margaret Ellard of Coolycarney, Wexford. Michael, like many others, took advantage of the Homestead Act to acquire 160 acres in Adrian, Minnesota; when he died in 1900. Margaret brought her two girls, Helen, and Mary, to Philadelphia where her family, who had emigrated from Wexford, were settled. After their marriage my father and mother raised a family of eight, five boys (John, the eldest boy, died at the age of four) and three girls. My sisters Margaret and Helen married and had families of their own while Madeleine became a nurse anesthetist. My brother Michael, a Franciscan priest, taught mathematics at Siena College in New York State before becoming a missionary in Brazil. Denis, a priest of the Archdiocese of Philadelphia, challenged racist attitudes and championed the cause of the black minority in Chester before finishing his career as a member of the Pastoral Department of St. Mary's Seminary, Baltimore. William taught philosophy at St. Norbert College, Green Bay, Wisconsin, and his son John currently teaches philosophy at the University of Notre Dame.[31] As the fifth son, I pursued a career as an historian. The example of the Philadelphia O Callaghans is just one of many that illustrate the process whereby Irish immigrants to America and their descendants created new lives for themselves, acquiring farms or other property, entering business, the priesthood, the law, or the academic world.

Joseph T. O Callahan, S.J., Naval Hero

In an entirely different manner Joseph Timothy O Callahan, S.J. (1905-1964), professor of mathematics at Holy Cross College, Worcester, Massachusetts, gained distinction as a chaplain in the United States Navy in World War II. After serving as chief morale officer on the aircraft carrier USS Ranger during the invasion of North Africa, he was transferred to the carrier USS Franklin in the Pacific Ocean, with the rank of Lieutenant Commander. During the horrendous bombardment of the Franklin on 19 March 1945 by Japanese air planes off Kobe, Japan, he helped to save the ship while ministering to the wounded and the dying. President Harry S. Truman honored his heroic behavior on 23 January 1946 by conferring on him the Congressional Medal of Honor, the highest award given by the United States. The citation read in part: "He organized and led fire-fighting crews into the blazing inferno on the flight deck; he directed the jettisoning of live ammunition and the flooding of the magazine; he manned a hose to cool hot, armed bombs rolling dangerously on the listing ship, continuing his efforts despite searing, suffocating smoke." The captain said that Fr. O Callahan "was the bravest man I ever saw." He responded: "any priest in like circumstances should do and would do what I did." Returning home after the war with the rank of captain he resumed his teaching career at Holy Cross until ill health forced his retirement. Meantime he wrote an account of his experiences entitled, *I was Chaplain on the Franklin.* He died on 16 March 1964. On 20 October 1965 at Bay City, Michigan, his sister Alice, a Maryknoll missioner known in religion as Sister Rose Marie, christened a new destroyer escort, the USS O Callahan, named in his honor. The first nun ever to christen an American warship, she had been interned in the Philippines by the Japanese; after liberation she taught at

---

[31] William's colleagues in philosophy dedicated to him *Conflict and Community: New Studies in Thomistic Thought*, ed. Michael B. Lukens (New York: Peter Lang, 1992). His son John authored *Thomistic Realism and the Linguistic Turn: Toward a More Perfect Form of Existence* (Notre Dame, IN: University of Notre Dame, 2003).

Maryknoll college in Quezon. The O Callahan Science Library at Holy Cross is named in her brother's honor.[32]

Rev. Joseph T. O Callahan, S.J., Naval Hero

(Courtesy of Jay O'Callahan)

Two other Jesuit priests attained their own degree of renown. Roger O Callaghan, S. J. (1912-1953), a native of New York City, ordained in 1939, became a student of Semitic languages and taught at the Pontifical Biblical Institute in Rome from 1946 to 1952. An exceptional linguist, he conversed easily in Hebrew and Arabic as well as trhe languages of Western Europe, and even acquired a facility in Irish. While Professor of Archaeology at Fordham University, New York, he received a Fulbright Fellowship that enabled him to study in Iraq, but his career was abruptly terminated when he was killed there in an automobile accident. Another Jesuit, John J. O Callaghan, was elected as one of the four general assistants at the Jesuit curia in Rome. A native of Chicago, he entered the Jesuits in 1949 and served as rector of the seminary there and also as president of the Jesuit Conference in Washington.[33] Many other priest members of the family served the Church throughout the world.

---

[32] Joseph Timothy O Callahan, S.J. *I Was Chaplain on the Franklin* (New York: Macmillan, 1956); *Boston Pilot*, 30 October 1965; *Boston Globe*, 29 October 29, 1965; Matthew Ashe, S.J., "Conspicuous Gallantry," *Company: A Magazine of the American Jesuits*, Winter 1989, 18-19.

[33] Roger Timothy O Callaghan, S. J., *Aram Naharaim. A Contribution to the History of Upper Mesopotamia in the Second Millenium B.C.* (Rome: Pontificum Institutum Biblicum, 1948); *New York Times*, 6 March 1953; F. L. Moriarty, *Catholic Biblical Quarterly* 16 (1954): 328-329; "In Memoriam Roger T. O'Callaghan, S. J.," *Bulletin of the American Schools of Oriental Research* 134 (April 1954): 3-4; Arthur Jones, "A Close Look at Jesuit Order uncovers a Rich History and Challenging Future," *National Catholic Reporter*, February 19, 1

Admirals Daniel and William Callaghan

In addition to Fr. Joseph O Callahan, two other members of the family, the Admirals Daniel and William Callaghan, played exceptional roles in the American armed forces during the Second World War. They were the great-grandsons of Daniel Callaghan who arrived in Boston from Cork in 1845 and joined his brother Jeremiah in California in 1852. By providing supplies to miners attracted by the Gold Rush they achieved wealth and prominence in the affairs of San Francisco.

Admiral Daniel J. Callaghan   Admiral William M. Callaghan

Both Daniel and William were graduates of the United States Naval Academy at Annapolis and served during the First World War. Rear Admiral Daniel Callaghan (1892-1942), a naval aide to President Franklin D. Roosevelt from 1938 to 1941, represented the president at the funeral of Cardinal George Mundelein of Chicago in 1939. Three years later he was placed in command of a force sent to intercept the Japanese in the Solomon Islands. In the naval battle of Guadalcanal on 13 November 1942, his flagship, the cruiser San Francisco, moved into the enemy with her guns blazing, causing one enemy ship to sink, and disabling a battleship. Admiral Callaghan, whom the President described as "my close personal friend," was killed on the bridge of his flagship. The Congressional Medal of Honor "for extraordinary heroism and conspicuous intrepidity" was awarded to him posthumously. The citation commended his "ingenious tactical skill and superb coordination of the units under his command . . . his courageous initiative, inspiring leadership, and judicious foresight in a crisis of grave responsibility. . . . He gallantly gave his life in the defense of his country." The destroyer USS Callaghan, launched in his honor in August 1943, was sunk by a Japanese kamikaze attack on 28 July 1945. In August 1981 a new USS Callaghan was commissioned.[34]

---

[34] Francis Trevelyan Miller, *History of World War II* (Philadelphia: John Winston, 1945), 527-

Daniel's brother, William (1898-1991), who served on a destroyer guarding convoys in the North Atlantic during World War I, helped to organize the delivery of petroleum to Britain during World War II. When the new battleship Missouri, of 45,000 tons, was put into service in 1944, he was given command and participated in naval actions off Iwo Jima, Okinawa, and Tokyo. When the Japanese surrendered in 1945 the ceremony presided over by General MacArthur took place on the battleship Missouri, with Captain Callaghan still in command. After the war he organized the Military Sea Transportation Services and also commanded American naval forces in the Far East. Retiring with the rank of Vice-Admiral in 1957, he became Vice-President of American Export Lines, and acted as chairman of the Maritime Transportation Research Board under the National Academy of Sciences. A recipient of the Legion of Merit as well as several other honors, he was also a Knight of Malta. His son Rear Admiral William Callaghan, Jr. (1925-2013) continued the family tradition of naval service.[35]

An O Callaghan Miscellany

The reader is surely aware of the impossibility of recording the actions of all those O Callaghans who attained some measure of excellence At best I can only offer a miscellany, far from complete, demonstrating that members of the family, given the opportunity, have achieved success and even renown in diverse endeavors. The nineteenth-century architect J. J. O Callaghan designed numerous churches, usually in the Gothic style, as well as the first synagogue in Dublin and all Ireland. Sir Francis Langford O Callaghan (1839-1909) gained distinction as an engineer, while Sir George Callaghan (1852-1920) commanded the British Home Fleet in 1914 just before the outbreak of World War I.[36] In the world of American politics Donal O Callaghan (1929-2004), usually known as Mike, was perhaps the most popular governor in the history of the State of Nevada (1971-1978). Born in Wisconsin, he received the Silver Star for heroism in the Korean War, but also lost his left leg below the knee. Later as executive editor of the Las Vegas Sun he had a strong influence on the life of his state.[37]

In an entirely different vein, John O Callaghan of Mallow wrote a street ballad on the French recapture of Orleans during the Franco-Prussian war. Each verse ended with a line in Irish, "Fagamaid suir mar ata shea," - "let's leave things as they are."[38] Another balladeer, Teige O Callaghan (1890-1955) praised the beauties of Kilshannig and of his own place:

528; F. X. Murphy, *Fighting Admiral: The Story of Dan Callaghan* (New York: Vantage, 1952); *The Catholic Standard and Times*, 20 November 1942; *Dictionary of American Naval Fighting Ships*, ed. James L. Mooney (Washington: Naval Historical Center, 1991); Richard Connors, "Rear Admiral Daniel Judson Callaghan," www.microworks.net/pacific/biographies/daniel_callaghan.htm.

[35] *New York Times*, 9 July 1991.

[36] *Dictionary of National Biography, Supplement.*

[37] A. D. Hopkins, "Mike O Callaghan, The Popular Pugilist," in *The First 100 Persons who Shaped Southern Nevada*; Ed Koch, "O Callaghan Engenders Inspiration," *Las Vegas Sun 50th Anniversary Issue*; *International Who's Who*, 38th ed. (London, 1974-75), 1286; *New York Times*, 8 March 2004.

[38] John O Callaghan, *A New Song on the Recapture of Orleans by the French* (Dublin: P. Brereton, 1871); William Barry, "The Current Street Ballads of Ireland," *Macmillan's Magazine* 25 (November 1871-April 1872): 190-199, esp. 198.

When I gaze in gay pleasure upon mountain and dell,
There's a land famed for beauty which none can excel,
The home of my childhood. May I ne'er see the morrow,
If I'd live as an exile from my own Lackendarra.[39]

Other notable figures include: the theologian, Michael C. O Callaghan; Owen O Callaghan, the successful Cork-born property developer; Miriam O Callaghan, presenter of RTE's Prime Time; Donncha O Callaghan, international rugby star; William O Callaghan, the distinguished chef at Longueville House; Daniel Callahan, the ethicist; the historians, Margaret O Callaghan, Jerry A. O Callaghan, Dennis Brynley O Callaghan, and Timothy J. O Callaghan; Mark A. J. O Callaghan, scientist; North Callahan, biographer of Carl Sandburg; the poet Julie O Callaghan; the journalist, Sheila Mary O Callaghan; Fr. Donal O Callaghan, O. Carm., an active supporter of Irish independence; the artists, Clinton Clement O Callaghan and his son Juan; Rosemary O Callaghan-Westropp, the equestrian portrait painter; Lt. General James T. Callaghan of the United States Air Force; Morley Callaghan, the Canadian novelist; the philosopher, John P. O Callaghan of the University of Notre Dame; Harry Callahan, the photographer; Robert Callahan, former Chief Justice of the Connecticut Supreme Court; the Spanish jurist, Xavier O Callaghan; the handball champion Xavier O Callaghan Ferrer; and the storyteller Jay O Callahan, nephew of Fr. Joseph O Callahan already mentioned. Continuing the tradition of the Irish *seanchaidhe* or storyteller, Jay reminds us that "Storytelling is an art that is fun, intimate and simple, yet underneath it's a fiery art of soul and language and human beings." Finally, we must not forget the many women who married into the O Callaghan family and contributed their wisdom and love to the enhancement of the clan. Among them was Anne Drummey O Callaghan, catechist and advocate for the retarded, honored by her family after her death by the creation of The Annual Anne Drummey O Callaghan Lecture on Women in the Church at Fairfield University.

Surely thousands of other O Callaghans, Callaghans, and Callahans have contributed in their own way to the well-being of our society through their work as farmers, teachers, social workers, mechanics, musicians, artists, craftsmen and women businessmen and women, mothers and fathers of children. Would that I could recognize them all!

The Chieftainship in the Twentieth Century

The question of the chieftainship of the O Callaghans, effectively dead since the seventeenth century, came to the fore again, at least in certain quarters. Putting forward his own claim, Colonel George O Callaghan-Westropp (1864-1944), the only son of Colonel John O Callaghan of Maryfort (Lismehane) and Bodyke, in 1937 placed a newspaper advertisement inviting all the O Callaghans to assemble in a Mallow hotel to elect him as chief. A festive crowd gathered and duly acclaimed him as titular head of the family, though few in the room were actually O Callaghans. A captain in the Royal Irish

---

[39] See examples of Teige's poems in Kavanagh, Kilshannig, 94, and Murphy, Mount Hillary, 87, 243-244. I am indebted to Cornelius O Callaghan of Cork City who sent me typescripts of Teige's poems.

Rifles, he served as an aide-de-camp to three kings. In 1919 he was High Sheriff of CountyClare and was a member of the Senate of the Irish Free State in 1921-1922. In accordance with the will of his maternal uncle, Captain Ralph Westropp, he changed his surname to O Callaghan-Westropp in 1885. During the war of independence when nationalists were accused of burning the big houses or mansions that dotted the countryside, Colonel George, believing that landowners had to take firm measures to protect their property wrote "Notes on the defence of Irish country houses." By that time, according to Mark Bence-Jones, Maryfort was in decline; enamel jugs were set to catch drops of water from a leaky roof, as wallpaper peeled off the walls, furniture warped, and carpeting grew threadbare. In 1943 Edward MacLysaght, the Chief Herald in Dublin Castle, acknowledged Colonel O Callaghan-Westropp as The O Callaghan; but his descent from the principal branch of the family could not be established beyond question. Nevertheless, he continued to be recognized as chief of his name until his death on 30 July 1944.

The O Callaghan-Westropp Papers, presented to the Irish Manuscripts Commission, are housed in the National Library of Ireland. Given the expense of maintainng Maryfort, Colonel George's son, Colonel Conor J. O Callaghan-Westropp, the last member of the famiy to reside there, in 1967 demolished the mansion, a final vestige of this era.[40]

The Spanish O Callaghans asserted a claim to the chieftainship that was acknowledged as preferable and more solidly established. In the nineteenth and twentieth century members of this family continued to enjoy distinction in various professions as notaries, advocates, physicians, chemists, friars, Jesuits, nuns, and railway officials.[41]

Seventh in descent from Cahir of Leatherdon, Juan O Callaghan Martínez (1903-1979), the son of a notary, pursued a career as an advocate in Tortosa, and was acknowledged as chief of the name on 23 December 1944. His arms were certified as follows:

> Argent in base a mount vert on the dexter side a grove of trees therefrom
> issuant a wolf passant towards the sinister all proper. For Crest: A dexter
> hand couped at the wrist holding bendwise a sword entwined with a snake
> all proper; and for Mottoes *In virtute vincere* and *Fidus et audax*.[42]

This description tallies exactly with those of the eighteenth century already cited. The motto *In virtute vincere* means "to conquer in virtue." Don Juan's pedigree, now preserved in the Genealogical Office in Dublin Castle, traces his direct descent from

---

[40] Mark Bence-Jones, *Twilight of the Ascendancy* (London: Constable, 1987), 261-262; Burke, *Gentry,* 519-520; *BIFR*, 888, 890; Arthur Charles Fox-Davies, *Armorial Families: A Directory of Gentlemen of Coat Armour*, 2 vols. (Rutland, VT: Tuttle, 1970), 2:1456; Dublin, GO, MS 110, pp.75-76, and MS 153, pp. 503-508; Terence Dooley, *The Decline of the Big House in Ireland: A Study of Irish Landed Families, 1860-1960* (Dublin: Wolfhound Press, 2001), 181-182.

[41] Dublin, GO MS 182, p. 569-570.

[42] Edward MacLysaght, Genealogical Officer and Principal Herald of Ireland, on 16 July 1946, certified and declared that Don Juan was O Callaghan Chief of the Name and that he was entitled to use the O Callaghan arms; Dublin, GO, MS 111G, fol. 33; New York Times 14 April 1945; *BIFR* 888-890.

Donough O Callaghan of Dromaneen. His son Juan O Callaghan Casas (b. 1934), an electrical engineer and Vice-President of the Catalan Electric Power Company, was subsequently acknowledged as Chief of his Name and presided over the O Callaghan Clan reunion in the summer of 1988, attended by about 220 persons from all over the world. Reenacting an ancient custom, Lord Muskerry, representing MacCarthy Mór, who anciently invested the O Callaghan chieftains, presented him with the wand of authority at Longueville House on 30 July. Michael O Callaghan, the proprietor of Longueville House, recounted how he had cut the wand from a hazel bush earlier in the day.

Investiture of Juan O Callaghan as Chief of his Name

Canon Denis O Callaghan of Mallow, the noted moral theologian and author, presided at the liturgy celebrated in the ruins of Ballybeg Abbey, where many O Callaghans are buried. In his homily Canon Denis reminded his hearers that they were standing on holy ground. The concelebrant was Canon Neil O Callaghan of Stockton, England. The chalice given in the seventeenth century by the chieftain Callaghan O Callaghan and his wife Joanna Butler to the priory of Kilmallock was used during the mass. The language of the mass was Irish with music composed by Micheál Ó Ceallacháin. In 1994 Juan O Callaghan attended the annual meeting of the Standing Council of Irish Chiefs and Chieftains at Cashel.

The gathering at Longueville in 1988 not only recalled the triumph and tragedy of the past but also gave renewed emphasis to common familial bonds that remain firm and steadfast despite the scattering of the O Callaghans and Callaghans throughout the world.

CHAPTER 10

EPILOGUE

The O Callaghan family is an ancient one, tracing its descent from the tenth-century king, Cellachán of Cashel, celebrated in the annals and in the mists of legend. From their original homeland around Cashel, the O Callaghans migrated into County Cork where they became, and remain today, one of the largest family groups. A few laconic entries in the annals and long genealogical lists are the principal sources of our knowledge about the family in the Middle Ages. The penchant of the English authorities to determine landholding and other rights presents us with much more detailed information from the sixteenth century onward.

The main branch of the family settled in the barony of Duhallow in North Cork. There they controlled an extensive swath of land known as Pobul Uí Cheallacháin or O Callaghan's Country along both banks of the Blackwater River from Mallow westward to Kanturk. In the twelfth century the O Callaghans of Uí Echach were located in the southernmost part of County Cork and one of their number, Máel Sechnaill Ua Cellacháin, hailed as "king of the south of Ireland," had his name inscribed on the celebrated shrine of St. Lachtín's arm. Still another band descended from Cellachán of Cashel were the MacCallaghans (later O Callaghans) of Muskerry. In time these families tended to become indistinguishable from one another. Indeed those of Duhallow and Muskerry shared the same coat of arms.

The extension of English control throughout the island during the course of the sixteenth century brought significant changes. In 1594 the chieftain, Conor of the Rock, surrendered the clan lands, including the castles of Clonmeen and Dromaneen, to the crown, receiving them in return to be held thereafter under English law as a personal estate for himself and his immediate family. This alteration of the traditional clan system transformed the chieftain into a landlord whose property would be inherited according to the English law of primogeniture. Throughout this period the O Callaghans seem to have followed an ambivalent policy toward church and state. While the chieftain professed his loyalty to the crown and paid lip service to the Established Church, his younger sons and brothers frequently participated in rebellion. Early in the seventeenth century a quarrel between Conor of the Rock of Clonmeen and Cahir Modarta of Dromaneen resulted in the division of O Callaghan's Country. Issues relating to Conor's surrender and regrant were resolved in court in *The Case of Tanistry*, resulting in the condemnation of the ancient custom of tanistry and its attendant rules for succession to power and landholding.

That breach in the family was repaired by the marriage of Donough Mór of Dromaneen and Ellen of Clonmeen, but the old order soon suffered a grievous blow that changed the family's fortunes forever. When the English Civil War spilled over into Ireland Donough and his brother Callaghan played prominent roles in the Confederation of Kilkenny, pursuing a moderate policy of accommodation with the Stuart monarchy in the hope of gaining civil rights for Catholics. For his trouble Donough was dispossessed and transplanted to Clare, while the ancestral lands were transferred to English adventurers. The male line of his descendants in Clare terminated in 1791, but their estates passed to the O Callaghans of Lismehane (Maryfort), who later claimed the headship of the family. Meantime, among the exiles in France seeking to fix the blame for the debacle was Fr. John MacCallaghan of Muskerry.

Following the treaty of Limerick in 1691 many O Callaghan soldiers went abroad to serve in the armies of France, Spain, and Germany and to set down new roots. Among them were Captain Matthew and Colonel Julian, both representatives of the O Callaghans of Muskerry. Chief among the O Callaghans in Spain were the descendants of Donough Mór's second son, Cahir of Leatherdon. Meantime, in Ireland a few, in order to preserve their lands, conformed to the Established Church and intermarried with the planters who had displaced their ancestors. This was true of the O Callaghans of Banteer and Dromskehy in County Cork, Lismehane in County Clare, and Clogheen in County Tipperary. Nevertheless, they displayed traces of the ambivalence of their predecessors in matters of religion. The O Callaghans of Tipperary eventually were raised to noble rank with the titles of baron and then of viscount Lismore; both titles became extinct in 1898.

Members of the family who remained loyal to the Catholic faith suffered under the harshness of the Penal Laws in the eighteenth century and were deprived of essential civil rights. Although the laws were gradually ameliorated and Catholic Emancipation in 1829 gave everyone the right to participate fully in society, the rural population had still more to suffer from repressive landlords. Not only did they demand exorbitant rents, but they also moved quickly to evict whole families if the rent was not paid. This coupled with overpopulation and the subdivision of tenements into tiny plots contributed to the misery of peasant life. The failure of the potato crop and the Great Famine at mid-century decimated the population and stimulated emigration. Colonel John O Callaghan of Bodyke in Clare gained notoriety for hostile relations with his tenants, while the O Callaghans of Dromcummer in Cork exemplified the many who were evicted for failure to meet their rental obligation. Agitation by the Land League, however, eventually led to a series of laws enabling tenants to purchase their farms, thereby putting an end to the troublesome era of landlordism.

As the twentieth century opened the failure to gain Home Rule dealt a severe blow to the parliamentary tradition and prompted the Easter rebellion in 1916. In the struggle for independence Michael O Callaghan, former Lord Mayor of Limerick, assassinated by the Black and Tans, and Donal O Callaghan, Lord Mayor of Cork, represented the family. The treaty of 1921 creating the Irish Free State gave Ireland a measure of autonomy until full independence was gradually achieved during the next twenty-seven years.

Epilogue

Meantime, the great migration of the late nineteenth century to England, America, Canada, Australia, and elsewhere was on. Seeking to escape wretchedness at home and to find better lives for themselves and their children, thousands of O Callaghans (most identified as Callaghans) took part in this diaspora. They or their descendants achieved a measure of prosperity unknown at home and some achieved great distinction as historians, theologians, biblical scholars, mil military heroes, and in nearly every other form of human endeavor. In 1944 Juan O Callaghan of Barcelona was acknowledged as head of the family and in 1988 his son Juan, in the presence of so many exiles and their Irish cousins, presided over the O Callaghan reunion at Longueville House overlooking the Blackwater River.

As the O Callaghan family enters the twenty-first century, it is my fond hope that this book, which seeks to place their history in the context of the wider world, will help to strengthen the bonds of those still settled in Cork and the far greater number dispersed throughout the four continents. May each one of them continue to exemplify the family motto, *Fidus et Audax, Faithful and Courageous*!

APPENDIX I

PARDONS GRANTED TO O CALLAGHANS OF DUHALLOW, 1573-1601

Recorded in the *Calendar of Fiants*, published in the *Reports of the Deputy Keeper of the Public Records and Keeper of the State Papers of Ireland*, vols. 7-22 (Dublin: Public Record Office, 1875-1890); abbreviated *RDK*. See *12 RDK* (Twelfth Report), 92-98, 132, 138, 145, 193, nos. 2243 (5 May 1573), 2248 (6 May), 2251-2252 (6 May), 2257 (6 May), 2264 (8 May), 2464 (30 September 1574), 2515 (17 November 1574), 2576-2577 (3 May 1575), 2928 (16 November 1576); 13 *RDK*, 17, 29, 41, 44, 70, 117, 175, nos. 2941 (21 November 1576), 3031 (20 May 1577), 3083 (6 September 1577), 3095-3096 (7 September 1577), 3257 (24 April 1578), 3553 (6 June 1579), 3974 (24 August 1582); 15 *RDK*, 25, 41, 111, 120, nos. 4318 (27 February 1583/4), 4415 (3 June 1584), 4722 (26 June 1585), 4751 (16 July 1585); 16 *RDK*, 161, no. 5598 (19 June 1591); 17 *RDK*, 75, 83-84, 101-102, 125, 130, 147, 153, 165, 187-190, 245, 264. 269, nos. 6173 (25 November 1597), 6198 (17 February 1597/8), 6302 (24 July 1599), 6407 (15 June 1600), 6431 (11 September 1600), 6465 (27 January 1600/1), 6467 (17 February 1600/1), 6481 (18 March 1600/1), 6499 (25 April 1601), 6539 (29 May 1601), 6555 (22 June 1601), 6558 (5 July 1601).

1. Cahir O Callaghan, alias Cahir Moddir, Dromaneen, gentleman, 6481 (18 March 1600/1); 6499 (25 April 1601)
2. Cahir Óg O Callaghan, Dromaneen, gentleman, 2248 (6 May 1573); Cahir Óg O Callaghan, Banteer, 3095 (7 September 1577).
3. Cahir McCallaghane McDermod, 6499 (25 April 1601)
4. Callaghan O Callaghan, 3096 (7 September 1577)
5. Callaghan McConoghor, Clonmeen, gentleman, 2248 (6 May 1573); Callaghan McConoghor, Dromaneen, gentleman, 3095 (7 September 1577)
6. Callaghan McConoghor I Callaghan, 6407 (15 June 1600)
7. Callaghan McDermod O Callaghan, Leitrim in Condon's Country, 2464 (30 September 1574)
8. Callaghan McDonnell McShane, Ardamadan, 6539 (29 May 1601)
9. Callaghan McOwen of Dromrastill, 2941 (21 November 1576), 3553 (6 June 1579)
10. Callaghan McOwen I Challaghan, Dromdowney, 3974 (24 August 1582)
11. Callaghan McOwen I Callighan, 6407 (15 June 1600)
12. Callaghan McTeige O Kallaghan, Pallas, gentleman, 2252 (6 May 1573)
13. Conoghor O Callaghan alias O Kallaghan, Dromaneen, 4751 (16 July 1585); Conoghor O Callaghan alias O Calghan, Clonmeen, 6407 (15 June 1600)
14. Conoghor McDonnell I Kellichan, 6555 (22 June 1601)
15. Conoghor Gancagh McKroeghane O Callegan, 6499 (25 April 1601)
16. Conoghor Roe McMorierto I Callaghan, Killcalley, 6539 (29 May 1601)
17. Conoghor McHowny I Callaghan, 4751 (16 July 1585)
18. Conoghor McOwnie O Kallahan, 6465 (27 January 1600/1); 6499 (25 April 1601)
19. Conoghor McShane McDonogh I Callaghan, 4751 (16 July 1585)
20. Conoghor McShane McTeige, Kanturk, 2248 (6 May 1573)
21. Conoghor McTeige O Callaghan, Dromore, 2251 (6 May 1573)

22. Conoghor McTeige Ehowllaghan, 6198 (17 February 1597)
23. Conoghor McTeige McDonogh, Pallas, yeoman, 2948 (21 November 1575)
24. Conoghor McTeige McOwen, Gortmore, 6558 (5 July 1601)
25. Connor Garraf alias McDonogh O Callaghan, yeoman, 2251 (6 May 1573)
26. Cornelius O Callaghan, Dromore, gentleman, 2252 (6 May 1573)
27. Cornelius McOwen McThomas, Kilcranathan, yeoman, 2257 (6 May 1573)
28. Daniel McTeige, 6302 (24 July 1599)
29. Dermot O Callaghan, Kenalbeick [Kinalmeaky], 4415 (3 June 1584)
30. Dermot O Kallaghan, Ballymckowe, 6465 (27 January 1600/1)
31. Dermot O Kallaghan, 6465 (27 January 1600/1)
32. Dermot Óg O Callaghane, 6302 (24 July 1599)
33. Dermot O Callaghan, Annagh, 6539 (29 May 1601)
34. Dermot O Callaghane alias Squincy, 6407 (15 June 1600)
35. Dermot McConoghor, Kilcaskan, brother of Donogh ny Tully McConoghor, 4751 (16 July 1585)
36. Dermot McConoghorMcThomas O Callaghan, 6499 (25 April 1601)
37. Dermot McDonel, son of Donell McThomas McTeige, Kilcranathan, yeoman, 2257 (6 May 1573)
38. Dermot McDonogh O Calloughan, 6198 (17 February 1597)
39. Dermot McIrelagh O Kealeghane, 6499 (25 April 1601)
40. Dermot McMorrice McDonnell, 6555 (22 June 1601)
41. Dermot Boy McOwen, Dromaneen, 2928 (16 November 1575)
42. Dermot McOwen O Callaghan, alias baron of Dromore, 2251 (6 May 1573)
43. Dermot McOwen I Challaghan, Dromdowney, 3974 (24 August 1582)
44. Dermot Ygearhie McOwen Y Kallaghan, 3553 (6 June 1579)
45. Dermot McShane McDonogh Y Kallaghain, 3995 (16 July 1585)
46. Dermot McShane McTeige O Callaghan, 6499 (25 April 1601)
47. Dermot McTeige O Callaghan, Garrymcowny, yeoman, 2251 (6 May 1573); Dermot McTeige O Callaghan, Gortnagross, 2928 (16 November 1575); Dermot McTeige O Callaghan, 3095 (7 September 1577); Dermot McTeige I Callahane, 6302 (24 July 1599)
48. Dermot O Callaghan McTeige, Cloghroe, 6539 (29 May 1601)
49. Dermot Leigh McTeige, Clonmeen, 6558 (5 July 1601)
50. Dermot McTeige McCahir O Callaghan, 6499 (25 April 1601)
51. Dermot McTeige McDermot O Callaghan, the Creg, 2243 (5 May 1573); Dermot McTeige McDermod O Callaghan, the Kreg, a kern, 2577 (3 May 1575)
52. Dermot McTeige McDermod O Kealeghan, 6499 (25 April 1601)
53. Dermot McThomas, Roskeen, yeoman, 2928 (16 November 1575)
54. Donald McDermod, Clontyne [Cloonteen], 2928 (16 November 1575)
55. Donell O Callaghan, 6467 (17 February 1600/1)
56. Donnell McDermond McShane I Callaghan, Gortincarrall, 5598 (19 June 1591)
57. Donnell McDonell Roe I Callaghan, Blarney, 6539 (29 May 1601)
58. Donell McMorrice I Kelichan, 6555 (22 June 1601)
59. Donell McSakeruan, Clonmeen, 6558 (5 July 1601)
60. Donell McTeige McDonogh O Callaghan, Pallas, yeoman, 2248 (6 May 1573); Donald McTeige McDonogh, Pallas, 2941 (16 November 1575); Donnell

McTeige McDonogh, Clonmeen, 4751 (16 July 1585)

61. Donel McTeige McOwen, Gortmore, 6558 (5 July 1601)
62. Donald McThomas Riogh, Roskeen, 2251 (6 May 1573); Donald McThomas, Roskeen, 2928 (16 November 1575), 3257 (24 April 1578)
63. Donell McThomas McTeige, Kilcranathan, yeoman, 2257 (6 May 1573)
64. Donogh McCahir O Callaghan, Dromaneen, gentleman, 2248 (6 May 1573)
65. Donogh ny Tully McConoghor, Kilcaskan, 4751 (16 July 1585)
66. Donogh McDermod, Clontyne [Cloonteen], 2928 (16 November 1575)
67. Donogh McDermot, Dromaneen, 6173 (25 November 1597)
68. Donogh McDermod I Callahane, 6302 (24 July 1599)
69. Donogh McDermot McTeige O Callaghane, 6499 (25 April 1601)
70. Donogh McDermot O Callaghan, alias Donogh Oleighie (O Leahy), Killianiskie, 6539 (29 May 1601)
71. Donogh McDonell McTeige O Callaghan, Clonmeen, 6539 (29 May 1601)
72. Donogh Óg McDonogh McMahowne, Bellaballagh, yeoman, 2251 (6 May 1573)
73. Donogh Óg McDonogh McShane I Callaghan, Ardamadan, 6539 (29 May 1601)
74. Donogh McShane McTeige, Kanturk, 2248 (6 May 1573)
75. Donogh McTeige I Callaghane, 6302 (24 July 1599)
76. Donogh McTeige McDonogh, Gortroe, 2928 (16 November 1575)
77. Donogh McTeige McDonogh O Callaghan, Pallas, yeoman, 2248 (6 May 1573); Donogh McTeige McDonogh, Pallas, 3095 (7 September 1577)
78. Donogh McThomas McOwen, Ballymacmurragh, 4751 (16 July 1585)
79. Ellen ny Tirrelagh, wife of Callaghan McOwen I Callighan, 6407 (15 June 1600)
80. Elinor Kallaghan, wife of Edmond FitzRichard Stackbolde, 6465 (27 January 1600/1)
81. Eliza ny Callaghan, wife of James Barrett FitzWilliam, Lackenteonyne, 6431 (11 September 1600)
82. Irrelagh O Callaghan, Leitrim in Condon's Country, 2464 (30 September 1574); Irrelagh O Callaghan, Dromore, gentleman, 3096 (7 September 1577); Erilagh O Callaghan, 4722 (26 June 1585)
83. Irielagh O Calleghane, 6499 (25 April 1601)
84. Johanna ny Tirrelagh, wife of Conoghor O Callaghan of Clonmeen, CPRC, 2:563-4, no. 51 (15 June 1600)
85. John McDonell, Kilcranathan, yeoman, 2257 (6 May 1573)
86. John McDonogh McOwen O Kallaghan, 6465 (27 January 1600/1)
87. John McDonogh O Callaghan, 6499 (25 April 1601)
88. John Óg McShane I Callaghane, Loughnane, 6539 (29 May 1601)
89. Kennedy O Callaghan, Dromaneen, 6173 (25 November 1597)
90. Kennedy Óg McKennedy O Callaghan, 2515 (17 November 1575)
91. Kennedy Óg O Callaghan, Clonmeen, 6558 (5 July 1601)
92. Mahown McSheane, Clonmeen, 6558 (5 July 1601)
93. Owen McConoghor, Rath, yeoman, 3095 (7 September 1577)
94. Owen Ballagh McEgan, Kildorrery, 3095 (7 September 1577)
95. Owen McDonell, Kilcranathan, yeoman, 2257 (6 May 1573)
96. Owen McDonell McTeige, 4751 (16 July 1585)
97. Owen McDonnell McTeige O Callaghan, Clonmeen, 6539 (29 May 1601)
98. Owen McDonogh McOwen O Kallaghan, 6465 (27 January 1600/1)

99. Owen McDonogh McOwen O Callaghan, 6499 (25 April 1601)
100. Owen McThomas, Ballymacmurragh, 2248 (6 May 1573)
101. Owen McTeige McDonogh, Pallas, yeoman, 2941 (21 November 1575)
102. Owen McTeige O Callaghan, 6198 (17 February 1597); 6302 (24 July 1599)
103. Ownhy McDonogh McCahir, 6499 (25 April 1601)
104. Owny McDonogh McTeige O Callaghan, Gortmore, yeoman, 2264 (8 May 1573)
105. Shane McTeige McBrian O Callaghan, 6499 (25 April 1601)
106. Teige O Callaghan, 6467 (17 February 1600/1)
107. Teige Óg O Challaghan, 6302 (24 July 1599)
108. Teige McCahir O Callaghan, Kilpadder, horseman with Lord Muskerry, 2576 (3
     May 1575); Teige McCahir O Callaghan, Gortmolire, 3257 (24 April 1578);
     Teige McCahir Y Kellighane, Gortmolire, 4751 (16 July 1585)
109. Teige Gankagh McConor O'Callaghan, Dromore, yeoman, 2257 (6 May 1573)
110. Teige McDermod of Gortmore (later tanist to Conor of the Rock), 3095 (7
     September 1577)
111. Teige McOwnhy O Calleghane, 6499 (25 April 1601)
112. Teige McShane McTeige O Callaghan, 6499 (25 April 1601)
113. Thady Roe McCroghe, Roskeen, yeoman, 2928 (16 November 1576)
114. Thady McOwen McDonogh, Gortmore, yeoman, 2928 (16 November 1576)
115. Thady McTeige O Callaghan, Gortnagross, 2928 (16 November 1576)
116. Thomas Riogh O Callaghan, Roskeen, yeoman, 2251 (6 May 1573)
117. Thomas McConoghor McThomas O Callaghan, 6499 (25 April 1601)
118. Thomas McDonnell O Callaghan, 6465 (27 January 1600/1)
119. Thomas McDonell McTeige O Callaghan, Clonmeen, 6539 (29 May 1601)
120. Thomas McOwen McMorrogho, Ballymacmurragh, 2248 (6 May 1573)
121. Thomas McTeige McDermod, Gortnagross, yeoman, 2928 (16 November 1576)

APPENDIX II

PARDONS GRANTED TO O CALLAGHANS AND MACCALLAGHANS OF MUSKERRY, 1573-1601

1. Callaghan McDonogh McCallaghan, Carrigadrohid, yeoman, (2941 (21 November 1576)

2. Callaghan McOwny O Callaghan, Carrigadrohid, yeoman, 2264 (8 May 1573); Callaghan McOwney O Callaghan, Carrigadrohid, 2941 (21 November 1575); Callaghan McOwny, Carrigadrohid, yeoman, 3083 (6 September 1577)

3. Dermot Roe McCallaghan, 6198 (17 February 1597)

4. Dermot McConoghor McCallaghane, Killysall, 5598 (19 June 1591)

5. Dermot McDonogh McCallaghan, Carrignamuck, yeoman 3031 (20 May 1577)

6. Dermot Roe McDonogh McCallaghan, Donaghmore, 6539 (29 May 1601)

7. Donald McShane McMelaghlin O Callaghan, Blarney, 2264 (8 May 1573); Donald McShane O Callaghan, Blarney, 3083 (6 September 1577)

8. Donogh McShane O Callaghan, Great Castle, Co. Cork, husbandman, 3083 (6 September 1577)

9. Fineen McOwen O Callaghan, Carrigadrohid, clerk, 3083 (6 September 1577)

10. Molronie McShane I Callaghane, Loughnane, 6539 (29 May 1601)

11. Owen McMoriertagh O Callaghan, Castleinch, yeoman, 2264 (8 May 1573)

12. Shane McDermod O Callaghan alias Mcny Flahy, Blarney, 2264 (8 May 1573)

13. Teige McOwen Brycke O Callaghan, Gorte Donoghy moyr [Donoughmore], yeoman, 2941 (21 November 1576)

14. Teige McShane I Callaghane, Loughnane, 6539 (29 May 1601)

Genealogical Tables

1. The Descendants of Cellachán of Cashel to about 1500

2. The Chieftains of the 16th Century

3. The Chieftains of the 17th Century

4. The O Callaghans of Rathmore

5. The O Callaghans of Dromore, Gortmore, and Ballymacmurragh

6. The O Callaghans of Kilpadder and Kilcranathan

7. The O Callaghans of Clare to 1791

8. The O Callaghans of Spain

9. The O Callaghans of Banteer

10. The O Callaghans of Tipperary

11. The O Callaghans of Glynn, Dromskehy, Cahirduggan, and Killeenleigh

12. The O Callaghans of Lismehane, County Clare

13. The MacCallaghans of Muskerry

14. The O Callaghans of Carrigadrohid in Spain

15. The O Callaghans of Carrignavar in Spain

16a. The O Callaghans of Dromcummer and Philadelphia

16b. The O Callaghans of Dromcummer and Philadelphia

1. THE DESCENDANTS OF CELLACHÁN OF CASHEL TO ABOUT 1500

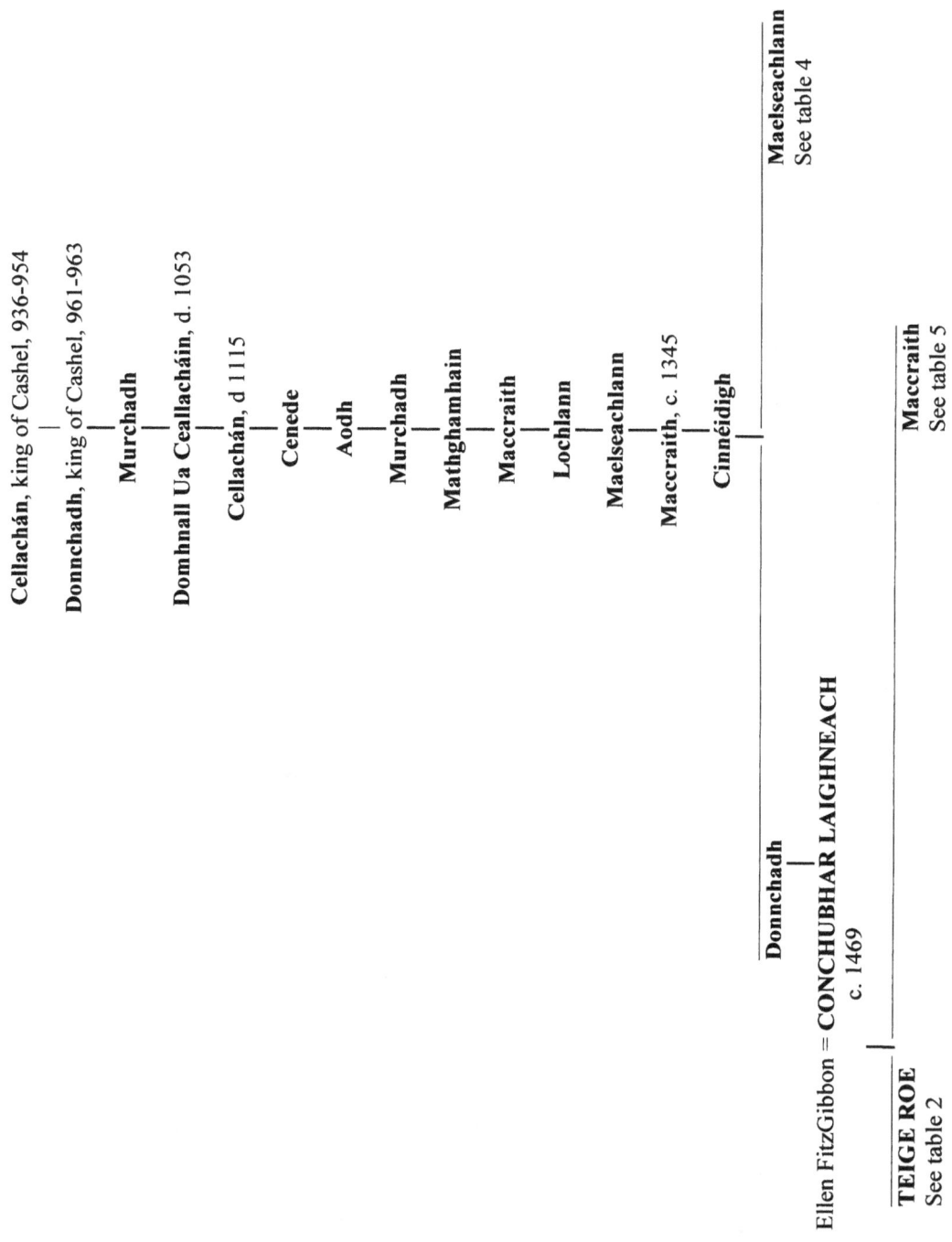

Cellachán, king of Cashel, 936-954

Donnchadh, king of Cashel, 961-963

Murchadh

Domhnall Ua Ceallacháin, d. 1053

Cellachán, d 1115

Cenede

Aodh

Murchadh

Mathghamhain

Maccraith

Lochlann

Maelseachlann

Maccraith, c. 1345

Cinnéidigh

Maelseachlann
See table 4

Maccraith
See table 5

Donnchadh

Ellen FitzGibbon = **CONCHUBHAR LAIGHNEACH**
c. 1469

TEIGE ROE
See table 2

231

2. THE CHIEFTAINS OF THE 16TH CENTURY

TEIGE ROE = Ellen d. of Donough Óg MacCarthy of Duhallow
d. 1537
See table 1

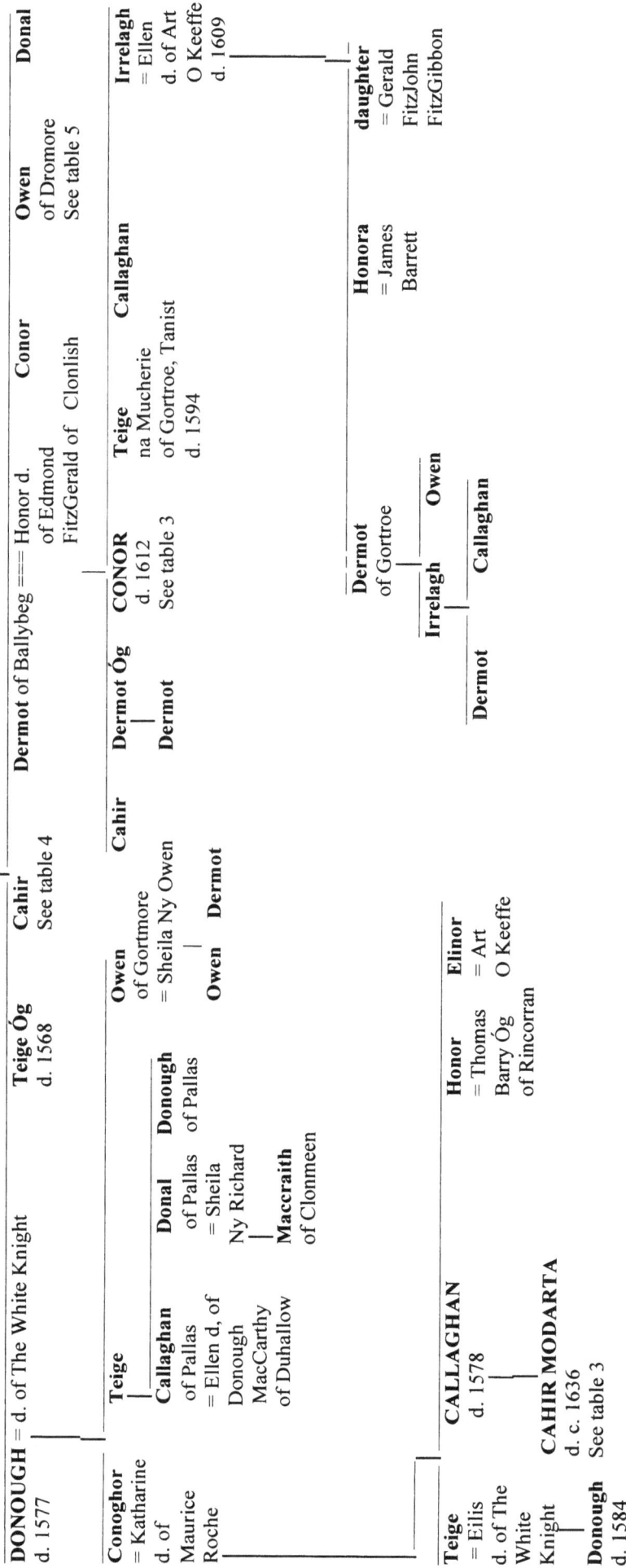

DONOUGH = d. of The White Knight
d. 1577

Teige Óg
d. 1568

Cahir
See table 4

Dermot of Ballybeg === Honor d.
of Edmond
FitzGerald of Clonlish

Conor

Owen
of Dromore
See table 5

Donal

Conoghor
= Katharine
d. of
Maurice
Roche

Teige

Callaghan
of Pallas
= Ellen d, of
Donough
MacCarthy
of Duhallow

Donal
of Pallas
= Sheila
Ny Richard

Donough
of Pallas

Maccraith
of Clonmeen

Owen
of Gortmore
= Sheila Ny Owen

Owen   Dermot

Cahir

Dermot Óg

Dermot

CONOR
d. 1612
See table 3

Teige
na Mucherie
of Gortroe, Tanist
d. 1594

Callaghan

Honora
= James
Barrett

daughter
= Gerald
FitzJohn
FitzGibbon

Dermot
of Gortroe

Owen

Irrelagh   **Callaghan**

Dermot

Irrelagh
= Ellen
d. of Art
O Keeffe
d. 1609

Honor
= Thomas
Barry Óg
of Rincorran

Elinor
= Art
O Keeffe

CALLAGHAN
d. 1578

CAHIR MODARTA
d. c. 1636
See table 3

Teige
= Eilis
d. of The
White
Knight

Donough
d. 1584

232

3. THE CHIEFTAINS OF THE 17TH CENTURY

TEIGE ROE
d. 1537
See table 2

Dermot of Ballybeg

CONOR OF THE ROCK ===== Joan d. of Turlough MacSweeney
d. 1612

Teige
= Mary d. of
Brian Mac Owen
MacSweeney
of Mashanaglass

CALLAGHAN
d. 1631
= Joan d. of
James Butler
Lord Dunboyne

Conor
of Abbeydorney
d. 1638

Teige   Elinor

Cahir   **Donough**   **Calvagh**   **Kedach**   **Morgan**

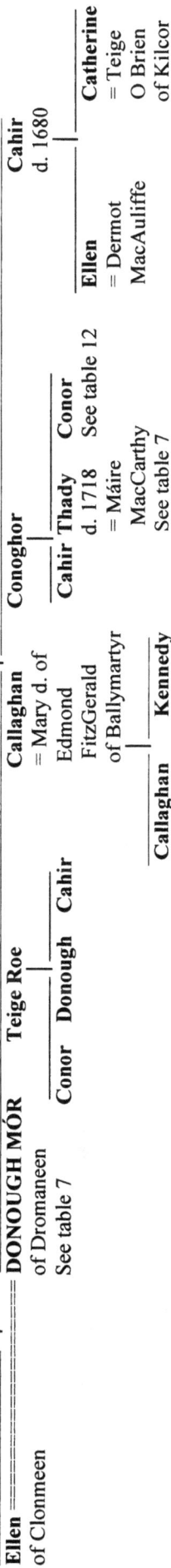

CAHIR MODARTA = Ellen, d. of Callaghan MacCarthy
d.c. 1636   of Carrignamuck
See table 2

Conoghor

Callaghan
= Mary d. of
Edmond
FitzGerald
of Ballymartyr

Callaghan   Kennedy

Cahir
d. 1680

Ellen
= Dermot
MacAuliffe

Catherine
= Teige
O Brien
of Kilcor

Cahir   **Thady**   **Conor**   See table 12
         d. 1718
         = Máire
         MacCarthy
         See table 7

Ellen ===== **DONOUGH MÓR**   **Teige Roe**
of Clonmeen   of Dromaneen
                 See table 7

Conor   Donough   Cahir

233

4. THE O CALLAGHANS OF RATHMORE

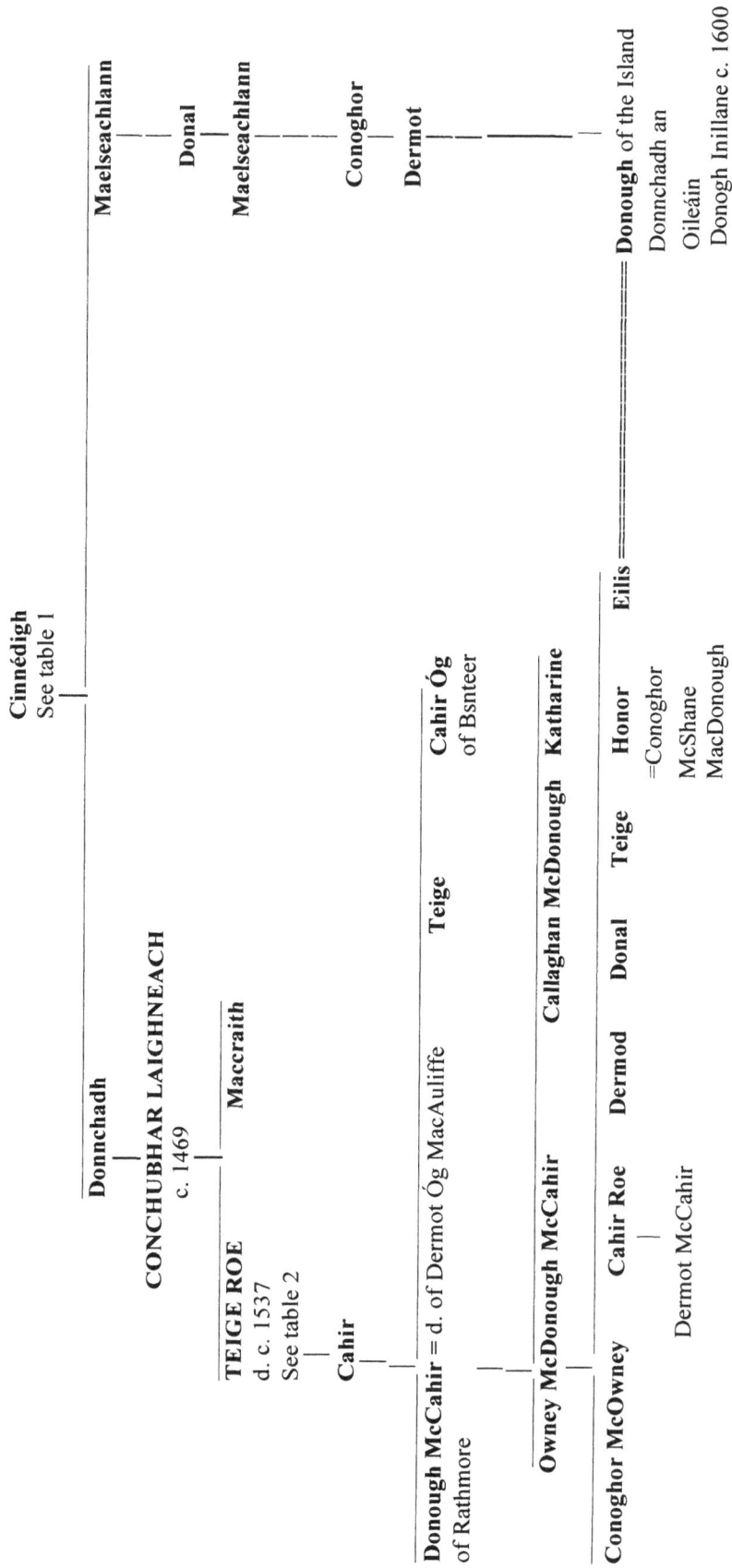

Cinnédigh
See table 1

Donnchadh

CONCHUBHAR LAIGHNEACH
c. 1469

Maccraith

Maelseachlann

Donal

Maelseachlann

TEIGE ROE
d. c. 1537
See table 2

Cahir

Donough McCahir = d. of Dermot Óg MacAuliffe
of Rathmore

Cahir Óg
of Bsnteer

Teige

Conoghor

Dermot

Owney McDonough McCahir

Callaghan McDonough

Katharine

Conoghor McOwney

Cahir Roe

Dermot McCahir

Dermod

Donal

Teige

Honor
=Conoghor
McShane
MacDonough

Eilis ========= **Donough** of the Island
Donnchadh an
Oileáin
Donogh Inillane c. 1600

5. THE O CALLAGHANS OF DROMORE, GORTMORE AND BALLYMACMURRAGH

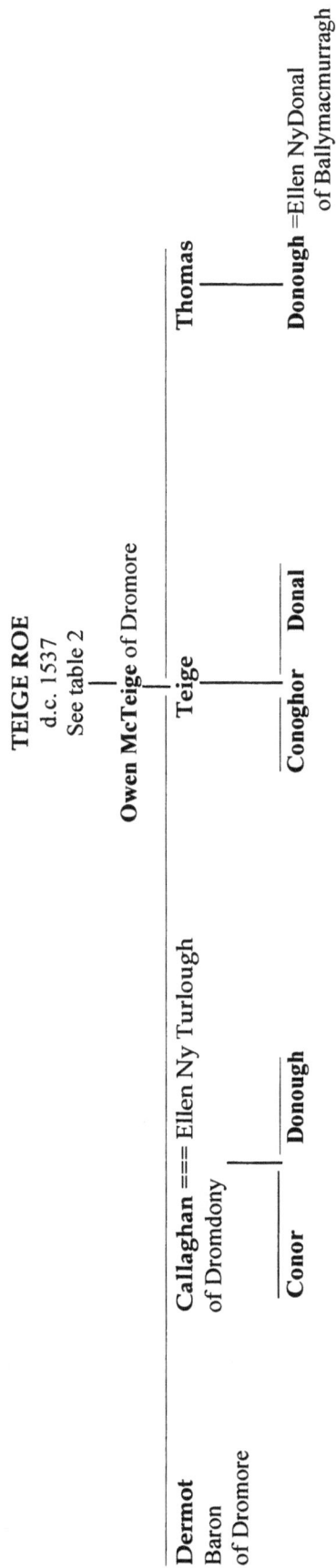

TEIGE ROE
d.c. 1537
See table 2

Owen McTeige of Dromore

Dermot
Baron
of Dromore

Callaghan === Ellen Ny Turlough
of Dromdony

Conor　　**Donough**

Teige

Conoghor　**Donal**

Thomas

Donough =Ellen NyDonal
of Ballymacmurragh

235

6. THE O CALLAGHANS OF KILPADDER AND KILCRANATHAN

CONCHUBHAR LAIGHNEACH
See table 1

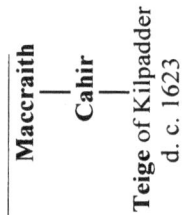

TEIGE ROE
d. c. 1537
See table 2

Maccraith

Cahir

Teige of Kilpadder
d. c. 1623

Murrogh McTeige

Dermot Roe McTeige = Sarah d. of Fineen O Mahony of Kinalmeaky
d. 1636

Teige = Ellen d. of Teige MacCarthy
d. ante 1679   of Kilballyvorrihy

Callaghan
priest
"beyond seas"

Conor = Eilis d. of John Daly
of Clonmeen

Donough = Mary d. of Paul Melleric
of Kilcranathan   of Castlemore

Ellen   Joan
= Dermot
MacCarthy
of Dooneen

Cahir
of Kilpadder
and Curragh
d. 1679
= 1. Ellen, d. of John Power
of Carrickphilip, Waterford
2. Joan, d. of Teige MacCarthy

Dermot of Glenkelleney

Teige

Dermot   Donough   Callaghan

7. THE O CALLAGHANS OF CLARE TO 1791

Ellen ════════════ **DONOUGH MÓR**
of Clonmeen   of Dromaneen
               d. ante 1683
               See table 3

Teige   **DONOUGH ÓG** == Máire   **Cahir** of Leatherdon   **Callaghan**   **Morrogh**   **Patrick**   **Joan**
       of Mountallon   d. of Cormac   See table 8
       d. c. 1698   MacCarthy
                 See table 3

Callaghan   **Charles**   **Donough**   **Michael**   **DANIEL** ══════ Catherine, d. of Nicholas Purcell   **Teige**   **Connor**
d. 1708   d. 1708   of Mountallon   d. 1724   Baron of Loughmoe

1. Hannah d. of Christopher O Brien ══ **DONOUGH** of Kilgorey ══════ 2. Marcella d. of Richard Burke   **Eilis**   **Jane**
                           d. 1779

Mary   **Hannah**   **Daniel**   **EDMOND** = Ellen d. of Denis O Brien   **Marcella**   **Mary**   **Catherine**   **Helen**
                      d. 1772   d. 1791

Bridget = Thomas O Reilly   **Catherine** = Thomas Brown, earl of Kenmare   **Ellen** = James Bagot   **Elizabeth** = Gerald Dease   **Marcella**

Edmond O Reilly, S. J.

8. THE O CALLAGHANS OF SPAIN

DONOUGH MÓR
d. ante 1683
See table 7

Cahir of Leatherdon = Ellen, d. of Maurice FitzGerald of Inchiracrannagh

Cornelius = Paula de Dameto of Spain
1693-1741

John
d. 1712

James Louis
of Baden-Baden

Louis Denis
of Baden-Baden

Maria Louisa
= von Weistersheim

Mariana Mauricio = Carlos
1730-74

Dionisio
1732

Francisca

Elena = John Nixon
1738-75

Maria Anna
= von Hornstein

RAMÓN = Rosa Alguero
1798-1844

RAMÓN = Francisca Antonia Tarragó
1765-1833

Maria Ana = Francisco Pamies
1766-1830

Carlos
1791-94

Ramón
1796

Salvador
1801-44

Pedro
1803-69

José ==== Mla Forcadell
1806-81

Carlos
1812-36

Raimunda
1793

Maria Teresa
1794-1864

Maria Ana
1810-12

Francisca Antonia   Rosa

Ramón
1834-1911

JUAN
1836-1921
= Rosa
Vizcaino

José
1839-1911

Tomás
1841-57

Manuel
1845-1923
= E. Martí

1. L. Vives = Carlos ===2. Joaquin
1847-99

Agustín = J. Vilanova

Gl. Rodríguez = Carlos
d. 1921

Ramón
d. 1921

José

JUAN
1868-1940
= Gabriela
Martínez

Amado
1870-73

Justo
1872-1903

Dolores
1869

José
1887-1936

Carlos
1890-91

Juana
1883-1936

Francisca
1885-1932

Dolores
1885-88

Manuela
1893-95

Ramón
1886-
=1. María Pons = 2. María Muñoz

Tomás
1889-90

Pilar
1882

Josefa
1891

JUAN = E. Casas
1903-79

Pedro = M.L. Mestre
1904-

J. Ramón
1879

Joaquin
1880

Justo
1907-09

Ramon
1919-

José
1922-2002

Rosa
1910-5

Antonia
1912-

Concepción
1914-

Dolores
1924-

Luis
1920-

Ángel
1925-

Gabriel
1926-

Ramón
1929-

JUAN
1934-

Esteban
1936-

Salvador
1937-

Concepción
1940-

Carlos
1942-

Mercedes
1941-

Pedro
1942-

238

9. THE O CALLAGHANS OF BANTEER

CONOR OF THE ROCK
d. 1612
See table 2

Teige McConoghor
d. 1624

Conoghor McTeige
d. c. 1638

Donal Mór of the Pálach

Sheila? ===== **Owen** of Kilcranathan

Joan d. of Robert Williams = **Conor or Cornelius Sr.**
d. 1739

Teige?

Teige of Coolroe
See table 9

Mary = Francis Power of Roskeen

Margaret = Nicholas Chinnery

Eleanor = Robert Holmes

Richard   Elizabeth   David   Cornelius   Pierce

Timothy = Mary Gould of Bregoge
d. 1759

Mary Towgood === **Robert**
d. 1727

Cornelius Jr.
d. c. 1737

Cornelius III
d. 1772

Mary

1. Henry Daunt = **Mary** = 2. Denis O Callaghan of Glynn
See table 11

Joan = Thomas Knolles of Killeighy

Robert = Ann Brady
d. 1778   d. 1780

Meliah = Thomas Morgell

Margaret = John Craggs

Margaret = Thomas Morgell

Crosbie

Mary

Cornelius
d. 1731

10. THE O CALLAGHANS OF TIPPERARY

Timothy of Banteer (Teige of Coolroe)
See table 9

Cornelius of Shanbally = Maria d. of Robert Jolley

Cornelius
d. 1782

Robert = Alicia Worth   1. Sarah d. of John Davis = Thomas of Shanbally = 2. Hannah d. John Rogerson
d. 1761

Frances d. of John Ponsonby = Cornelius
Baron Lismore
1740/1-1797

Elizabeth = Robert Longfield

Elizabeth = John Hyde   Mary = Thomas Scott
d.1824

Eleanor d. of John Butler === Cornelius
Duke of Ormonde   1st Viscount Lismore
                               1775-1857

Robert William   1777-1849

George
1787-1856

Louisa = William Cavendish   d. 1863

William Frederick
d. 1836

George ============ Mary d. of George Norbury
2d Viscount Lismore
1815-98

Cornelius
1809-49

Rosina d. of W.H. Williams = George
                             1846-85

William
1852-77

11. THE O CALLAGHANS OF GLYNN, DROMSKEHY, CAHIRDUGGAN AND KILLEENLEIGH

Denis of Glynn

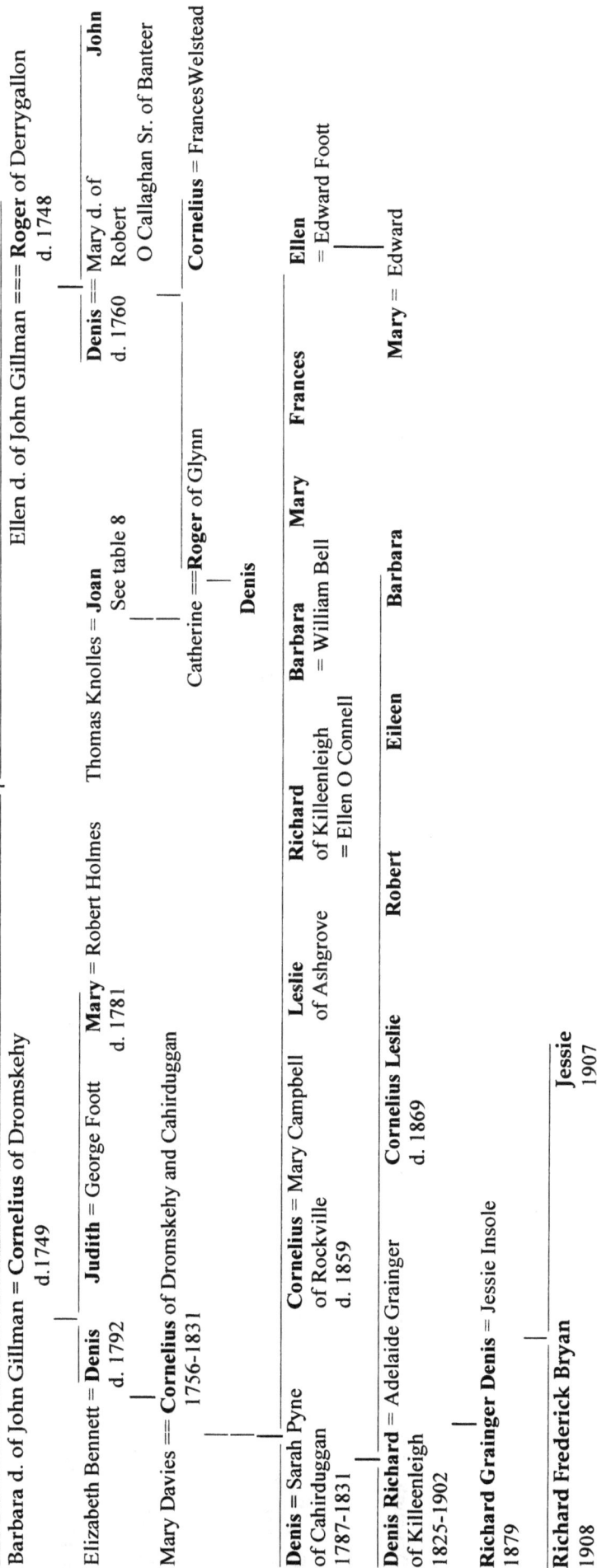

Barbara d. of John Gillman = **Cornelius** of Dromskehy d.1749   Ellen d. of John Gillman === **Roger** of Derrygallon d. 1748

Elizabeth Bennett = **Denis** d. 1792   **Judith** = George Foott   **Mary** = Robert Holmes d. 1781   Thomas Knolles = **Joan** (See table 8)   **Denis** == Mary d. of Robert O Callaghan Sr. of Banteer, d. 1760   **John**

Mary Davies == **Cornelius** of Dromskehy and Cahirduggan 1756-1831   Catherine == **Roger** of Glynn   **Cornelius** = Frances Welstead

Denis

Denis = Sarah Pyne of Cahirduggan 1787-1831   **Cornelius** = Mary Campbell of Rockville d. 1859   **Leslie** of Ashgrove   **Barbara** = William Bell   **Mary**   **Frances**   **Ellen** = Edward Foott

Denis Richard = Adelaide Grainger of Killeenleigh 1825-1902   **Cornelius Leslie** d. 1869   **Richard** of Killeenleigh = Ellen O Connell   **Robert**   **Eileen**   **Barbara**   **Mary** = Edward

Richard Grainger Denis = Jessie Insole 1879

Richard Frederick Bryan 1908   **Jessie** 1907

12. THE O CALLAGHANS OF LISMEHANE, COUNTY CLARE

CAHIR MODARTA
See table 3

Conoghor

Conor?
See table 3

Denis of Liscullane = Helen ?

Cornelius of Coolready and Liscullane = Olivia d. of Henry Brady of Kilconry
d. 1793

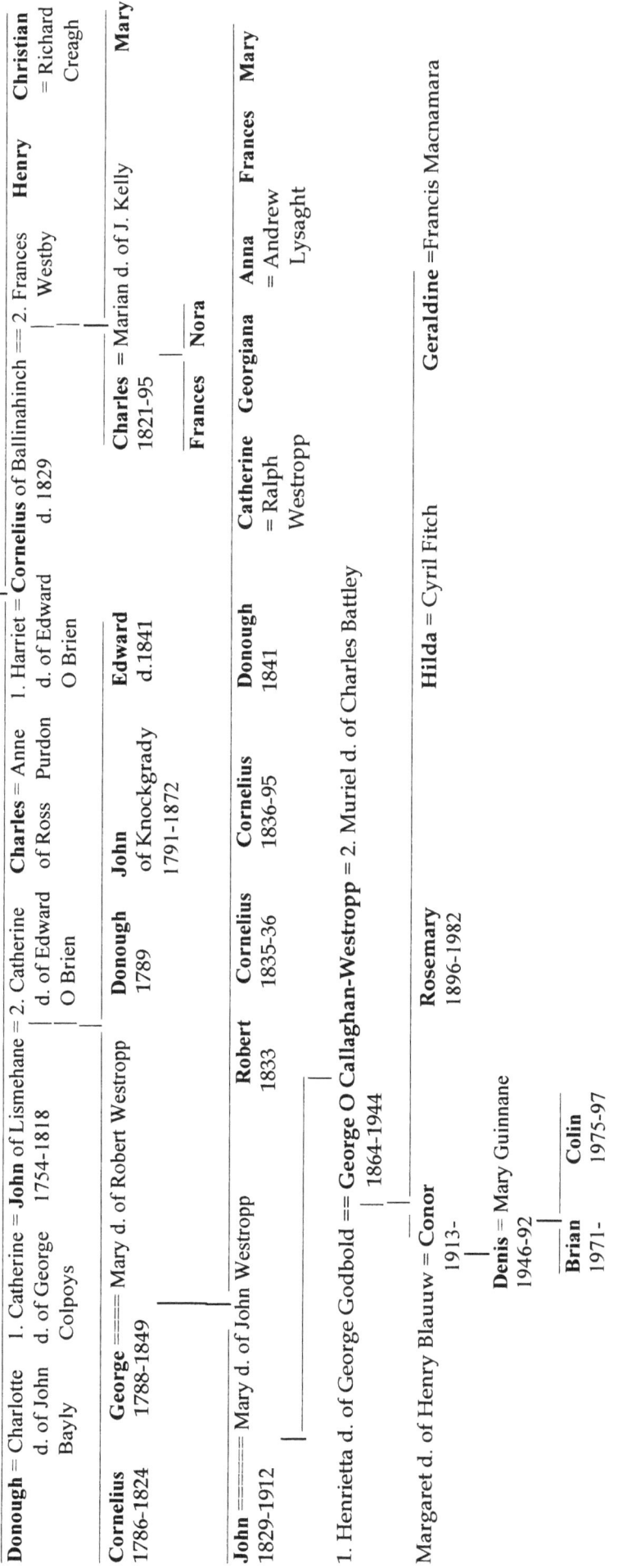

Donough = Charlotte   1. Catherine = **John** of Lismehane = 2. Catherine   **Charles** = Anne   1. Harriet = **Cornelius** of Ballinahinch == 2. Frances   **Henry**   **Christian**
d. of John   d. of George   1754-1818   d. of Edward   of Ross   Purdon   d. of Edward   d. 1829   Westby   = Richard
Bayly   Colpoys   O Brien   O Brien   Creagh

Cornelius   **George** ==== Mary d. of Robert Westropp   **Donough**   **John**   **Edward**   **Charles** = Marian d. of J. Kelly   **Mary**
1786-1824   1788-1849   1789   of Knockgrady   d.1841   1821-95
   1791-1872

Frances   **Nora**

John ======= Mary d. of John Westropp   **Robert**   **Cornelius**   **Cornelius**   **Donough**   **Catherine**   **Georgiana**   **Anna**   **Frances**   **Mary**
1829-1912   1833   1835-36   1836-95   1841   = Ralph   = Andrew
   Westropp   Lysaght

1. Henrietta d. of George Godbold == **George O Callaghan-Westropp** = 2. Muriel d. of Charles Battley
   1864-1944

Margaret d. of Henry Blauuw = **Conor**   **Rosemary**   **Hilda** = Cyril Fitch   **Geraldine** =Francis Macnamara
   1913-   1896-1982

Denis = Mary Guinnane
1946-92

Brian   **Colin**
1971-   1975-97

13. THE MACCALLAGHANS OF MUSKERRY

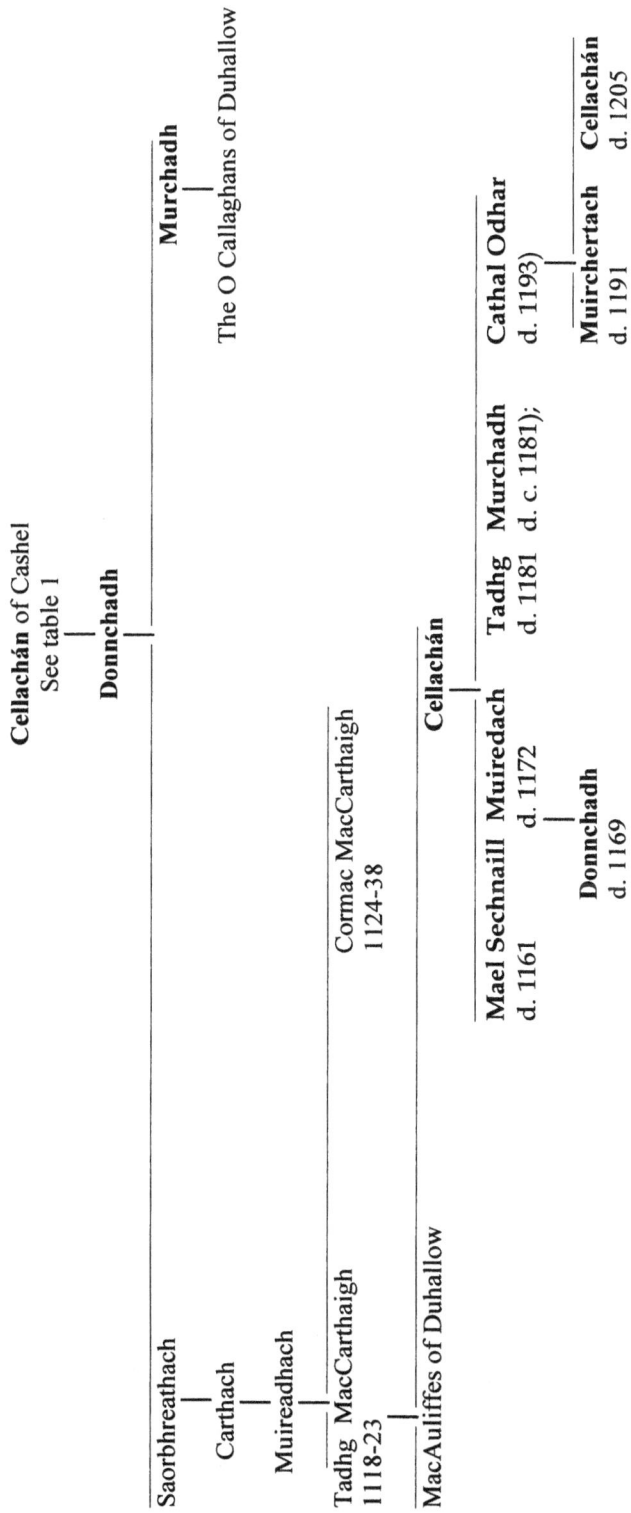

Cellachán of Cashel
See table 1

Donnchadh

Murchadh

The O Callaghans of Duhallow

Saorbhreathach

Carthach

Muireadhach

Tadhg MacCarthaigh
1118-23

Cormac MacCarthaigh
1124-38

MacAuliffes of Duhallow

Cellachán

Mael Sechnaill
d. 1161

Muiredach
d. 1172

Donnchadh
d. 1169

Tadhg
d. 1181

Murchadh
d. c. 1181);

Cathal Odhar
d. 1193

Muirchertach
d. 1191

Cellachán
d. 1205

14. THE O CALLAGHANS OF CARRIGADROHID IN SPAIN

Cornelius of Carrigadrohid === Ellen MacCarthy of Macroom

David Power of Torbeagh === Joanna Condon of Torbeagh

Eugene ===Catherine

Mathew b. 1666

15. THE O CALLAGHANS OF CARRIGNAVAR IN SPAIN

Teige of Castleinch and Carrignavar b.c. 1619 "*conde de Clanscarti*" === Margaret MacCarthy of Carrignavar

Patrick MacCarthy of Muskerry = Winifred White of Cork

Denis of Castleinch and Carrignavar b.c. 1652 === Mary

IgnatiusWhite marquess of Albeville count of Albi === Maria Heron

Julian of Carrignavar b. c. 1685 - 1727

Anna Christina d. 1732

Dionisio b. 1718

16a. THE O CALLAGHANS OF DROMCUMMER AND PHILADELPHIA

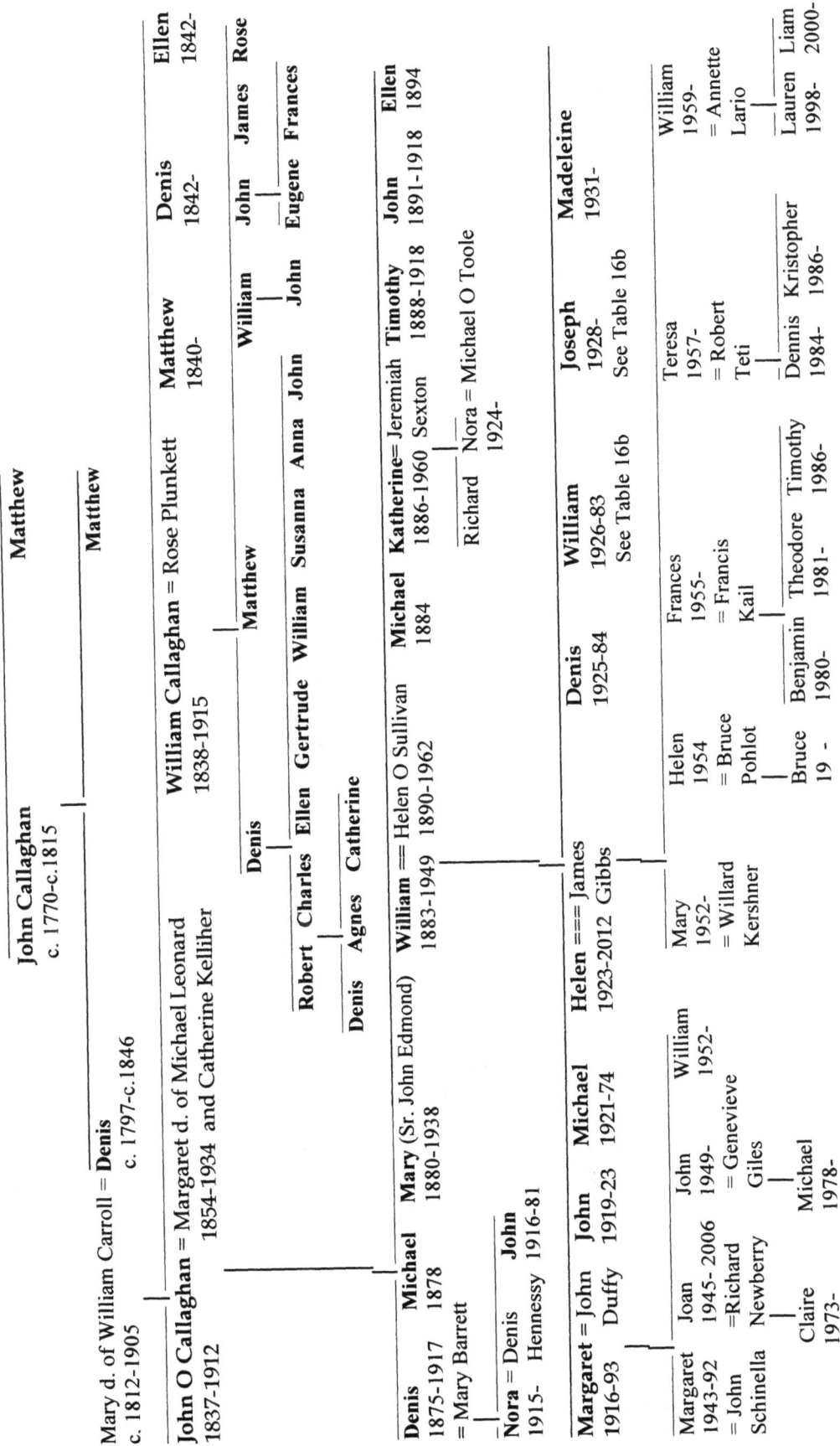

Matthew

John Callaghan
c. 1770-c.1815

Matthew

Mary d. of William Carroll = **Denis**
c. 1812-1905   c. 1797-c.1846

William Callaghan = Rose Plunkett
1838-1915

Matthew   Denis   Ellen
1840-   1842-   1842-

William   John   James   Rose
Eugene   Frances

Matthew

Denis

Robert   Charles   Ellen   Gertrude   William   Susanna   Anna   John

Denis   Agnes   Catherine

John O Callaghan = Margaret d. of Michael Leonard
1837-1912   1854-1934 and Catherine Kelliher

Michael = Helen O Sullivan   **Katherine** = Jeremiah   **Timothy**   **John**   **Ellen**
1884   1886-1960 Sexton   1888-1918   1891-1918 1894

Richard   Nora = Michael O Toole
1924-

Denis   **Michael**   **Mary** (Sr. John Edmond)   **William** = Helen O Sullivan
1875-1917   1878   1880-1938   1883-1949   1890-1962
= Mary Barrett

Nora = Denis   **John**
1915- Hennessy 1916-81

William   **Denis**   **Joseph**   **Madeleine**
1926-83   1925-84   1928-   1931-
See Table 16b   See Table 16b

Helen === James
1923-2012 Gibbs

Margaret = John   **John**   **Michael**   **William**   Teresa   William
1916-93   Duffy   1919-23   1921-74   1952-   1957-   1959-
= Robert   = Annette
Teti   Lario

Mary   John   Frances   Helen
1952-   1949-   1955-   1954
= Willard   = Genevieve = Francis   = Bruce
Kershner   Giles   Kail   Pohlot

Dennis   Kristopher   Lauren   Liam
1984-   1986-   1998-   2000-

Benjamin   Theodore   Timothy
1980-   1981-   1986-

Bruce
19 -

Margaret   Joan
1943-92   1945- 2006
= John   =Richard
Schinella   Newberry

Claire   Michael
1973-   1978-

16b. THE O CALLAGHANS OF DROMCUMMER AND PHILADELPHIA

William === Helen O Sullivan
1883-1949 1890-1962
See table 16a

William = Mary Ann
1926-83 Phelps

Joseph = Anne
1928- Drummey

Mary
1958-
= Todd
Hamiter

Michael
1960-
= Cheryll
Neuser

Joan
1960-

John
1962-
= Mary
Scherzinger

Joseph = Daniela Ialeggio
1965-

Harry
1994-

Liam
1983-

Lauren
1984-

Ian
1986-

Kayleigh
1987-

William
1993-

Kathryn
1995-

Caroline
1999-

Daniel
2004 -

Michael
1994-

Megan
1995-

Matthew
2002-

William
1958-

Catherine = Gurudharm Singh Khalsa
1961-

Anne = Timothy Stephens
1962-

Rónán
1997-

Thomas
1996-

Peter
1999-

Daniel
2003-

ABBREVIATIONS

AH – Analecta Hibernica

AI - Annals of Inisfallen. Ed. and tr. Seán Mac Airt. Dublin: Institute for Advanced Studies, 1951.

AICC -Archaeological Inventory of County Cork. Vol. IV - North Cork. Parts 1-2. Comp. Denis Power, Sheila Lane, Elizabeth Byrne, Ursula Egan, Mary Sleeman, Eamon Cotter, and Judith Monk. Dublin: Stationery Office, 2000.

AU - Annals of Ulster. Ed. And tr. William M. Hennessy. 4 vols. Dublin: Her Majesty's Stationery Office, 1887.

Betham Abstracts – Dublin PRO Prerogative Will Abstracts by Sir William Betham

BIFR - Burke's Irish Family Records. London: Burke's Peerage Ltd. 1976.

Calendar Ormonde – Calendar of the Manuscripts of the Marquess of Ormonde, K. P., preserved at Kilkenny Castle. New series. 8 vols. London: Historical Manuscripts Commission, 1902-1920.

CCP - Calendar of Carew Papers in the Lambeth Library, 1515-1624. 6 vols. Ed. J. S. Brewer and W. Bullen. London: Public Record Office, 1867-1873.

CGH - Corpus Genealogiarum Hiberniae. Ed. M. A. O Brien. 1 vol. thus far. Dublin: Dublin Institute for Advanced Studies, 1976.

CE – Cork Examinerxxxxxxxxxx

CH – Collectanea Hibernica

CPCRC - Calendar of Patent and Close Rolls of Chancery in Ireland in the Reigns of Henry VIII, Edward VI, Mary, and Elizabeth. 3 vols. Ed. James Morrin. Dublin: A. Thom and Sons, 1861-1863.

CPCRC Charles I - Calendar of the Patent and Close Rolls of Chancery in Ireland of the Reign of Charles I. First to Eighth Year 1631 Inclusive. Ed. James Morrin. Dublin and London: Her Majesty's Stationery Office, 1863.

CS - Chronicon Scotorum. A Chronicle of Irish Affairs from the Earliest Times to 1135. Ed. and tr. W. M. Hennessy. Rolls Series, 46. London: Longman, 1866.

CSPIreland. Henry VIII - Calendar of the State Papers relating to Ireland. Henry VIII, Edward VI, Mary, Elizabeth, 1509-1603. 11 vols. Ed. H. C. Hamilton, E. G. Atkinson, R. P. Mahaffy. London: Public Record Office, 1860-1912.

CSPIreland. James I - Calendar of the State Papers relating to Ireland of the Reign of James I. 5 vols. Ed. C. W. Russell and John P. Prendergast. London: Public Record Office, 1872-1880.

CSPIreland. Charles I - Calendar of the State Papers relating to Ireland of the Reign of Charles I. 4 vols. Ed. R. P. Mahaffy. London: Public Record Office, 1900-1904.

CSPIreland. Charles II - Calendar of the State Papers relating to Ireland. Charles II 1660-1670. 4 vols. Ed. R. P. Mahaffy. London: Public Record Office, 1905-1911.

Dublin, GO - Dublin, Genealogical Office

Dublin, PRO. – Public Record Office

Egmont MSS - Report on the Manuscripts of the Earl of Egmont. 2 vols. London and Dublin: Historical Manuscripts Commission. 1905-1909.

FM - Annals of the Kingdom of Ireland by the Four Masters from the Earliest Period to 1616. 2d ed. and tr. John O Donovan. 7 vols. Dublin: Hodges and Smith, 1856.

Grehan Papers - Cork, University College, Boole Library

Abbreviations

ITQ – Irish Theological Quarterly

JCHAS - Journal of the Cork Historical and Archaeological Society

JRSAI - Journal of the Royal Society of Antiquaries of Ireland

JAPMD - Journal of the Association for the Preservation of Memorials of the Dead in Ireland

LM - An Leabhar Muimhneach. Ed. Tadhg Ó Donnchadha. Dublin: Irish Manuscripts Commission. 1941.

MFCJ – Mallow Field Club Journal

NHI - A New History of Ireland. Ed. T. W. Moody, F. X. Martin, vols. 2, 3, 5, part 1 thus far. Oxford: Oxford University Press. 1976, 1987, 1992.

O Callaghan-Lismehane Papers – Dublin, National Library Reports on Private Collections, no. 110: J. F. Ainsworth, Report on the O Callaghan-Westropp Papers (from 1635) now in the National Library of Ireland relating to the O Callaghan and Westropp Families and to lands in Cos. Clare and Tipperary.

Ormonde MSS - The Manuscripts of the Marquis of Ormonde preserved at the Castle of Kilkenny. Historical Manuscripts Commission. Fourteenth Report. Appendix. Part 7. London: Historical Manuscripts Commission, 1895.

RDK - Reports of the Deputy Keeper of the Public Records and Keeper of the State Papers in Ireland. vols. 7-22. Dublin: Public Record Office, 1875-1890.

RIA – Royal Irish Academy

RIA, O.S. - Royal Irish Academy, Ordnance Survey Inquisitions

SD - Seanchas Dúthalla

TAB – Dublin, PRO Tithe Applotment Books

Thrift Abstracts– Dublin, PRO Abstracts of Wills by Miss Thrift

TIG – The Irish Genealogist

BIBLIOGRAPHY

Manuscript Sources

Cork, University College, Boole Library. Grehan Papers.

Dublin, National Archives. *Books of Survey and Distribution.*

Dublin, National Library

Reports on Private Collections, no. 110: J. F. Ainsworth, Report on the O Callaghan-Westropp Papers (from 1635) now in the National Library of Ireland relating to the O Callaghan and Westropp Families and to lands in Cos. Clare and Tipperary.

Reports on Private Collections, no. 205: J. F. Ainsworth, Interim Report on the O Callaghan-Westropp Papers (from 1727) the property of Mr. C. J. O Callaghan-Westropp, Lismehane, O Callaghan's Mills, Co. Clare, deposited in the National Library of Ireland.

Report on Private Collections, no. 343: J. F. Ainsworth, Report on the Shanbally Estate Office Papers (from 1736) Clogheen, Co. Tipperary, relating to the O Callaghan family, Lords Lismore, and to lands in Co. Tipperary.

Dublin, National Library. Genealogical Office. MSS 110, 111G, 147, 153, 170, 177, 178, 179, 182, 289.

Dublin, Public Record Office. Books of Survey and Distribution

Tithe Applotment Books

Abstracts of Wills by Miss Thrift

Prerogative Will Abstracts by Sir William Betham

Testaments.

Dublin, PRO, VII B/2/21. IA 41 657, pp. 93-103, 107-119. Records of the Diocese of Cloyne. Religious Census 1766. Copy of Transcripts by Rev. Bartholomew O'Keeffe.

The Church of Ireland Parish of Kilshannick, Cork, Register of Baptisms, Deaths, and Marriages.

The Return of the Hearth Money Collectors in the Different Portions of the Diocese of Cloyne, A.D. 1764-1765.

Richard Griffith, Primary Valuation of Tenements, 1848-1864, 200 vols.

Richard Griffith, *Primary Valuation of that Portion of the Barony of Duhallow comprised in the Union of Kanturk,* Parts I-III. Dublin, 1852.

Index to Griffith's Valuation of Ireland, 1848-1864. CD No.188, Family Tree Maker, Family Archives, Broderbund Software 1997.

Dublin, Royal Irish Academy. Ordnance Survey Inquisitions, Cork, 1:52-54, 137-148, 325-331, nos. 6, 12, 40.

Karlsruhe, Badische Generallandesarchiv, 173, nos. 40, 42, 220/513, 2575-2576, 2685-2686.

Madrid, Archivo Histórico Nacional. Asiento de consulta sobre que se permite a D. Julián O Callaghan, don Antonio Sartine, don Antonio Álvarez de Bohorque, don Simón Connock, y don Guillermo Lacy el uso del título de Conde de Albi y

Marqués de Albiville, mercedes imperiales. Libro 2757, año 1725, núm. 4, fols. 136v-137r.

Ordenes Militares. Pruebas de Caballeros. Alcántara, Expediente 1080. Calatrava, Expediente 614. Santiago, Expediente 5795.

Madrid, Biblioteca Nacional, 807. O Callaghan y de Gournay, Francisco. Datos para escribir la historia de la isla de Cuba durante el mando de los Generales Dulce y Caballero de Rodas, Año 1869.

Narrative Sources

A Contemporary History of Affairs in Ireland 1641-1652. Ed. John T. Gilbert. 3 vols. Dublin: Irish Archaeological Society 1879.

Annals of Inisfallen. Ed. and tr. Seán MacAirt. Dublin: Dublin Institute for Advanced Studies, 1951.

Annals of Loch Cé. A Chronicle of Irish Affairs from A.D. 1014 to A.D. 1590. Ed. and tr. William Hennessy. 2 vols. Rolls Series. London: Longman, 1871.

Annals of the Kingdom of Ireland by the Four Masters from the Earliest Period to 1616. 2d ed. and tr. John O'Donovan. 7 vols. Dublin: Hodges and Smith, 1856.

Annals of Ulster. 4 vols. Ed. and tr. William Hennessy. Dublin: Her Majesty's Stationery Office, 1887-1901.

Bellings, Richard. *A History of the Irish Confederation and the War in Ireland, 1641-1643.* 7 vols. Ed. John T. Gilbert. Dublin, 1882-1891; reprint New York: AMS, 1972.

Brisacier, Jean, S.J. *Le Jansenisme confundu dans l'advocat du Sr. Callaghan.* Paris 1651.

Callaghan, John. *Lettre de Monsieur Callaghan docteur en theologie de la Faculté de Paris et curé prieur de Cour Cheverny, a un docteur de Sorbonne de ses amis, touchant les principales impostures du P. Brisacier Jesuite. Avec une lettre d'un Seigneur Catholique d'Hibernie [Richard Bellings], qui le justifie . . . de toutes les calomnies de ce Jesuite regardent ce royaume.* Paris 1652.

_____ *Vindiciarum Catholicorum Hiberniae authore Philopatro Irenaeo ad Alithophilum Libri duo, quorum primus rerum in Hibiernia gestarum ab anno 1641 ad annum 1649 verissimam et actorum publicorum fide munitam synopsim, secundus libelli famosi in Catholicos Hiberniae proceres qui honestissimam cum regium partium hominibus pacem inierunt confutationem continet. Ne confudaris dicere verum. Eccles. 4.* Paris: Vidua I. Camusat et Petrum le Petit, 1650.

Castlehaven, Earl of. *Memoirs or his Review of the Civil Wars in Ireland.* Dublin, 1815; reprint, Delmar, NJ: Scholars Facsimiles, 1974.

Chronicon Scotorum. A Chronicle of Irish Affairs from the Earliest Times to 1135. Ed. and tr. W. M. Hennessy. Rolls Series 46. London: Longman, 1866.

Commentarius Rinuccinianus. De sedis apostolicae legatione ad foederatos Hiberniae Catholicos per annos 1645-1649. Ed. Fr. Richard [Barnabas O Ferrall] and Fr. Robertus [Daniel O Connell]. New ed. Fr. Stanislaus Joannes Kavanagh. 6 vols. Dublin: Irish Manuscripts Commission 1932-1949.

Gilbert, John T. *A Jacobite Narrative of the War in Ireland, 1688-1691.* Dublin, 1892; reprint New York: Barnes and Noble, 1971.

Gillman, Herbert W. "The Rise and Progress in Munster of the Rebellion, 1642." *JCHAS* 1 (1895): 529-542; 2 (1896): 11-29, 63-79.

Keating, Geoffrey. *Forus Feasa ar Éirinn. History of Ireland.* 3 vols. Ed. and tr. David Comyn and P. S. Dineen. Dublin: Irish Texts Society, 1901-1908.

"MacCarthaigh's Book." In *Miscellaneous Irish Annals.* 2-115.

Meyer, Kuno. "The Laud Synchronisms. *Zeitschrift für celtische Philologie* 9 (1913): 482.

Miscellaneous Irish Annals (A.D. 1114-1437). Ed. and tr. Séamus Ó hInnse. Dublin: Institute for Advanced Studies, 1947.

Nunziatura in Irlanda di Monsignor Giovan Battista Rinuccini arcivescovo di Fermo negli anni 1645 a 1649. Firenze: Tipografia Platti, 1844.

O Kelly, Charles. *Macariae Excidium.* Ed. John C. O Callaghan. *Narratives Illustrative of the Contests in Ireland in 1641 and 1690.* Ed. Thomas Crofton Croker. Camden Society. 14. London: J. B. Nichols, 1841.

Spenser, Sir Edmund. *A View of the Present State of Ireland.* Ed. W. L Renwick. Oxford: Oxford University Press, 1970.

Stafford, Thomas. *Pacata Hibernia. Ireland Appeased and Reduced or a History of the Wars of Ireland in the Reign of Queen Elizabeth.* 2 vols. (London, 1633; reprint, London: S. and R. Bentley, 1821.

The Embassy in Ireland of Monsignor G. B. Rinuccini. Archbishop of Fermo in the Years 1645-1649. Tr. Annie Hutton. Dublin: A. Thom, 1873.

The Life and Letters of Florence MacCarthy Reagh, Tanist of Carbery, MacCarthy Mór. Ed. Daniel MacCarthy. London: Longman, 1867.

The Memoirs of Edmund Ludlow, Lieutenant-General of the Horse in the Army of the Commonwealth of England, 1625-1672. Ed. C. H. Firth. 2 vols. Oxford: Clarendon Press, 1894.

Vigors, Philip D. "Rebellion 1641-2 described in a Letter of Rev. Urban Vigors to Rev. Henry Jones, with a note of Officers engaged in the Battle of Liscarroll (From a Manuscript in Trinity College, Dublin)," *JCHAS* 2 (1896):

Documentary Sources

A Catalogue of the Bradshaw Collection of Irish Books in the University Library. 3 vols. Cambridge: Cambridge University, 1916.

A List of the Claims as they are entred with the Trustees at Chichester-House on College-Green Dublin, on or before the tenth of August, 1700. Dublin: Joseph Ray 1701.

Ahern, Dennis J. "Index of Occupiers in Griffith's Valuation for Mallow in the Barony of Fermoy." *MFCJ* 17 (1999): 160-186.

Ainsworth, John. *The Inchiquin Manuscripts.* Dublin: Irish Manuscripts Commission, 1961.

Brady, W. Maziere. *Clerical and Parochial Records of Cork, Cloyne and Ross.* 3 vols. Dublin: A. Thom, 1863-1864.

z, 1515-1624. 6 vols. Ed. J. S. Brewer and W. Bullen. London: Public Record Office, 1867-1873; reprint New York: Kraus, 1974.

Calendar of Papal Letters relating to Great Britain and Ireland. Vol. 16. Ed. Anne P.

Fuller. Dublin: Irish Manuscripts Commission, 1986. Vol. 19. Ed. Michael J. Haren. Dublin: Irish Manuscripts Commission, 1998.

Calendar of the Manuscripts of the Marquess of Ormonde, K. P., preserved at Kilkenny Castle. New series. 8 vols. London: Historical Manuscripts Commission, 1902-1920.

Calendar of the Patent and Close Rolls of Chancery in Ireland in the Reigns of Henry VIII, Edward VI, Mary, and Elizabeth. 2 vols. Ed. James Morrin. London and Dublin: A. Thom & Sons, 1861-1862.

Calendar of the Patent and Close Rolls of Chancery in Ireland of the Reign of Charles I. First to Eighth Year 1631 Inclusive. Ed. James Morrin. Dublin and London: Her Majesty's Stationery Office, 1863.

Calendar of the State Papers relating to Ireland preserved in the Public Record Office, 1625-1670. 8 vols. Ed. Robert P. Mahaffy. London: Public Record Office, 1900-1910.

Calendar of the State Papers relating to Ireland. Henry VIII, Edward VI, Mary, Elizabeth, 1509-1603. 11 vols. Ed. H. C. Hamilton, E. G. Atkinson, R. P. Mahaffy. London: Public Record Office, 1860-1912.

Calendar of the State Papers relating to Ireland of the Reign of James I. 5 vols. Ed. C.W. Russell and John P. Prendergast. London: Public Record Office, 1872-1880.

Calendar of the State Papers relating to Ireland of the Reign of Charles I. 4 vols. Ed. R. P. Mahaffy. London: Public Record Office, 1900-1904.

Calendar of the State Papers relating to Ireland. Charles II. 1660-1670. 4 vols. Ed. R. P. Mahaffy. London: Public Record Office, 1905-1911.

Calendar of the Stuart Papers belonging to His Majesty the King preserved at Windsor Castle. 6 vols. Ed. F. H. B. Daniell. London: Historical Manuscripts Commission, 1902.

Carrigan, William. "Catholic Episcopal Wills in the Public Record Office, Dublin 1683-1812." *Archivium Hibernicum* 4 (1915): 68-95.

_____ "The Old Priests. Part II. Gleanings from Documents in the Public Record Office." *JCHAS* 4 (1898): 212-221.

Casey, Albert E., and Thomas E. Dowling. *O Kief, Coshe Mang, Slieve Lougher and Upper Blackwater in Ireland.* 14 vols. Birmingham, AL: Knocknagree Historical Fund, 1952-1968.

Catálogo alfabético de los documentos referentes a Títulos del Reino y Grandezas de España conservados en la Sección de Consejos suprimidos. 3 vols. (Madrid: Archivo Histórico Nacional, 1952.

Caulfield, Richard. *The Council Book of the Corporation of the City of Cork from 1609 to 1643 and from 1690 to 1800.* Guildford, Surrey: J. Billing, 1876.

_____. *The Council Book of the Corporation of Kinsale from 1652 to 1800.* Guildford, Surrey: J. Billing, 1879.

Census of Ireland 1851. General Alphabetical Index to the Townlands and Towns, Parishes, and Baronies of Ireland. Dublin: Alex Thom, 1861.

Collins, John T. "Extracts from the Caulfield MSS, University College, Cork." *JCHAS* 66 (1961) 51-54.

Conlon, M. V. "Will of Roger Brettridge, 1683." *JCHAS* 61 (1956):110-14.

Corish, Patrick J. "Irish College, Rome. Kirby Papers. Guide to Material of Public and

Political Interest 1884-1894 with Addenda 1852-1878." *Archivium Hibernicum* 32 (1974):

Cork Defence Union, The. *Boycotting in the County Cork: What Boycotting Means.* Cork: Purcell, 1886.

Curtis, Edmund, and R. B. McDowell. *Irish Historical Documents, 1172-1922.* London, 1943; reprint New York: Barnes and Noble, 1968.

Davies, Sir John. *A Discovery of the True Cause why Ireland was never brought under Obedience of the Crown of England.* Dublin, 1787; reprint: Shannon, Irish University Press, 1969.

_____ *Les reports des cases et matters en ley resolvés et adjudgés en les courts del rey en Ireland 1604-1612 et digest per Sir John Davies, chivaler, attorney general del rey en cest realm.* London: E. Flesher at al, 1674.

_____ "The Case of Tanistry." In *A Report of Cases and Matters in Law resolved and adjudged in the King's Courts in Ireland.* Dublin: Sarah Cotter, 1752. 78-115.

Dunlop, Robert. *Ireland under the Commonwealth, being a Selection of Documents relating to the Government of Ireland from 1651 to 1659.* 2 vols. Manchester: Manchester University Press, 1913.

Edwards Cork Remembrancer or Tablet of Memory. Cork: Anthony Edwards, 1792.

Filby, P. William, and Mary K. Meyer. *Passenger and Immigration Lists Index: A Guide to Published Archival Records of about 500,000 Passengers who came to the United States and Canada in the Seventeenth, Eighteenth and Nineteenth Centuries.* Detroit: Gale, 1981.

Foster, Joseph, The Register of Admissions to Gray's Inn, 1521-1889, together with the Register of Marriages in Gray's Inn Chapel, 1695-1754. London: Hansard Publishing Union, 1889.

Francis Guy's County and City of Cork Directory for the Years 1875-1876. *Cork: Francis Guy, 1875.*

Giblin, Cathaldus. "A List of the Personnel of the Franciscan Province of Ireland, 1700." *CH* 8 (1965): 47-57.

_____ "Catalogue of Material of Irish Interest in the Collection Nunziatura di Fiandra, Vatican Archives, Part 6, vols.133-135 Gg." *CH* 10 (1967): 99-101.

_____, "Miscellaneous Papers," *AH* 16 (1965): 62-98.

Gillman, Herbert W. *Index to the Marriage Licence Bonds of the Diocese of Cork and Ross, Ireland, for the years from 1628-1750 preserved in the Public Record Office of Ireland.* Cork: Guy & Co, 1896.

Glazier, Ira, and Michael Tepper. *The Famine Immigrants: Lists of Irish Immigrants arriving at the Port of New York, 1846-1851.* 7 vols. Baltimore: Genealogical Publishing Co., 1983.

Firth C. H., and R. S. Rait, *Acts and Ordinances of the Interregnum, 1642-1660.* 3 vols. London: His Majesty's Stationery Office, 1911.

Harris, P. R. *Douai College Documents, 1639-1794.* Dublin: Catholic Record Society Publications, 1972.

Henchion, Richard. "The Gravestone Inscriptions of Cork. I. Aghinagh Burial Ground." *JCHAS* 72 (1967): 101-121.

Hickson, Mary. *Ireland in the Seventeenth Century, or the Massacres of 1641, their*

Causes and Results. 2 vols. London: Longmans, Green, 1884.

Hosler, Matthäus. "Irishmen ordained at Prague, 1629-1786." *CH* 33 (1991): 7-54.

Hussey de Burgh, U. H. *The Landowners of Ireland. An Alphabetical List of the Owners of Estates of 500 Acres or £500 Valuation and Upwards.* Dublin: Hodges, Foster, and Figgis, 1878.

Inquisitionum in Officio rotulorum Cancellariae Hiberniae asservatarum Repertorium. 2 vols. Dublin: George and John Grierson and Martin Keene, 1826.

"Irish Wills from Barcelona. Second Series." *TIG* 6:4 (1983): 473-474.

Jennings, Brendan. *Wild Geese in Spanish Flanders. Documents relating chiefly to Irish Regiments.* Dublin: Irish Manuscripts Commission, 1964.

Journals of the House of the Commons of the Kingdom of Ireland from the Eleventh Year of King James the First to the Twenty-fifth Year of the Reign of his Majesty King George the Second Inclusive. 9 vols. Dublin: Abraham Bradley, 1753-1757.

Landowners in Ireland. Return of Owners of Land of One Acre and Upwards in the Several Counties, Counties of Cities and Counties of Towns in Ireland . . . Presented to both Houses of Parliament by Command of Her Majesty 1876. Baltimore: Genealogical Publishing Co. 1988.

Lascelles, Rowley, ed. *Liber Munerum publicorum Hiberniae ab anno 1152 usque ad 1827 or The Establishments of Ireland from the nineteenth of King Stephen to the seventh of George IV.* 2 vols. London, 1824-1830.

Macgeagh, Henry, and H. A. C. Sturgess. *Register of Admissions to the Honourable Society of the Middle Temple: From the Fifteenth Century to the Year 1944.* 3 vols. London: Middle Temple, 1949.

MacLysaght, Edward. *Calendar of the Orrery Papers.* Dublin: Irish Manuscripts Commission, 1941.

_____ *The Kenmare Manuscripts.* Dublin: Irish Manuscripts Commission, 1942.

_____ "Survey of Documents in Private Keeping: Second Series. Doneraile Papers," *Analecta Hibernica* 20 (1958): 3-361, 363-393.

MacSwiney, Marquess of Mashanaglass. "The Casualty List of the Infantry Regiment of Albemarle in the Battle of Luzzara, 15th August 1702." *JRSAI* 60 (1930): 84-90.

Millett, Benignus. "Calendar of Volume 16 of the Fondo di Vienna in the Propaganda Archives, Part 3, ff. 217-280." *CH* 41 (1999): 10-35.

_____ "Copies of some Decisions from the Missing Discretorial Registers of St. Isidore's College, Rome, 1652-1739." *CH* 43 (2001): 86-111.

O Byrne, Eileen, ed., *The Convert Rolls.* Dublin: Irish Manuscripts Commission, 1981.

O Connell, Maurice, ed. *The Correspondence of Daniel O Connell.* 8 vols. Dublin: Irish Manuscripts Commission, 1972-1980.

O Doherty, D. J. "Students of the Irish College, Salamanca (1619-1700)," *Archivium Hibernicum* 3 (1914): 4 (1915):

Ó Suilleabháin, O.F.M., Pádraig. *Wexford Friary.* Wexford, 1950.

_____ "Documents relating to Wexford Friary and Parish, 1733-1798." *CH* 8 (1965):

Pender, Seamus. *A Census of Ireland circa 1659 with supplementary Material from the Poll Money Ordinances (1660-1661).* Dublin: Irish Manuscripts Commission 1939.

Bibliography

Report on Franciscan Manuscripts preserved at the Convent, Merchants' Quay, Dublin. Dublin: Historical Manuscripts Commission, 1906.

Report on the Laing Manuscripts preserved in the University of Edinburgh. 2 vols. London: Historical Manuscripts Commission, 1914-1925.

Report on the Manuscripts of the Earl of Bathurst preserved at Cirencester Park. London: Historical Manuscripts Commission, 1923.

Report on the Manuscripts of the Earl of Egmont. 2 vols. London and Dublin: Historical Manuscripts Commission. 1905-1909.

Report on the Manuscripts of the Lord de L'Isle and Dudley preserved at Penshurst Place. 6 vols. London: Historical Manuscripts Commission, 1925-1966.

"Report on the State of Popery in Ireland 1731." *Archivium Hibernicum* 1 (1912) 10-27; 2 (1913) 108-156.

Reports of the Deputy Keeper of the Public Records and Keeper of the State Papers in Ireland. Vols. 7-22. Dublin: Public Record Office, 1875-1890.

Rotulus Pipae Clonensis. Ed. Richard Caulfield. Cork:George Nash, 1859.

"Royal Visitation of Cork, Cloyne, Ross, and the College of Youghal." *Archivium Hibernicum* 1 (1913): 173-215.

Simms, J. G. "Irish Jacobite Lists from TCD MS N.1.3." *AH* 22 (1960): 11-230.

Skehan, W. G. "Extracts from the Minutes of the Corporation of Fethard, Co. Tipperary." *TIG* 4 (1971): 308-322.

Statutes at Large passed in the Parliaments held in Ireland, 1310-1785. 20 vols. Dublin: B. Grierson, 1786-1801.

Simington, R. C. *The Civil Survey, A. D. 1654-1656.* 10 vols. Dublin: Stationery Office, 1936-1961.

_____ *The Transplantation to Connacht, 1654-1658.* Dublin: Irish Manuscripts Commission, Irish University Press, 1970.

Swords, Liam. "Calendar of Irish Material in the Files of Jean Fromont, notary at Paris, May 1701-24 January 1730 in the Archives Nationales, Paris: Part 2, 1716-1730." *CH* 36-37 (1994-95):

The Diary of Humphrey O Sullivan, 1827-1835. Trans. by Tomás de Bhaldraithe. Cork: Mercier, 1979.

The Irish Parliament of 1775 from an Official and Contemporary Manuscript. Ed. William Hunt. Dublin: Hodges Figgis, 1907.

The Letters of Oliver Plunkett, 1625-1681, Archbishop of Armagh and Primate of All Ireland. Ed. Msgr. John Hanly. Dublin: Dolmen Press, 1979.

The Lismore Papers (Second Series). Selections from the Private and Public (or State) Correspondence of Sir Richard Boyle, First and 'Great' Earl of Cork. Ed. Rev. Alexander B. Grosart, 5 vols. N.P. 1887-1888.

The Manuscripts of the Marquis of Ormonde preserved at the Castle of Kilkenny. Historical Manuscripts Commission, Fourteenth Report, Appendix, Part 7. London: Historical Manuscripts Commission, 1895.

The Manuscripts of his Grace the Duke of Portland preserved at Welbeck Abbey. 10 vols. London: Historical Manuscripts Commission, 1891-1931.

The Manuscripts of S. H. Le Fleming, Esq. of Rydal Hall. London: Historical Manuscripts Commission, 1890.

The Martyrology of Donegal. Ed. J. H. Todd and W. Reeves. Dublin: A. Thom, 1864.

The Statutes of the United Kingdom of Great Britain and Ireland 1 & 2 Victoria 1838. London: Her Majesty's Printers, 1838.

The Walsingham Letter Book or Register of Ireland, May 1578 to December 1579. Ed. James Hogan and N. McNeill O Farrell. Dublin: Irish Manuscripts Commission, 1959.

Tepper, Michael, ed. *New World Immigrants: A Consolidation of Ship Passenger Lists and Associated Data from Periodical Literature.* 2 vols. Baltimore: Genealogical Publishing Co., 1979.

Tierney, Mark. "Dr. Croke, the Irish Bishops and the Parnell Crisis, 18 November 1890- 21 April 1891: Some Unpublished Correspondence." *CH* 11 (1969):

_____ "A Short Title Calendar of the Papers of Archbishop Thomas William Croke in Archbishop's House, Thurles, Part 2, 1886-1890." *CH* 16 (1973):

Genealogical Sources

An Leabhar Muimneach. Ed. Tadhg Ó Donnchadha. Dublin: Irish Manuscripts Commission, 1941.

Burke, Sir Bernard. *A Genealogical and Heraldic History of the Landed Gentry of Ireland.* Ed. A.C. Fox Davies. London, 1912; reprint London: Burke's Peerage, 1958.

Burke's Irish Family Records. London: Burke's Peerage Ltd., 1976.

Cokayne, George E. *The Complete Peerage of England, Scotland, Ireland, Great Britain and the United Kingdom.* New ed. 13 vols. London: St. Catherine, 1910-1959.

Corpus Genealogiarum Hiberniae. Ed. M. A. O'Brien. 1 vol. thus far. Dublin: Dublin Institute for Advanced Studies, 1976.

Corpus Genealogiarum Sanctorum Hiberniae. Ed. Pádraig Ó Riain. Dublin: Dublin Institute for Advanced Study, 1985.

Fox-Davies, Arthur Charles. *Armorial Families: A Directory of Gentlemen of Coat Armour.* 2 vols. Rutland, VT: Tuttle, 1970.

Pine, Leslie G. *The New Extinct Peerage, 1884-1971.* London: Heraldry Today, 1972.

The Pedigrees and Papers of James Terry, Athlone Herald at the Court of James II in France 1725. Ed. Charles E. Lart. Exeter: William Pollard, 1938.

Literary Sources

Caithréim Cellacháin Chaisil. The Victorious Career of Cellachán of Cashel. Ed. and tr. Alexander Bugge. Christiana, Sweden: J.Chr. Gundersens Bogtrykkeri, 1905.

Cogadh Gaedhel re Gallaib (The War of the Gaedhil with the Gaill). Ed. and tr. James H. Todd. Rolls Series. London: Longman, 1867.

De hÓir, Eamonn. "Caithréim Dhonnchaidh mhic Thaidhg Rua Uí Cheallacháin." *North Munster Studies: Essays in Commemoration of Monsignor Michael Molony.* Limerick: Thomond Archaeological Society, 1967. 505-525.

Leabhar na g-Ceart, or the Book of Rights. Ed. John O Donovan. Dublin: Celtic Society, 1847.

Lebor Gabála Érenn. The Book of the Taking of Ireland. Ed. and tr. R. A. S. Macalister. 5 vols. Dublin: Irish Texts Society, 1938-1956.

O Daly, Aongus. *The Tribes of Ireland. A Satire.* Ed. John O'Donovan. Tr. James Clarence Mangan. Dublin, 1852; reprint Cork: Tower Books, 1976.

Bibliography

Ó Tuama, Seán, and Thomas Kinsella. *An Duanaire: An Irish Anthology, 1600-1900: Poems of the Dispossessed.* Philadelphia: University of Pennsylvania, 1981.

The Circuit of Ireland by Muirchertach mac Néill, Prince of Aileach. A Poem written in the year 942 by Cormacán Eigeas, Chief Poet of the North of Ireland. Ed. and tr. John O Donovan. In *Tracts relating to Ireland* 1 (Dublin: *Irish Archaeological Society*, 1841): 1-68.

The Poems of Egan O'Rahilly. Ed. and tr. Patrick Dineen. Dublin: Irish Texts Society, 1900.

The Topographical Poems of John O Dubhagain and Giolla na-Naomh O Huidhrin. Ed. and tr. John O Donovan. Dublin: Irish Archaeological and Celtic Society, 1862.

Topographical Poems by Seaán Mor Ó Dubhagáin and Giolla na Naomh Ó Huidhrín. Ed. James Carney. Dublin: Institute for Advanced Studies, 1943.

Newspapers
Cork Examiner
Cork Journal
Irish Examiner

Modern Works
A New History of Ireland. Ed. T. W. Moody, F. X. Martin. Vols. 2, 3, 5, part 1 thus far. Oxford: Oxford University Press. 1976, 1987, 1992.

Archaeological Inventory of County Cork. Vol. IV - North Cork. Parts 1-2. Comp. Denis Power, Sheila Lane, Elizabeth Byrne, Ursula Egan, Mary Sleeman, Eamon Cotter, and Judith Monk. Dublin: Stationery Office, 2000.

Archdall, Mervyn. *Monasticon Hibernicum. A History of the Abbeys, Priories and other Religious Houses in Ireland.* Ed. Patrick F. Moran. 3 vols. Dublin: W. B. Kelly, 1873-1876.

Ashe, Matthew, S.J., "Conspicuous Gallantry." *Company: A Magazine of the American Jesuits.* Winter 1989, 18-19.

Bagwell, Richard. *Ireland under the Stuarts and during the Interregnum.* 3 vols. London: 1909-1916; reprint London: Holland Press, 1963.

_____ *Ireland under the Tudors.* 3 vols. London: Longman, 1885-1890; reprint London: Holland Press 1963.

Barnard, T. C. *Cromwellian Ireland. English Government and Reform in Ireland 1649-1660.* London: Oxford University Press, 1975.

_____ "Histories of the 1640s." In Micheál Ó Siochrú, ed. *Kingdoms in Crisis: Ireland in the 1640s: Essays in Honour of Donal Cregan.* Dublin: Four Courts Press, 2001.

Barrington, Jonah. *Rise and Fall of the Irish Nation.* New York: Sadlier, 1833.

Baudrillart, Alfred. *Philippe V et la cour de France.* 5 vols. Paris: Firmin-Didot, 1870.

Bence-Jones, Mark. *A Guide to Irish Country Houses.* London: Burke's Peerage, 1988.

_____ *Twilight of the Ascendancy.* London: Constable, 1987.

Berry, Henry F. "Justices of the Peace for the County Cork," *JCHAS* 3 (1897): 58-65, 105-112.

_____ "The English Settlement in Mallow." *JCHAS* 12 (1906): 1-25.

_____ "The Parish of Kilshannig and Manor of Newberry, Co. Cork." *JCHAS*

11 (1905): 31-38, 53-64.

Bitel, Lisa M. *Isle of the Saints. Monastic Settlemnt and Community in Early Ireland.* Ithaca: Cornell University Press, 1990.

Blackall, Sir Henry. "The Memorandum Book of David Rochfort." *JCHAS* 67 (1962): 54-56.

Bolster, Evelyn. *A History of the Diocese of Cork from the Earliest times to the Reformation.* New York: Barnes and Noble, 1972.

Bolton, G. C. *The Passing of the Irish Act of Union: Study in Parliamentary Politics.* Oxford: Oxford University Press, 1966.

Bottigheimer, Karl. *English Money and Irish Land. The Adventurers in the Cromwellian Settlement of Ireland.* Oxford: Oxford University Press, 1971.

Bowman, Michael J. *Place Names and Antiquities of the Barony of Duhallow.* Ed. Jean J. MacCarthy. Duhallow, 2000.

Boylan, Henry. *A Dictionary of Irish Biography.* 3d ed. Niwot, CO: Roberts Rinehart, 1998.

Boyle, Patrick. *The Irish College in Paris from 1578 to 1901.* London: Benziger, 1901.
_____"A Jansenist Agent in Ireland in 1646. John Callaghan, D.D." *Irish Ecclesiastical Record.* Series 5, 22 (1923): 1-9.

Bradshaw, Brendan. *The Dissolution of the Religious Orders in Ireland under Henry VIII.* Cambridge: University Press, 1974.

Breen, Dan. *My Fight for Irish Freedom.* Dublin: Anvil, 1981.

Buckley, David. "Two Stone Alignments in Kilshannig Parish." *SD* 7 (1989): 61-62.

Burke, Thomas. *Hibernia Dominicana sive Historia Provinciae Hiberniae Ordinis Praedicatorum.* Cologne, 1762; reprint Westmead, England: Gregg, 1970.

Burke, William P. *The Irish Priests in the Penal Times (1660-1760). From the State Papers in H. M. Record Offices, Dublin and London, the Bodleian Library and British Museum.* Waterford, 1914; reprint Shannon: Irish University Press, 1969.

Butler, William F. T. *Gleanings from Irish History.* London: Longman, 1925.

Buttimer, Cornelius G. "Gaelic Literature and Contemporary Life in Cork, 1700-1840." In O Flanagan and Buttimer. *Cork.* 585-654.

Callahan, Nelson. *A Case for Due Process in the Church: Father Eugene O Callaghan, American Pioneer of Dissent.* Staten Island, NY: Alba House, 1971.

Canning, Bernard J. *Bishops of Ireland, 1870-1987.* Ballyharrow, Donegal: Donegal Democrat, n.d.

Canny, Nicholas. "The 1641 Depositions as a Source for the Writing of Social History: County Cork as a Case Study," in O Flanagan and Buttimer, *Cork.*

Casway, Jerrold. *Owen Roe O Neill and the Struggle for Catholic Ireland.* Philadelphia: University of Pennsylvania Press, 1984.

Ciadoncha, Marquesa de. *Los caballeros portugueses en las Ordenes militares españolas* Lisbon: Sociedade Cestíoria, 1946.

Clark, Dennis. *The Irish in Philadelphia: Ten Generations of Urban Experience.* Philadelphia: Temple University Press, 1973.

Clark, Ruth. *Strangers and Sojourners at Port Royal.* Cambridge: Cambridge University Press, 1932.

Clarke, Aidan. *The Old English in Ireland 1625-1642.* Ithaca: Cornell University Press, 1966.

_____ "Selling Royal Favours, 1624-32." *NHI*, 3:233-242.

Coffey, George. *Guide to the Celtic Antiquities of the Christian Period preserved in the National Museum.* 2d ed. Dublin: Hodges, Figgis, 1910.

Coghlan, Daniel. *The Land of Ireland.* Dublin: Veritas, 1931.

Collins, John. "Gleanings from Old Irish Newspapers." *JCHAS* 69 (1964): 56-59.

_____ "Some Cork Wills, Deeds and Indentures." *JCHAS* 64 (1959): 104-108.

_____ "Some MacCarthys of Blarney and Ballea," *JCHAS* 59 (1954): 82-88.

Connolly, S. J. *Priests and People in Pre-Famine Ireland, 1780-1845.* New York: St. Martin's, 1982.

Coogan, Tim Pat. *The IRA: A History.* Niwot, CO: Roberts Rinehart, 1994.

Coonan, Thomas L. *The Irish Catholic Confederacy and the Puritan Revolution.* New York: Columbia University Press, 1954.

Cooney, James. *Macroom People and Places: A Brief Historical Sketch.* Macroom: Macroom and District Literary, Historical and Archaeological Society, 1976.

Corish, Patrick. "The Rising of 1641 and the Catholic Confederacy," *NHI*, 3:289-316.

_____ "Ormond, Rinuccini and the Confederates," *NHI.* 3:317-335.

_____ "The Cromwellian Conquest, 1649-1653." *NHI.* 3:336-352.

_____ "John Callaghan and the Controversies among the Irish in Paris 1649-1654." *Irish Theological Quarterly* 21(1954):32-50.

_____ "The Irish in Paris." *Irish Theological Quarterly* 21(1954): 35-50.

Co. Cork, North and East, Cork City. Naas: Irish Tourist Board, 1982.

Corkery, Daniel. *The Hidden Ireland: A Study of Gaelic Munster in the Eighteenth Century.* Dublin: Gill and Macmillan, 1967.

Coughlan, A. J. "The Whiteboys' Origins," *MFCJ* 17 (1999): 63-79.

_____ *"A Riot in Kilshannig and Glantane,"* *MFCJ* 28 (2010): 101-114.

Craigen, Jessie, and Robert John Buckley. "A Visit to Bodyke." in Brian Ó Dálaigh. *The Stranger's Gaze: Travels in County Clare, 1534-1950.* Ennis: Clasp Press, 1998. 291-294, 308-313.

Croker, Thomas Crofton. *Researches in the South of Ireland.* London, 1824; reprint New York: Barnes and Noble, 1969.

Crowe, Rev. J. "Notice of the Kilmallock Chalice." *JRSAI* 9 (4th series 1889): 216-217.

Crowley, Seamus. "An Old Ground Sketch of Mallow." *MFCJ* 5 (1987): 6-17.

_____ "Mallow Map: 1831." *MFCJ* 9 (1991): 85-98.

Curtis, Edmund. *A History of Ireland.* London: Methuen, 1961.

_____ *A History of Medieval Ireland.* London: Methuen, 1938.

Curtis, Jr., L. P. *Coercion and Conciliation in Ireland, 1880-1892.* Princeton: Princeton University Press, 1963.

D'Alton, Ian. *Protestant Society and Politics in Cork, 1812-1844.* Cork: Cork University Press, 1980.

_____ "Keeping the Faith: An Evocation of the Cork Protestant Character, 1820-1920." In O Flanagan and Buttimer. *Cork.* 759-792.

D'Alton, John. *Illustrations Historical and Genealogical of King James' Irish Army List* Dublin: The Author, 1855.

Daly, Matthew. "Duhallow," *Seanchas Duthalla* 1 (1976-7):1-4.

Day, Robert. "Additional Notes on the Kilmallock Chalice, with a Notice of the Midleton Chalice." *JRSAI* 9 (4th series 1889):217-220.

_____ "Licensed Beggars," *JCHAS* 4 (1898): 318-320.

Denham-Jephson, Maurice. *Anglo-Irish Miscellany. Some Records of the Jephsons of Mallow.* Dublin: Allen Figgis, 1964.

Dolley, Michael .*Anglo-Norman Ireland.* Dublin: Gill, 1972.

"Distinguished Corkmen." *JCHAS* 11 (1905): 194.

Donnelly, Jr., James S. *The Land and the People of Nineteenth-Century Cork: The Rural Economy and the Land Question.* London: Routledge & Kegan Paul, 1975.

_____ "The Whiteboy Movement, 1761-5." *Irish Historical Studies* 21 (1978): 20-54.

_____ "The Rightboy Movement, 1785-88." *Studia Hibernica* 18 (1977-78): 120-202.

Dooley, Terence. *The Decline of the Big House in Ireland: A Study of Irish Landed Families, 1860-1960.* Dublin: Wolfhound Press, 2001.

Dowling, P. J. *The Hedge Schools of Ireland.* Cork: Mercier, 1968.

Duggan, John P. *A History of the Irish Army.* Dublin: Gill and Macmillan, 1991.

Early Modern Ireland 1534-1691. Oxford: Oxford University Press, 1976. In *A New History of Ireland.* Ed. T. W. Moody, F. X. Martin, F. J. Byrne. Vol. 3.

Edwards, R. Dudley. *Ireland in the Age of the Tudors: The Destruction of Hiberno-Norman Civilization.* London: Croom Helm, 1977.

Eldridge, Jim. "Banteer History Project, 1995." *SD* 10 (1996): 74-77.

Ellis, Peter Berresford. *Hell or Connaught! The Cromwellian Colonisation of Ireland 1652-1660.* New York: St. Martin's Press, 1975.

Ellis, Steven G. *Tudor Ireland. Crown, Community and the Conflict of Cultures, 1470-1603.* London: Longman, 1985.

Esson, D. M. R. *The Curse of Cromwell. A History of the Ironside Conquest of Ireland, 1649-1653.* Totowa, NJ: Rowman and Littlefield, 1971.

Eubel, Konrad, et alii. *Hierarchia Catholica Medii et Recentioris Aevi.* 8 vols. Padua: San Antonio, 1910-1968.

Fitzpatrick, Brendan. *Seventeenth-Century Ireland: The War of Religions.* Totowa, NJ: Barnes and Noble, 1989.

Forde, Rev. Robert. "Lieutenant General William Callaghan." *MFCJ* 5 (1987): 18-21.

Foster, R. F. *Modern Ireland, 1600-1972.* New York: Penguin, 1989.

_____ ed. *The Oxford History of Ireland.* Oxford: Oxford University Press, 1992

Frost, James. *The History and Topography of the County of Clare from the Earliest Times to the Beginning of the Eighteenth Century.* Dublin: Sealy, Breyers and Walker, 1893.

Gallagher, Thomas. *Paddy's Lament: Ireland 1846-1947. Prelude to Hatred.* San Diego: Harcourt, 1982.

Gallwey, Herbert. "Irish Officers in the Spanish Service: III. The Regiment of Waterford." *TIG* 6:1 (1980): 18-21.

_____ "Irish Officers in the Spanish Service: IV: The Regiment of Irlanda." *TIG* 6:2 (1981): 204-211.

_____ Irish Officers in the Spanish Service: VI. The Regiment of Hibernia.", , *TIG* 6:4 (1983): 461-468.

Gaughan, J. Anthony. *Listowel and its Vicinity.* Cork: Mercier, 1973.

_____ *The Knights of Glin. A Geraldine Family.* Mount Merrion:

Kingdom Books, 1978.

General Alphabetical Index to the Townlands and Towns, Parishes, and Baronies of Ireland. Dublin: Alex Thom, 1861.

Gibson, C. B. *The History of the County and City of Cork.* 2 vols. London: T. C. Newby, 1861.

Gillman, Herbert W. "The Chieftains of Pobul I-Callaghan, Co. Cork," *JCHAS*, Series 2, 3 (1897): 201-220.

Good, Jo. "The Grehans of Clonmeen: Portrait of an Irish Catholic Unionist Family." *SD* 12 (2000): 46-52.

Green, E. R. R. "The Great Famine, 1845-1850." In Moody and Martin. *Course.* 263-274.

Grove-White, James. *Historical and Topographical Notes, etc. on Buttevant, Castletownroche, Doneraile, Mallow and Places in their Vicinity.* 3 vols. Cork: Guy & Co. 1911.

Guiney, David. "Once a Duhallow Man – Always a Duhallow Man." *SD* 4 (1980-1981): 89-92.

Hartnett, P. J. "Holy Wells of East Muskerry, Co. Cork." *JCHAS* 52 (1947): 9-10.

Hayes McCoy, G. A. "The Completion of the Tudor Conquest and the Advance of the Counter-Reformation, 1571-1603." *NHI.* 3:94-141.

Hennessy, Maurice N. *The Wild Geese: The Irish Soldier in Exile.* London: Sedgwick and Jackson, 1973.

Henry, Françoise. *Irish Art.* 3 vols. Ithaca: Cornell University Press, 1965-1970.

Hayes, Richard. *Manuscript Sources for the History of Irish Civilization.* 11 vols. Boston: G.K. Hall, 1965. Supplement I (1965-1975). Boston: G.K.Hall, 1979.

Hayes, Richard F. *Irish Swordsmen of France.* Dublin: Gill, 1934.

Hogan, Edmund. *Onomasticon Goedelicum locorum et tribuum Hiberniae et Scotiae.* Dublin, 1910; reprint Dublin: Four Courts Press, 1993.

Hoppen, K. Theodore. *Ireland since 1800: Conflict and Conformity.* London: Longman, 1989.

Hughes, Kathleen. *Early Christian Ireland: Introduction to the Sources.* New York: Cornell University Press, 1972.

Hyland, C. P. "Father Jeremiah O Callaghan, A Man of Principle." *MFCJ* 17 (1999): 135-140.

Jackson, Alvin. *Ireland 1798-1998: Politics and War.* Oxford: Blackwell, 1999.

Johnson, Swift Paine, and T. A. Lanham, eds. "On a Manuscript Description of the City and County of Cork, cir. 1685." *JRSAI* 32 (1902): 361-362.

Johnston, Edith Mary. *Ireland in the Eighteenth Century.* Dublin: Gill, 1974.

Johnston-Liik, Mary. *History of the Irish Parliament 1692-1800.* 6 vols. Belfast: Ulster Historical Foundation, 2002-2003.

Joyce, P. W. *The Origin and History of Irish Names of Places.* 3 vols. Dublin: 1901-1913; reprint New York: Blom, 1968.

Kavanagh, John J. *A Sense of History and Heritage of Kilshannig and Surrounds.* Kanturk: Kanturk Printers, 1996.

_____ "The Antiquities of Kilshannig." *MFCJ* 1 (1983): 39-50.

_____ "Excerpts from the History of Kilshannig." *MFCJ* 2 (1984): 55-69.

_____ "Some Kilshannig Place Names." *MFCJ* 5 (1987): 30-33.

_____ "Some Places and Names in Duhallow." *SD* 7 (1989): 89-96.

_____ "Kilshannig: The Changing Times." *MFCJ* 8 (1990): 82-94.

_____ "Kilshannig, Mythology, Tales and Beliefs." *MFCJ* 9 (1991): 15-22.

Kelly, John S. *The Bodyke Evictions.* Scariff, Co. Clare: Fossabeg Press, 1987.

Laffan, Thomas. "Fethard, County Tipperary. Its Charters and Corporation Records, with some Notice of the Fethard Everards." *JRSAI* 36 (1906) 143-153.

Large, David. "Irish House of Commons in 1769." *Irish Historical Studies* 11 (1958-1959): 18-28

Larkin, Emmet. *The Roman Catholic Church and the Creation of the Modern Irish State 1878-1886.* Philadelphia: University of Pennsylvania Press, 1975.

_____ *The Roman Catholic Church in Ireland and the Fall of Parnell, 1888-1891.* Chapel Hill, NC: University of North Carolina Press, 1979.

Lenihan, Pádraig, *Confederate Catholics at War, 1641-1649.* Cork: University Press, 2001.

Lewis, Samuel. *A Topographical Dictionary of Ireland.* 2 vols. London: S. Lewis, 1837.

Linehan, Michael P. *My Heart Remembers How, being the Story of Muscraidhe O Donegan.* Dublin: J. Duffy, 1944.

Lucas, A. T. *Treasures of Ireland: Irish Pagan and Early Christian Art.* New York: Viking, 1974.

MacCarthy, C. J. F. "Seanchas." *MFCJ* 5 (1987): 138-154; 8 (1990): 101-110.

_____ "Some Researches in Ancient Irish Law: A Complementary Note." *JCHAS* 54(1949): 11-16.

MacCarthy, Jean J. "The Ancient and Noble Families of Duhallow." *SD* 10 (1996): 63-73.

MacLysaght, Edward. *Irish Families: Their Names, Arms, and Origins.* 3d ed. New York: Crown, 1972.

_____ *The Surnames of Ireland.* Dublin: Irish Academic Press, 1980.

MacNeill, Eoin. *Celtic Ireland.* Dublin: M. Lester, 1921.

_____ *Phases of Irish History.* Dublin: Gill, 1919.

Magner, Thomas F. "Irish Convicts in America and Australia. *MFCJ* 13 (1995): 116-131.

Mahr, Adolf and Joseph Raftery. *Christian Art in Ancient Ireland.* 2 vols. Dublin: Stationery Office of Saorstat Eireann, 1932-1941.

McCaffrey, Lawrence J. *The Irish Diaspora in America.* Bloomington: Indiana University Press, 1976.

McCarthy, Donogh. "Mass Rocks and Altar Sites in Duhallow." *SD* 8 (1991): 83-97.

McCarthy, William P. "The Litigious Earl." *JCHAS* 70 (1965): 7-13.

McCartney, Donal. "From Parnell to Pearse (1891-1921)." In Moody and Martin, *Course,* 294-312.

McCuaig, Carol Bennett. "Farewell to Old Ireland: The Voyage of the 'John Barry.'" *MFCJ* 13 (1995): 137-150.

MacDermott, Anthony. "The Irish Regiments in the Spanish Service." *TIG* 2:9 (1952): 259-268.

McDowell, R. B. "The Protestant Nation (1775-1800)." In Moody and Martin, *Course,* 232-247.

McLaughlin, Mark. *The Wild Geese: The Irish Brigades of France and Spain.* London: Osprey, 1980.

McNamara, Maedhbh, and Paschal Mooney. *Women in Parliament 1918-2000.* Dublin: Wolfhound Press, 2000.

McOwan, Rennie. "Alasdair MacDonald." *SD* 11 (1997):11-14.

Meagher, Jim. "Duhallow's Hidden Coal Wealth." *SD* 2 (1976-77): 25-28.

Meehan, Charles P. *The Confederation of Kilkenny.* New ed. Dublin: J. Duffy, 1882.

Michell, John. *Eccentric Lives and Peculiar Notions.* Secaucus, NJ: Citadel Press, 1989.

Miller, Francis Trevelyan. *History of World War II.* Philadelphia, 1945.

Moody, T. W. "Fenianism, Home Rule and the Land War (1850-1901)." In Moody and Martin, *Course,* 275-293.

Moody, T. W., and F. X. Martin, ed. *The Course of Irish History.* Cork: Mercier, 1967.

Mooney, Canice. *Irish Franciscans and France.* Dublin: Clonmore and Reynolds, 1964.

Moran, Gerard. *Sending out Ireland's Poor: Assisted Emigration to North America in the 19th Century.* Dublin: Four Courts Press, 2004.

Mullins, Mary. "Colonel John O Callaghan - Landlord of Bodyke," Local Ireland: Clare: Bodyke; www.clarelibrary.ie colas coclarehistory bodyke

Murphy, F. X. *Fighting Admiral: The Story of Dan Callaghan.* New York: Vantage, 1952.

Murphy, Pat. *The View from Mount Hillary: A Chronicle History of Banteer, Lyre and Duhallow from 1886 to 2003.* Banteer: Pat and Eileen Murphy 2003.

Nicholls, Kenneth. *Gaelic and Gaelicised Ireland in the Middle Ages.* Dublin: Gill, 1972.

Nolan, William, and Thomas McGrath. *Tipperary History and Society: Interdisciplinary Essays on the History of an Irish County.* Templeogue, Dublin: Geography Publications, 1985.

Oakland, John. "Irish Officers in the Spanish Service: V. The Regiment of Irlanda (concluded)." *TIG* 6:2 (1982): 328-333.

O Brien, Donough. *History of efthe O Briens from Brian Boroimhe, A.D. 1000 to A.D. 1945.* London: Batsford, 1949.

O Brien, William, and Desmond Ryan. *Devoy's Post Bag, 1871-1928,* 2 vols. Dublin: Academy Press, 1948.

Ó Buachalla, Liam. "Some Researches in Ancient Irish Law." *JCHAS* 53 (1948): 1-12. x75-78.

O Brien, Niall. "Roger Brettridge, the 1662 Act of Settlement and Duhallow Affairs at the Court of Claims." *Seanchas Dúthalla* 25 (2011): 10-16.

O Callaghan, Antóin. *The Lord Mayors of Cork, 1900 to 2000.* Cork: Inversnaid Publications, 2000.

O Callaghan, Jeremiah. *Usury or Interest proved to be repugnant to the Divine and Ecclesiastical Laws and Destructive to Civil Society.* London, C. Clement, 1825.

O Callaghan, John Cornelius. *A History of the Irish Brigades in the Service of France from the Revolution in Great Britain and Ireland under James II to the Revolution in France under Louis XVI,* Cameron and Ferguson Edition. Glasgow: R. & T. Washbourne, 1870.

O Callaghan, John. *A New Song on the Recapture of Orleans by the French.* Dublin: P. Brereton, 1871.

O Callaghan, José, S.J. *El nuevo testamento en las versiones españolas.* Rome: Biblical Institute, 1982.

_____ *La vida en los primeros siglos según las cartas cristianas.* San

Cugat del Vallés: Papyrologica Castrooctaviana, 1964.

_____ "¿Papiros neotestamentarios en la cueva 7 de Qumran?" *Biblica* 53 (1972): 91-100.

O Callaghan, Joseph F. "The O Callaghans and the Rebellion of 1641." *JCHAS* 95 (1990): 30-40.

_____ "The O Callaghans of Killcranathan, County Cork." *JCHAS* 92 (1987): 106-112.

O Callaghan, Kathleen. *The Limerick Curfew Murders of 7 March 1921: The Case of Michael O Callaghan, Councilor and ex-Mayor presented by his Widow* N.p.n.d.

Michael O Callaghan, 1879-1921: First Republican Mayor of Limerick 1920. Requiescat. Dublin: Dun Emer Press, 1921.

O Callaghan, M. Murray. "A Fenian Officer: Captain Edward O Meagher Condon and his American Envoy Visit Millstreet." *SD* 2 (1876-77): 53-58.

O Callaghan, Roger Timothy, S. J. *Aram Naharaim. A Contribution to the History of Upper Mesopotamia in the Second Millenium B.C.* Rome: Pontificum Institutum Biblicum, 1948.

O Callaghan, Seán. *Down by the Glenside: Memoirs of an Irish Boyhood.* Cork: Mercier, 1992.

_____ *Execution.* London: Muller 1974.

_____ *The Easter Lily: Story of the IRA.* London: Wingate, 1956.

_____ *The Jack Boot in Ireland.* London, 1958.

O Callaghan, Seán. *The Informer: The Real Life Story of One Man's War against Terrorism.* London: Corgi, 1999.

O Callaghan, Joseph Timothy, S.J. *I Was Chaplain on the Franklin.* New York: Macmillan, 1956.

Ó Ciardha, Eamonn. *Ireland and the Jacobite Cause, 1685-1766: A Fatal Attachment.* Dublin: Four Courts Press, 2002.

O Connell, Basil. "Catherine O Mullane, Mrs. O Connell, mother of Daniel O Connell, the Liberator." *TIG* 2:10 (1953): 311-316.

O Connell, Mary Anne Bianconi. *The Last Colonel of the Irish Brigade. Count O Connell and Old Irish Life at Home and Abroad.* 2 vols. London: Kegan, Paul, Trench, 1892.

Ó Corráin, Donncha. *Ireland before the Normans.* Dublin: Gill, 1972.

_____ "*Caithréim Chellacháin Chaisil*: History or Propaganda?" *Eriu* 24 (1974): 1-69.

_____ and Fidelma Maguire. *Irish Names.* Dublin: Lilliput, 1990.

Ó Dálaigh, Brian. *The Stranger's Gaze: Travels in County Clare, 1534-1950.* Ennis: Clasp Press, 1998.

O Donnell, Patrick. *The Irish Faction Fighters in the Nineteenth Century.* Dublin: Anvil, 1975.

O Donovan, R. "To Hell or to Clare: Donogh O Callaghan, Chief of his Name, A Transplanter." *The Other Clare* 9 (1985): 68-75.

Ó Faoláin, Seán. *King of the Beggars: A Life of Daniel O Connell, the Irish Liberator in a Study of the Rise of Modern Irish Democracy (1775-1847).* New York: Viking, 1938.

O Ferrall, E. G. More. "The Dispossessed Landowners of Ireland 1664. Part II. Munster and Ulster." *TIG* 4 (1972): 434-436.

O Ferrall, Fergus. *Catholic Emancipation: Daniel O Connell and the Birth of Irish Democracy, 1820-1830.* Dublin: Gill and Macmillan, 1985.

O Flanagan, James Roderick. *The Blackwater in Munster.* London: J. How, 1844.

O Flanagan, Patrick, and Cornelius G. Buttimer. *Cork History and Society: Interdisciplinary Essays in the History of an Irish County.* Dublin: Geography Publications, 1993.

O Hart, John. *Irish Pedigrees or the Origin and Stem of the Irish Nation.* 2 vols. New York: Murphy & McCarthy, 1923.

_____ *The Irish and Anglo-Irish Landed Gentry when Cromwell came to Ireland.* Dublin, 1884; reprint as *The Irish and Anglo-Irish Gentry.* New York: Barnes and Noble, 1969.

O Kelly, Charles. *Macariae Excidium.* Ed.and tr. John Cornelius O Callaghan. In *Narratives Illustrative of the Contests in Ireland (1641-1690).* Ed. Thomas Crofton Croker. London: Camden Society Publications, vol. 14, 1841.

O Leary, John. *Recollections of Fenians and Fenianism,* 2 vols. London, 1896; reprint New York: Barnes and Noble, 1969.

O Leary, Joseph S. "The Irish and Jansenism in the Seventeenth Century." In Swords. *The Irish-French Connection.* 21-43.

O Leary, Peter. *My Story.* Trans. Cyril Ó Céirín. Oxford: Oxford University Press, 1987.

O Mahony, Colman. *In The Shadows: Life in Cork, 1750-1930.* Cork: Tower, 1997.

Ó Muimneacháin, Tadhg, and Mícheál Ó Léanacháin. "The Athletic and Historical Triangle." *SD* 10 (1996): 27-28.

O Murchadha, Diarmuid. *Family Names of County Cork.* Dún Laoghaire: Glendale Press, 1985.

_____ "The Formation of Gaelic Surnames in Ireland: Choosing the Eponyms." *Nomina. Journal of the Society for Name Studies in Britain and Ireland* 22 (1999): 25-44.

O Mullane, Denis. "Ballybahallow." *SD* 3 (1978-1979): 37-40.

Ó Riordáin, John J. "Investigating St. Latiaran of Cullen." *SD* 6 (1986): 31-35.

O Shea, James. *Priests, Politics and Society in Post-Famine Ireland: A Study of County Tipperary, 1850-1891.* Dublin: Wolfhound Press, 1983.

Ó Siochrú, Micheál. *Confederate Ireland, 1642-1649: A Constitutional and Political Analysis.* Dublin: Four Courts Press, 1999.

O Sullivan, Patrick S. "Papist and Protestant in Wild Goose Time." *SD* 4 (1980-81): 96-97.

_____ "The 1847 Crisis within Kanturk Union." *SD* 11 (1997): 37-46.

_____ "Out of Darkness 2: The Fight for the Land 1850-1882: Tenant Right and Land League." *SD* 13 (2003): 63-71.

Patterson, Nerys. *Cattle, Lords, and Clansmen. The Social Structure of Early Ireland.* 2d ed. Notre Dame, Ind.: University of Notre Dame Press, 1994.

Perceval- Maxwell, M. *The Outbreak of the Irish Rebellion of 1641.* Montreal: McGill-Queen's University Press, 1994.

Pigot & Co.'s Directory 1824 – Cork City, Co. Cork; Kanturk.

"Pigott's Directory 1824." *MFCJ* 8 (1990): 137-140.

Bibliography

Piveronous, Peter J. "Sir Warham St. Leger and the First Munster Plantation, 1568-1569." *Eire-Ireland* 14 (1979):

Power, Denis. "Dromaneen Castle: An O Callaghan Stronghold." *MFCJ* 17 (1999): 5-17.

Power, Patrick C. *History of South Tipperary*. Cork: Mercier, 1989.

Power, Thomas P. *Land, Politics, and Society in Eighteenth-Century Tipperary*. Oxford: Clarendon Press, 1993.

Quinn, D. B. "The Munster Plantation: Problems and Opportunities," *JCHAS* 71 (1966):

Roberts, Paul E. W. "Caravats and Shanavests: Whiteboyism and Faction Fighting in East Munster 1802-11." In Samuel Clark and James S. Donnelly. *Irish Peasants, Violence and Poltical Unrest, 1780-1914*. Madison: University of Wisconsin Press, 1983.

Ryan, John. "The Historical Content of *Caithréim Ceallacháin Chaisil*." *JRSAI* 71 (1941): 89-100.

Pawlisch, Hans S. *Sir John Davies and the Conquest of Ireland. A Study in Legal Imperialism*. Cambridge: Cambridge University Press, 1985.

Petrie, George. *Christian Inscriptions in the Irish Language*, 2 vols. Dublin, 1872-1878.

P.[urcell], R. J. "Jeremiah O Callaghan." *Dictionary of American Biography* 13:613-614.

Roche, Christy. "Mallow and the Robinson Settlements." *MFCJ* 8 (1990): 52-59.

"St. James's Cemetery, Mallow." *MFCJ* 8 (1990): 141-162.

"St. Mary's Cemetery, Mallow." *MFCJ* 13 (1995): 151-168.

Sadleir, T. N. "The Register of Kilkenny School (1685-1800)." *JRSAI* 54 (1924): 152-169.

"Salute to a Sporting Legend: Dr. Pat O Callaghan." *SD* 9 (1993): 7.

Shaw, Francis Guy. *Edmund Bailey O Callaghan: A Study in American Historiography (1797-1880)*. Washington: Catholic University of America, 1934.

Sheehan, A. J. "The Population of the Plantation of Munster: Quinn reconsidered." *JCHAS* 87 (1982):

Shoosmith, Teresa. *Settlement and Social Change in the Barony of Tulla, c. 1650-1845*. Galway: Nationl University of Ireland, 2015.

Silke, John. *Kinsale. The Spanish Intervention in Ireland at the End of the Elizabethan Wars*. New York: Fordham University Press, 1970.

_____ "The Irish Abroad in the age of the Counter-Reformation, 1534-1691," *NHI*, 3:587-633.

Simms, J. G. *Jacobite Ireland, 1685-1691*. Dublin: Four Courts Press, 2000.

_____ *War and Politics in Ireland, 1649-1730*. London: Hambledon Press, 1986.

_____ "The Restoration, 1660-85," *NHI*, 3:420-453.

_____ "The Restoration and the Jacobite War," in Moody and Martin, *Course*, 204-216.

_____ "The War of the Two Kings, 1685-91." *NHI*, 3:478-508.

Simms, Katharine. *From Kings to Warlords: The Changing Political Structure of Gaelic Ireland in the Later Middle Ages*. Wolfeboro, NH: Boydell, 1987.

Slater's National Commercial Directory of Ireland 1846 – Kanturk.

Sleeman, Mary. "A Lost Tradition: The Forgotten Kiln." *MFCJ* 8 (1990): 95-100.

Smith, Charles. *The Ancient and Present State of the County and City of Cork*. 2 vols. Cork: John Connor, 1815.

Stokes, Margaret. *Early Christian Art in Ireland*. Dublin: Chapman and Hall, 1894.

Swords, Liam, ed. *The Irish-French Connection, 1578-1978*. Paris: The Irish College, 1978.

Tansill, Charles Callan. *America and the Fight for Irish Freedom: An Old Story based on New Data*. New York: Devin-Adair, 1957.

Tarrant, Con. "Alaster MacDonnell," *SD* 2 (1976-77): 38-42.

_____ "House Building: Its Art and Culture in Duhallow over the past 150 Years." *SD* 4 (1980-81): 64-66.

_____ "How the Planting of Clonmeen Failed," *SD* 7 (1989): 39-40.

_____ "Matchmaking in Duhallow at the Turn of the Century." *SD* 4 (1980-81): 14-16.

_____ "Terror and Counter-Terror." *SD* 7 (1989): 81-84.

_____ "The Battle of Knockbrack," *SD* 6 (1986): 54-56.

_____ "The Chieftains of Pobul Uí Cheallacháin, Co. Cork." *SD* 5 (1984): 19-27.

Treasures of Early Irish Art, 1500 B.C. to 1500 A.D. New York: Metropolitan Museum of Art, 1977.

Tuckey, Francis H. *The County and City of Cork Remembrancer or Annals of the County and City of Cork*. Cork: O. Savage & Son, 1837.

Verney, Jack. *O Callaghan: The Making and Unmaking of a Rebel*. Ottowa: Carleton University 1994.

_____ "Edmund Bailey O Callaghan, Rebel and Writer." *MFCJ* 5 (1987): 79-101.

Wall, Thomas. "Irish Enterprize in the University of Paris, 1651-1653." *Irish Ecclesiastical Record*. Series 5, 74(1944): 94-106, 159-172.

Wall, Maureen. "The Age of the Penal Laws (1691-1778)." In Moody and Martin, *Course*, 217-231.

Walsh, Micheline. *Spanish Knights of Irish Origin: Documents from Continental Archives*. 3 vols. Dublin: Irish Manuscripts Commission, 1970.

Walsh, Thomas. *History of the Irish Hierarchy*. New York: Sadleir, 1854.

Watt, John. *The Church in Medieval Ireland*. Dublin: Gill and Macmillan, 1972.

Westropp, T. J. "The Colpoys of Ballycarn." *JRSAI* 28 (1898): 71-72.

Woodham-Smith, Cecil. The Great Hunger: Ireland 1845-49. London: NEL 1970.

Aldworth, Sir Richard, 106

Barry family, 19, 23; Barry Mór, 20, 23, 24, 25, 37; Barrymore, Lord, 44, 107; Barry Óg, 23, 24, 26, 37; David, 16; David, archdeacon of Cloyne, 20; General, 77, 85, 94; John, sheriff, 51; Nicholas, 16; Robert, bishop of Cork, 97; Thomas, 20; William, 101
Barton family, 153, 158
Bellings, Richard, 80, 84, 97, 98, 99
Bettesworth, Thomas, 59, 75, 78
Blunte, Sir James, 67
Brettridge, Roger, 89, 91, 93, 94, 102, 187, 190
Brian Boru, 2, 5, 6, 7, 8
Brisacier, Jean, Jesuit, 98
Broghill, Lord, 69, 84, 117
Burghley, Lord, 19
Butler family, 18, 75; James, lord of Dunboyne, 62, 72; Joanna, wife of Callaghan O Callaghan, 63, 72, 117, 219; William, historian, 50. See Ormond

Callaghan, Charles, of Ballynamona, 69; Cornelius of Carragoon, 109, Adm. Daniel, 215, 216; Daniel, Cork merchant, 102, 162-163; Daniel, M.P., 163-164; Daniel, refusal to testify against Bishop Creagh, 106; Gerard, M.P., 163-164; George, 175; Adm. George, 216; James, priest of Armagh, 105; John, priest, Jansenist, 95-99; Neale, tory, 105; Owen, priest, 105; Thady of Carrignameragh, 69; Thady, agent for Lord Kilmallock, 108; Adm. William, 215, 216; Gen. William, 199-2022
Callaghan Ranch, 208
Callahan, James Hughes, Texas Ranger, 208
Carew, Sir George, 34, 45, 46, 47

Castlehaven, earl of, 76, 77, 83
Cecil, Sir Robert, 45
Cellachán, king of Cashel, 2-9, 11, 14, 70, 73, 157, 220
Charles I, 59, 68, 72, 74, 78, 81, 83, 85, 87, 103, 113, 119
Charles II, 83, 84, 87, 95, 100, 102, 103, 104, 106, 119
Chichester, Sir Arthur, 54
Chinnery, Lieut. John, 74, 94, 101, 102, 105, 147; Nicholas, 147
Clare, Lord, 102, 107, 136
Cliodhna, fairy, 16, 17, 138, 139
Condon, Edmond, of Marshaltown, 69, 70; Edward, Fenian, 192; Joanna, 117
Corkery, Daniel, historian, 139
Coppinger, Walter, 5, 59; William, bishop of Cloyne, 171
Corish, Patrick, historian, 83, 95, 97, 98
Cosabone, Capt. Thomas, 101
Creagh, Bishop Pierse, 106
Croke, Archbishop Thomas, 192
Croker, Thomas Crofton, 127, 165
Cromwell, Oliver, 84, 87, 93, 99, 161

Dál Cais, 2, 4, 5, 6, 7
Davies, Sir John, 33, 48, 49, 52; 53; family, 151
Davitt, Michael, 183
De hÓir, Eamonn, historian, 23
De Valera, Eamon, 195, 197
Delany, bishop of Cork, 192, 193
Devoy, John, Fenian, 192
Donnchadh, king of Cashel, 7, 8
Drury, Sir William, 36
Dwyer, Gen. Anthony, 115; Dermot, Jesuit, 96

Elizabeth, Queen, 19, 24, 26, 32, 34, 36, 38, 39, 43, 48, 49, 50, 52, 53, 60, 70, 72, 117, 143
Eoghanacht, 2, 4, 5, 6, 7, 8, 9, 10, 12, 13
Everard, Sir Redmond, 153; Sir Richard, 82
Essex, earl of, 45, 51

Fenton, Dame Elizabeth, 89, 90, 91,
    93, 94, 145; Sir William, 59
FitzGerald family; earls of Desmond, 13,
    18, 19, 22, 23, 24, 26, 36, 38;
    Desmond's Revolt, 35-39; earls
    of Kildare, 18, 20, 22; Edmond,
    lord of Clonlish, 34; Edmond of
    Ballymartyr, 73; James
    FitzThomas, 44, 45; John
    FitzEdmond, sheriff, 56
FitzGibbon, Ellen, 14; David, 28; Gerald
    FitzThomas, 34; John, 28
FitzMaurice, Sir James, 22, 23, 24, 26,
    36, 38; Maurice FitzThomas, 23
Forbes, Lord, 77

Gillman family, 151; Herbert, historian,
    20, 24, 28, 33, 43, 45, 50, 58, 60,
    68
Gould, James, justice, 39; Nicholas Fitz
    Christopher, 54, 55; Thomas,
    solicitor, 39; Thomas
    FitzWilliam, 62, 63
Grehan family, 149; George, 182, 191
Grey, Leonard, 22

Henry VII, 20
Henry VIII, 22, 23, 24
Hingston, John, rector of Clonmeen,
    132, 134, 168

James I, 48, 52, 54, 55, 56, 66, 67, 72
James II, 69, 86, 106, 107, 108, 109,
    110, 111, 112, 113, 117, 119,
    126, 132, 136, 144, 158
James III, 118, 119
Jephson, Sir John, 56; Mary, 101

Kavanagh, John, historian, 61, 178
Keating, Geoffrey, historian, xiii, 153
Kilmallock, Lord, see Dominick
    Sarsfield
King, Paul, priest, 97
Kingston, Lord, 88, 89, 90, 91,
    92, 93, 94, 102, 144, 145, 157
Kyrle, Sir Richard, 88, 89, 94,

101, 145, 146

Lacy, Maria Francisca, 122; Robert,
    bishop of Limerick, 131; Col.
    William, 120, 121, 122
Lismore, Baron, Viscount, 128, 143,
    150, 158, 159, 161, 167, 168,
    177, 182, 183, 184, 191, 201,
    202, 203, 204, 222
Lombard, David, 63; Edmond, 167;
    James, 62, 63; Nicholas, 63;
    William, 88, 89, 90, 932
Longfield, John, 69, 91, 166, 197;
    Richard, 182, 183
Louis XIV, king of France, 80, 111, 112,
    113, 114, 122
Ludlow, Gen. Edmund, 78, 84, 86

MacAuliffe, 11, 12, 18, 19, 24, 27,
    36, 37, 45; John, 46; Teige, 77
MacCallaghan, see Callaghan, John
MacCallaghans of Muskerry, 11-13,
    27, 70, 87, 95, 107, 108, 171,
    220; Owen, 126; Callaghan, Lt.
    Col., of Caherlag, 109, 110, 124.
MacCarthy (MacCarthaigh), Callaghan
    of Carrignamuck, 59; Cormac,
    king, 6, 9; Denis, bishop of Cork,
    118; Domhnall, king, 8; Tadhg,
    king, 9; Teige McOwen of
    Drishane, 39
MacCarthy Mór, 18, 22, 23, 24, 33, 45,
    54, 62, 219; Donal, earl of
    Clancarthy, 18, 22, 34, 53, 116;
    Florence, 45, 62
MacCarthy of Muskerry
    Cormac Óg, 22, 24, 26; Cormac
    McTeige, sheriff, 28, 37;
    Cormac, Viscount Muskerry, 70;
    Donough, Viscount Muskerry,
    76, 81- 83, 97, 119;
    Joan nyTeige, wife of Cahir O
    Callaghan, 73
MacCarthy Reagh, 18, 23, 37
MacDonnell, Alasdair MacColla, 73, 81,
    82, 91, 92

MacDonough MacCarthy, 18, 19, 24, 169, 173; Dermot, 74, 75, 79, 80; Donough 21,24

MacNeill, Eoin, historian, 4, 7

MacSweeney, Brian McOwen, 49, 50, 51, 52, 53, 54, 63; Denis, priest of Carrigadrohid, 117; , wife of Conor of the Rock, 34, 45, 56, 62; Turlough Bacach, 34, 50

MacSwiney, Terence, mayor of Cork, 196, 197

Mangan, James Clarence, 35

Mountgarret, Lord, 74, 76, 77, 79, 97

Muirchertach mac Néill, 2, 3

Neville, Msgr., 192, 193

Newman, John, 182; Richard, 69, 88, 89, 94, 101, 145

Normans, 5, 12, 13, 15, 16, 48, 74

Norris, Sir Thomas, 39, 43, 44, 56

Norsemen, 2, 4, 5, 6, 15

O Brien, Gen. Arthur, 117; Donal, earl of Lismore, 112; Morrogh, baron of Inchiquin, 77, 78, 81, 82, dking her em,ail now.83; Muirchertach Ua Bríain, 7; Gen. Murrough O Brien, 112

O Callaghan, Ambrose, bishop of Ferns, 129-130; Brian McOwen, 50; Cahir of Leatherdon, 103, 109, 112, 116, 218, 221; Cahir Modarta, 29, 44, 50, 51, 59, 69, 72, 73, 75, 76, 113, 160, 220; Callaghan McConoghor, chieftain, 26, 28-29, 32, 45, 50, 51, 52, 53, 62; Callaghan, brother of Donough Mór, 73-87,100, 101; Callaghan, son of Conor of the Rock, chieftain, 62-64; Ceadach, son of Conor of the Rock, priest, 65; Christy, of Tincoora, song, 195; Conor of the Rock, chieftain, 32-47, 48-58, 59, 62, 65, 66, 67, 68, 69, 103, 143, 229; Conoghor Reagh, agent of Sir Philip Perceval, 75-80, 100, 127, 162; Cornelius, attorney, of Tipperary, 151-156; Cornelius, first baron Lismore, 128, 158-159; Cornelius, second baron Lismore, viscount Lismore, 161, 201-202; Cornelius, Sr., of Banteer, 136-142; Cornelius, of Liscullane, 142; Cornelius, J.P, Millstreet, 192; Daniel, chieftain, 16, 137-140; Denis, canon of Mallow, 219; Dermot, prior of Ballybeg. 33, 66; Dermot McWogny, vicar of Kilshannig, 64; Dionisio, knight of Alcántara, 118-122; Donal, governor of Nevada, 216; Donal Óg, mayor of Cork, 196-198; Donnchadh, chieftain, 22-28, 50, 53, 54; Donough, Franciscan, 16; Donough Mór, chieftain, 72-94, 100-104, 107, 108, 116, 134-136, 142-143, 205, 221; Donough Óg, chieftain, 74, 103-104, 107-109, 134-137, 144; Donough McTeige McConoghor, 50; Edmond, chieftain, 140-142, 184, 205; Edmund Bailey, historian, 208-210; Eleanor, wife of Art O Keeffe, 50, 54; Ellen of Clonmeen, wife of Donough Mór. 71, 72, 84, 97, 101, 212; Eugene, priests' champion, 210-211; Francis Langford, engineer, 216; George, of Bodyke, 184; George Ponsonby, viscount Lismore, 201; Irrelagh. of Pallas and Roskeen, 26, 27, 34, 38, 41, 66-68; Irrelagh, grandson of Irrelagh, 77, 87, 103; J. J., architect, 216; James, Fenian, 191; James, priest, assassinated, 194; Jeremiah, priest, opponent of usury, 171-172; Jeremiah, poor law guardian, 165; Jerry, Irish volunteer, 194; John, balladeer, 216; John, Fenian, 191; John, awarded Medal of Honor, 208; Col. John, of Bodyke, 185-187; John Cornelius, historian, xiv, 203; José, Jesuit, biblical scholar. 206-207; Juan, chieftain, 218, 219; Julian, governor of Balaguer, 116, 119-122, 221; Kathleen, widow of Michael, mayor of Limerick, 196; Kennedy, nephew of Donough Mór, 74, 101; Leo, Irish volunteer, 194; Mathew, knight of Santiago, 117-118; Michael, mayor of Limerick, 195-196; Michael, of Tipperary, 194; Michael, proprietor of Longueville, 198, 219; Murrough McBrian, plaintiff, tanistry case, 50-52; Owen of Dromore, 23, 67; Patrick, Olympic athlete, 198-199; Ramón, claimant to chieftainship, 205; Ramón, Carlist leader, 205-206; Ramón, historian, 206; Robert, the elder, of Banteer, 132, 145-146; Robert, the younger, of Banteer, 146-150; Robert of Tipperary, 156-157; Robert William, general, 159, 203; Roger, biblical scholar, 214; Seán, IRA informer, 199; Seán, journalist, 195; Síle (Sheila) of Kilcranathan, xv, 137; Teige, balladeer, 216; Teige, "conde de Clanscarti," 119; Teige, of Coolroe More, 69, 144, 146, 148, 151; Teige na Muchorie, tanist, 26, 41, 66; Teige Reagh, of Rossline and Ballybahallagh, 109, 127; Teige Roe, chieftain, 20-24, 26-28, 33, 38,41, 45, 50, 55, 66-70; Capt. Thady, envoy to France, 118, 122; Capt. Thady, of Clare, 135-137; Thomas of Shanbally, 158-159; Thomas Alphonsus, bishop of Cork, 192-194; Thomas O Donnell, Fenian, 191; Wilfrid, M.P., 1913; William, proprietor of Longueville, 197-198; William, chef, Longueville, 217; William, of Dromcummer, 211-213

O Callaghan-Westropp, George, 217-218; Rosemary, 217

O Callaghan's Country, 15, 16, 19, 22, 23, 27, 35, 41, 42, 45, 46, 53, 54, 56, 57, 63, 65, 75, 128, 162, 170, 174, 178, 182, 220

O Callaghans, of Baden-Baden, 112-113; of Banteer, 69, 136-143; of Carrigadrohid, 70, 95, 117, 122; of Carrignavar, 70, 118-119; of Clare, 134-142; of Dromcummer, 211-213; of Dromskehy, 150-151; of Glynn, 150-151; of Gortmore and Ballymacmurragh, 67; of Kilcranathan, 41, 68, 81, 91, 94, 112, 144; of Kilpadder, 68; of Liscullane, Lismehane, 142; of Pallas, 65-66; of Rathmore, 65; of Roskeen, 68; of Spain, 103, 112-116, 205-207; of Tipperary, 151-1597; converts, 160; in census of 1766, 132-133. 149; in French service, 111, 127, 135; in Griffith's Valuation, 179, 189, 201; in James II's army, 107-108; in Spanish army, 113-116; in Spanish Military Orders, 116-122; in Tithe Applotment Books, 167-171; in towns, 173-176; landowners in 1870, 181-172; outlawed in 1689, 108; peasants, 124-126, 128-129, 164-166; priests and schoolmasters, 128-132; repeal rent contributors, 175; restored to estates, 109; tories and rapparees, 126; transplanted to Clare, 67, 86-87,

102, 103, 112, 134, 140, 221

O Callahan, Joseph, Medal of Honor, 213

O Connell, Daniel, 156, 157, 168, 189, 194; Denis, 160; Maurice, 150; Richard, 150; Owen, 126

Ó Corráin, Donnchad, historian, 8

Ó Dálaigh, Aongus, poet, 34

O Donnell, Hugh Roe, 44

O Donovan, Donal, chieftain, 39; John, historian, 21, 102

O Ferrall, Richard, historian, 98

O Garvan, Conoghor Óg, 56, 60; Donough, 56; Teige, 56

O Hartigan, Matthew, Jesuit, 96

O Keeffe, 12, 18, 19, 23, 24, 28, 30, 36, 37, 39, 44, 45, 53; Art, chieftain, 50, 53, 54, 67; Daniel of Dromagh, 60, 63, 73, 74, 75, 145; Ellen wife of Irrelagh O Callaghan, 67; Manus, chieftain, 50, 53, 54; Manus of Knocknagehy, 126

O Mahony family, 11, 12, 13; Conor, chieftain, 37

O More, Owny MacRory, 51; Rory, 74

O Mullane, Dermot, 145; Jean-Baptiste, 108; John, 86, 86

Ó Muirgheasáin, Maol Domhnaigh, poet, 73

Ó Murchadha, Diarmuid, historian, xiv, xv, xvi, 68

O Neill, Felim, 74; Hugh, earl of Tyrone, 22, 44-45; Owen Roe, 80, 81, 82, 111

O Rahilly, Egan, poet, 1, 17, 133, 134

O Sullivan, Humphrey, 125

O Sullivan Beare, 24, 25, 37; O Sullivan More, 24, 25

Oates, Titus, 104

Ormond, earl of, 18, 24, 37, 73, 77, 78, 80, 81, 82, 83, 93, 194; duke of, 99, 103, 104, 105, 113, 115

Orrery, Roger Boyle, earl of, 101, 104, 126

Parnell, Charles Stewart, 183, 184, 194

Pelham, Sir William, 37

Perceval, Sir John, 55, 69, 87, 123, 144; Sir Philip, 59, 69, 77, 78, 79, 80, 94, 97, 100, 190, 127

Petty, Sir William, 71, 87, 89, 90, 94, 103, 145, 176

Phaire, Emmanuel, 65, 76; Robert, 69, 85

Philip V, king of Spain, 114, 115, 118, 120, 121, 122

Pilkington, Laetitia, 158

Plunkett, Archbishop Oliver, 105

Power, Denis, archaeologist, 61

Redmond, John, 194

Reymond, Capt. Thomas, 78

Rinuccini, Archbishop Giovanni Battista, 80, 81, 82, 83, 94, 95, 96, 97; *Commentarius Rinucinnianus*, 97

Roche, 19, 23, 24, 25, 26, 32, 36, 37; James, 63; Katherine, 28, 32, 33; David, Viscount of Fermoy, 59; Maurice, Viscount of Fermoy, 28, 45, 57, 75, 76, 843; Maurice, 61

St. Lachtín, 9, 15, 188, 220

St. Leger, John, 69, 89; Sir William, 59, 76

Sarsfield, Sir Dominick, 53, 108

Saxey, William, chief justice, 39, 51

Shaftesbury, earl of, 104, 105

Sidney, Sir Henry, 27, 28

Smith, Charles, historian, 108, 125, 146

Spenser, Edmond, poet, 32, 37

Taafe, Lord, 81

Terry, James, King of Arms, 118

Tudors, 18, 20

Tyrconnell, earl of, Richard Talbot, 106, 112

Ua Cellacháin, Aed, king, 9; Cellachán,

8, 9; Domhnall, 9; Máel
   Sechnaill, king, 9-11, 220
Ua h-Uidhrín, Giolla na Naomh, 12
Uí Echach Muman, 9-11, 13, 221
Uí Néill, 2, 4, 5, 7

Wadding, Fr. Luke, 96
White, Anna Christina, 117, 118;
   Ignatius, 117, 118; Theresa, 116,
   118, 119; Winifred, 116, 118, 119
William of Orange, 107, 119, 145

Index of Places

Abbeydorney (Mainistir Ó dTorna), 64
Aldworth (Úllord, Owlert, Oulert
        Itallord; An tAbhallort), 40, 87,
        88, 101, 133, 169
Annagh (An t-Eanach), 36
Aughrim (Eachroim), battle of, 109, 112,
        144
Awbeg River (An Abha Bheag), 19, 69,
        149

Ballybahallagh (Béal Átha Bathlach),
        79, 80, 104, 128
Ballybeg (Baile Beag, Small Town),
        priory, 22, 33, 34, 64, 67, 77, 211
Ballycarty castle, 77
Ballyclough (Baile Cloch, Stone Town),
        12, 19, 23, 39, 77, 81, 87, 92, 93,
        128, 131, 167, 171, 180, 183
Ballyheen (Baile Choinn), 21, 27, 28,
        33, 40, 54, 94, 103
Ballyhest (Baile Hoiste), 54, 94
Ballymacmurragh (Baile Mhic
        Mhurchú, MacMurragh's Town),
        21, 38, 40, 41, 59, 62, 66, 67, 68,
        93, 95, 101
Ballynafeaha (Baile na Féithe), 40, 54,
        73, 92
Ballynamona (Baile na Móna,
        Moorestown), 69
Ballynoe (An Baile Nua, New Town), 42
Ballysimon (Baile Shíomoin), 134
Bandon (Droichead na Bandan), 131,
        162
Bannagh (An Bheannaigh), 93, 94, 149,
        150, 183
Banteer (Bán Tír), 16, 21, 26, 27, 28, 40,
        41, 42, 53, 56, 57, 58, 59, 62, 63,
        66, 67m 69, 79, 82, 84, 89, 90,
        91, 103, 127, 143, 144, 145, 147,
        150, 151, 152, 153, 158, 160,
        163, 169, 174, 192, 181, 183,
        200, 213, 222
Barnehely (Bearn na hÉille), 68, 127
Barretts, barony, 87
Bawnmore (An Bán Mór), 80
Barrinclay (Barr an tSléibhe;

Bearnyinclynowe, Bear Icanhin),
        42
Bearnymoher, 42
Byalahabwy (Bealachbuí), 40, 41
Benburb (An Bhinn Bhorb), battle, 81
Blackwater River (Abhann Mór), 12, 13,
        14, 16, 18, 19, 21, 22, 27, 29, 30,
        37, 38, 39, 40, 41, 42, 46, 56, 57,
        58, 60, 61,63, 65, 66, 67, 68, 72,
        84, 87, 89, 92, 93, 95, 105, 133,
        142, 140, 147, 148, 149, 169,
        171, 188, 198, 221, 223
Blarney (An Bhlarna), 13, 27, 70, 77,
        110
Bodyke (Lúbán Díge), 185-187, 218,
        222
Boggeragh Mountains (An Bhograch),
        13, 42
Bregoge (An Bhréagóg), 150, 158
Brittas (An Briotás) 40, 88, 89, 112, 134,
        170, 171
Boula (An Bhuaile), 42, 56, 171
Boyne, battle, 109
Buttevant, 19, 22, 23, 24, 26, 74, 132,
        150, 200
Bweeng (Na Boinn), 42, 56, 163, 173,
        174, 191

Cahirduggan (Cathair Dhúgáin), 151,
        152, 176, 177
Cameraure, 40, 41
Cappengyrryn, 40, 41
Carrigadrohid (Carraig an Droichid), 13,
        27, 70, 95, 118, 123
Carrigcleena (Carraig Chlíona), 16, 33,
        40, 42, 56, 134, 170
Carrignameragh, 69
Carrignavar (Carraig na bhFear), 13, 70,
        119, 121
Carrignamuck (Carraig na Muc). 59, 70,
        137
Carrigaline (Carraig Uí Leighin), 131,
        132
Carrigolane, 21, 40, 59, 87, 88, 112
Cashel, 1-9, 11, 14, 16, 73, 81, 108, 120,
        142, 153, 157, 161, 195, 220, 221

Castle Inch (Caisleán Insé) 70, 120

Castle MacAuliffe, 76, 77, 81

Castlemagner (Caisleán an
Mhaignéaraigh), 12, 19, 39, 59,
65, 75, 87, 93, 94, 131, 132, 133,
147, 167, 171, 177, 179, 180,
181, 189, 190, 194

Castlemaine (Caisleán na Mainge), 37

Castlemore (Caisleán Mor, Great
Castle), 49, 50, 51, 54

Clogheen (an Chloichín, The Little
Stone), 129, 154, 155, 157, 178,
202, 222

Cloghleigh (An Chloch Liath, The Gray
Stone), battle of, 77

Clonmeen (Cluain Mín, Smooth
Meadow), 12, 16, 17, 19, 21, 22,
23, 27, 28, 38, 39, 40, 41, 42, 46,
50, 51, 53, 54, 55, 57, 58, 60, 61,
62, 63, 64, 65, 66, 67, 68, 69, 70,
72, 73, 76, 77, 78, 80, 81, 82, 83,
84, 86, 87, 88, 89, 90, 95, 100,
102, 104, 109, 116, 118, 119,
123, 131, 132, 133, 134, 135,
139, 140, 143, 144, 145, 146,
147, 148, 149, 150, 151, 152,
153, 158, 167, 168, 169, 170,
173, 176, 178, 179, 180, 183,
193, 221, 222

Cloonteens (Na Cluaintíní), 21, 40, 55,
56, 57, 103

Cloyne (Cluain), diocese of, 15, 16, 20,
64, 65, 96, 107, 132, 133, 161,
172

Clydagh River, 19, 41, 42, 62, 67

Coarryneybesye (Coarrineyesye), 40

Condon's Country, 26

Coolageela (Cúil an Gheimhligh), 77,
78, 80, 128

Coolavota, 77

Coolekeelt (Koolekiltyh ny Monane,
Cowlenykilty), 55, 63

Coolnahane (Cúil an Átháin), 40, 56,
145

Coolroe Beg (An Cúil Rua Bheag), 147,
168, 169

Coolroe More (An Cúil Rua Mór), 69,
145, 147, 149, 152, 168, 169

Corbally (An Corrbhaile), 69

Cork City (Corcaigh), 13, 87, 102, 103,
111, 145, 146, 150, 163, 174,
188, 196, 197

Cork, Cloyne, and Ross, diocese, 64

Curragh (Currach), 70, 92, 93, 107

Curraghbower (An Currach Bodhar), 55

Curraghraigue (An Chorrghráig), 182

Curraghrour (An Currach Ramhar), 16,
62, 63, 73, 133, 146, 149, 169

Derrygallon (Doire Ghealbhan), 151,
184, 199

Donoughmore (Domhnach Mór), 9, 13,
15, 42, 178, 189

Dowkile (Dubh Coill. Black Wood), 40,
41

Drishane (An Driseán), 39, 75. 95

Dromahane (Drom Átháin), xvi, 21, 40,
54, 68, 87, 88, 102

Dromalour (Drom an Lobhair), 69, 101,
109, 144, 177

Dromaneen *(An Dromainnín)*, 20, 21,
22, 26, 27, 28, 33, 39, 40, 41, 42,
43, 44, 46, 50, 51, 52, 53, 54, 55,
59, 60, 61, 63, 66, 70, 72, 73, 74,
76, 76, 77, 86, 87, 88, 95, 100,
102, 104, 109, 114, 119, 134,
139, 143, 144, 146, 147, 152,
153, 170, 183, 198, 220, 221, 222

Dromcummer (Drom an Chomair), 40,
55, 62, 63, 89, 91, 103, 133, 145,
146, 149, 150, 169, 170, 188-
190, 212-213, 222

Dromeragh, 41, 55, 62, 63, 89

Dromore (An Drom Mór) , 16, 21, 23,
26, 27, 28, 36, 39, 40, 41, 42, 43,
46, 54, 62, 67, 87, 88, 102, 134,
135, 173, 179, 183

Drompeesh (Drom Físe), 18, 40, 102

Dromrastill (Drom Rastail), 21, 40, 41,
92, 18476

Dromsecane (Drom Seacán), 148

Dromskehy (Drom Sceiche), 151-152,

183, 202, 222
Duagh (Duach), 195
Duhallow (Dúiche Ealla), 12, 13, 14,
15, 18, 20, 22, 23, 24, 25, 30, 36,
37, 38, 39, 42, 47, 55, 71, 79, 86,
94, 97, 100, 121, 122, 130, 137,
143, 159, 179, 192, 199, 212

Farredorisse (Farrdorisse, Farderis), 40,
41
Fermoy (Mainistir Fhear Maí), 19, 45,
59, 77, 101, 175
Fermoyle (Formaoil), 40, 55, 57, 62, 63,
89, 91, 101, 132
Fethard (Fiodh Ard), 152, 153, 156, 157,
158, 159, 161

Galway (Gallimh), 4, 84, 86, 105,
110, 183
Garranasath, 21, 40, 92
Garrane (An Garrán), 40, 92, 169
Garrymcowney (Garraí Mhic Uaithne,
The Garden of Uaithne's Son),
21, 40, 54, 59, 92, 93, 95, 101,
183, 198
Gearanaskagh (Gaorthadh na Sceach,
(Townland of the Hawthorn), 21,
40, 54, 67
Gill abbey, 13
Glanda Ieyghe, 42
Glanminane (Gleann Meannán), 134
Glannaharee River (Gleann an Charria),
42
Glantane (An Gleanntáin), 57, 89,
133, 134, 163, 168
Glankitinere, Glawnyketenerick (Gleann
an Chitinéaraigh), 21, 55
Glen River, 42, 135
Glentaneatnagh (Gleanntán an tSnátha),
42, 169
Glynn (An Gleann, The Glen), 133, 151,
169, 206
Gortavoher (Gort an Bhóthair) 133
Gortbofinna (Gort Bó Finne, Field of the
White Cow), 21, 40, 67
Gortinibrahalye, 40

Gortincowley, Gortnecolly,
Gortnachonolye (Garrymcvouhy), 21, 59
Gortnynagh, 40, 41
Gortmolire (Gort Mhaoluír), 38, 40, 41,
54, 55, 56, 63, 88, 89, 93
Gortmore (GortMór, the Big Field), 16,
21, 26, 27, 28, 34, 39, 40, 41,
55, 56, 62, 67, 68, 77, 88, 89, 90,
145, 146, 147, 169, 182, 183,
184
Gortnagross (Gort na gCros, field of the
crossroads) 21, 28, 40, 41, 43,
54, 59, 59, 92, 171
Gortneleiragh, 80
Gortnascragga (Gort na Screige), 80
Gortroe (Kilegortroe), (An Gort Rua,
The Red Field), 21, 28, 40, 41,
54, 55, 56, 67, 75, 88, 89, 95,
101, 102, 134, 149, 168
Gurteenard (Goirtín Airde, Little Field
on the Height) 40, 89, 91, 183
Gurteenbeha (Goirtín Beathach, 21, 34,
55, 56, 57, 62, 93, 145, 146
Gurteenacloona (Goirtín na Cluana,
Little Field of the Meadow), 133

Inchidaly (Inse Uí Dhálaigh, O Daly's
Island) 59, 69, 143, 145, 148,
167, 168, 199

Kanturk (Ceann Toirc, The Boar's Head)
xvi, 16, 19, 20, 38, 63, 68, 69,
72, 75, 79, 81, 109, 128, 144,
151, 152, 163, 166, 167, 174,
175, 176, 177, 178, 182, 183,
184, 199, 211, 221
Kilavoy (Cill an Mhaí, Church of the
Plain), 39, 55
Kilbarrahan (Cill Bhearcháin,
Bearchán's Church;
Knockyveraghane), 40, 54,
55
Kilberrihert (Cill Bheircheirt,
Berrichdert's Church), 15, 40,
57, 79, 80

Kilbrin (Chill Bhrain, Bran's Church),
  75, 77, 79, 87, 94, 103, 131, 167,
  179, 180, 181
Kilcaskan (Cill Cháscann), 15, 21, 28,
  40, 41, 55, 56, 57, 89, 91, 131,
  145, 146, 147
Kilcolman (Cill Cholmáin, Colman's
  Church) , 15, 32, 40, 41, 87, 88,
  128, 134, 135, 170, 179
Kilcranathan (Cill Chranatan,
  Chranatan's Church), 21, 40, 41,
  66, 68, 77, 81, 92, 95, 113, 145,
  171
Kileaskith, 40, 41
Kilebeg (Coill Bheag, Small Wood), 40,
  41
Kilecurenane, 40, 41
Kileknockeigowney (Coill Chnoc an
  Ghabha, The Wood on the
  Smith's Hill, Smithfield), 40
Kiletra (Kileoughteragh, An Choill
  Íochtarach, The Lower Wood),
  40
Kiltylane, 39, 40
Kiletany, 40, 41
Kilgobban (Cill Ghobáin, Goban's
  Church), 39, 40, 59, 92
Kilgobnet (Cill Ghobnait, Gobnait's
  Church), 15, 39, 40
Kilgory (Cill Ghuaire, Guauir's Church),
  vii, 103, 105-110, 113, 135, 138,
  141, 142, 143, 158, 160, 185
Killavaher (Coill an Bhóthair, The Wood
  by the Road), 55, 56
Kilmallock chalice (Cill Mocheallóg,
  Mocheallóg's Church), 64, 220
Kilmichael (Cill Mhichíl, Michael's
  Church) , 15, 40, 60, 73, 90
Kilknockagaur, 134
Kilpadder (Cill Pheadair, Peter's
  Church), 15, 21, 26, 27, 33, 40,
  41, 54, 66, 68, 69, 77, 88, 89, 95,
  101, 102, 134, 163, 173, 183
Kilpatrick (Cill Phádraig, Patrick's
  Church), 15, 40
Kilroe (Cill Ruadh, Red Church), 39, 40,

41, 100, 160. 170

Kilshannig (Cill Seanaigh, Seanach's
  Church), 12, 15, 16, 19, 39, 61,
  64, 65, 75, 76, 87, 88, 89, 128,
  131, 132, 133, 134, 136, 151,
  168, 170, 179, 180, 181, 217
Kilvealaton (Kilbealade), (Cill
  Bhéalada), 21, 40, 54, 87, 88,
  102, 134, 170, 183
Killarush (Cill an Rois, Church of the
  Height) 40, 62, 63, 89, 91, 133
Killavallig (Cill an Bhealaigh, Church
  on the Way), 59, 93
Killeenleigh (Cillín Léith, The Little
  Gray Church), 152, 182, 183,
  184
Kinalea (Cineál Aodha). 12, 13
Kippagh (Ceapach, plot of land), 21, 34,
  40, 55, 56, 59, 62, 93, 94, 103
Kinsale (Cionn tSáile, Head of the Sea)
  12, 23, 47, 77, 108, 110
Knockacappul (Cnoc na gCapall, Hill of
  the Horse) 133
Knockaneroe (Cnocán Rua, Red Hill),
  177
Knockaney (Cnocán or Gleann an
  Chnocáin, Glenaknockane), 40,
  41
Knockansweeney, (Cnocán Mhic
  Suibhne, MacSweeney's Little
  Hill), 170
Knockardsharriv (An Cnoc Ard Searbh),
  103, 171
Knockavilla (Cnoc an Bhile, Hill of the
  Tree), 13, 70
Knockbrack (Cnoc Breac, Speckled Hill)
  (Knockiclashy), battle, 84
Knockdrislagh (Cnoc Drisleach), 170
Knockeenatuder, Knockyneytadyry
  (Cnoicín an tSúdaire), 40, 57
Knockelly, 153
Knocknacolan (Cnoc na Comhlann) 69
Knocknagehy (Cnoc na Gaoithe, Windy
  Hill), 131
Knocknamona (Cnoc na Móna, Hill of

the Bog), 40, 100
Knocknanagh, 182
Knocknanuss (Cnoc na nOs), battle, 81, 92, 113
Knocktemple (Cnoc an Teampaill, Hill of the Church), 79
Knockycarig (Knockycarry), 40, 41

Lackaleigh (Leaca Liath. Gray Stone), 94
Lackendarragh (Leacain Darach), 40, 55, 88, 95, 134, 170, 179
Limerick (Luimneach), 2, 5, 12, 16, 18, 23, 34, 36, 37, 51, 63, 64, 68, 85, 87, 105, 108, 110, 112, 113, 116, 118, 121, 125, 129, 132, 136, 150, 158, 160, 164, 183, 192, 196, 197, 202, 208, 222
Liscarroll (Lios Cearúill), battle, 77-79, 127
Liscullane, 135, 136, 137, 141, 143
Lismehane, 143, 185, 218, 222
Lismohilie, 40, 41
Lisnaherey, 62, 63
Lisyvogholy, 40, 41
Lissaghvohilly, 54
Lohort (Caisleán an Lóthairt), 36, 82
Lombardstown (Baile Lombaird), 40, 56, 63, 112, 128, 134, 198
Longueville, 21, 40, 59, 92, 93, 142, 144, 167, 183, 198, 199, 218, 220, 223
Loughrea (Baile Locha Riach), 86, 105

Macroom (Maigh Chromtha), 13, 63, 70, 80, 84, 85, 118, 120, 172
Maine, Money (Móin, The Bog), 21, 22, 55, 56

Mallow (Mala), 15, 16, 18, 19, 24, 26, 36, 39, 42, 44, 45, 46, 51, 58, 59, 60, 65, 66, 67, 68, 72, 73, 74, 75, 76, 78, 79, 83, 84, 87, 88, 92, 102, 103, 109, 119, 126, 129, 161, 166, 167, 170, 175, 176, 177, 178, 181, 189, 198, 200, 209, 217, 218, 220, 221
Marshalstown, 69, 70
Maryfort, 184-186, 202, 218, 219, 222
Mohereen (An Mothairín) 34, 57, 62, 87, 88, 134, 135, 170, 171
Molyne Intremane, 42
Monasternenagh, battle of, 36
Moorestown, 70
Mount Hillary, 90, 133, 169
Mountallon, 86, 102, 102, 103, 104, 105, 109, 110, 135, 136, 137, 138, 150
Mourne abbey, 16, 19
Mullahalaree, see Mount Hillary
Muskerry (Múscraí), see MacCallaghans of, and MacCarthys of

Nad, Nad Beg, Nad More (Nead an Iolair, The Eagle's Nest), 40, 62, 63, 169, 170, 196
Nadrid (Nead Druide, The Druid's Nest), 176
Narroure, 40
Newberry, 15, 60, 102, 179, 183
Newmarket (Áth Trasna, Ford of the Trasna), 76, 79, 80, 107, 174, 176

O Callaghan's Mills, 137

Pallas, 21, 26, 27, 28, 40, 41, 65, 66, 67, 89, 133
Poble O Callaghan, 21, 28, 41, 43, 55
Portidieth, 42
Portaghadav, 42

Raheen (An Ráithín, The Small Fort), 70
Rathbeg (Rath Beag, Little Fort), 21, 40, 66, 93, 95

Rathcomane, 21, 28, 40, 41, 54, 55, 56, 63, 89

Rathmaher (Ráth Mhachaire, Fort on the Plain), 9, 59, 82, 94, 103, 183

Rathmore (Rath Mór, Big Fort), 21, 40, 66, 93, 95

Roskeen (Ros Caoin, Pleasant Wood), 12, 19, 21, 26, 27, 40, 55, 56, 65, 66, 67, 68, 69, 75, 89, 91, 95, 101, 103, 133, 138, 145, 146, 147, 148, 169, 171, 179, 181, 183

Rossline (Ros Fhlainn, White Wood), 110, 128

Ruanes (Na Ruáin), 59, 77, 92

Shanakill (An tSeanchill, The Old Church), 133

Shanyvyaloid, 40, 41

Shanevolaghe, 56

Shanavoher (An Seanbhóthar, The Old Road), 42, 55, 160

Shanbally Castle (An Seanbhaile, The Old Town), 129, 150, 154, 156, 159, 160, 178, 184, 202, 204, 205

Skarragh (Scarbhach) , 21, 40, 41, 43, 54, 57, 73, 77, 87, 89, 101, 192, 134, 170, 198

Smerwick (Ard na Caithne), 36

Subulter (Sobaltair), 16, 59, 94, 110, 128, 179

Tipperary (Tiobraid Árann), 1, 24, 35, 51, 84, 120, 129, 152-162, 176, 183, 184, 193, 195, 200-206, 222

Torbeagh, 118

Trelairtynytonyh, 40, 41

Tyhyngyeryh, 40, 41

Yellow Ford, battle of, 44

Index of Subjects

Act of Settlement (1652, 1662, 1665),
    69, 85, 100-101
Act of Uniformity, 48
Act of Union, 161-162, 175
Annals of Loch Cé, 7
Annals of the Four Masters, 9, 18, 20, 28, 29
Annals of Inisfallen, 9

Beggars, 127
Black and Tans, 194,195, 196, 221
Board of Claims, 109
Bodyke evictions, 184-187, 217, 221
Book of Munster, 11, 13, 14, 20, 134,
    139
Books of Survey and Distribution, 87
Boyne, battle of, 109
Brehon Law, 5, 48, 106

Caithréim Cellacháin Chaisil, 4
Caithréim Dhonnchaidh, 23
Census of Parishes 1766, 132
Census of 1841, 181. 188
Chalice of Clonmeen, 146, 178, 219
Confederation of Kilkenny, 63, 72-99,
    103, 111, 221
Convert Rolls, 124, 140

Declaration of Indulgence (1672, 1687),
    104, 106
Decrees of Innocents, 100

Emancipation, Catholic, 160, 161, 162, 163,
    164, 167, 221
Emigration, 180, 207, 208, 221

Famine, 125; Great Famine, 161, 165, 166,
    172, 173, 174, 175, 176-180, 189,
    190, 191, 208, 210, 221
Fenians, 161, 191-192, 194

Glorious Revolution, 69, 106-108, 124
Griffith's Valuation, xv, 179, 189, 201

Hearth money, 132, 134
Holy Wells, 16, 166
Home Rule, 161, 191, 194, 203, 221

Inquisition of 1594, 20; 1609, 20, 21, 28, 29,
    33, 53, 66; 1617, 62; 1618, 55; 1631,
    62; 1637, 59; 1638, 59, 69, 143;
    1641, 70
Irish Colleges, 95, 128
Irish Parliamentary Party, 194
Irish Republican Brotherhood, 191

Jansenism, 98

Land League, 161, 180-184, 186, 190, 192,
    194, 221
Lebor Gabála, 1

Military Orders of Spain, 117

Nine Years War, 35, 39, 44-47, 49, 51

O Callaghan Coat of arms, xiv, 139, 147,
    154, 220
Ormond Peace, 81

Peasantry, 124-126, 128-129, 164-166, 171,
    186, 189
Pipe Roll of Cloyne, 16
Poor Law, act of 1838, 164, 194
Popish Plot, 104-106
Population, 1, 4, 23, 45, 48, 125, 134, 161,
    164, 166, 173, 174, 176, 178, 179,
    180, 189, 221
Priests, 65, 98, 105-106, 128-132, 172,
    192, 194, 206, 209, 210, 211
Pyrenees, treaty, 114

Rapparees, 126
Regiments, Irish, in French Service, 111;
    in Spanish Service, 114, 116
Repeal Association, 175
Report on the State of Popery in Ireland,
    131

Schoolmasters, 129-130, 172
Sinn Fein, 195

Tanistry, 5, 32, 33, 42, 48-54, 106, 221
Tenant Right League, 183

280

Index of Subjects

Test Acts 1673, 1678, 106
Tithe, 125, 127, 166-171, 188
Tithe Applotment Books, xv, 167, 188
Tithe War, 166-170
Tories, 84, 105, 110, 126,164
Transplantation to Clare, 86-93, 100, 142

USS Callaghan, 215

War of the Spanish Succession, 114
Westminster, 161, 162
Whiteboys, 128
Wild Geese, 110-123

www.ingramcontent.com/pod-product-compliance
Lightning Source LLC
Chambersburg PA
CBHW080231270326
41926CB00020B/4203